Warren Spahn and Johnny Sain. The rallying cry of the 1948 National League champion Braves was "Spahn, Sain, and Pray for Rain." The lefty-righty duo combined for thirty-nine victories and helped the Braves to their first pennant in thirty-four seasons. Courtesy of the Sports Museum of New England

The
BOSTON BRAVES
1871–1953

By Harold Kaese

Introduction and photo selection
by Richard A. Johnson

NORTHEASTERN UNIVERSITY PRESS

Boston

Northeastern University Press edition 2004
First published in 1948 and 1954 by G. P. Putnam's Sons

Index copyright 2004 by Jonathan S. Fine

Kaese, Harold.
The Boston Braves, 1871–1953 / by Harold Kaese; introduction and
photo selection by Richard Johnson.—Northeastern University Press ed.
p. cm. — (The sportstown series)
Originally published: New York: Putnam, 1948.
ISBN 1-55553-617-4 (pbk.: alk. paper)
1. Boston Braves (Baseball team) —History.   I. Title.   II. Series.
GV875.B59   K34   2004
796.357'64'0974461—dc22   2003026908

Printed and bound by Edwards Brothers, Inc., in Lillington, North Carolina.
The paper is EB Natural, an acid-free sheet.

MANUFACTURED IN THE UNITED STATES OF AMERICA
08   07   06   05   04   5 4 3 2 1

CONTENTS

ILLUSTRATIONS

SPORTSTOWN SERIES PREFACE

It's been said that you can judge a city by its newspapers, bars, ballparks, and bookstores. By this reasonable standard Boston is world-class. Boston is to sports and literature what Paris is to painting and romance, London to drama and royalty, and Rome to ruins and traffic.

Sporting traditions dictate both the landscape and the social calendar of Bostonians. They literally plan their lives around The Marathon, The Beanpot, The Country Club, The Green Monster, and The Game. Not only has Boston produced and embraced the talents of such athletes as John L. Sullivan, Bobby Orr, Sam Langford, Joan Benoit, Bill Russell, and Ted Williams, but it is also the city that boasts of writers such as Phillis Wheatley, Nathaniel Hawthorne, William Dean Howells, Henry James, John Updike, and Edwin O'Connor, to name but a few.

It is no surprise that sportswriting talent developed in Boston and that the talented writers documenting the local sports scene have nearly matched the accomplishments of both their writing and athletic counterparts. For generations the sports pages of Boston's many newspapers have been among the best in America. Likewise, books depicting Boston's colorful and unparalleled array of athletes, events, and teams are among the best of world sports literature.

For years many of these books have been out of print. The Sportstown Series from Northeastern University Press, selected and edited by myself, an author and the curator of the Sports Museum in Boston, will reprint selected works among these classics and publish original titles that illuminate one of the world's great sports regions.

Following our well-received first volume, *Ted Williams: Reflections on a Splendid Life*, edited by Lawrence Baldassaro, came *Dynasty's End: Bill Russell and the 1968–69 World Champion Boston Celtics*, by Tom Whalen, an original work and a dynamite story. Now we offer Harold Kaese's classic *The Boston Braves*, as volume three of our developing Sportstown Series.

Richard A. Johnson

FOREWORD

The Boston Braves were a team of tradition, full of unforgettable characters. It was my privilege to have been one of their number. My old friend Harold Kaese of the *Boston Globe* told their story in a book that was published following our pennant-winning season in 1948, and later updated after we moved to Milwaukee in 1953. Harold looked like a college professor and was considered the last word on Boston baseball history. I'm pleased that after fifty years his only book, *The Boston Braves*, is being reprinted.

Prior to signing my first pro contract in 1940, I knew I was coming to Boston. Scout Bill Myers made the case to his Red Sox superiors that a lanky, high-kicking southpaw from Buffalo was worth the risk of several hundred dollars. When Red Sox brass didn't agree, Myers switched over to the Braves and the rest, as they say, is history.

My American dream started in Boston. I was a member of the organization when I went into the service in '42 and was wounded at Remagen Bridge, when I married Lorene in 1946, and when my son, Greg, was born in 1948. I loved the loyalty of the Boston fans, the size of Braves Field, and the weather, which reminded me of my hometown of Buffalo.

When I think of Boston I think of Casey Stengel, Bob Coleman, Sibby Sisti, Johnny Sain, Torgy, Al Dark, Nelly Potter, Phil Masi, Tommy Holmes, and so much more. I also think of our World Series against the Indians in '48, which should have been a streetcar series against the Red Sox. And who can forget my diner on Commonwealth Avenue? I started work on it after I was assured by the front office that the team was staying in Boston. Needless to say, it opened adjacent to an empty Braves Field after we moved to Milwaukee.

It hardly seems possible that fifty years have passed since we left Boston. And though our time in Milwaukee was magical and brought two pennants, a world championship, and new major-league attendance records, I will always keep Boston close to my heart. For those of you who didn't see us play in Boston or are too young to remember the Boston Braves, I suggest you read this wonderful book. We may not have been the best team in the National League, but Kaese makes it clear we had the best history. Enjoy.

Warren Spahn
October 2003

PREFACE

This is the story of a big-league baseball club that followed the sage's advice to young men and went West to fame and riches. An old club, one that had belonged to Boston for eighty-two years, and then suddenly—on March 18, 1953—belonged to Milwaukee. When living became too difficult or boring on their seaboard farms, men gathered their families and packed their belongings, and, hitting the trails that led to the lands of the setting sun, became the pioneers of the West.

The Braves were baseball pioneers when they left Boston for Milwaukee. Theirs was a daring venture, one untried in the major leagues since 1903 when the American League entered New York by shifting the Baltimore franchise to that city. The Braves' reward, of course, was an acceptance fantastic in its wealth and warmth, for Milwaukee set unexpected records for hospitality in its welcome to the displaced ball club.

Although the Braves did not know what they were letting themselves in for when they settled in Wisconsin, they knew what they were getting away from when they left Massachusetts. They were leaving an indifferent population, an ugly ball park, and the Red Sox. Ever since the American League had played its first game in Boston in 1901 it had been an American League city, although the Braves had made spasmodic bids to regain popularity in 1914, 1933, and 1948. It is not frivolous to say that Boston had become the home of the bean, the cod, and the Red Sox.

Thus, when the Braves were abruptly moved to Milwaukee by President Louis R. Perini and his National League confreres, only a minority of New England fans were outraged. They expressed by voice and pen their anguish over losing their favorite team, referring to Perini as a drummer who carried his franchise in a valise. But they got little for their pains except the smirks of Red Sox fans who said, "Nobody will miss the Braves. A minor-league outfit. As long as we still have the Red Sox, let them go."

Mismanaged and poorly promoted though they often were, the Braves—and through them the National League—were sporting, business and cultural assets to Boston, but the majority did not know or care. Now they are sporting, business and cultural assets to Milwaukee, and the majority—according to attendance records—cares very much.

Those who thought Boston was losing something precious in the Braves were proved right when the team finished second in 1953. Those who grieved when the Red Sox sold Babe Ruth and Carl Mays to the Yankees were no more right than those who lamented when Ed Mathews and Warren Spahn were transferred to Milwaukee.

"We lost Ruth and Mathews, two of the best sluggers," said one bitter Boston fan. "How did we ever hang onto Ted Williams?"

The Braves' move to Milwaukee is as significant as any development in modern baseball—the change from the dead ball to the lively ball after World War I, the Supreme Court ruling in 1953 upholding the Holmes decision of 1921, the pension plan for players, night baseball, and the growth of a television audience.

For many years, chiefly because of the Browns' misfortunes in St. Louis, the question had been asked: Could a big-league team move successfully to a new territory?

Milwaukee's attendance of 1,826,397 in 1953 answered with an emphatic "Yes," and six months later the American League let the Browns move from St. Louis to Baltimore. That the big leagues will expand to other cities ripe for the best in baseball is a certainty. This is not so much a movement as a revolution, and it will change the map of baseball.

The man who probably deserved the honor of being the first modern magnate to shift a club was Bill Veeck. As president of the Browns, he was refused permission by the American League to move to Baltimore. Just two days before, the National League gave Perini permission to move the Braves from Boston to Milwaukee. But while Perini has the distinction of being the first to move, credit must be given to the man who forced him into a corner where he had to make the decision—Russ Lynch, sports editor of the *Milwaukee Journal*. Through the powerful medium of the press, Lynch put the issue squarely to Perini: Quit Milwaukee, or move the Braves there. Choose now—Boston or Milwaukee.

Lacking neither foresight nor nerve, as his business record attested, and feeling no moral obligation to keep the Braves in Boston, Perini boldly chose Milwaukee. All early indications are that he made the right choice for himeself, for his players, and for baseball. For everybody, possibly, except Boston. This, then, is the story of the Braves: of their first eighty-two years in the historic old Bay State, as I have told it.

Harold Kaese, 1954

INTRODUCTION

As curator of the Sports Museum, I receive many curious phone calls. Several months ago, I received an urgent phone message from one of Boston's prominent television anchors. When I returned her call, she asked breathlessly when "the Braves became the Red Sox." It was an example of the collective memory (or lack thereof) of the legacy of North America's oldest continually operated sports franchise, Boston's most successful major league baseball team. After eighty-two colorful and often glorious seasons, a half-century absence, and one dumb question, their history, as told by the estimable Harold Kaese, is back in print to set the record straight.

Boston claims to embrace history, but it often manufactures and embraces myth. This paradox spawned the notion of Paul Revere's overstated role on the famed midnight ride, abolitionists hiring blacks and Irish to work in their Beacon Hill mansions—the list goes on. And so it goes with our baseball heritage. When the painstaking mining of history has proved too difficult for the sportswriting community, curses are conjured and fable is passed off as the real deal to an audience none the wiser.

Unlike the Red Sox, the Braves are a team that escaped the mantle of myth only to be forgotten within a generation. What a pity, for the Braves are Boston's most storied and decorated team besides the Celtics. They were a stodgy as well as progressive team. Their early owners crafted the reserve clause, yet their last owner, the contractor Lou Perini, signed an African American named Sam Jethroe (rejected with Jackie Robinson by the Red Sox after a 1945 tryout). He won National League Rookie of the Year honors in 1950. Not only were they the first Boston professional team to integrate, but years earlier they opened the doors of Braves Field to barnstorming Negro League teams. In 1952, the Boston Braves signed a young shortstop named Henry Aaron to a minor-league contract. Neither Aaron nor the Yankee-slaying, 1957 world champions (whose lineup featured six players of color) played in Boston. Perhaps that is the true curse of Beantown. The Red Sox were the last team to integrate, two seasons later.

The Braves represented the entrenched establishment and the non-Irish immigrant wave of the late nineteenth and early twentieth centuries. Old-time fans remembered the swagger of the dynasty led by Kid Nichols and Hugh Duffy. First-generation, immigrant kids from Dorchester and Mattapan cherished the "knothole gang" cards that admitted them to Braves Field for a nickel. The Braves further endeared themselves to Boston's ethnic working class with the presence of Judge Emil Fuchs, a settlement house boy himself, who rose through the legal and judiciary ranks to be recognized as one of America's greatest attorneys. He was beloved when he moonlighted as team manager in 1929, and was the first Jewish owner in Boston sports.

The Braves spent their years in Boston (five in the National Association, seventy-seven in the National League) on the other side of the tracks. Their best seasons, achieved at the end of the nineteenth century, were played at the South End Grounds, which were hard by the tracks of the Boston and Providence railroad.

By the turn of the century, their magnificent ball yard burned. It was replaced by a drab facsimile because the old park had been underinsured. Boston fans crossed the tracks with Boston Nationals superstar Jimmy Collins to the Huntington Avenue Grounds, home of the newly formed Boston Americans. The hastily constructed yard was built on the site of a water park. It stood across from the South End Grounds, barely the width of the railbed away. The new team charged half the price the Nationals asked. That, and the presence of Collins (player/manager of the Americans), marked the end of National League dominance in Boston and Boston's preeminence (except for seven seasons from 1912 to 1918) over major league baseball.

Baseball history is divided by the year 1900. There is the vibrant world of the post-1900 game, in which film footage documents the action from Mathewson to McGuire. The post-1900 stars, their records, and the rules under which they were achieved hold great significance and stand in contrast to the popular perception of the musty world of nineteenth-century hardball. It was in this latter world, preserved in wood engravings and sepia stills, that the franchise still known as the Braves enjoyed their greatest success, with eleven pennants in twenty-nine seasons.

The Braves play a far more significant role than that of "America's Team," a term born in the marketing department of Ted Turner's entertainment colossus. The Braves are the oldest continually operated professional sports franchise in North America. Their early success forced the founding of the National League and big league baseball as we know it. They begat the infamous reserve clause, which governed baseball for nearly a century. They were the first team in any professional sport to relocate in the twentieth century. The Braves deserve the title "History's Team." Their heritage is as rich with championships, superstars, characters, and color as any in sports. In the nineteenth century they made Boston the baseball capital of America.

With G. P. Putnam's Sons' publication of Harold Kaese's *Boston Braves* in 1948, their series in major league team histories reached the high watermark. It was also a splendid example of the perfect author matched with the ideal topic.

Several books in the series were written in the golly-gosh prose common to mid-century sportswriting. Many are also questionable works of "history" compromised by the personal agendas and biases of men paid to report on games, and not to craft serious accounts. Fred Lieb's history of the Red Sox, for example, misrepresents important details of the Babe Ruth sale while perpetuating such myths as Harry Frazee's rape of the team.

In contrast, Kaese writes clearly and accurately as he brings the Wright brothers, King Kelly, and Frank Selee, among countless others to life. He unearths the rich history of the team's twin dynasties of the nineteenth-century, while chronicling the many hapless and colorful seasons that followed.

Kaese, the longtime baseball beat man for the *Boston Evening Transcript* and the *Boston Globe*, brought an unusual perspective to his task. He had been an outstanding third baseman and a scholar at Tufts University. He knew the game from the remote reach of the press box, and he also related to the game as a former collegiate all-star. The Lynn native absorbed the history of the Braves on long train trips and countless hours spent in the company of legendary Boston writers such as "Uncle" Jim O'Leary, Paul Shannon, and Melville Webb.

Bud Collins remembers Kaese as "a stoic, spare in appearance and always dressed in a suit and hat." Collins made his first trip to Wimbledon in 1959 on a busman's holiday with Kaese. Both were sent by their respective newspapers (Collins was then with the *Boston Herald*) to cover Harvard at the Royal Henley Regatta. Kaese gave Collins a tutorial on the finer points of rowing, and the two bonded as "Yanks abroad" in their search for hotel rooms, meals, and stories.

Collins recalled that Kaese, a former national champion in squash, was the last man to wear white flannel trousers while playing tennis at Longwood. Following his retirement, he met his future bride at the opera. Kaese's dry sense of humor suited a gentleman as comfortable in the reading room at the Athenaeum as he was in the press box.

Tim Horgan, a fellow Tufts graduate, remembers that the bespectacled and studious Kaese was called the "gray ghost" by his fellow writers in "earache alley," a name that perfectly described the Braves Field and Fenway Park press boxes. Horgan, and the half-dozen contemporaries I interviewed, remarked on Kaese's pioneering use of statistics in his chronicling of the game. Leigh Montville, a *Globe* colleague, recollects that Kaese's statistical files made him one of the fathers of SABR-metrics. Such were the powers of Kaese's recall that Ted Williams, upon his return to Boston as manager of the Washington Senators, bet Kaese a dollar regarding the particulars of Williams's first Fenway Park homer. Montville was present when Williams grumpily but good-naturedly paid Kaese the following day.

Bob Ryan recalled a fastidious and reserved Kaese who handed in perfect, typed copy every day at 5 P.M. sharp before taking the bus to the Union Club for his daily squash match. Those work habits earned him the additional nickname of the "ribbon cutter." Montville smiled as he remembered a man who barely spoke to him but didn't forget to leave a wedding gift at the home of Montville's mother-in-law. "In a room of fifty men," Montville relates, "Harold was the last man you'd have guessed was a sportswriter."

His love of the history and tradition of the team was never more evident than in an open letter he penned to the citizens of the beer-brewing city of Milwaukee shortly after the club moved from Boston. He wrote:

March 20, 1953

Dear Sudsy:

Welcome to the big leagues. May your party for the Braves be a smashing success; may they reward you by retiring the last batter in every game.

You are rolling out a red carpet for the Braves today, a lovely gesture toward a bunch of callous-toed, ball-playing mercenaries. I hope you don't feel like burying them in that same carpet come August.

The Braves may be a big league team, but big or little as Gertrude Stein might have said, a loser is a loser is a loser. If you think finishing seventh with the Braves is more thrilling than finishing first with the Brewers [these Brewers were the AAA minor league team of the American Association], you are someday going to be surprised.

Your wild joy submerges my grief over losing the Braves, but there is one thing I want to know: Can you take it?

If the Braves lose their first three games and eight of their first ten, never reach .500, drop 13 games in arrears of Memorial Day, lose 13 straight to the Dodgers, are eliminated from the race August 31st, and lose ten games in succession as they did last season, will you still be joyous?

Or will you feel like rolling out a red carpet studded with spikes and glowing with red hot coals for them in October?

I hope you are not put to such a trial by torture, and doubt that you will be this season. The Braves look like an improved team, probably a stronger team than the Red Sox you were kind enough to leave us.

As a big leaguer, you will have to pay higher prices, but there are compensations. You will see the best in baseball and you will be able to stage a real big league baseball dinner next winter.

Ford Frick may visit you and preach solemnly about the right of the American boy to take a baseball bat to bed with him. And you can give awards. Do you need any awards? We have some extra ones now.

You have had the Braves 1952 attendance of 281,000 thrown at you so much in recent weeks you must think Boston fans a lot of cold-blooded, tight-fisted, hard-hearted ingrates.

We have been misrepresented. We have turned out 14,000 strong for basketball and hockey games in recent weeks. We will turn out 14,000 strong for a lightweight title fight between Tommy Collins and Jimmy Carter with a $20 top.

We demand nothing except quality. Are you any different, Sudsy old boy?

Do you know that since the war, five teams drew fewer than the Braves (6,500,000), Phillies (6,250,000), Washington (5,540,000), Cincinnati (4,880,000), Athletics (4,700,000), Browns (2,500,000)?

Do you know that since the war, Boston supported two teams better than did Chicago, Philadelphia, and St. Louis?

Do you think, Sudsy old boy, that Milwaukee will soon equal the attendances Boston gave the Braves in five consecutive years 1946–51—969,000, 1,277,000, 1,455,000, 1,081,000, and 944,000?

Don't make fun of Boston. Wait until you have had a taste of big league decrepitude when it is not subsidized by your city government or your big business.

Meanwhile, good luck. Treat our team well. Treat it better then we did. It lasted only 82 consecutive seasons in Boston.

But if anyone at tonight's dinner refers to the Braves as a "sacred trust," you may snicker. The Braves were not sacred in Boston. They won't be sacred in Milwaukee. Only as sacred as the money in your pants pocket, Sudsy old boy.

Little did Kaese know at the time that his words foreshadowed the Braves' move from Milwaukee just thirteen seasons after their historic and painful relocation from Boston.

His account of their years in Boston is comprehensive and readable. It has been improved with the addition of fifty photographs and illustrations, as well as an index by Jonathan S. Fine of the Boston Braves Historical Association. I trust readers will find it a fitting record of one of the great franchises in all of sports.

Richard A. Johnson
August 2003

For further information on the Boston Braves readers are urged to contact and join the Boston Braves Historical Association at P.O. Box 5668, Marlborough, MA 01752

The Boston Braves

CHAPTER 1

TOO GOOD TO LAST

There once was a baseball team so remarkably good that to end its parade of successes it was found advisable to dissolve the league it played in. Thus, cries of "Break up the Yankees!" so common a few years ago, amused the few Bostonians still living who remembered the Boston Red Stockings of 1871–75. How quaint a remedy! There had been no idle talk of breaking up those powerful old Boston champions. They just slipped the rug from under the Red Stockings by breaking up the league instead, then started all over again from scratch.

The club that broke up a league still flourishes today as the Atlanta Braves. It is the only club that has been continuously represented since the first professional league was formed in 1871. It is the oldest club, and in tradition, the glory of past achievement, and the pride of the illustrious players, to say nothing of promise of the future, it is one of the richest clubs.

The Boston Red Stockings won four successive championships, from 1872 to 1875, in the first professional league, the National Association of Professional Base Ball Players. In 1875 they lost only 8 out of 79 games and won the pennant by 20 games.

It was through no accident that Boston monopolized the championship of the first professional circuit. Boston had a rich baseball heritage to start with. Albert Goodwill Spalding once said, "Just as Boston was the cradle of liberty for the Nation, so also was it the cradle in which the infant game was helped to a healthy maturity."

The exact age of baseball in Boston is not known. The boys who first played Rounders on the Common did not bother to erect a tablet commemorating the event Dr. Oliver Wendell Holmes, however, once told a reporter than he had played baseball while at

3

Harvard, and he graduated from Harvard in 1829. Dr. Holmes must have been mistaken, of course, for history says that Abner Doubleday did not invent baseball until 1839, or ten years after Dr. Holmes thought he had played it. Dr. Holmes must have played Rounders, Three Old Cat, One Old Tomcat, or some other vulgar form of today's national game.

Spalding, never wanting in boldness, without hesitation traced baseball back to Plymouth Colony, where Governor William Bradford three centuries ago was alleged to have broken up a ball game while it was being played on Christmas Day by men who refused to work because it was "against their conscience." As yet, however, no Boston historian had suggested that the Pilgrim Fathers jumped off the *Mayflower* to play a game of baseball, using Plymouth Rock for home plate.

Early baseball split into two major branches, the Massachusetts game and the New York game. The Massachusetts game, as played by Boston's West End teamsters, firemen, and mechanics, was a virile sport in which a runner could be retired by being "soaked," or hit, by a thrown ball. After a quarter century or so of serving as live targets, even Boston players welcomed the more effete game when it was introduced by a New Yorker, E. G. Satzman, who infiltrated their lines in 1857. Somehow, it seemed a more congenial way to spend an afternoon.

The first clubs organized to play the Massachusetts game were the Olympics in 1854, the Elm Trees in 1855, the Green Mountains in 1857, and the Hancocks in 1857. The Olympics and Elm Trees met in the first recorded match in 1855. Satzman organized the Tri-Mountain Club in 1857, and the first game under the New York rules was played on the Common in 1858, the Portland Club of Maine beating the Tri-Mountains, 47–42. Other clubs were soon organized to play the New York game, including the Baseball Club of Harvard College, the Bowdoins, the Lowells, and the Flyaways of East Boston. The Lowells, most famous of these clubs, lasted until December, 1873. The first college game, involving several Boston boys, was played at Pittsfield, Massachusetts, July 1, 1859. Amherst defeated Williams, 73–33, with each side using its own ball while at bat. Nobody knows yet if the better team or the livelier ball won.

4

In June, 1870, the Cincinnati Red Stockings, first professional baseball team, visited Boston and defeated such spirited broad-A rivals as the Lowells, Tri-Mountains, and Harvards by such lopsided scores as 40–12 and 46–15. Harry Wright's team opened the eyes of Boston baseball followers. The Boston amateurs were comparative novices beside the Cincinnati players when it came to batting, throwing, and catching a baseball.

"Why can't we have a team like that?" asked Boston fans.

"Why not indeed?" said Ivers Whitney Adams, a leading businessman and sports lover. He resolved that Boston should have such a team. He sold the idea to his friends.

"Where will we get the players?" he was asked.

"Don't worry. We'll get them some place," promised Adams. Then the Cincinnati Red Stockings lost their first game, after having won 87 consecutive victories in two seasons, to the Atlantics in Brooklyn. A few weeks later, the Red Stockings disbanded. Adams knew then where he would get his players.

The first meeting and organization of the Boston Red Stockings Club took place at the Parker House, January 20, 1871. The club was incorporated with a capital of $15,000, with Adams elected as its first president. Stockholders included Henry L. Pierce, John F. Mills, Eben D. Jordan, Edward H. White, James A. Freeland, F. G. Welsh, Harrison Gardner, John A. Conkey, and others. Harry and George Wright were present at the meeting, and arrangements were made for Harry to secure players for Boston's first professional team.

Boston can now boast of possessing a first class professional Base Ball club, as all the efforts tending to establish an institution of this kind culminated yesterday, when at a meeting of the shareholders in the organization, the business transactions of Mr. Ivers W. Adams, who has been laboring for the last twelve months to establish such an institution in this city, were heartily approved and the club regularly organized, the officers chosen for the ensuing year, and all preliminary steps taken looking toward an animated base ball campaign in this section, in which the model club of the country, the Boston Base Ball Club, will constitute the main attraction.

So wrote the *Boston Journal* of January 21, 1871, in one of the longest sentences ever dedicated to baseball up to that time.

The Wrights were sons of an English cricketeer who had come to this country and settled in New York. George was born near the present site of the Polo Grounds, at 110th Street and Third Avenue, January 28, 1849. Of the brothers, he became the most famous, although the tenacious Harry was the most natural leader. A third brother, Sam, excelled only at cricket.

When he was sixteen years old, "Little Georgie" visited Boston as a bowler and "mid-wicket-off" on the famed St. George Cricket Club. Craving more action than cricket offered, he and Harry turned to baseball, first playing with the Gothams in New York. In 1867 he took a job as a government clerk in Washington, to play with the Nationals, and in 1868 he rejoined Harry with the Unions of Morrisania, New York.

They hit the jack pot with the first outright professional nine, the Cincinnati Red Stockings, in 1869 and 1870. Harry was captain of the team, pitching and playing center field. George was the shortstop. George was paid $1,400, more than any other player, while Harry received $1,200. Harry seemed always destined to be outdone by his younger brother.

If Harry Wright had not stubbornly insisted on playing extra innings, the Cincinnati Red Stockings would not have lost to the Atlantics, 8–7, in eleven innings in 1870, and their winning streak might be going yet. It was in this game that George started the first double play. Instead of catching an infield fly with two Atlantics on base in the tenth inning, he trapped the ball and forced out runners at third and second.

Harry Wright, playing at Newport, Kentucky, in 1867, had hit seven home runs in a game, but George had a better reputation as a hitter. He hit 59 homers in 52 games in 1869, when the ball was dead, fields were open, and the pitchers delivered the ball underhand from a distance of 45 feet. He batted .518 and scored 339 runs. James O'Wolfe Lovett wrote of him: "He assisted one hundred and seventy-nine times and made eighty-two fly catches out of eighty-six chances, thus making good his title to 'King.'" George W. Howe, early Cleveland authority, called George "incomparable" in the field.

George could and did play every position, although not simultaneously, but he settled down at shortstop. Only a little bigger than Rabbit Maranville, he had a powerful throwing arm, which enabled him to play deeper than most early shortstops. He was admired above all other players of his time in Boston, and was called, "Our George." But George had something in common with many modern players. He disliked curve-ball pitching. When pitchers started bending them around 1875, George's batting average nose-dived. Not only was George a star cricket and baseball player, but he pioneered the game of golf in this country.

Asked once which was the best game of them all, George surprised his interrogator by replying, "Tennis, because it is the hardest game to learn." His sons, Beals and Irving, were tennis champions.

George Wright, the model player of his age, the quiet little fellow who flashed his teeth in bright smiles under his mustache as he gave juggling exhibitions with Andy Leonard and Jim O'Rourke, lived to be ninety years old.

But it was Harry, christened William Henry Wright, who put the Boston Red Stockings together. George once said of him, "He had a quiet, gentlemanly bearing, but Harry also had a peculiar knack of securing the esteem of men in his charge." Harry was the first of the mental-giant managers. He was so shrewd that a rule was passed prohibiting the manager to sit on the bench unless he was also playing.

Harry was not a good hitter but he was a good center fielder and change pitcher. When he was made captain of the Boston Red Stockings, he at once visited Rockford, Illinois, where he signed Al Spalding, Ross Barnes, and Fred Cone, who had played for the Forest Citys. He added Charlie Gould and Cal McVey from the defunct Cincinnati Red Stockings and got Harry Schafer from the Philadelphia Athletics, Dave Birdsall from the Unions of Morrisania, New York, and Samuel Jackson, an Englishman, from the Flour City Club of Rochester, New York.

Most of these men were famous players in their day. Barnes was so clever an infielder that he was tried at shortstop ahead of George Wright, although soon moved to second base, where he was in a class by himself. Of Barnes it was written that he could run so fast that he could steal second and third without sliding, and only dirtied his pants when stealing home.

But the player on the first Boston team destined to become best known was Spalding, the pitcher. As a native of Rockford, Illinois, one of baseball's early capitals, Spalding was subsidized like a modern college football player. He went to work as a bill clerk in a wholesale grocery concern in Chicago, with the understanding that he would pitch for an amateur team every Saturday.

"I wasn't a very good bill clerk but I was a pretty good pitcher," Spalding once admitted.

Wright persuaded Spalding to come to Boston by giving him $2,500, $500 of it spot cash. He might have made a better bargain if he had known that Spalding was eager to visit Boston because of a Back Bay girl he had met while visiting in Rockford. The girl became Spalding's wife, and her father helped establish him in the sporting-goods business, which made him a millionaire.

When Harry Wright had signed up his players, the *Boston Journal* wrote: "This nine has been selected with great care, and is regarded as one of the strongest, if not the strongest, in the country."

Where was the new club to get its competition? Ivers Adams took care of that problem by entering the team in the National Association of Professional Base Ball Players, when the first professional league was formed in the congenial surroundings of Collier's Saloon in New York, March 4, 1871. The league was formed because pure amateurism was no longer possible in baseball, and because of the success of the Cincinnati Red Stockings in 1869 and 1870.

For a park, the Boston club had leased the grounds known as the Union Base Ball Ground at South End, near Milford Place. New seats were built, and the best seats even had a roof over them. The question of the uniform was left to Harry Wright, and naturally he borrowed from the Cincinnati Red Stocking pattern. "It consists of a white flannel suit, of shirt, knee breeches and cap, red stockings reaching to the knees, and a red belt," went a description. "On the shirt front the word 'Boston' in red German text will be worked, which, with the usual canvas gaiters, will complete the uniform."

By March 31, all the Boston players were in the city training from two to four hours daily at the Tremont Gymnasium as they awaited suitable weather for outdoor practice. The players lived in the Highlands, next to Harry Wright's house, so he could keep them "under his eye at all hours."

The opening match of the Boston club was against a picked nine April 6, 1871. The new professionals won, 41–10, with Spalding pitching. The *Boston Journal* expressed its satisfaction as follows:

The prediction that the establishment of a professional club in Boston would develop an interest in the game, hitherto unknown, bids fair to be proved true, for there assembled on the grounds of the club yesterday

8

afternoon, full five thousand persons to witness the opening game of the Boston Nine, this being the largest number ever assembled before in these grounds.

People stood on the top of the fence and watched from the roof tops. It was Boston's biggest crowd except for the Peace Jubilee. When Boston later played a game against Harvard, the crowd numbered 2,000 spectators. They saw George Wright at shortstop make stops and throws that excelled anything ever seen before in Boston. Furthermore, "the umpiring of Mr. Ellis of the Athletics was in strict accordance with the rules."

That was more than could be said of the umpiring of H. A. Dobson, baseball editor of the *New York Clipper*, who officiated at the first league game played by Boston. The game was played in Washington, and it was "generally remarked in the stands that Boston was playing both the Olympics and umpire." But Dobson had lost a leg in the Civil War, and credit was given him for moving about nimbly on crutches, although "the umpire received an ugly blow on his only leg in the eighth inning, which keeled him over on the grass, but he was soon recovered." Boston won its first league game, 20–18, by scoring five runs in the last of the ninth inning, the home team batting first.

Before returning to Boston for its home opener, the Red Stockings beat the Haymakers at Troy, New York, 9–5. However, the first official game in Boston was won by the Haymakers, 29–14, when George Wright was unable to play, and his brother Harry played shortstop instead. At Troy, George had injured the same leg he had broken in 1870. He called for a fly ball, but Fred Cone, the left fielder, could not hear him because of a passing train, and there was a collision.

George Wright was able to play only 27 games because of his injury. Birdsall and Cone also suffered injuries. This partially explained Boston's failure to win the pennant in its first season. Boston won 22 games and lost 10, while the Philadelphia Athletics won 22 games and lost only 7. It was a rather loose league, it not being clear whether games won or series won should decide the championship. And then, not all the teams that started the season were around for the finish. Boston took satisfaction from beating the Athletics 3 out of 4 games. Spalding actually shut out the Kekiongas of Fort Wayne, 20–0, June 21, and as the Red Stockings beat Chicago, 6–3, September 5, "Charlie Gould made the big hit over the fence, bringing in three men, and making a home run himself, which caused great excitement." The team drew well, and exhibition games played with amateur teams and even rival league teams increased gate receipts.

Late in the season, Harry Wright and Al Spalding chose up sides and tried to determine whether Wright's slow pitching was better than Spalding's fast pitching. Wright's team won, 9–7, but since both teams were makeshift affairs, nobody felt that anything was proved, least of all, A. G. Spalding.

It required a meeting of the league's Championship Committee to decide that Philadelphia had won the pennant, but Boston could hardly protest after the compliment paid it by the *New York Clipper:* "Though the Boston club did not win the whip pennant for 1871, they achieved a reputation for skillful play, and for honorable conduct and gentlemanly deportment, on and off the field, unsurpassed by any baseball club in the fraternity, and equalled by but few. It avoided many of the objectionable features which have characterized professional nines surrounded by betting influences."

3

The Boston Red Stockings won the first of four consecutive championships in 1872. They won thirty-nine of forty-seven championship games, which caused the *Boston Herald* to proclaim: "Their record is such as to honorably earn the right of flying the Whip pennant, the much coveted emblem for the championship." Philadelphia won as many games as the Red Stockings, but lost six more. A vital victory was scored by Boston at the South End Grounds, October 5, when Spalding shut out the Athletics, 10–0, on 3 hits. "Nine blinders for the champions," said the *Herald*. Later, when he pitched for the White Stockings, Spalding's shutouts inspired the phrase, "to 'Chicago' the opposition."

Replacing Cone and Jackson in the line-up were: Andy Leonard, one of the original Cincinnati Red Stockings; Fraley Rogers, a promising Brooklyn amateur; and Jack Ryan, of Philadelphia. Leonard and Rogers played the outfield, but Ryan wound up as the club's official scorer. Leonard became the best left fielder of his era, a fast man going back for a fly, and a long and accurate thrower. In a pinch, he could play second base or even shortstop.

Boston beat the Picked Nine on Fast Day, 32–0, and opened its

10

home season by beating the Brooklyn Mutuals, 4–2, scoring 3 runs off Arthur Cummings, one of the first curve-ball pitchers, in the ninth inning. Spalding pitched all the league games, as he had in 1871, and several of the many exhibitions the Red Stockings played with amateur and professional teams. In one exhibition they beat the Mutuals, 11–4, for $300 at the Weymouth Fair.

Having lost only two games up to July, the Red Stockings became a little cocky. They took a week's rest at Calf's Island, swimming, sun-bathing, and breathing in the good salt air. Then they came home to be trounced by Troy, 17–10, and by Philadelphia, 9–1. Harry Wright banned further vacations until after the season.

At the close of the season, the Bostons entered a tournament in Brooklyn, tying the Athletics for first prize. Unable to play off for the blue ribbon because of injuries, the Red Stockings were given the same amount of prize money as the Athletics, $1,400.

Ivers W. Adams had resigned as president of the club after the first season, being succeeded by John A. Conkey, a customhouse official. It was a poor year financially. The great Boston fire of 1872, coming after the season, almost wrecked the club. Spalding was owed $800 and he was so disillusioned and desperate that he went to work for the *New York Graphic*.

Rumors that Boston would not have a professional club in 1873 were ended in December, when a meeting of friends of the game was held at Brackett's Hall. Of the 150 friends who showed up, 50 volunteered to join the new club. Colonel Charles H. Porter, later mayor of Quincy, was elected president.

The flame of interest was fanned still higher when the first pennant was presented to the club in a meeting at Brackett's Hall, January 2, 1873. The flag measured all of 36 feet long, and was lettered, "CHAMPIONS, 1873," although it had been won in 1872.

To replace Gould, Rogers, McVey, and Ryan, Harry Wright signed up: Deacon Jim White, from the Cleveland club; Orator James O'Rourke, from the Mansfield club of Middletown, Connecticut; John Manning, the only Bostonian on the team and a graduate of the Boston Red Stocking Juniors; Robert Addy, a Canadian, who had not played in 1872, but previously starred for the Forest Citys; and Charles Sweasy, of the original Red Stockings.

White, who was ranked at the head of all catchers for 1873 by the *New York Clipper*, was "a quick, heavy hitter." O'Rourke, who dropped the "e" off his name to help typesetters, was "a heavy hitter

11

to third base and left field." Sweasy got into only one game, and "then fielded creditably his old position of second base." Addy played in only half the games, but his "steady play had a tendency to infuse confidence into the minds of his fellow players."

The Red Stockings beat the Picked Nine only 12–5, and lost their home opener to Philadelphia, 8–5. There was more bad news in 1873. The *Boston Globe* reported that, on June 14, "the Bostons met a Waterloo defeat, playing the first game of their existence in which they failed to score." With Dick McBride pitching a two-hitter, Philadelphia beat the Bostons, 3–0, at the South End. A few weeks later, Boston was beaten by Baltimore, 17–14, after having led, 14–4. This provoked the following letter to the editor of the *Boston Herald*:

We paid our money last year to see base ball played, but we are not so green as to imagine we see square games this year. Like a hundred or more we have spent our last half dollar on the Boston ground. As the land is in the market for sale, I presume we will not have to be humbugged more than this season. We don't believe the club exists that can fairly beat the Bostons in three innings, when the score stands, 14–4. We don't know, but we think, and are sorry that we must, that the Boston Club is on its make; but they cannot make fools of the public any longer. The club of '72 is not the club of '73, and we hope they will disband before they go backward any farther.

Fair Play

An answer was made by an official of the Boston Red Stockings:

Fair Play seems afraid to say that the Boston Club sells games, but if that is what he means, I will pay him $50 for every game he will prove was sold either by the club as a club or by individual players. I have heard that kind of talk in Philadelphia and New York from purchasers of pools, etc., but not from honest men.

B.B.C.

Boston won the 1873 race from Philadelphia by a margin of four games, to earn a lyrical tribute from the *Clipper*:

Boston will rest easier hereafter. Her victorious Reds have won it, won the base-ball championship, and all is serene. The championship question has caused more dispute, more cuss words, more wickedness, than it has entered into the heart of man to conceive. From one section of the country to the other the watchword has been—"Who's It?"—But the great problem was solved at last, and Boston is "it." What cares she for her great fire now? Of what avail is her liquor law, or her last wool crop? The Reds have won the base-ball championship.... All hail,

Boston! All hail, her noble Red men, whose honesty of purpose, and strict sense of right and justice against the most alluring temptation have enabled them to win and wear the laurel for another term!

And professional baseball was only five years old!

But a few days after winning the pennant, the Reds were humbled by the Harvard Nine, 21–19. In 3 seasons, they had won 95 consecutive games from amateur teams. This was their first defeat by amateurs and was attributed to overconfidence, the *Boston Globe* explaining: "The Reds went into the game as if they had a soft thing."

The season of 1873 was a great success in Boston. Barnes, who had led the league by hitting .404 in 1872, led it again by hitting .453. Spalding again pitched all the championship games. The team made an exhibition trip to Canada, as it had in 1872, and even played a cricket match in Ottawa. Receipts for 1873 were $27,832.38, the profit $4,245.63. These figures were announced at a meeting held December 3, in Hampshire Hall, when Nathaniel Taylor Apollonio, a public-spirited citizen, was elected president, succeeding Colonel Porter, who declined another term.

During this season, Spalding, the Wright brothers, and Barnes received $1,800 each for their services. White was paid $1,500, Leonard $1,400, Schafer $1,200, Birdsall $1,000, O'Rourke and Sweasy $800, and Manning $500. But the boys were amateurs at heart. On Christmas Day, 1873, Harry Wright and Spalding chose up sides, the Wrights winning, 18–16, in ten innings, in a game played before 450 spectators at the South End Grounds.

The National Association held its annual meeting in Boston in March, 1874. The Red Stockings were given their second pennant, which was inscribed, "BOSTON 1873-74. Champions of the United States." The flag measured thirty by ten feet. There was also the lighter whip pennant that snapped from the top of the pole.

To replace Birdsall, Manning, Addy, and Sweasy, Harry Wright, in 1874, added Tommy Beals, who had played under the name of Thomas for the Washington Olympics, and George Hall, a left-handed player from the Lord Baltimore Nine. Both were outfielders. Of Beals it was said: "He distinguished himself for covering a large space of ground when he played for the Unions, for it was then in the time of lively ball games, when an outfielder had more work to do than at the present time."

13

The 1874 race was thoroughly scrambled by an exhibition trip the Bostons and Athletics made to England in midseason, landing in Liverpool, July 27, and returning home September 9. The trip had been arranged by Spalding, a born promoter, who visited England the previous winter and talked the noble members of the Marylebone Cricket Club into approving a visit by two American baseball clubs. On his return home, Spalding had said: "I'm glad we arranged a game at Lord's Cricket Ground, because it is fenced in with a brick wall, where no holes can be cut through."

The Bostons won eight games, the Athletics six, playing at Liverpool, Manchester, London, Sheffield, and Dublin. But instead of selling baseball to the English, they found the English trying to sell cricket to them. Several tests were held, and the Americans, aided by such skilled cricketeers as George, Harry, and Sam Wright, won five out of six matches. Their victory over Marylebone, 107 to 105, was described as the greatest American victory over the English since the Revolution.

The trip was a financial failure, losing $1,679, according to one report. The players were happy to return to Boston and celebrated by clinching their third straight pennant. At least, they made money at home. Receipts for 1874 totaled $19,005, and the Boston club made a profit of $844.13—which today wouldn't even buy uniforms.

It was a loose league, with 96 of 232 scheduled games being ignored, but the Red Stockings won 52 games while losing 18, to beat out the Mutuals by 13½ games. By now, the Bostons had much better teamwork and discipline than their rivals. Even the experiment of playing ten innings and using a tenth man as an extra shortstop between first base and second, tried early in 1874, didn't bother the Red Stockings. And if Schafer could make seven errors in one game at third base, the Boston players knew that Harry was "a plucky facer of hotly thrown and batted balls." They just turned around and beat the Brooklyn Atlantics, 29–0.

Boston again ran away with the pennant in 1875, the year that saw the introduction of the catcher's mask and the elimination of the National Association. The Bostons won seventy-one and lost only eight games, for a record-setting .899 percentage. The second-place Philadelphians finished fifteen games behind. Between April 19 and June 3, Boston won twenty-six games in succession. Barnes slumped to .386, but Spalding finished with fifty-four victories, four defeats, and three ties. He won twenty-four games in

14

succession between April 29 and June 3, and twenty-two games in succession between July 3 and October 30.

The Boston team won all thirty-eight of its home games, as the Big Four outdid themselves after the news had leaked that they were going to play for Chicago in 1876. The Big Four were Spalding, Barnes, McVey, and White, who were damned as "dirty seceders" for their proposed dereliction, although present students of the game might consider this westward migration more prophetic than traitorous. But the Boston owners capitalized on the defection of their four stars by staging an exhibition game at the South End Grounds in October, in which the four seceders played for Chicago. Spalding did not "dare risk his reputation" and played left field. Cal McVey pitched for Chicago instead, and he stifled the taunts of the large Boston crowd by beating the Red Stockings, 14–0. Pitching for Boston was Josephs, whose real name was Joseph Borden. In July he had pitched the first no-hit game against Chicago for the Athletics, and Boston had signed him to succeed Spalding as their pitcher in 1876.

Spalding engineered the exodus of Boston's Big Four to Chicago, which resulted in the formation of the National League in 1876. Determined to have a winning club for Chicago, the wealthy William A. Hulbert won Spalding by appealing both to his pocketbook and to his pride.

"You're a Midwesterner, Al," he said, "and you should be playing in Chicago. I would rather be a lamppost in Chicago than a millionaire in any other city." So Spalding went to Chicago and became not a lamppost but a millionaire. He complained that winning pennants in Boston had become monotonous.

He signed up his Boston teammates: Ross Barnes, second baseman; Cal McVey, catcher; and Jim White, outfielder and catcher; and won over two of Philadelphia's best players, Adrian (Pop) Anson and Ezra Sutton. There was no rule then to prevent a player from signing with any club he chose, but there was talk of expelling the seceders from the National Association at the March meeting.

"We'll anticipate them," Hulbert said, as he found himself with a team but no league to play in. "We'll form a league of our own. Then let them try to expel us."

Hulbert formed his league, with Spalding's help, and its prospects were so attractive that five of the eight clubs were from the old National Association, which just curled up and died. Joining was the

15

Boston club—or what was left of it. Apollonio and Harry Wright both attended the New York meeting that produced the National League.

In five years the professional game had made great strides, although there was some resistance to progress. Asked by George Wright to try Fred Thayer's catcher's mask, Jim White had said, "I can't breathe in the damned thing." But White and other catchers were soon saving their teeth behind Thayer's invention.

Evidence of progress on the field was low-score games. Evidence of progress off the field was gambling pools in the back of the stands. About two thirds of the fans were betting on games. There was drunkenness and rioting, and worse still, players were being bribed to throw games.

"The gambling, cheating, stealing, and throwing of games going on now are horrible," said baseball leaders nearly three quarters of a century ago. "And so is that Boston club that can't be beaten. Baseball ought to be cleaned up."

So they abandoned the National Association and cheerfully joined the new National League. The Boston Red Stockings continued with Apollonio as president and Harry Wright as captain, but they were to miss the Big Four who had seceded to Chicago.

CHAPTER II

THE TRIUMVIRS

THE National League chose to be born in a year that was otherwise notable in the march of progress. In 1876 the first batch of Portland cement was put together, Custer's troops were massacred by Sitting Bull, and at 5 Exeter Place, Boston, Alexander Graham Bell was heard by his assistant in another room to say over a length of copper wire, "Watson, come here, I want you."

These words by Bell did not agitate some citizens of Boston as much as those of William A. Hulbert, founder of the White Stockings, who had said, "Spalding, come here, I want you," and repeated the command three times using the names of Barnes, McVey, and White.

Except for the loss of the Four Seceders, there is little doubt that the Boston club would have won seven pennants in succession, the last four in the National Association and the first three in the National League. The transfer of the Seceders meant first place for Chicago in 1876, fourth place for Boston. Loyal Boston rooters would gladly have seen Hulbert's scalp blowing like a pennant from the wigwam of one of Sitting Bull's braves.

The Four Seceders were the backbone of the Chicago champions. Spalding won over 75 per cent of the 60 games he pitched. White hit .335, McVey hit .345, and the remarkable Roscoe (Ross) Barnes hit .403. All four of these players ranked with the best of their day.

Even while finishing fourth, the Boston club had several distinctions in this inaugural season. It was the only club to play a full schedule of seventy games. The Philadelphia Athletics and New York Mutuals, by way of contrast, neglected to make their second western trip, with the result that both were expelled from the league.

Andy Leonard, the star Boston outfielder, endeavored to play second base June 14, and made eight errors in one game. As if this were not enough, he made three more errors in the next game, giving him a total of eleven errors for two consecutive games, beside which John Manning's five errors in the outfield on May 1 seemed insignificant. The game of June 14, played against St. Louis, was a rather loose affair, since the Boston team made twenty-four errors altogether, seventeen of them by the infield.

Boston also participated in the first extra-inning game in league history, being defeated, 3–2, by Hartford in ten innings, at Boston, April 29. Tom Bond outpitched Boston's prize flop, Joseph Borden, also known as "Josephus the Phenomenal." Mr. Knight, of Yale, umpired, and the game required three hours and ten minutes to play.

A distinction more prized was the 6-to-5 victory scored by the Boston club in Philadelphia, April 22. It was the first National League game ever played. On this occasion, the great Josephus rose to the occasion by outpitching Alonzo Knight, of Girard College, on the grounds at Twenty-fifth and Jefferson Streets. Admission was fifty cents. Boston's first victory was achieved by scoring two runs in the ninth inning.

The Boston line-up that day had: George Wright at shortstop; Andy Leonard at second base; Jim O'Rourke in center field; Tim Murnane (spelled without the "e" in the box score) at first base; Harry Schafer at third base; Tim McGinley catching; John Manning in right field; William Parks in left field; and Borden pitching under the name of Josephs.

The Athletics used: David Force, shortstop; David Eggler, center field; West Fisler, first base; Levi Meyerle, second and third base; Ezra Sutton, third base and right field; Coons, catcher; George Hall, left field; William Fowser, right field and second base; and Knight, pitcher.

The "f" in the Philadelphia team that day, however, did not stand for Force, Fisler, or Fowser, but foozle. The Athletics made thirteen errors, whereas the visiting Bostons made only seven.

Jim O'Rourke had the honor of making the first National League hit, a single to left. Tim McGinley scored the first run. John Manning batted in the first run with a fly to left field. Tim Murnane stole the first base. Unfortunately, there is no record of the first player to glare at an umpire, the first to lose a fly ball in the sun,

18

or the first to be picked off base. But McGinley was the first to strike out, and Ezra Sutton, Philadelphia third baseman, made the first error.

A crowd of about 3,000 spectators saw the game, which was nothing like the crowd that, on May 30, tore down the fences at the South End Grounds to see the Chicago White Stockings and the Four Seceders on their first visit to Boston.

The White Stockings, with Spalding on the mound, won the game, 5–1, a superiority they demonstrated all through the season by winning nine out of ten games from Boston. Boston fans had not groaned without reason when the Four Seceders jumped to Chicago.

2

Forced to change his line-up because of the dereliction of his four stars, Harry Wright used McGinley and Brown as catchers in place of White, O'Rourke and Leonard as second basemen in place of Barnes, Morrill as first baseman in place of McVey, and Borden and Frank Whitney as pitchers in place of Spalding. In no case did the new incumbents match their predecessors in performance or ability.

As long ago as 1876, the Boston Nationals discovered that unlovely flower of baseball now known as the "morning glory." Their find was the Philadelphia pitcher named Borden, who had hurled a no-hit, no-run game against Chicago in a National Association game. The Bostons had faced Borden, admired him, and when Spalding succumbed to the entreaties of Hulbert, Harry Wright could think of no better pitcher to take his place than Borden.

Borden was given a three-year contract calling for $2,000 a year. Any baseball player who could command such a fabulous income in 1876 deserved a distinctive nickname, so the baseball writers called him "Josephus the Phenomenal."

He was phenomenal in that he was the highest-paid errand boy then under contract in the country. For Josephus, once he put on the red stockings of the Boston team, could not pitch. The excuse was offered that he had changed his style and lost his cunning, but whatever the reason, Josephus could get no one out. Such high-priced uselessness irritated the Boston directors, and they set out to rid themselves of the impostor in their midst. They made Josephus the groundskeeper.

Did the grass need cutting? Josephus smiled and cut it. Did the fences need mending? Josephus smiled and mended them. Did the stands need fixing? Josephus smiled and fixed them. He fixed them happily. He held no rancor for the Boston directors. If they would not let him pitch for three years for $2,000 a year, then he would cut their grass for three years for $2,000 a year. Josephus was not proud. He felt no shame. And he knew a good job when he had one.

In the end, to be rid of him, the directors gave Josephus a flat sum to be gone and remain forevermore out of their sight. They disposed of William Parks, a substitute outfielder and change pitcher, somewhat more cheaply. Parks, like Josephus, was a burden to the club, and he too had a contract it could not break.

After several attempts to discourage Parks, one of the Boston players had a New York friend write to him, saying in effect: "I represent the St. Louis club, which will be here next week, and have been authorized to offer you one hundred dollars a month if you will join us. If you will come to New York, a contract for that amount will be given you to sign."

Parks was taken in by the ruse. Here was a fine chance to better himself, and to prove to these stupid Boston directors that he was a valuable and sought-after ballplayer. So he jumped the Bostons and went to New York, only to learn there that he had been duped. St. Louis certainly had never even thought of giving him one hundred dollars a month. So Parks returned to Boston, but instead of opening a lawsuit, he opened a barbershop. If not a good pitcher, at least he proved to be a very good barber.

The first player to have his name spelled wrong was Murnane, first baseman of the 1876 Red Stockings. Murnane was a famous baseball character for nearly a half century. Born in Waterbury, Connecticut, June 4, 1850, he first played as a catcher for Norwalk in his native state. He then was with Stratford, Connecticut, Savannah, Georgia, and the Mansfields of Middleton, Connecticut, before joining the Philadelphia Athletics, with whom he played for three years. He went to England with them in 1874.

While playing with the Athletics, Murnane made a sensational play against Boston. Attempting to steal second base, he found Andy Leonard waiting with the ball that had been fired to him by Jim White, so instead of sliding, as Leonard expected, Murnane leaped high over Leonard's head to reach the base safely.

Murnane was always the player's champion, being active in the

20

Union of 1884 and the National Brotherhood of Baseball Players. He scouted for Chicago and for years was president of the New England League, but his principal contribution to baseball was as a writer for the *Boston Globe*. Along with such early reporters as Jacob C. Morse and Edward F. Stevens of the *Herald,* Bertrand A. Smalley of the *Evening Record,* and Walter S. Barnes, Jr., and William D. Sullivan, of the *Globe,* he helped to carry the torch for baseball in Boston. A jovial man with a magnificent shock of white hair, Murnane knew baseball as few writers have known it, for he had played with the Boston Red Stockings of 1876 and 1877, and other big-league teams.

Another new player to join the Bostons in 1876 was Honest John Morrill, who was discovered in the Fast Day game. It was customary in those days to open the local season with a game played on Fast Day, a legal state holiday, between the Red Stockings and a picked nine. The game was the big preseason opener, as the city series games between the Braves and Red Sox are now.

On Fast Day of 1876, a Boston boy who had learned to play ball on the Common caught for the Picked Nine. He was not an unknown, for three years earlier he had organized a team known as the Stars, and they had won the junior championship of the state. He played third base on that team. In 1875, he played for Lowell, and his team won the state amateur championship. He was ready to become a professional player with Syracuse in 1876, when he caught against the Red Stockings.

So well did John Morrill play for the Picked Nine, that the next day Manager Harry Wright, of the Red Stockings, signed him to a three-year contract. Here was a find! It was Wright's intention to use Morrill as a catcher, since Tim McGinley gave little promise of filling the shoes of Jim White. But instead, he played Morrill at first base and signed another Boston boy, Lew Brown, as catcher.

As a lad, Morrill had played with such teams as the Beacons and Our Boys. Late in life he used to say, "Those were the good old days. I enjoyed most the years from 1872 to 1874, when I used to play with such fellows as Al McKinnon, Chub Sullivan, Curry Foley, Sam Crane, Lew Brown, Frank Holden, Dutch King, Jim Russell, Tom Keenan, and Bob O'Tool. We used to play after school and on Saturdays, and we had some fine old times on the Common."

When Morrill broke into baseball, he wore a mustache that

looked as though he had been eating blueberry pie and had forgotten to wipe his upper lip. Asked to explain this unsubstantial adornment, he later explained, "If you didn't have a mustache or beard in those days, they'd say you were too young to play and wouldn't put you on the team."

3

Boston won its first National League pennant in 1877, just by way of celebrating the beginning of one of baseball's famous regimes—the Triumvirs. The famed triumvirs of ancient Rome, Caesar, Pompey, and Crassus, were minor leaguers compared to the Triumvirs of the Boston Nationals, Soden, Conant, and Billings. Boston's threesome wielded fully as much power in the National League as their predecessors wielded in the Roman league, and they survived to live considerably longer and happier lives.

What Caesar was to the ancient triumvirs, Arthur H. Soden was to the moderns. Soden became a wealthy man, a leader in National League councils, and he did not die of multiple knife wounds, but lived to be eighty-two years old. He was the number-one Triumvir. Soden was president of the Boston club for thirty years, 1877-1906, and in those three decades his teams won eight championships, more than any rival club.

Soden, an amateur player, was one of some eighty fans who made the trip to England in 1874 with the Bostons and Athletics. He actually played one game in center field for the Bostons at Kensington Oval. George B. Appleton, a close friend, persuaded him to invest in the Boston team, which he did by purchasing three shares of stock from Appleton at the price of fifteen dollars per share. With this huge stake in the team, young Soden could not afford to relax his vigilance. Instead, his interest mounted, and so did his accumulation of stock in the club.

Before the 1877 season started, Soden and his friend James B. Billings, a shoe and leather man, owned a majority of the stock. As usually happens in such cases, an election was held and a new president chosen. His name was Soden. Billings was elected treasurer. The third Triumvir, William H. Conant, slipped in by a side door. Through an emissary named Captain Jones, he had quietly bought enough stock to be able to throw his weight around. Recognizing a powerful minority, Soden and Billings admitted Conant to the inner circle, electing him secretary of the club.

22

Soden, the ultraconservative, regarded baseball as a business but he once broke down and admitted: "Baseball is a game I love, whether it represents business with me or not. Keep it from the gamblers, and keep it from unprincipled speculators who would jockey with it and destroy its standing as was done in the '70's."

His voice was dominant in National League councils. He led the National League through three successful wars with rival leagues. Soden was described as "a man of singularly upright character, his integrity always being above discussion." When William A. Hulbert died in 1882, it was Soden who directed the league until a new president was elected.

Soden was born in Framingham, Massachusetts, April 23, 1843. When twenty-one years old, he enlisted and served with the Twenty-second Massachusetts Infantry as a hospital steward during the Civil War. After the war, he was a wholesale druggist, then entered the roofing business, in which he made most of his fortune. For fun he liked to fish, and he was president of the Boston Chess Club. Six days a week, from 8:30 A.M. to 4:30 P.M., he was to be found in his office in the firm of Chapman and Soden, at 150 Oliver Street. A true New Englander, Soden was frugal. He always brought his lunch with him from his Newtonville home. A hard worker, he was a director in several banks, and part owner of a railway, a supply company, a hardware firm, and a manufacturing company. Baseball was a financial investment to him, not merely a hobby.

Conant was a sporty fellow, who liked to smoke big cigars and drive behind a frisky span. He was born at Bridgewater, Massachusetts, March 15, 1834. He was closer to the players than Soden, but not as close to them as Billings. Conant frequently traveled with the club, and often scouted in the minor leagues. He knew a ballplayer when he saw one. Uncle Bill, as he was called, first manufactured hoop skirts. When they went out of fashion, he manufactured rubber goods, from which he made a fortune. Conant outlived his fellow Triumvirs, dying a few months after Soden, at the age of ninety-two, in 1926.

These two Triumvirs, rather than Billings, were responsible for the financial policies of the Boston club. Complimentary tickets were virtually unknown, each Triumvir having only one card-board pass, good for only two admissions. On big days, the Triumvirs themselves went to work selling and collecting tickets at the gate. Players were encouraged to enter the stands and wrestle fans for

foul balls. Firemen who jumped from their locomotive cabs to retrieve balls hit to the outskirts of the South End Grounds would
not have been worse thieves if they had snitched gold nuggets
off somebody else's claim.

Toward the end of its regime, Boston's famed triumvirate was
cussed and abused for penny pinching. Soden and Conant had
become wealthy and their baseball ambitions faded. They who had
fought so successfully against the challenges of the Union Association in 1884, the Brotherhood in 1890, and the American Association in 1891 were beaten down by the stunning success of the
American League as represented by the club now known as the
Boston Red Sox.

It was unfortunate that the Triumvirs, having brought Boston
its finest baseball teams, had to make a sorry exit when they sold
the club after the 1906 season. Cheers, not jeers, should have been
their parting salute.

CHAPTER III

THE FIRST PENNANTS

IT took just one year for the Bostons to recover from the loss of the Four Seceders to Chicago. Harry Wright knew that he had the nucleus of a good team but he needed a winning pitcher. Not a winning pitching staff, but a winning pitcher. In those days it wasn't asking too much of a man to pitch every game. A team played only fifty or sixty league games a season, which meant that there were days when he could rest, if he was so delicate that he needed rest.

Wright found his man in Thomas Bond, who in 1876 had pitched Hartford to second place behind Chicago, winning more than two thirds of his games. Since Soden had not yet introduced the reserve rule, Boston needed only to offer Bond sufficient inducement to lure him from Hartford, and this they did to their great profit. Bond brought Boston its first National League pennant in 1877.

Discovered by Bob Ferguson in 1874, Bond pitched his first professional game that year for the Atlantics of Brooklyn. During his career, he hurled thirty-six shutouts in the National League, a record bettered by only a handful of pitchers. His complete record is buried or lost in baseball's musty archives, but Tom Bond, the man with the iron arm, pitched Boston to its first two National League pennants. He must have been good.

Although one of the first to violate the straight-arm pitching rules of his day, Bond was a winner when the pitching distance was 45 feet, and again when it was 50 feet, as it was from 1881 to 1893. Bond had terrific speed, which troubled the bare-handed catchers of his era, but he also was one of the first successful exponents of the curve ball. For this reason he has been sometimes called the Father of Modern Pitching.

Some scientists had proved to their own satisfaction that it was possible to curve a thrown ball, but three quarters of a century ago scientists were not respected as they are now. Men who had never stood up to the plate claimed that the ball did not actually curve, but merely appeared to curve. They said Bond's curve was a trick, an optical illusion, he had picked up from such mound magicians as Arthur Cummings and Alphonse (Phonnie) Murphy. Columbus sailed toward the setting sun to prove that the world was round, but Harry Wright, manager of the Boston club, used merely two fences and one post to prove that Bond could make a baseball curve.

The experiment was made in Cincinnati in 1878. The two fences were placed twenty yards apart, with the post midway in the gap—all three being on the same line. Bond then stood to the left of one fence and made the ball curve around the post so that it passed the left of the second fence.

Cincinnati doubters watched Bond curve the ball around the post several times, then shook their heads, and said, "Nope. It's a good trick, but you can't get away with it. The wind is blowing the ball off its course."

But Wright wasn't considered the shrewdest baseball man of his time for nothing. He immediately called on a left-handed pitcher, one Lefty Mitchell, to make the ball curve against the wind. When Mitchell did this, all but a few of the most stubborn skeptics were converted to the theory that it was possible to make a ball curve. Baseball had passed another milestone.

Bond won thirty-one and lost seventeen games in 1877, hurling every game played by Boston. Counting exhibition games, in which he was sometimes aided by William White, he pitched about 120 games his first season with Boston.

Another newcomer who helped Boston win its first flag in 1877 was Uncle Ezra Sutton, third baseman, who in 1876 had made the first error in National League history while playing for the Athletics against Boston. Sutton replaced Harry Schafer, who was moved into the outfield, and he was soon regarded as the game's leading third baseman.

Sutton was a powerful hitter, as he demonstrated his first season by hitting three consecutive triples in one game. He had a strong throwing arm, and no third baseman showed more nerve facing "fair fouls" (balls that struck fair but went into foul territory before reaching third base, and which were then in play). Sometimes Sutton played in foul territory for notorious pull hitters, and he needed a strong arm to wing the ball all the way to first.

Sutton had been a cross-handed batter before coming to Boston, and a good one. But as the pitching became faster, he noted that he was hitting too many flies, so he took the more orthodox grip on his bat and improved his average. Although famed as a third baseman, he frequently helped at shortstop, especially in 1877, when George Wright played second base. If Sutton played third, Andy Leonard played shortstop. If Sutton played shortstop, John Morrill played third. Sutton was to play for the Boston champions of 1877, 1878, and 1883—and to die a penniless cripple years later in a Rochester, New York, hospital.

When Boston won the hand of Miss Pennant in 1877, close followers of the game could only assume that the fair young lady was keeping company with Deacon Jim White. White had joined the Bostons in 1873, coming from the Forest Citys, of Cleveland. He caught Spalding in 1873, played first base in 1874, caught Spalding again in 1875, and in all three seasons the Bostons finished first.

In 1876 he went to Chicago, catching Spalding, and again was with a winner. Back to Boston came White in 1877, but since Lewis Brown was catching Bond, White played first base and right field. He led the league in hitting with a mark of .385, and of course Boston finished first. This gave White a record of having played on five consecutive pennant winners. Little wonder, then, that Cincinnati, ambitious to finish on top, signed him for 1878. But, alas, the romance had ended. Cincinnati could finish only second.

It was many years before Deacon Jim White got back into the good graces of Miss Pennant. This wonderfully versatile player was thirty-nine years old when he played third base for the Detroit champions of 1887. By then, the fellow he used to catch on the old Boston Red Stockings, A. G. Spalding, was well on his way to a fortune.

The pitching of Bond, the hitting of White, and the all-round work of Sutton were all the help Boston needed to win the pennant in 1877 by a margin of three games over Louisville. Boston earned its victory by taking eight out of twelve games from the Kentucky team, yet nothing pleased Boston fans more than beating Chicago ten out of twelve games. Boston players to enter the record book

27

were Jim O'Rourke, who made five errors in the outfield in one game, and Harry Schafer, who accepted eleven chances in right field in another game.

But although Boston won the pennant in 1877, the team lost money. Besides Boston, only Louisville, Hartford, St. Louis, and Chicago finished the season. The Athletics, who had drawn big crowds at Boston the year before, and the Mutuals had been expelled for failing to make their second western trip in 1876. The National League lacked class in 1877.

2

There was more interest in the 1878 race, because one of the four new teams in the league was Providence, a natural rival of the Boston Reds. Three teams, Louisville, Hartford, and St. Louis, quit the National League after 1877, but Providence, Cincinnati, Indianapolis, and Milwaukee entered to give the circuit six teams in 1878.

There were several changes in the Boston line-up. Tim Murnane moved to Providence, where he paved the way for the later exodus of such Boston stars as George Wright, Jim O'Rourke, Lew Brown, and even Harry Wright. John Morrill played first base throughout the season for Boston. The return of George Wright to shortstop was made possible by the signing of Johnny Burdock, a Brooklyn second baseman who had played for the Atlantics and Hartford. The happy-go-lucky Burdock was to be Boston's second baseman for six years.

Genial John Manning, who had been loaned to Cincinnati in 1877 at a fancy salary of $2,500, was recalled against his wishes and played in the Boston outfield with Leonard and O'Rourke. The other new player was Charlie Snyder, a highly rated catcher who had been with Louisville the previous season. He proved his ability by holding Tom Bond's fastest pitches. Bond won forty-one of the fifty-nine games he pitched. This was a powerful team, finishing four games ahead of Cincinnati. But in their series with Cincinnati, the champions only broke even in a dozen games. They did better against Chicago, winning eight out of twelve.

The ball was deadened about this time, and low scores were the rule in 1878. Boston's leading batter, O'Rourke, hit only .274, while Burdock batted .260, and Morrill batted .240. Despite the

28

dead ball, in the eighth inning of a game with Providence, the Rhode Islanders scored twelve runs. Providence did a good job of getting in the hair of the champions, which was a profitable arrangement, since special trains were run to carry excited fans from one city to the other when the teams met. On May 8, 1878, Paul Hines, Providence outfielder, was credited with making the first big-league unassisted triple play when he caught a short line drive hit by Burdock and tagged second and third base to retire Boston players who had scampered home confident that the ball would not be caught. However, some authorities question if Hines made his play unassisted.

The Boston-Providence rivalry became still hotter in 1879. George Wright, Jim O'Rourke, and Lew Brown had jumped from Boston to Providence, which excited Boston fans almost as much as the secession of the Big Four to Chicago in 1876. Wright managed Providence to the pennant by a margin of six games over Boston, a notable triumph for Our George over his older brother Harry.

The teams closed the season with a six-game series. Boston needed to win five of the six games to tie for first place. Instead, with Bob Mathews and John Montgomery Ward outpitching Bond and Curry Foley, Providence won four games and clinched first place with successive 15-to-4 and 7-to-6 victories. Providence deserved the pennant after beating Boston eight out of twelve games.

Boston missed Our George most of all, for Sadie Houck, obtained from Washington, was a failure at shortstop. Bond also was showing the effects of too much pitching in previous seasons. He was able to hurl only sixty-two of seventy-eight contests, so there was little wonder that Boston slumped to second place. Orator Jim O'Rourke was replaced in the outfield by the unrelated John O'Rourke, who led the Boston team by hitting .341. The O'Rourkes were among baseball's first holdouts, refusing to sign with Boston because the club taxed its players twenty dollars a season for uniforms, and fifty cents a day for travel maintenance. When neither club nor players would give in, the fans took up a collection and paid the bill, but Jim O'Rourke was not satisfied and jumped to Providence.

Loss of George Wright, who had played on six Boston pennant winners in eight years, and Jim O'Rourke inspired Soden to write into baseball law the reserve clause, which is so often described as an enslavement device by today's Lincolns. In their eyes, Arthur

H. Soden fought in the Civil War to free the Negro, then turned around and sold the white man into baseball bondage.

Soden's reserve clause was adopted to curb the practice of "revolving." Prior to 1879, players were free to sign with whatever club they chose when their contracts expired. An owner who had built up a winning team frequently would find his personnel dispersed through the departure of star players for fairer fields.

"What man in his right mind will invest money in this kind of business?" asked Soden, after losing George Wright and O'Rourke. "Today he has some assets. Tomorrow he may have none."

The only protection possible for the owner, Soden thought, was to give him an option on the services of players after their contracts expired. That a player should be "owned" by a ball club and not be free to sell his talents where he wishes may seem undemocratic, but nobody yet has presented a practical alternative. When Soden's reserve rule was passed in 1879, it was to apply to only four players on each club, but the number grew steadily, until now every player is under option to the club with which he signs.

Soden's reserve rule should be known as Soden's Stabilizer, for that is what it proved to be for organized professional baseball. It was the first of several major contributions by Boston's number-one Triumvir to the game he served so well.

3

For three more years the Bostons were also-rans, finishing sixth in 1880 and 1881, and tying Buffalo for third place in 1882. Jim O'Rourke returned to Boston in 1880, and in two successive games hit four home runs. But George Wright remained in Providence, and the Bostons were weak in the infield as well as in pitching, for Bond was about through, and Jim Whitney was inexperienced.

On June 10, Charlie Jones is credited with having hit two home runs in the eighth inning, another feat doubted by some baseball authorities, but which if true made Jones the first big leaguer to hit two homers in one inning. On August 19, the Bostons for the first time took part in a no-hit game, but they took the wrong part, serving as stooges for Chicago's Larry Corcoran. For the first time in ten years, Boston's professional team failed to win half its games, winning only forty of eighty-eight contests.

The poor showing of the Bostons on the field was reflected by a low attendance, but every club in the league lost money in 1880 except Chicago, which won the pennant by finishing fifteen games ahead of Providence. Pop Anson's powerhouse began a record twenty-one-game winning streak by beating Boston, 5–4, on June 2.

The record of the Bostons was even worse in 1881. They lost ten out of twelve games to Chicago, the repeating pennant winners. Still, Whitney managed to get into the record book by making twenty-eight errors in sixty-three games, a tidy total for a pitcher, and Charlie Snyder had ninety-nine passed balls in fifty-eight games, even though the pitching distance had been increased from 45 to 50 feet. Joe Hornung, leading the league's outfielders for the first of four consecutive years, accepted eleven chances in left field, September 23. Boston outfielders had plenty of opportunity to star in these years.

The owners' answer to a losing team in the last century was the same as it is today: Get a new manager. By firing the old manager, past failures are instantly explained. By hiring a new manager, hope for the future again bursts into flame.

Before the season of 1882, the Triumvirs replaced Harry Wright as manager of the Bostons with Honest John Morrill, who was a native Bostonian. He had been with the team since it had entered the National League in 1876, and when George Wright went to Providence in 1879, Morrill succeeded him as captain of the Red Stockings. When Harry Wright went to Providence in 1882, Morrill succeeded him as manager.

In eleven seasons at Boston, Harry Wright had won six pennants, four in the National Association and two in the National League. He had put together Boston's first professional team in 1871, and more than anyone he had given Boston its triumphant start in professional baseball. He led the team off the field as well as on it. He was a player, captain, manager, and general manager all in one. He was the first of Boston's modest number of great baseball leaders.

The pennant did not follow Harry Wright. He left his luck in Boston. He managed Providence in 1882 and 1883, finishing second and third. Then he became manager of the Philadelphia Nationals in 1884, a job he held for ten years without ever finishing higher than third, although only once did his team finish below .500.

Under Morrill, Boston got back above the .500 level in 1882, tying Buffalo for third place with a 45-to-39 record, but finishing a full ten games behind victorious Chicago. Joe Hornung achieved another slight measure of fame by hitting two triples in the eighth inning on May 6. Boston might have challenged Providence for second place if it had been able to win more than four games from Troy City. Soden had more to worry about than his own ball club this season, for William A. Hulbert, president of the league, died in April. For the rest of the season, the Boston strong man served as league chairman.

CHAPTER IV

MORRILL STEALS A PENNANT

☒

THE modest flame of interest that accompanied the return of the Bostons to the first division under Morrill became a raging holocaust in 1883, when the Bostons roared from seventh place in June to clinch the pennant late in September. The pell-mell finish lifted the hats of Boston fans. The National League had never known such a fighting comeback, nor was it to know another as exciting until the 1914 Braves came along to put in the shadow every other club that has ever picked itself off the floor to win.

In the opinion of rivals, Boston stole the 1883 pennant: It was not the best club in the league; Sam Wise was a jittery shortstop; Joe Hornung was a good left fielder, but the Reds were weak in center and right, where they tried several men. When Grasshopper Jim Whitney and Big Charlie Buffington were not pitching, they had to play center field.

"Good pitching and catching, and lucky hitting won for us," admitted Honest John Morrill. "When the season started, I thought we would finish fourth or fifth. Our biggest surprise was Burdock, but Hackett deserves great credit for catching with his hands mangled."

Johnny Burdock, the second baseman who had joined the club in 1878, led the Red Stockings by hitting .330. In his first year with the team he had hit .226, in his second year .240. Ezra Sutton, third baseman, batted .323, Morrill .319. During the season, Morrill played all four infield positions, appeared in left field, and even pitched.

Other teams had better players at most positions, but the Red Stockings had two prime pitchers in Whitney and Buffington. Whitney was the better man in 1883, whether he was pitching, playing the outfield, or swinging a bat. He always batted fourth, even when pitching, while Buffington batted seventh or eighth. Whitney, a tall, lean fellow from Binghamton, New York, who had joined the Bostons in 1881, after having hurled for San Francisco in the California League, won forty games and batted .282 in 1883. With his great speed, he was the best strike-out pitcher in the league, having 309 whiffs to his credit. In one game he fanned sixteen Chicago batters. In another he fanned thirteen Detroit batters. Six times in Boston he fanned three men in an inning, and one day he fanned six men in succession. He could fire the ball, as the bent and broken fingers of the Boston catchers, Mertie Hackett and Mike Hines, painfully attested. And Grasshopper Jim could hit that ball, too. In 1883 he became the first man to drive a ball over Detroit's right-field fence.

His running mate was Big Buff, a twenty-two-year-old youngster from New Bedford, Massachusetts. This was only Buffington's first full season in the league. He was the change, or alternate, pitcher. He won twenty-three games and batted .237. Big Buff was famous for his downer. "He has the most perplexing curves in the country," wrote an expert. Besides, he was a student of pitching. Morrill said, "The fielders have an easy time when Buff pitches. His ball is easy to handle." But his curve that exploded into the dirt gave the catcher a workout. Mertie Hackett of Cambridge earned his letter catching Buff. In those days Buffington's name was always spelled without the "g."

While catching as a young amateur around Fall River, Buffington had been hit in the eye by a foul tip. Convinced that it was better to give than to receive, he thereupon became a pitcher. He broke in as a pro with Philadelphia in 1882, but was soon released and joined Boston. Pitching his first game for the Reds in 1882, he shut out Worcester, 4–0. While playing center field one day, he revealed the strength of his arm by throwing out a hitter at first base on a sharp hit over second. Before becoming a leading pitcher, Buffington had excelled at roller polo—which is field hockey on roller skates and was once extensively played around Fall River.

Boston got away to a miserable start in 1883. They opened the season by playing the first National League game played by the Giants in New York. Among the 12,000 spectators present was General Ulysses S. Grant. Whitney pitched; New York won, 7–5. The Reds won only four of their first fifteen games, and at the end of the fifth week of the season stood seventh. After ten weeks they were third, after fifteen weeks they were fourth, and after twenty weeks they were first. The Red Stockings won the pennant by winning fourteen of their last fifteen games.

The Red Stockings first took the lead September 4, when Whitney beat the Giants in New York, 8–2. The standing that night showed four teams, Boston, Cleveland, Chicago, and Providence, with forty-nine victories. Boston had thirty-two defeats, Cleveland and Chicago had thirty-three defeats, and Providence had lost thirty-four times. John Morrill's mustache would have covered the four teams.

Boston immediately fell from the top when Old Hoss Radbourne beat them on successive days, 6–1 and 8–1, in Providence. The umpire was Tom Bond, former Boston pitcher. The next day at Boston, Radbourne tried to make it three straight, but Whitney, who had lost the second game, came back and beat Old Hoss, 4–3, in eleven innings, before a crowd of 4,000 fans that filled the small South End Park. Boston won by scoring two runs in the last of the eleventh, on a missed third strike by Radbourne's catcher, Hornung's triple, and Sutton's single. Radbourne complained that his arm was sore, and fortunately for the Red Stockings, it stayed sore for the rest of the season.

This vital victory over Radbourne had put Boston in third place when the crucial four-game series opened against Chicago at South End on September 10. The Red Stockings rose to the occasion by sweeping the series, regaining first place, and all but clinching the pennant. A reporter pointed out, "Boston needs a new flag badly to replace without expense the ragged reminder of bygone days, which floats so proudly from the masthead." The tatters he referred to were the pennant of 1878.

Whitney won the first game from the White Stockings, 4–2, before 3,500 fans, and Boston trailed the league leaders by only a half game. It was a good game, except that the Chicago catcher, one Mike Kelly, "was as conspicuous and farfetched in his conduct as ever. He was the only one of the visiting Chicago players who found any delight in making himself ridiculous. Too bad that such a good player has to act so little like a gentleman."

The Red Stockings won the second game, 3–2, and for the second time during the season were leading the race. Whitney was off form, allowing six hits. He had allowed only three the day before. Batting first, Boston trailed, 1–2, entering the ninth. Their only run

35

was Sam Wise's fourth homer of the season. But Hornung singled off Chicago's Larry Corcoran to start the ninth, Anson made a two-base error on Sutton's grounder, and Burdock singled to drive in the tying and winning runs. The Boston players were given an ovation after retiring the White Stockings in the last of the ninth. Canes, hats, and cushions were showered on the field by excited Bostonians. Players were surrounded, their hands shaken, their backs slapped.

Morrill's team had caught fire. The next day Buffington beat the White Stockings, 11–2. For the first time since 1879, Boston had won more games than any other club. The Red Stockings led Providence by a full game. The series with Chicago closed September 13, with Whitney hurling his third victory in four days, a 3-to-1 four-hitter for the Grasshopper. The game was played in a drizzle, but a band livened things up. So did Mike Hines, who made three hits.

Eight consecutive games were won by the Red Stockings before Buffalo beat them, 3–2. Whitney lost this game when Wise made two errors. "The umpiring was simply wretched. The audience was in a fever of rage." Rumors spread that Wise had thrown the game. They were branded as ridiculous by the newspapers, which pointed out that Wise was young and erratic, and only two years in the league.

There was no need for alarm. The Red Stockings won their last six games. Providence collapsed with Radbourne's arm. On September 27, four days before the season's end, the Red Stockings clinched the pennant, their first in five years. Whitney beat Cleveland, 4–1; Buffalo beat Providence. It wasn't a front-page story, but Boston was rather pleased. Jim Galvin, Buffalo pitcher, was given a forty-five-dollar overcoat for beating Providence. Jim White, Buffalo player who knocked in the run against Providence, was given fifteen dollars.

Boston fans blew raspberries at their Rhode Island friends, who ultimately lost second place to Chicago. One of them wrote an ode to Harry Wright, the old Red Stocking leader, managing Providence, that began:

> We ne'er shall see his like again,
> Bluff Captain Harry Wright.
> He left our nine for Providence,
> And bade us all good night.

Boston players were feted for days. They got no sixteen-cylinder sedans, or even mules, mink, or turkeys, but they seemed quite satisfied with the rings, watches, and engraved mustache cups showered upon them by their adoring rooters. Johnny Burdock should have received a lasso, for in Detroit one day the Boston second baseman threw his arms around the rival catcher so the latter could not pursue a foul fly off Johnny's bat. Burdock was fined twenty dollars on the spot by the umpire.

The Boston club drew 138,000 fans at home, a record attendance, and an average of 2,760 fans per game. The Red Stockings won forty-two of fifty games at home. It was Boston's best season, and not only at the gate. "The habits of the nine have been better this year than last," wrote a reporter soberly, "and there has been no trouble between the directors and the players, or the captain and the players." Only two players had to be disciplined all season.

President Soden expressed his extreme pleasure, saying that he had not thought the Red Stockings capable of finishing even as high as third. He was so exhilarated that he wildly promised to rebuild the shoddy South End Grounds, and he gave each player an envelope containing one hundred dollars, a generous bonus for their splendid work. But despite the profits, there would be no dividends declared, Soden announced. The profits would be set aside for future use. Soden was at that time still buying out small stockholders, and he sought to discourage them by withholding dividends, a plan that succeeded admirably.

The Red Stockings closed the season with a three-game exhibition series against Buffalo, instead of the championship series that had been promised with the Philadelphia Athletics, American Association champions. The Athletics, losing seven of their last eight games, declined to play the torrid Boston nine.

2

It was to be eight years, four managers, and many headaches, before Boston was to win its fourth National League and eighth professional pennant. These were stormy years for the Triumvirs, but not only did Soden keep the Boston club going, he frequently lent a financial shoulder to the weaker clubs.

As if the Bostons, still called the Reds and Red Stockings, did not have enough trouble on their hands with Providence in 1884, they also had to fight a Union Association team formed by George Wright, Tim Murnane, and Frank Winslow. Backed by Harry V. Lucas, St. Louis millionaire, the Union was organized to fight the National League's reserve rule, which had been conceived by Soden in 1879.

On the Boston Unions were such popular old Red Stockings as Tom Bond, Lew Brown, and Merton Hackett. Murnane played first base and right field, and served as captain and manager. Hackett, who had caught for the Reds the year before, was the shortstop. Playing on the Congress Street Grounds, the Unions chipped in with some thrills for Boston fans. On July 7, nineteen of the Boston Unions struck out against Hugh Daily, one-armed Chicago pitcher. Two weeks later, Fred (Dupee) Shaw, Boston southpaw, struck out eighteen St. Louis hitters, allowed only one hit, and lost, 1–0.

Murnane's Union team tried to win Boston support by playing twenty-five-cent ball, but the reduced fare and a fourth-place finish in a loose league were not sufficient inducements for fans to quit the Red Stockings, who fought hard but unsuccessfully to defend their championship against Frank Bancroft's Providence Grays. Boston had a two-game lead at the end of July, but could not keep up with a Providence team that won seventeen of eighteen games in August. With Radbourne winning 60 of the 72 games he pitched, Providence finished ten and one-half games ahead of Boston.

Radbourne had pitched a no-hit game in 1883 against Cleveland, and in 1882 he had beaten Detroit, 1–0, by hitting a home run in the eighteenth inning, but 1884 was the Iron Man's best season. He had to work overtime because of the defection of Charles Sweeney, Providence's other pitcher, in midseason. Sweeney, on June 7, at Boston had set a record by striking out nineteen Red Stockings. He fanned every Boston player except Sutton and whiffed Burdock four times. Jim Whitney pitched for Boston, struck out ten Providence hitters, and was beaten only 2–1. Radbourne played first base for Providence.

Several weeks later in Providence, Sweeney was ordered out of the box to right field by Manager Frank Bancroft. Instead, he walked off the field. Radbourne went in and finished the game with only two outfielders behind him. Sweeney jumped the club and joined the St. Louis Unions. Left with only one pitcher, Providence directors considered closing shop, but the thirty-one-year-old Rad-

38

bourne told them he would carry on. Carry on he did, for he pitched in twenty-two consecutive games. From August 7 until September 6, he won eighteen games in succession, before being stopped, 2–0, by Jim Galvin of Buffalo. His arm nearly killed him. It took him two hours to warm up, but Radbourne pitched Providence to the pennant. He faced Boston four times during the season, hurling three shutouts, allowing one run and seventeen hits. He had 411 strike-outs for the season.

One of Providence's outfielders was Paul Revere Radford, who had been with Boston in 1883. The Providence captain was a South Boston boy, Arthur Irwin, a shortstop. Playing against Boston at the South End Grounds, with two out in the sixteenth inning and the score, 0–0, Irwin won the game with a home run that passed through a hole high in the right-field fence. This delighted critics of the Triumvirs, one of whom had written in the *Clipper* in February: "The Boston grounds are the worst in the country." The field was untidy, and the fences and stands were unpainted, despite promises that the park would be repaired. The Triumvirs had been criticized, too, for raising the price of a season ticket from twenty to thirty dollars, because Boston won the pennant in 1883. In Providence a season ticket still cost only twenty dollars.

It was a disappointing season for the Red Stockings. Sutton hit .349, but Burdock dropped to .267 and Morrill to .265. Such new players as William Annis, Martin Barrett, and Tom Gunning did not live up to advance notices. Buffington made the most notable contribution of the campaign when he struck out seventeen Cleveland hitters September 2, eight of them in succession. A reporter wrote: "Buff struck out eight men in succession yesterday, twelve of the last fifteen outs in the last five innings were made on three strikes."

That the Bostons were on the downgrade was demonstrated further when they finished fifth in 1885, far below .500. The club could not hit a lick, with the result that Whitney lost thirty-two games and Buffington suffered twenty-seven defeats. The Chicago White Stockings, pennant winners, shellacked Boston, 24–0. Big Buff had one good day when he pitched a one-hitter and fanned sixteen men against Philadelphia. Tom Gunning tied a catching record with three passed balls in one inning.

The Bostons again finished fifth in 1886. They had a new pitcher in Bill Stemmyer, who uncorked sixty-four wild pitches in forty-one

39

games, and a new catcher in Pat Dealey, who had ten passed balls in one game. Boston had acquired Hoss Radbourne from Providence, when that club folded after the 1885 season, but he was thirty-three years old and nearly pitched out. Radbourne was paid $4,500 in 1886, and he stayed with the Red Stockings until 1890.

Boston figured ingloriously in the close race between Chicago and Detroit for the 1886 pennant. Chicago won the flag the last day of the season by beating Boston, while Detroit was losing two games to Charlie Ferguson in Philadelphia. Pop Anson, Chicago manager, bought each Philadelphia player a suit of clothes, but he didn't buy the helpful Boston players even a pair of socks. This was the season Anson had first taken his White Stockings to Hot Springs for spring training. The Red Stockings had trained in the loft of Soden's store.

These were rough days for Honest John Morrill, whose faculty for making friends came in handy. His luck was running out, but Honest John never lost his temper and he never took a dishonest advantage of an opponent. One day a ground ball was hit to him at first base. The ball struck a pebble as he reached for it, and hopped over his glove. The official scorer gave him an error, but, his conscience troubling him, he later asked Morrill if he had ruled correctly.

After a moment's reflection, Morrill replied, "Yes, it was an error. It hit a pebble, but what of it? I'm supposed to stop those drives. When I don't, you should give me an error."

Such a fine fellow deserved a better fate. Morrill released Buffington because of a sore arm after the 1886 season, only to see Big Buff enjoy three excellent seasons with Philadelphia. But this was only a mild headache for Morrill compared to that which accompanied the appearance of Mike Kelly in 1887. Trouble was Kelly's shadow, and it was a dark day for Honest John Morrill when that shadow fell on him.

CHAPTER V

HIS ROYAL HIGHNESS

⊖

MEN still live who say that the greatest of all baseball players was not Ty Cobb, Honus Wagner, Babe Ruth, Eddie Collins, Tris Speaker, Napoleon Lajoie, Joe DiMaggio, or any player of this century. They are old men, to be sure. Men whose memories penetrate the haze of sixty years. Men who remember Michael J. Kelly—King Kelly.

"If you had ever seen him play, you would have no trouble remembering him," said Hugh Duffy of the Red Sox, as he sat one day in Fenway Park. "Kelly was in a class by himself. There has never been anyone like him since he passed away."

Kelly passed away November 8, 1894. He died of pneumonia at the Emergency Hospital in Boston. By the records, he was only thirty-seven years old, having been born in Troy, New York, in 1857. If so, he was sixteen years old when he first played for the Haymakers of Troy in 1873. But anything was possible with King Kelly. When only three years old he could hit a ball over the back-yard fence, when four he could peg a ball to second, and when five he was chewing tobacco. If this seems a little farfetched, it is at least as creditable as some of the stories told about the King.

In an exhibition game played at Austin, Texas, Kelly hit a ball into the tall grass behind the right fielder. The right fielder couldn't find it, so Kelly ran out from first base and helped him look for it.

"Well, I can't waste me time no longer," said Kel at last, and he trotted in and touched second. From there he went out and circled the left fielder, then returned to third. He started for home, but the ball had been found, and he was trapped. There ensued a long rundown, but just as the third baseman yelled, "I gotcher now, Kel," the King replied, "The hell yer have, me bucko," and he took

41

off for right field. With the third baseman pursuing him hotly, Kelly dashed through a gate in the fence and kept on running until he had reached the hotel. By then the third baseman had given up the chase, so Kelly did the only thing a sensible man could do under the circumstances. He sat down and had a drink.

Kelly was the John L. Sullivan of baseball. He wasn't the greatest hitter or fielder the game has known. Far from it. But he was a wonderful base runner, a quick thinker, an incomparable competitor, and a born comedian. It is an old story how he put himself in a game so that he could catch a foul fly even while the ball was in the air. It happened while he was playing for Boston. Charlie Ganzel was catching, and Kelly, the captain, was sitting on the bench.

The batter hit a high foul fly. Ganzel had trouble finding it, and Kelly was quick to see that he would not catch the ball. Shouting to the umpire, "Kelly now catching for Boston," the King leaped off the bench and caught the ball. It was another ten years before a rule was passed requiring all line-up changes to be announced to the spectators by the umpire.

Kelly was quick to take advantage of a situation. If the lone umpire was watching a ball hit to right field, Kelly invariably cut inside of third base on his way to the plate. Kelly was never in any danger, his opponents said, of spraining an ankle from stepping on a base.

In a series between Boston and Cleveland, Jesse Burkett, known as "The Crab," was on third base for Cleveland with two out.

The batter hit to Herman Long at shortstop, but Long's throw to Tommy Tucker at first base was too late to retire the runner. Burkett started for home when Long threw to first, but as he neared the plate, he suddenly stopped running. Kelly had dropped his mitt as though the batter was out at first, and the side retired. As Burkett turned to take the field, Kelly called for the ball, caught Tucker's throw barehanded, and tagged out The Crab.

Bobby Lowe, old Boston second baseman, tells of a similar play by which he and Kelly broke up an attempted double steal. As the man on first started for second, Lowe cut in front of second base and took Kelly's throw. When the runner on third broke for the plate, Lowe returned the ball to Kelly, who took the ball barehanded and tagged out the runner.

"Why did you take off your glove, Kel?" asked Lowe later.

42

"Because that feller was goin' ter try ter make me drop the ball, and I didn't want ter be bothered by no damn glove," said Kelly.

Tommy McCarthy, one of Boston's Heavenly Twins of the 1890's, once said, "King Kel was the greatest player I ever knew. He was better than Ewing, Bennett, and Ganzel. He had the most baseball brains, and invented new rules. He wasn't so very fast, but he was a great slider."

His Royal Highness, as he was called in Boston, demonstrated his base-running ability at the expense of a young Washington catcher, a tall, skinny fellow named Connie Mack. Hank O'Day, pitching for Washington, had a one-run lead as Kelly came to bat leading off for Boston.

"Don't waste any balls on Kelly," O'Day was told by Ted Sullivan, Washington manager. O'Day promised, "Every pitch will be a strike."

But Kelly worked the count to three balls and two strikes, fouled off four pitches in succession, then walked. He stole second on Mack and daringly went to third on a short fly to the center fielder. With the infield in, Kelly looked like a dead duck when he dashed for home on a grounder to shortstop, but although the throw was ahead of him, Kelly fooled Mack with a feint and then made his famous curving slide to touch the plate with his hand.

"It surpassed anything I have ever seen on the ball field," Sullivan wrote. Boston won the game in the fourteenth inning, with Kelly driving in the winning run.

Sullivan recalled a game played in Washington when Hoss Radbourne and King Kelly were the Boston battery, and John Kelly was the umpire. All three had been out on a party the night before and were still slightly inebriated when the game started. Curiously, all three gave impeccable performances, and while Washington had beaten Radbourne on a previous trip when he was sober, they could not beat him this day when he was intoxicated.

Kelly was probably the most popular player in all Boston baseball history. He was the darling of the fans because of his aggressiveness, his good nature, and his daring. Hugh Duffy, who played with him, was once asked to compare Honus Wagner and Nap Lajoie. He said: "I think that a pitcher would rather face Wagner than Lajoie, but it's my opinion that Mike Kelly was the greatest player ever to put on a uniform. There never was a player so outstanding, despite his many limitations. Mike had a wonderful head.

43

He was not a fast runner, yet he was the best base runner the game ever knew. A wonderful light went out when he was lost to the game. No one ever put as much life and snap into a game as he did. He was a winning ballplayer, and he infused his spirit into every man who played with him."

The King was big, but not huge, standing six feet and weighing 190 pounds. He was strong. Fred Tenney once saw him reach over a seat in a train, pick up Jack Doyle by the elbows, and drop him on the seat beside him. In the Brown University gymnasium one day, Kelly challenged two Boston players to turn him over on his back. They couldn't do it.

Mike was a hit with the fans because he taunted them. Playing right field in St. Louis on Queen Victoria's birthday, in 1886, he told the fans in the bleachers, many of whom came from the Kerry Patch district: "So yer Kerry Patchers, eh? Well, this is the twenty-fourth of May. God save the Queen! I'm coming up yer way tonight and start an Orange lodge. I expect all of yez ter join up."

He was a good friend and a poor enemy. There was no meanness in the man. Jim Hart, who had managed him in Boston and was later president of the Chicago National League club, once said: "Kelly was the hardest of all players to discipline. He never lied. He confessed his faults. He borrowed money, only to give it away."

George A. Tuohey in his book on the Braves, written in 1897, says that Kelly probably never had a payday while he was in Boston. From the directors' room adjoining the clubhouse, J. B. Billings would pay the players from a beaten-up black bag before the game. When it came Kelly's turn, he collected canceled receipts, but no cash. He was always in debt. Boston fans once gave him a house in Hingham. Within a few days, the house was mortgaged to the hilt. They also gave the King a horse and buggy, which he wasted no time cashing in.

When he stole eighty-four bases in 1887, his first season in Boston, he was given a medal by General Charles H. Taylor, publisher of the *Globe*. It was inscribed: "Champion Base Runner, Boston Baseball Club. National League, 1887. Presented by the *Boston Globe* to Michael J. Kelly." Nearly twenty years after it was given to Kelly, it was found in a New York hock shop by John Driscoll of Plymouth, Mass. He gave the relic to Michael T. (Nuf Ced) McGreevey, one of the original Royal Rooters and proprietor of a spa on Columbus Avenue near Ruggles Street, which was popular with ballplayers early in the century. Nuf Ced's granddaughter, Miss Alice Ann Thompson, gave the medal to Melville E. Webb, *Globe* baseball writer, a few years ago, and soon it will be on display at Cooperstown's baseball museum.

So beloved was the spectacular Kelly in Boston that J. W. Kelly, the Rolling Mill Man, wrote a comic song about him in 1889, which was repeatedly sung by the popular songbird of her day, Miss Maggie Cline. The lyrics went:

> I played a game of baseball, I belong to Casey's Nine!
> The crowd was feeling jolly, and the weather it was fine.
> A nobler lot of athletes, I think were never found,
> When the omnibuses landed, that day upon the ground.
> The game was quickly started, they sent me to the bat.
> I made two strikes. Says Casey, "What are you striking at?"
> I made the third, the catcher muff'd, and to the ground it fell;
> Then I ran like the divil to first, when the gang began to yell;

> Chorus:
> "Slide, Kelly, slide! Your running's a disgrace.
> Slide, Kelly, slide! Stay there, hold your base!
> If someone doesn't steal you, and your batting doesn't fail you,
> They'll take you to Australia! Slide, Kelly, slide!"

> 'Twas in the second inning, they'd call'd me in, I think,
> To take the catcher's place, while he went to get a drink,
> But something was the matter, sure I couldn't see the ball,
> And the second one that came in, broke my muzzle, nose and all.
> The crowd up in the grandstand, they yelled with all their might.
> I ran toward the clubhouse, I thought there was a fight.
> 'Twas the most unpleasant feeling, I ever felt before,
> I knew they had me rattled, when the gang began to roar:

> Chorus

> They sent me out to center field, I didn't want to go;
> The way my nose was swelling up, I must have been a show!
> They said on me depended, vict'ry or defeat.
> If a blind man was to look at us, he'd know that we were beat.
> "Sixty-four to nothing!" was the score when we got done.
> Ev'rybody there but me, said they had lots of fun.
> The news got home ahead of me, they heard I was knock'd out;
> The neighbors carried me in the house and then began to shout:

> Chorus

Some experts thought Kelly a mediocre player who stole the act through his showmanship, but John McGraw thought enough of

Kelly to name him as his all-time catcher. He was weak on easy flies in the outfield, but good on the hard ones. He excelled as a coach because he had a loud voice and liked to use it. Not only was he a good hitter but he was unsurpassed as a team man, one year leading the league with fifty-two sacrifice hits.

After having played for the Haymakers of Troy, the Olympics of Paterson, the Buckeyes of Columbus, and the Reds of Cincinnati, Kelly joined the Chicago club in 1880. For seven years he was Pop Anson's right-hand man, and his fame spread quickly throughout the land for his many heroic deeds. Stories were told of him that would have done credit to Paul Bunyan. He was constantly drinking his way into trouble, and just as constantly laughing his way out of it.

In Kelly's opinion, the Chicagos of 1882 were the greatest of all teams. "There were seven of us six feet high," he boasted. "Fred Pfeffer, the second baseman, could lay on his stomach and throw a ball a hundred yards. We wore silk stockings and the best uniforms money could git. We had 'em whipped before we even threw a ball. We had 'em scared ter death."

In 1886 Kelly led the National League hitters with an average of .388. One of the Triumvirs, J. B. Billings, thought, "Why can't we get a player like King Kelly? We need somebody like him to liven things up around here. Why can't we get Kelly himself? I wonder. . . ."

Billings proposed to his partners, Soden and Conant, that they buy Kelly from Chicago. They were skeptical. Such a thing had never been done before. Billings talked them into approaching Spalding, president of the Chicago club. There was an exchange of telegrams between the clubs. The Triumvirs bid $5,000 for Kelly, but Spalding demanded $10,000.

First, Spalding talked to Kelly. Would he agree to being "sold" to Boston? The great Kel didn't like the idea. Horses were sold. So were dogs. But not ballplayers.

"You'll get more money," promised Spalding. Kelly had been getting $3,000 a year, although in 1881 with Chicago he was paid only $1,300.

Kelly agreed to go if he could get more money. He forgot about the horses and dogs, and said, "If you can get me five thousand dollars, I don't care a damn if you sell me for a hundred thousand." Kelly wanted to get away from Chicago because Spalding would

46

not return him the money he had been fined the previous season.

Kelly was Billings's boy, so Soden and Conant let J. B. make the deal. Billings met Kelly at Poughkeepsie, New York, Feb. 14, 1887. With Billings was Billy Sullivan, *Globe* sports editor who sent the electrifying news of the unprecedented $10,000 deal back to Boston.

Five minutes after Kelly and Billings had met at the Nelson House, Billings asked the player to sign a contract. Kelly said he would—for $5,000.

"So," wrote Sullivan, "they began a philosophical discussion on the value of ballplayers. Mike sat in the corner of the reading room, and a tight-fitting Prince Albert coat set off his finely built athletic figure, while he told why 'diamonds cannot be bought with shoe-strings.' He toyed with a diminutive cane and puffed a cigarette. For an hour and a half the discussion went on. But just before noon it came to an end. Mr. Billings had come here to sign Kelly and was not going away without doing so.

"The contract was drawn up for two thousand dollars, the limit, and then Mr. Billings said that the Boston club wanted a picture of their new player and would pay well (three thousand dollars) for it."

"Well, I am with you," said Kelly to Sullivan. And Billings tucked the contract away, saying heavily, "Good things come high, but we must have them."

Billings had worked on the deal since January. He said to Sullivan, "Ten thousand dollars is quite a sum for one player, isn't it? We thought so, and considered the price decidedly high."

There was great enthusiasm in Boston over the acquisition of the "king of players." It was baseball's biggest deal since the Four Seceders had left Boston in 1875 for Chicago. It also brought commercialism into baseball on a grand scale, but few people in 1887 ever thought that players within the next fifty years would be bought for as much as $250,000. Like Soden's reserve clause, the practice of buying players was a major contribution to the game by the Triumvirs.

Kelly's reaction to his sale to Boston was, "You always guyed us fearfully here, but for all that, you turned out big ter see us play ball."

He could do everything but pitch, Kel said, and he had even tried that once against Buffalo. "But," he explained, " 'Old Brouth,' he made a homer the very first thing, and then Jack Rowe put in a

47

three-bagger, and I retired. No, I ain't no pitcher, but in a pinch I might make 'em hustle. I'd have some fun, anyhow!"

"He's one of the jolliest fellows in the world," Sullivan told his Boston readers. "Mike boils over with enthusiasm on the field. He cannot fail to inspire every man. Just such a spirit has long been wanted on our nine."

But for every ounce of joy in Boston, there was one ounce of bitterness in Chicago, where Kelly had first been given the crown that became him so well. Spalding was accused of being money-mad. When Kelly played his first game for Boston in Chicago in 1887, papers gave columns to the return of the King. But His Royal Highness was not at his best. He lost a silver service to Pop Anson when the Bostons were beaten because he was thrown out at first on a single to center field. He had such a bad Charley horse that he was scarcely able to run.

The Triumvirs exploited His Royal Highness, calling him "the ten-thousand-dollar beauty" and encouraging people to come out and see the great Kelly, but the King entered the picture much too soon. Playing in this era, he might have rivaled Babe Ruth as a gate attraction.

CHAPTER VI

THREE IN A ROW

INSTEAD of a pennant, King Kelly brought dissension to the Boston Nationals, who about this time were being called the Beaneaters as the league's baseball writers sought to get away from Reds and Red Stockings, which seemed to belong to Cincinnati. Famed for its baked beans, Boston was inevitably associated with Beaneaters by out-of-towners. Kelly helped make the name popular by calling himself a "beaneater."

Kelly's presence immediately became onerous to John Morrill. Although Morrill remained as manager in 1887, Kelly replaced him as captain, a position that then carried more prestige. The Bostons finished fifth in a seesaw pennant race that was won by Detroit. Their chief boasts were scoring ten runs in the tenth inning to beat New York the morning of June 17, and hitting eight home runs in one game against Washington.

Striving for harmony, the Triumvirs made Morrill captain as well as manager in 1888. Striving for some badly needed pitching, they bought John Clarkson from Chicago for $10,000. Clarkson, who had been born across the Charles River in Cambridge in 1861, was a superb pitcher, having won fifty-three games for Chicago in 1885, thirty-six games in 1886, and thirty-eight games in 1887. In 1885 he had pitched a no-hit game against Providence. He stood next to Kelly and Pop Anson in popularity in Chicago. Spalding was a brave man to sell Clarkson, after having sold Kelly. In Boston they called Clarkson and Kelly "the twenty-thousand-dollar battery."

"Clarkson is one of the greatest of pitchers," Anson once said, "but it takes a lot of encouragement to keep him going. He won't pitch if scolded, but if praised he'll pitch three days in a row."

49

Clarkson won thirty-three games for the Beaneaters in 1888, a poor season for Handsome John, who was one of the most scientific of the early pitchers. He depended on curves and control and he studied hitters and pitched to their weaknesses. With his wonderfully supple fingers and wrists, he could spin a billiard ball so that it would make a complete circle on the table. Of the five Clarkson boys of Cambridge, John was by far the most famous. Although high-strung, he was to win three hundred and twenty-eight and lose one hundred seventy-six games in eleven seasons.

Despite Clarkson's presence, the Beaneaters of 1888 could finish no better than fourth. The Triumvirs, especially Conant and Billings, became cold toward Manager Morrill. When he held out for more money before the 1889 season, the temperature of their regard dropped even lower. Billings, when he purchased Kelly, had said, "Morrill is too sensitive, and in losing does not play the game of which he is capable."

In March, Morrill signed his contract, saying, "I'm perfectly satisfied. I appreciate the many kind words spoken in my behalf by the baseball public." Asked where he would play, the manager replied, "I don't feel timid about being placed in any infield position." There was no lively ball then, of course.

But the issue was not resolved. On Fast Day, the Triumvirs asked Morrill to captain the picked team, while Kelly captained the Beaneaters. Morrill was outraged, and refused. The next day, he and Sam Wise, infielder, were sold to Washington. President Soden made a statement:

"The directors saw yesterday that the patrons of the game were divided between Morrill and Kelly. It came down to who should go. Morrill has many friends in this city and is a perfect gentleman. Kelly is a ballplayer. So it was for us to choose between the men, and we picked out Kelly as the one who could win the most games."

Soden dismissed Wise by saying: "He has too many friends here. He will play better in Washington."

The next day Tim Murnane wrote in the *Boston Globe*: "Some of the best known business men in the city called at the *Globe* office last evening to condemn the action of the Boston directors in allowing Mike Kelly to drive Honest John Morrill out of his home."

50

The Triumvirs chose James A. Hart, who had managed Milwaukee in 1888, to replace Morrill as manager. Besides the twenty-thousand-dollar battery, Hart inherited the Big Four—Charlie Bennett, Charlie Ganzel, Hardie Richardson, and Dan Brouthers—who had been bought for $26,000 when the Detroit club went out of business because of poor attendance. With these purchases, sensational in their day, Soden introduced and established the practice of buying ballplayers.

The judgment of the Triumvirs in releasing Morrill was vindicated. The Washington club finished in last place. Morrill, its captain and manager, broke a finger and was released in July, the Washington president saying bluntly, "Morrill was no use to us as a player or manager. He did not produce."

But when Morrill made his first visit in a Washington uniform to the South End Grounds on June 13, he knew one of the great moments of his life. Murnane described his reception:

"Morrill was given the greatest ovation ever given to a ballplayer in this country. He went to bat in the second inning, and the crowd rose with a shout that might have been heard a mile away. Cheers were given with a will, hats were thrown in the air. Then came a steady round of cheering for fully five minutes, while Mr. Morrill stood with bowed head at home plate."

Morrill, when he retired as a player, became a sporting-goods dealer and the author of weekly articles on baseball for the *Boston Journal*. He acquired some fame for such accessories as the Morrill pneumatic water bottle, the football nose mask, and laced-front football pants, and for predicting that spring training trips by big-league teams would be a failure, there being too much danger for the players in the balmy Southern weather.

Hart proved to be a conservative and capable manager for the Beaneaters in 1889, being content to remain in the background while King Kelly, captain of the team, performed from the front of the stage. Hart was a close friend of Spalding, having accompanied him to England on the baseball junket of 1874.

On the 1889 Beaneaters besides the Big Four were: Joe Quinn, second baseman who had been bought the previous August from Des Moines for $4,000; Billy Nash, third baseman; Dickie Johnston, handsome left fielder; Pop Smith, shortstop; Tom Brown, outfielder; Clarkson; and, of course, the great Kelly. The original Big Four, for which Detroit had bought the entire Buffalo franchise

51

in 1885, was comprised of Brouthers, Richardson, Jim White, and John Charles Rowe.

The mighty Dennis Brouthers, six foot two and weighing 200 pounds, hit .373 in 1889, his only season with the Boston Nationals, to lead the league. Brouthers believed in moving around. He had played with Buffalo five years and Detroit three years before coming to the Beaneaters, but in 1890 he was with the Boston Brotherhood team, in 1891 with the Boston team in the American Association, and in 1892 with Brooklyn in the National League, before going to Baltimore during the 1893 season. Thus, Brouthers played with six different big-league clubs in six seasons.

But for all of Brouthers's hitting and for all of Clarkson's pitching, the Beaneaters had to be satisfied with second place in 1889. Clarkson pitched in seventy-two games, winning fifty and losing nineteen of them. On September 12, he won two games. At the end of August, Boston had a two-game lead over New York, but the Giants, defending champions under James J. Mutrie, took the lead late in September, after playing furious 9-to-9 and 4-to-4 ties with Boston, and staved off the final rush of the Beaneaters in one of the closest of races.

Entering the last week of the season, Boston trailed by three percentage points, New York's record being 79–42 .653 and Boston's 80–43 .650. At Cleveland on September 30, Boston trailed 2–3 in the seventh. It was raining, and it was dark. There were only 300 spectators present. The umpire wanted to call the game, but King Kelly shouted, "We can see to play. I'll show you I can see the ball." He promptly doubled, and Boston went on to score four runs, win the game, 6–3, and keep pace with New York, which won in Pittsburgh. Clarkson allowed only six hits.

The next day, October 1, Boston again beat the Spiders, 8–5, while Pittsburgh beat New York, 7–2. Boston was now leading the league by a full game. Clarkson allowed twelve hits, and Kelly proclaimed, "If Clarkson should win the pennant, they ought to erect a monument to him in Boston."

But it was second place again for Boston the next day. The Spiders beat them, 7–1, with Beatin holding the Beaneaters to only four hits. New York beat Pittsburgh, 6–3, to regain the lead by three tiny percentage points. This was the day Boston lost the pennant, and, alas, what a way to lose it! Captain Mike Kelly could not play because of "a jollification during last night with several

52

theatrical friends." The great King could only sit on the bench in a light overcoat, and he did not sit there long.

Richardson was called out at the plate by Umpire McQuaid, and Kelly arose to tell the umpire flatly that he was stealing the championship from Boston. Said Kelly, "You're bound to do the Bostons out of the championship."

McQuaid resented the tone of Kelly's remarks and asked police to put him out of the park. The police dealt rather roughly with Kelly, and as one of them held a billy poised over his noggin, one of the Cleveland players protested, "Say, you're dealing rather roughly with him, aren't you? You'd think he was a murderer."

"We've heard of this chap and think he's a disgrace to the business," Tim Murnane quotes the officer. Kelly was released outside the park. Manager Hart bought him a ticket so he could return, but the police wouldn't let him in.

There was quite a rhubarb about Kelly's ejection. Triumvir Bill Conant, who had just got in from a scouting trip on which he had picked up a young pitcher named Nichols, admitted that more than one league magnate had suggested blacklisting Kelly. But he added, "I think they're mistaken in their man." For his Boston readers, Murnane explained that Cleveland was Kelly's bad town. A friend named Al Johnson had cracked a few bottles of Pomery Sec the night before, and Kelly had imbibed rather freely. But Murnane hastened to explain, "Kelly is not the only Boston player who has enjoyed life in Cleveland."

Kelly's absence from the line-up at this stage of the race was a terrible blow to the people back in Boston who were filling the Music Hall each afternoon to see the game replayed from telegraphic reports. Even the famed "Hi! Hi!" cheer of General Arthur Dixwell, for thirty years a faithful follower of the Bostons, was momentarily silenced that awful day in Cleveland.

Clarkson, that day pitching his seventh successive game, "had no speed whatever," according to Murnane, but he only pitched eight innings, moving to third base while Billy Nash pitched the ninth. Thus, he was well rested the next day, when the Beaneaters opened in Pittsburgh with a 7-to-2 victory. Clarkson was thought foolish to go to the box for the eighth successive time, "but John intended to fight for the old rag as long as there was the slightest show to get it." The opposition was "piping off" Clarkson's signals, but wily John crossed them up.

53

Although back in the line-up, "not a smile lit up the usually jolly Kelly." He muffed a fly and was cheered by the Pittsburgh fans. On some careless base running he was caught between second and third. The Bostons won, but what good did it do? New York beat Cleveland, 9–0, and kept the lead.

Clarkson took a whole day off on October 5, complaining of a cold in his chest, but Madden pitched the Beaneaters to a 4-to-3 victory. Brouthers singled in Bennett with the winning run with two out in the last—yes, the home team usually batted first in those days—of the ninth. But New York beat Cleveland, 6–1, and so the teams came down to the last day with New York still ahead by three whiskers.

Before the final game, General Charles H. Taylor, publisher of the *Globe*, promised the Beaneaters $1,000 if they won the pennant.

Perhaps this offer is what prompted Hart and Clarkson to send a telegram to the Cleveland manager: "We will give your team $1,000 if Boston wins the pennant, $500 to the battery in today's game, and the like amount to the rest of the team."

The inducement was not sufficient to inspire Cleveland. New York won, 5–3, to clinch the pennant. In Pittsburgh, "Clarkson was so downhearted when he saw the Cleveland score that he had very little speed." Pitching his ninth game in ten days, Clarkson also was slightly stiff. Pittsburgh scored three runs off him in the first inning and went on to win, 6–1. Kelly played right field and also caught, made three hits, and scored Boston's only run.

Loss of the pennant hurt in Boston. Editorials were written blaming Hart, the manager. Hadn't he let Kelly make an exhibition of himself in Cleveland? Yet Conant had told Hart he was the best manager Boston had ever had. Hart complained that Boston on its western trip had to face all the best pitchers, while New York faced soft touches, in several places green amateurs. Charlie Bennett blamed the umpires, and Kelly—why, Kelly blamed the league officials, saying, "We didn't win the pennant because we were outplayed off the field, not on it." That certainly applied to Kelly.

The players were cheered a little when Murnane got a telegram from the *Globe* publisher: "Tell the boys that the *Globe* will pay that $1,000 because they worked so hard for it. Defeat never scares the *Globe*." They were so cheered up that they chipped in and bought a present for General Dixwell, their loyal mascot.

The Triumvirs did not suffer very much. The Beaneaters had

54

drawn 295,000 fans into the South End Grounds for a $100,000 profit.

2

The Beaneaters had a new manager in 1890, a leader in the true Harry Wright tradition. Frank Selee was born in Amherst, New Hampshire, and lived in Truro on Cape Cod, but he had spent most of his youth at Melrose, Massachusetts. He played some as a professional at Waltham and Lawrence in 1884, but in 1885-86 had turned to managing Haverhill, in the New England League. He won the Northwestern League pennant with Oshkosh in 1887, and moved to Omaha in 1888, winning the pennant there in 1889.

Conant had contacted Selee while scouting Kid Nichols, Omaha pitcher, in 1889. Besides recommending Nichols, Selee had tipped off Conant on a promising young player in Milwaukee named Bobby Lowe. The Triumvir bought Lowe for $700, one of baseball's biggest bargains.

Selee was a fine judge of players. Among his finds were Fred Tenney, Jimmy Collins, Charles Sylvester Stahl, Ted Lewis, Martin Bergen, and Fred Klobedanz. Like several other shrewd baseball men, he made one major mistake. He turned down a rawboned Fall River Frenchman named Napoleon Lajoie, who subsequently broke in with the Philadelphia Nationals and became an all-time second baseman.

"He was a good judge of players," Lowe once said of Selee. "He didn't bother with a lot of signals, but let his players figure out their own plays. He didn't blame them if they took a chance that failed. He believed in place-hitting, sacrifice-hitting, and stealing bases. He was wonderful with young players."

Under Selee, Boston teams acquired a reputation for playing inside baseball. His teams outthought the opposition, besides outplaying it.

The son of a Methodist clergyman, Selee was a quiet, courteous gentleman, mild of manner and not robust physically. George Tuohey attributes "the gentlemanly deportment" for which the Bostons were noted to Selee, with Ed Hanlon of Baltimore the most successful manager of the 1890-1900 era.

"If I make things pleasant for the players, they reciprocate," Selee once explained. "I want them to be temperate and live properly. I do not believe that men who are engaged in such exhilarating

55

exercise should be kept in strait jackets all the time, but I expect them to be in condition to play. I do not want a man who cannot appreciate such treatment."

Selee's methods brought results. In twelve seasons, his Boston teams finished in the first division nine times, winning five pennants, and never finished below fifth place.

Although the Beaneaters had finished a close second in 1889, Selee faced a hopeless task in 1890, because the National Brotherhood of Base Ball Players, a fraternal order organized by John Montgomery Ward in 1885, went on a rampage and formed the Players' National League. The Beaneaters lost ten of their most important players from the team of 1889 to the rival league.

King Kelly was manager and captain of the Brotherhood team in Boston, which played at the Congress Street Grounds. Dan Brouthers was active in signing players for Boston. Honest John Morrill was a minor club official. The chief grievance was Soden's reserve rule, which prevented the players from shopping around each season. The players argued that the owners were becoming rich at their expense. The players were mere slaves, limited to salaries of $2,000 a season.

Players who transferred their allegiance from the Boston Nationals to the Boston Brotherhood team included Kelly, Hardie Richardson, Billy Nash, Brouthers, Joe Quinn, Dickie Johnston, Charles (Hoss) Radbourne, Tom Brown, Bill Daley, and Mike Madden. Players who were loyal to the Beaneaters included Clarkson, Charlie Bennett, Charlie Ganzel, and Charles (Pop) Smith. This was a slim nucleus for Selee.

Boston won the pennant in the Brotherhood, but finished fifth in the National League. Yet it was the Brotherhood that couldn't stand the gaff. The teams played at home on the same days, with the result that attendances were small. Both teams lost money, but the Triumvirs had more to lose. National League owners kept luring back players who had seceded to the new league. King Kelly was offered $10,000 to return to the Boston Nationals, but after wrestling with his conscience, he turned it down. He said, "I'll stick with the boys."

The Brotherhood served one good purpose in Boston. It forced the Triumvirs to find new players. They found some good ones—good enough to help the Beaneaters win three successive pennants in 1891, 1892, and 1893. There was Tommy Tucker, gamest of all first basemen because he played with a fingerless mitt, who was bought from Baltimore for $3,000 and signed for $4,000 and a $1,500 bonus. And Bobby Lowe, bought from Milwaukee for $700 by Conant. And Herman Long, bought from Kansas City early in the season for $6,300, who became one of the game's greatest shortstops. And there was Charlie (Kid) Nichols, who had pitched for Selee in Omaha, in 1889. The Triumvirs had much to be thankful for in their war against the Brotherhood, although they did not think so in 1890.

Kid Nichols was born at Madison, Wisconsin, September 14, 1869. He won attention by pitching for the amateur Blue Avenue Club in Kansas City, in 1886. He pitched his first professional game for Kansas City in the Western League in 1887, a year in which he won twenty-one and lost eleven games. He pitched for Memphis and Kansas City in 1888, and in 1889 for Frank Selee at Omaha, in the Western Association, winning thirty-six and losing twelve games.

He was scouted by Conant, one of the Triumvirs, late in 1889, and bought for $3,500. When Conant joined the Beaneaters in Cleveland, he told John Clarkson: "John, I have a good man to help you. This Nichols is a strapping fellow and looks very much as Buffington did when he first came to Boston."

But the Beaneaters were not much interested in the new pitcher. They were fighting for the pennant and they were scheming for the Brotherhood League they planned to form. And, of course, Cleveland was a very sociable town for King Kelly and a few of the boys.

Conant wasn't talking through his hat. Nichols became a perfect running mate for Clarkson. He pitched for all of Boston's five pennant winners in the 1890's, and his record indicates that he is the best pitcher ever to wear a Boston uniform in any league. It is a mystery to the fans of his era why Nichols had not, up to 1947, been elected to baseball's Hall of Fame.

Selee's makeshift team was second as late as August, but a September slump during which they won only six of twenty-one games dropped them to fifth place. But Nichols had won twenty-seven games in his first season, Long had hit two home runs in his debut against Brooklyn, and Lowe and Tucker had looked like potential stars. Except for injuries to Clarkson, Long, Lowe, and Patsy Donovan, the center fielder, Selee's first team would have finished in the first division. That the 1890 Beaneaters had a 76-to-57 record while finishing fifth was explained by the terrible showing of the Pittsburgh club, which won twenty-three while losing one hundred and fourteen games. The Bostons this season won more games on the road than at home.

Besides Long's two homers in his first game, off Bobby Caruthers and Bill (Adonis) Terry of Brooklyn, Boston highlights of the 1890 season were five bases on balls and one hit-by-pitcher in a game for Pop Smith, Boston's second baseman; and the 1-to-0 defeat for Kid Nichols in the Polo Grounds, May 12. Mike Tierney, according to eyewitnesses, hit the ball 500 feet over the center-field flagpole, with two out in the eleventh inning, to give Amos Rusie the victory.

But with Nichols winning twenty-seven and losing nineteen games, and finishing all forty-six games he started during the season, there was no doubt that the Beaneaters had picked up quite a pitcher. And since Charlie (Pretzel) Getzein had won twenty-three and lost fifteen games, and John Clarkson's record was 25–18, Boston prospects for 1891 were rosy indeed when the Brotherhood magnates bought the Cincinnati National League club and closed up their league.

3

There was another war in 1891, this one brought on by that good old Boston sharpshooter Arthur H. Soden. The American Association, then rated a big league, had stood on the side lines watching the war of 1890, now and then getting kicked in the teeth, as innocent bystanders are apt to do while hanging on the outskirts of a free-for-all fight. Players jumped to the Brotherhood from the American Association, as well as from the National League.

Two of these jumpers were Harry D. Stovey and Louis Bierbauer of the Philadelphia Athletics. Stovey played on Boston's pennant-winning Brotherhood team in 1890. When peace was declared, the Athletics failed to put either Stovey or Bierbauer on their reserve list. As soon as Soden learned of the oversight, he signed Stovey for the Beaneaters. The Pittsburgh club did as much for Bierbauer. When the Board of Control upheld Boston and Pittsburgh, the American Association declared war on the National League.

A team was formed in Boston to fight the Beaneaters, with Arthur A. Irwin, South Boston resident who had once been Provi-

58

dence's captain, as manager; and Charles Alfred Prince as president. Prince was an upper-crust lawyer, a Harvard graduate, who nearly went broke trying to buck the Triumvirs, and wanting to put the Atlantic between himself and baseball, took a long vacation in France.

Both the Beaneaters and the Reds won pennants for Boston in 1891, but only the Beaneaters survived the costly war. Two valuable players returned to them, Billy Nash and Joe Quinn, and late in the season Mike Kelly came back after managing in Cincinnati.

Captain of the Reds was Hugh Duffy, and they had such familiar players as Brouthers, Daley, Buffington, Tom Brown, and Hardie Richardson. They also had a young pitcher named Clark Calvin Griffith, who was to become a leading hurler, and eventually owner of the Washington Senators. The Boston Reds of 1891 were one of baseball's finest teams.

The Beaneaters of 1891 had an infield composed of Tucker at first, Quinn at second, Nash at third, and Long at shortstop. Lowe played some at second base, but usually patrolled left field, while Stovey played right, and Walter Brodie, bought from Hamilton, Ontario, for $1,000 before the 1890 season, played center. Bennett and Ganzel were the catchers; Nichols, Clarkson, Getzein, and Harry Staley the pitchers. A youngster from Cambridge named Joe Kelley, who was later to star for the Baltimore Orioles and still later to manage the Boston Nationals, played a few games in the outfield. Nash, captain of the team, received a three-year contract at $5,000 and a $2,500 bonus to return to the Beaneaters.

Clarkson had a good season, winning thirty-four and losing eighteen games, while Nichols in his second season won thirty and lost seventeen games. Getzein slumped badly, but Staley was a winner with a 19-to-8 record. While Brouthers was hitting .349 for the Boston Reds, to lead the American Association, the Beaneaters did not have a single .300 hitter. Long led them with .287, and he also stole fifty-eight bases.

Beaneater fans were treated to the extremes in offensive potency when Stovey went to bat five times and struck out five times in one game; while in another game, Lowe made six hits—four singles, a double, and a homer—in six times at bat.

Chicago led the 1891 race through May, June, July, and August, but the Beaneaters took the lead in September, a month in which they won twenty-three out of thirty games. Boston clinched the pennant the last week of the season by beating Buck Ewing's Giants in Boston. There were some wild rumors after this series, because Ewing had not publicized the extent of New York injuries. The defeats of the Giants looked phony to the suspicious, and especially to those with money on Chicago.

For the first time in three seasons, Boston had only one professional team in 1892. They were the Beaneaters. This was a banner season for the Triumvirs. In June, the clubs were given permission to cut abnormally high salaries brought on by the wars with the Brotherhood and American Association. As if this were not balm enough, the Beaneaters won the pennant by eight and a half games over Cleveland; and then beat Cleveland in a postseason play-off for the championship without losing a game.

The Beaneaters were good in 1891, but they were better in 1892. They used the same infield of Tucker, Quinn, Long, and Nash. But to go with Lowe in the outfield, they had the Heavenly Twins, Hugh Duffy, from the Boston Association team, and Tommy McCarthy, from the St. Louis Association. Stovey and Brodie were released.

Selee had three fine catchers in Mike Kelly, Bennett, and Ganzel; and he had three superb pitchers in Nichols, Staley, and Happy Jack Stivetts. A huge, good-natured fellow from the Pennsylvania coal mines, who was only twenty-four years old when he joined the Beaneaters, Stivetts looked like Cy Young. He was a hard hitter and a good outfielder, as well as a fine pitcher.

To Stivetts went the distinction of being the first Boston pitcher to hurl a no-hit game. In the first fifteen years of their existence, the Bostons had participated in only one no-hit game, that being pitched against them in 1880 by Larry Corcoran of Chicago. But on August 6, 1892, Stivetts pitched a no-hitter against the Bridegrooms at Brooklyn. He won, 11–0, but it was far from a perfect game. Stivetts gave five bases on balls, and the Beaneaters made three errors.

During the season, the high-strung John Clarkson drew his release because of a sore arm. His willingness to sacrifice himself on the pitching altar for the good of the team had caught up with Handsome John. He signed with Cleveland and pitched twice against the Beaneaters in the postseason series, losing both games. Like Hoss Radbourne, Clarkson's big-league career spanned only eleven years.

60

But the Beaneaters did not need Clarkson in 1892, for Nichols won thirty-five and lost sixteen games; Staley won thirty-three, lost fourteen games; and Stivetts won twenty-four, lost eleven games. Because there were twelve teams in the National League in 1892, the season was divided into halves, the winners to meet at the end of the season. This was the only time the National League ever split its season.

Boston won the first half by a margin of two and a half games over Brooklyn. The Beaneaters opened by winning eleven of thirteen games in April and went on to win easily. "Too exhilarated," as one expert put it, the Bostons got away slowly in the second half, and though they won fifty games while losing only twenty-six, they trailed Cleveland by three games. Since Boston's over-all standing was 102–48 and Cleveland's 93–56, the Beaneaters won the pennant. The Triumvirs said they did not want to play the postseason series, arguing that fans would claim the Beaneaters had purposely lost the second half, but league officials insisted that the series be held.

The series was to be the best of nine games, with the first three games scheduled for Cleveland, the next three for Boston, and the final three, if necessary, for a neutral park. It was not unprecedented for a championship series to be played on neutral ground. In 1887, Detroit, of the National League, had beaten St. Louis, of the American Association, ten out of fifteen games, in a series that visited Boston, as well as Pittsburgh, Brooklyn, New York, Philadelphia, Baltimore, Washington, and Chicago.

The first game of the Boston-Cleveland series, played before 6,000 fans at Cleveland, was a 0-to-0 tie, being called after eleven innings because of darkness. The Beaneaters made six hits off Cy Young; Cleveland made only four hits off Stivetts. There was a horrible example of poor sportsmanship by King Kelly in this game, which was explained by one observer as follows:

"Zimmer [Cleveland catcher] was debarred from making an easy catch owing to the dirty ball playing characteristically indulged in by Kelly, who had a heavy bet on Boston's winning the first game. This was exhibited in the ninth inning, when Stivetts popped up a fly ball that Zimmer ran to catch, he being called to take the ball. Just then, Kelly called for Virtue [Cleveland first baseman] to take the ball, and in consequence both ran for it, and the result was a collision, as Kelly intended, and the ball was missed. It did not

61

benefit the Bostons, however, as they scored a blank, despite Kelly's dirty work. He was fined ten dollars for the call."

Boston won the second game, 4–3, as Staley outpitched Clarkson. With the score tied, 2–2, Boston scored a run in the fifth and added another in the eighth. Duffy made three hits, McCarthy and Tucker two each.

Boston also won the third game, 3–2, with Stivetts beating Young, as the Beaneaters broke a 2-to-2 tie in the eighth inning. Stivetts fanned six men and walked eight.

The series shifted to Boston, and the Beaneaters won, 4–0, as Nichols pitched a seven-hit shutout against Cleveland's Coppy. Duffy again made three hits.

Cleveland blew up in the fifth game, after Clarkson was given a 6-to-0 lead. Clarkson himself hit a home run, with two men on base in the third inning. Then Boston batted him all over the lot, scoring three runs in the fourth, two in the fifth, four in the sixth, and three in the seventh. Tucker hit a home run, one of his three hits, while Stivetts, who pitched for the Beaneaters, and McCarthy made two hits each. A crowd of 3,466 Boston fans enjoyed this slug fest.

Nichols beat Young again, 8–3, in the sixth game, to give Boston a sweep of the series. Cleveland took a 3-to-0 lead in the third, but the Beaneaters went ahead in the fourth and won going away.

Hugh Duffy, who had led Boston hitters during the season by hitting .302, also led them in the series by making twelve hits in six games. Kelly caught two games, but failed to hit safely. Thus ended the best season the Triumvirs had ever enjoyed.

The Beaneaters gave their competitors some more of the same punishment in 1893, winning the pennant by five games from Pittsburgh. The Beaneaters made a trip to Charlottesville, Virginia, during spring training and got away to a flying start. It was such a runaway by the middle of July that the Beaneaters began to coast, and in September they had to win a series from Pittsburgh in Boston to assure themselves the pennant.

It was in this series that Connie Mack, Pittsburgh catcher, had his leg broken by Herman Long, Boston shortstop. Long scored from third base on a single to left, and although there was no play being made on him, he crashed into Mack and put him out of the game for the rest of the season. There seems to be difference of opinion as to whether Long intentionally gave Mack the works, or whether Connie was blocking the plate.

62

Selee had changed his team slightly, trading Joe Quinn to St. Louis for Cliff Carroll, a left fielder, and putting Bobby Lowe at second base. Bill Merritt replaced King Kelly as third-string catcher, behind Bennett and Ganzel; Harry Gastright helped Nichols, Staley, and Stivetts with the pitching. Nichols had another fine season, winning thirty-two and losing fourteen games. The records of the other pitchers were: Stivetts 21–12, Gastright 12–4, and Staley 19–10. Not a player was released from the start of the season to the finish—a record.

Duffy led the league by hitting .378, while the other Heavenly Twin, McCarthy, hit .360. This season the pitching distance was increased to sixty feet six inches, and flat bats were abolished. The swap was a bargain for the hitters, according to the averages, which soared like stock shares in a bull market.

The Beaneaters of 1893 were so far ahead of their rivals that John Montgomery Ward, manager of the Giants, said, "The Bostons could have beaten any all-star nine the league could have put together this season."

The Boston team had everything—pitching, hitting, fielding, speed on the bases. But most of all it had teamwork and headwork. The Beaneaters perfected the use of the hit-and-run play. Whereas other teams were still sacrificing runners from first to second, the Beaneaters were running and hitting at the same time, to draw rival infielders out of position. The Beaneaters of 1893 were the first team to emphasize the big inning. It was no accident that they scored 1,003 runs to lead the league.

The Beaneaters made great use of signals, with runners on second telling the hitters what to expect from the pitchers. "And the chief schemer," said Ward, "is McCarthy. He sets the pace for Duffy, Long, Lowe, and Carroll when it comes to thinking up something new."

McCarthy found time to set an outfielding record of fifty-three assists in one hundred and seven games. Tommy Tucker made four doubles in one game. In the second inning of a game against Pittsburgh, August 19, four Boston batters were hit by pitched balls— a certain sign of a lack of affection between these teams. But the record the Triumvirs liked best was made at the gate. The club made money, as well as base hits, and the Triumvirs rejoiced, as well they might after several lean and hard years during which they had practically carried the whole National League on their dollar-padded shoulders. Time after time, Nick Young, president of the National League, called on Soden to rescue a sinking club during these years, and always Soden threw out a life preserver filled with ten thousand or more bills. Soden loaned some sixty thousand dollars to John B. Day, president of the Giants, taking bonds and common stocks in that club as security. He later redeemed the bonds, but he held onto the stock for years. Thanks largely to Soden's nerve, judgment, and bankroll, the National League won the baseball wars of 1884, 1890, and 1891.

CHAPTER VII

THE HEAVENLY TWINS

HAVING won the pennant in 1891, 1892, and 1893, there seemed to be no reason why the Beaneaters could not win it indefinitely. Selee and the Triumvirs had assembled an all-star team in the uniforms of the Boston Nationals, and yet this powerhouse not only failed to win the pennant in 1894, but finished third, eight games behind the Baltimore Orioles. Entering the final month of the season, the Beaneaters trailed the Orioles by a half game, but while they were winning fourteen and losing eleven games, the clan of Hanlon, McGraw, Jennings, and Robinson was winning twenty out of twenty-three games. Even the Giants passed the Beaneaters.

How could the Beaneaters of 1894, who set wholesale batting and scoring records, finish third? George Tuohey writes, "A tendency to noisy coaching had an ill effect." *Spalding's Guide* says that the team became unpopular because of excessive bickering and use of profanity. The pitching staff was thin, and the Beaneaters felt the loss of their prized catcher, Charlie Bennett.

Baseball has had few more tragic accidents than that which befell Bennett, a superb catcher who had played on one pennant winner at Detroit and three at Boston. On January 10, 1894, a Santa Fe passenger train ran over Bennett at Wellesville, Kansas, and he lost both lower limbs. Bennett, on his way from Kansas City to Williamsburg, got off the train to speak to a friend. It was cold. The platform was icy. As he started to swing aboard the moving train, Bennett slipped beneath the wheels.

Bennett, who was thirty-eight years old at the time of the accident, had been counted on to handle Nichols, Stivetts, Gastright, and Staley in 1894. He was rugged, tough, and smart. A native of New Castle, Pennsylvania, Bennett first caught for Milwaukee and

65

Worcester. Like other early catchers, he wore only a fingerless kid glove. He once showed the spunk of a Spartan by catching game after game with a split finger, sponging it with antiseptic between innings. His hands were as knotted and gnarled as limbs off an old oak tree. He was born to take physical punishment, and nothing could stop him—nothing but the wheels of a train.

Bennett was one of the Big Four bought from Detroit by the Triumvirs in 1889. They admired him so in Detroit that they named the first American League field there after him. He had led the 1887 Detroit champions by hitting .363, but he was not a particularly robust hitter for Boston. In 1890, however, he won a memorable 1-to-0 victory for Kid Nichols by hitting a home run in the twelfth inning. During the baseball wars of 1890 and 1891, Bennett remained with the Beaneaters. He demanded $5,000, a $500 bonus, and a $5,000 advance to join the Brotherhood, but didn't get it.

The loss of Bennett was a shock to Boston fans and an irreparable blow to the Beaneaters. They used Haverhill's Jack Ryan, Frank Connaughton, and Bill Merritt behind the plate, as well as Ganzel, but not one was another Charlie Bennett. Selee was so desperate for a receiver that he signed a left-handed Brown University catcher, Fred Tenney, but found him inexperienced and playing out of position.

A benefit game was held for Bennett, August 27, 1894, at the Congress Street Grounds. It was a pathetic scene, as the great catcher stood speechless and legless at home plate. The Beaneaters met a picked college nine. Gentleman Jim Corbett, Heavyweight Champion of the World, played several innings at first base for the Beaneaters, who won, 17–12. A crowd of 6,000 fans attended. Bennett was given the receipts—$6,000. He went to Detroit and opened a pottery business, and though he had lost a couple of legs, he had lost none of his toughness. He lived to be seventy-two years old.

What a pity that the carnage wrought by the 1894 Beaneaters had to be wasted! Baseball had never seen such hitting. Seven Boston players scored more than one hundred runs during the season, and the team set a record with twelve hundred and twenty-one runs. Not once were the Beaneaters shut out. They scored sixteen runs in the first inning of a game against Baltimore. In one inning they hit four homers and two doubles off Bill Lampe, Cincinnati pitcher. Bobby Lowe hit four home runs in one game. Hugh

Duffy batted .438, hit safely in twenty-six consecutive games, hit two doubles in one inning, and drew two bases on balls in one inning. Duffy, Lowe, Long, and McCarthy went to bat three times in one inning. Duffy hit eighteen home runs, and Lowe hit fifteen— and still the Beaneaters could not win their fourth consecutive pennant.

There must have been dynamite in the ball in 1894. No fewer than fifty-two National League regulars hit .300 or better. Sam Thompson of Philadelphia could hit .403 and not even come close to Duffy. The Beaneaters got a taste of what was in store for them at Baltimore on April 24. They went into the first of the ninth inning with a 3-to-1 lead and Nichols pitching. Before the Orioles were retired they had scored fourteen runs.

On June 22, Washington scored in all nine innings. The Beaneaters scored in only six. Washington won, 26–12. Pittsburgh beat the Bostons 27–11, hitting seven home runs, and scoring twelve runs in the third inning and nine runs in the fourth. If Stivetts, Duffy, and Saugus's Jimmy Bannon could hit successive homers for the Beaneaters, Baltimore could come back with four homers in one inning against the Beaneaters.

As if 1894 were not sufficiently bewildering in Boston, the South End Grounds had to burn down while the Beaneaters were playing the Orioles the afternoon of May 16. According to Leo Goulston, a Braves official during Bob Quinn's regime nearly a half century later, the fire at first got a cool reception from the fans because of a fight that was taking place on the field between John McGraw and Tommy Tucker.

While the fire was raging in the fifty-cent right-field bleachers, having been started by a cigar or cigarette dropped among old peanut shells, the attention of the fans was riveted on the McGraw-Tucker mix-up. Murnane wrote: "The game was full of excitement and the dirty playing of McGraw of Baltimore created a great deal of ill feeling because of its deliberateness."

With Tucker on third and Ganzel on first, the Beaneaters started a double steal, but Robinson threw to third instead of second. As Tucker slid safely back to third, McGraw kicked him in the face. Tucker resented the effort to dislodge a few of his teeth, and for a while the ensuing fight was hotter than the fire. In the end, however, the fire prevailed. The game had to be called with Boston leading, 5–3, in the first half of the third inning. The fire destroyed the bleachers, the $75,000 grandstand, Sullivan's Tower, and some 170 buildings covering twelve acres around the park. The total damage was estimated at one million dollars.

Sullivan's Tower was an architectural monstrosity that stood outside the right-field fence. From it spectators for ten cents could see a game that would otherwise have cost them a half dollar. It was a source of annoyance to the Triumvirs, who fought it by raising their right-field fence. But the higher they built the fence, the higher soared the tower. Bets were made on which would topple first, fence or tower, but the fire played no favorites. It leveled them both.

Also lost in the fire was the 1893 pennant. But J. B. Billings, one of the Triumvirs, said cheerily, "Don't worry. We'll win another one just as good." They did, but it was not in 1894.

Some of the Boston games were transferred to other cities, but most of them were played at the old Brotherhood Grounds on Congress Street. The Boston Reds in the Association had used the park in 1891, after which it was used for auctioning off wild horses brought in from the West, except for a short period during which the Lowell team of the New England League played there. A great many claims have been made for transcontinental home runs made via the railroads, but at the Congress Street Grounds, which was adjacent to a pier on Boston Harbor, a home run is alleged to have landed on a packet bound for Australia and been carried halfway around the world.

Final proof that 1894 was one of Boston's queerest seasons occurred the morning of June 18, Bunker Hill Day, when the Beaneaters scored sixteen runs in the first inning off Tony (Count) Mullane, the ambidextrous pitcher of Baltimore, on eleven hits, including three homers, seven passes, and one hit batsman. At the end of the inning, Wilbert Robinson, Baltimore catcher, retired, but Mullane had to pitch until the seventh inning. Nowadays they relieve the pitchers and let the catchers take it.

Soon after the season ended Boston was saddened by the death of a great favorite. Released to the Giants before the 1893 season opened, King Kelly soon had trouble with Ward and retired to manage Allentown, of the Pennsylvania State League. After the 1894 season, he went on the stage, but while in New York caught cold. He spent four days in bed, then took the Fall River boat to Boston. The great Kelly had returned to the city that loved him

68

best, for all his failings, but it was only to die in bed at the Emergency Hospital, November 8, 1894. He was interred in the Elks' lot in Mount Hope Cemetery, not, as Billy Sunday for a long time preached in his fiery sermons on the evils of drink, in a pauper's grave.

You may find his grave today, but it is an old grave. Few are the pilgrimages, now, to the last resting place of His Royal Highness. Mike Kelly made his last slide many years ago, and few now know, or care, where he is buried—once the king of players.

2

"In this year Duffy led the league in hitting."

This is George Tuohey's rather casual comment on Duffy's .438 batting average in 1894, which caused no great commotion. No one thought that fifty years and more would pass, and Duffy's .438 would still stand as the big-league record. In any event, averages were not publicized then as they are now. Duffy himself did not know if he was hitting .438 or .428 when the season ended.

"All I knew was that I had led the league, and that was the important thing," says Boston's venerable champion. He laughs when aspersions are cast on his record. It makes him happy to have modern players say that bases on balls must have counted in 1894. This was not so. Bases on balls counted as base hits in 1887, when James F. O'Neil of the St. Louis Browns hit .492, but they did not count as hits when Duffy batted .438 in 1894. Duffy set his record by making 236 hits in 539 times at bat.

Long after he was through playing, and when he was helping Bill Carrigan train the Red Sox at Bradenton, Florida, Duffy was trying to show some rookies how to hit. One of them, Bill Rogell, became exasperated by this little old man with the sharp tongue, and asked, "Who is this old fossil who thinks he knows so much about hitting?"

"His name is Duffy," Rogell was told. "He was a big leaguer once, and a pretty good hitter. He only hit .438 one season. Do you know anyone who has ever done better?"

Rogell's reply was recorded as one deep gulp.

"And Duffy hit .438 against good pitchers and bad baseballs," Rogell was further informed.

Although he carefully guards the secret of his age, early records

69

say that Duffy was born at River Point, Rhode Island, November 26, 1867. "If people knew how old I am," says Duffy, who is still employed by the Boston Red Sox as a tutor of sand-lot players, "nobody would give me a job."

Duffy first played amateur ball in his home town, wearing his uniform under his best suit when he went to church on Sundays. He was a catcher for Hartford in 1886, and for Springfield early in 1887. He was scouted there by George Fessenden, manager of Salem in the New England League, and his release was bought for twenty-five dollars. The Salem owner, George Vickery, thought this an outrageous price, and would promise to pay Duffy only five dollars a week and board, with the five dollars to be omitted if he made a poor showing.

Duffy was placed in center field for his first game in Salem, at the old Bridge Street Grounds, where center field ran uphill toward second base. It was the afternoon game against Lynn on Decoration Day, but they had no occasion to decorate Duffy, who missed five chances in the outfield and fanned three of his four times at bat. Vickery immediately fired both Duffy and Fessenden, but that night Vickery sold the club and Duffy was given another trial by the new owner. Of course he made good. The next day he made several one-handed catches while standing on his ear, and in five times at bat he hit a single, two doubles, a triple, and a home run.

Duffy was bought by Lowell in midseason, and the feats credited to him would have made Hercules envious. At Manchester, for instance, he hit a home run that went nearly to the top of a small mountain behind center field. The next day, at Lowell, he made three home runs off Mike McDermott, Manchester pitcher, his first three times at bat. His fourth time up, Jimmy Canavan backed out among the carriages in left field and held Duffy to a mere triple when he hit the ball into the 1887 parking lot.

In August, the Chicago scout, Tim Murnane, signed Duffy for $1,200. A few weeks later Mike Kelly of the Bostons offered him $2,250. He finally went to Chicago for $2,000, of which $500 was advanced. Pop Anson, who believed that beef won pennants, turned a frosty eye on the bag of peanuts from Lowell when Duffy reported in 1888, saying: "Duffy, you fall about five inches and twenty-five pounds short of major-league size."

Duffy sat on the bench until July, then played right field. He hit .282 his first season, and it was written that: "He strikes free

70

and hits the ball hard almost every time. He is not a giant in stature, being about 5-6 in height, but he has big, broad shoulders, and evidently possesses great strength."

In 1889 Duffy hit .311 for Chicago, and then he traveled around like a janizary during the baseball wars. He played for Chicago in the Brotherhood in 1890, hitting .328; and for the Boston Reds in the Association in 1891, hitting .349. In August he was made captain of the Reds and given a gold-headed cane by stockholders of the club. All through his playing career, the little Irishman was to get gold-headed canes, silver loving cups, floral horseshoes, or complimentary banquets at which his friends sung "Auld Lang Syne" and "For He's A Jolly Good Fellow." After he hit .438 in 1894, the Bleacher Club gave him a supper at the United States Hotel, where his friends presented a "splendid gold watch and a gold and platinum chain to the great run-getter." Run-getter! His fellow players gave him a watch charm studded with five good-sized diamonds, which was inscribed: "Presented to Hugh Duffy, champion batsman of the world, by his fellow players and manager."

Oliver Tebeau, Cleveland manager in the 1890's, ascribed to Duffy the most remarkable play he had ever seen. The Boston Reds were playing in St. Louis in 1891. Duffy was on second base with one out, when Farrell hit a long fly to Hoy, the St. Louis center fielder. Duffy took off for third when the ball struck Hoy's hands, but instead of stopping there, he kept going for the plate, sliding safely in with a magnificent slide. Two bases on a fly to the outfield? Exceptional, but others have done it.

According to Fred Tenney, Duffy was a right-handed Mel Ott, a little powerhouse who cocked his forward foot like a trigger when he took his cut. Tenney added: "Hughie showed plenty of guts the year he hit four-thirty-eight, because his teammates asked him not to play the last day of the season, after he hit safely his first two times up. But Hughie said, 'If I can't lead it on the level, I don't want to lead it at all.' And he made three more hits, every one of them a line drive over the third baseman's head."

Duffy rarely drank, and his roughest expression was, "By Jingoes." Tom Cogan once invited him to have a beer in Drach's Cafe in Cincinnati, but the little outfielder replied, "I'm not drinking." So they went to the Mecca and had a glass of Apollinaris. While standing at the bar, a tremendous explosion sent them dashing for the doors. Duffy ran so fast he fell and landed on his head. In the street they learned that Drach's Cafe had blown up, which for once gave Cogan adequate cause to rejoice in Duffy's temperance.

A favorite argument in the 1890's was whether Duffy or Jimmy McAleer was the greatest of outfielders. Duffy was the better hitter of the two and he played his position cannily. It was sometimes claimed that he never had to move more than ten feet for a fly ball, a slight exaggeration, because once at the South End Grounds he had to pursue the ball to the fence, where it rolled into a tin can. Unable to extricate it, Duffy threw can and all to the infield, with what result posterity has not recorded.

Duffy's own nomination as the greatest outfielder was his bosom pal Tommy McCarthy. Born in South Boston, July 24, 1864, Thomas Francis M. McCarthy was several years older than Duffy. They did not join forces until the American Association folded in 1891. Both joined the Beaneaters in 1892. So stylish were they, cavorting in the Boston outfield for four years, that they became known as the Heavenly Twins.

"It was McCarthy who was the heavenly one," Duffy insists. "He was a wonderful, heady player, thinking and doing things all the time. He and Mike Kelly were the smartest players of them all."

Bill Klem recalled Tommy McCarthy during the 1947 World Series in New York, saying: "McCarthy was responsible for changing the rule on when a man could leave his base on a fly ball. The rule used to be that a man couldn't leave his base until the fielder held the ball and was ready to throw it. But McCarthy would get under a long fly and keep bouncing it off his hands as he ran toward the infield, until he could throw out any runner trying to advance. Because of McCarthy, they had to let the runner leave his base the instant the ball struck the fielder's hands."

McCarthy won greater fame for being the first outfield to trap a fly ball. Playing against Pittsburgh, August 15, the batter raised a short fly to the outfield, with two men on base and nobody out. McCarthy came in, but instead of catching the ball in the air, he took it on a short hop and by whipping it to first started a double play. McCarthy was just as original when at bat or on base, faking a bunt at the third baseman so the runner on second could steal third, or working the double steal with his friend Duffy on third, a play on which Duffy remembers being thrown out only once.

McCarthy was discovered on the Boston sand lots by Tim Murnane, who gave him his first professional job with the Boston

72

Unions of 1884, for whom he pitched and played the outfield. He played forty games for the Boston Nationals in 1885, but then moved to the Philadelphia Nationals. In 1887 he helped Oshkosh win the Northwestern League pennant, and when the club's millionaire owner surrendered the franchise, joined the St. Louis Browns in the Association. He was with that team four years, stealing 109 bases in 1888 and hitting .351, and managing the team briefly in 1890.

Getting higher salaries out of the Triumvirs was always an ambition of the Heavenly Twins. They were stubborn holdouts before the 1894 season, when Tim Murnane, then a newspaperman, offered to intercede for them with Soden if they would promise to sign. They agreed.

"What is wrong with Duffy and McCarthy?" Murnane asked Soden.

"They want more money than we can afford to pay them," replied the club's president. "They're being stubborn about it."

"Oh, I think they'll come around. I think I can sign them for you," said Murnane.

"If you can, I'll give you a new hat."

So Murnane saw Duffy and McCarthy, who were waiting on a corner for him to come out of the office, and told them that they had better accept the terms offered. They took his advice and autographed their contracts. Later Duffy remarked, "We didn't get the money we wanted, but Tim got his new hat, so it was all right."

3

Only three men played on all of Boston's five pennant winners in the 1890's—Nichols, Robert Lincoln Lowe, and Herman C. Long. Hugh Duffy and Jack Stivetts missed 1891, being in the Association, and Charlie Ganzel and Tommy Tucker missed 1898, having been released.

Bobby (Link) Lowe, 155-pound second baseman and a man who hit only fifty-nine home runs in fourteen seasons, was the first big-league player to hit four home runs in one game. The place: the Congress Street Grounds, which were larger than the park that had burned down at Walpole Street. The date: May 30, 1894, afternoon game. The pitcher: Elton (Iceberg) Chamberlain, of the Cincinnati Reds.

Lowe was the Boston lead-off man, an indication that he was not considered a power hitter. He was retired in the first inning. Leading off the third inning, he hit the ball over the left-field fence. Later in the third inning, in which Boston scored nine runs, Lowe again hit the ball over the fence, with Jack Ryan on base.

"Two homers in one inning. That must be a record!" shouted Frank Selee on the Boston bench. The crowd cheered. Kid Nichols left the bench to shake hands with Lowe.

Lowe came up in the fifth with nobody on base. Bugs Holliday backed against the fence, but Lowe hit the ball over his head and out of the park—homer number three. Lowe had equaled a record held by six big leaguers, among them Dan Brouthers, Cap Anson, and John Manning. In the sixth inning, Lowe hit his fourth homer over the left-field fence. All four homers went over the same part of the barrier. All four were hit off curve balls. The delighted crowd showered $160 worth of silver on the plate for Lowe. When he singled in the eighth inning, the crowd laughed. So did Elton Chamberlain. Was Lowe getting weak?

Only three other big leaguers have hit four home runs in one game—Ed Delahanty in 1896, Lou Gehrig in 1932, and Chuck Klein in 1936. Only Gehrig hit his consecutively, as did Lowe. Lowe and Delahanty still hold the record for seventeen total bases in one game.

Lowe was modest. At St. Petersburg in the spring of 1928, he asked Babe Ruth and Lou Gehrig of the Yankees to autograph a ball for some bashful boys. They obliged, and he thanked them, but Lowe did not tell them his name or that he was the first player to hit four home runs in a big-league game. If he had, they probably would have looked at him and thought, Nobody that skinny ever hit four home runs in one game.

After Gehrig hit his four homers in 1932, Lowe put on his old Boston uniform and went out to the Detroit park and posed for photographs with him. Lowe said, "I feel complimented to share the record with so grand a boy as Gehrig."

Born at Pittsburgh, July 10, 1868, Lowe first played ball for Witherow's plant in New Castle, Pennsylvania. As a boy he used to look through a knothole in the fence and marvel at the great catcher Charlie Bennett. He never dreamed that someday he would play on the same team with Bennett at Boston. Lowe then played for the Archie Reeds and Neshannocks of New Castle, catching for the latter team because he hoped to be another Bennett.

He first played professionally for Eau Claire in 1887, where he was an outfielder and shortstop. He was with Milwaukee in 1888 and 1889, playing left field most of the time, and in 1889 was bought by Conant of the Triumvirs for only $700. He was recommended not only by Frank Selee of Omaha, but by Jim Hart, Boston leader in 1889, who had managed him at Milwaukee in 1888.

In 1890, his first season with Boston, Lowe played most of his games at third base. His salary was $1,800. On the pennant winners of 1891 and 1892, he usually played the outfield, but in 1893 he replaced Joe Quinn at second base. This was his favorite position because there were more chances to be handled.

Lowe never made more than $3,000 a season while playing for Boston, yet he thought clubs treated players well enough in those days. The team stayed at the best hotels, and each player was given $3 per day meal money in trains. After he hit .316 in 1893, the Triumvirs even gave him a $200 raise.

Many years after he had stopped playing, and was working for the Department of Public Works in Detroit, Lowe became friendly with Ty Cobb, then managing the Tigers. One evening when visiting, Mrs. Lowe and Mrs. Cobb were startled while looking over some linens upstairs to hear their husbands shouting angrily below. As they dashed down, prepared to separate the combatants, they heard some vehement remarks being exchanged.

"I touched you when you came in."

"The hell you did. You missed me."

"I got a little piece of your foot."

"You didn't. I didn't feel it."

The wives found Cobb sprawled on the floor with Lowe standing over him. Lowe had told Cobb that modern infielders were pretty dumb when they would let a fellow like Cobb fool them with a slide. And Cobb had said, "Is that so? Well, I can fool you, too."

So they moved aside the furniture, used a hassock for a base, and Cobb slid in with his most deceptive slide, immediately provoking an argument as to whether or not Lowe had touched him. Asked later if he had been able to tag Cobb, Lowe said, "Well, part of the time."

Lowe once had occasion to introduce his wife to Larry Lajoie, long after both players had retired.

"I'm proud to meet the greatest second baseman the game has ever known," said Mrs. Lowe.

"That's very nice of you to say so," replied Lajoie gallantly, "but it's not true. The greatest second baseman was your husband."

Reference has been made to the lamentable tendency to "noisy coaching" by the Beaneaters of 1894. The man who made the biggest noise was Herman (Germany) Long, frequently called the Dutchman. With the possible exception of Hugh Jennings, Long was the best shortstop of his age, being fast, acrobatic, and daring. Walter S. Barnes, Jr., former *Globe* sports editor, used to say that Long played shortstop like a man on a flying trapeze.

He had a strong arm and a wonderful ability to get the ball away. He made a remarkable play in 1894 when, unable to reach a ball hit over second base with his glove, he deflected the ball into the air with the toe of his left foot, caught it, and tossed it to second base for a force play. Sometimes in practice Long would deflect ground balls into the hands of his second baseman by using his feet. Old-timers say Long could field ground balls better with his feet than some modern shortstops can with their hands.

But Long was a noisy player. A *Boston Herald* reporter chided him for such uncouth coaching as: "Git er long thar!" "Don't stick tew the base!" "Dig up the dust and fly!" "Git back tew yer base, ye lunkhead!" and "Make a beeline fur home, and don't let the beans parboil under yer feet."

Little wonder that the Beaneaters could not win the pennant in 1894 with a shortstop using such distasteful language. On several occasions, even President Arthur H. Soden felt obliged to shut him up, but no man could keep the Dutchman quiet in the heat of a ball game. He was all ballplayer, a cool customer in the pinches whether at bat or in the field.

Long was born in Chicago, April 3, 1886, being of German parentage. When twenty-one years old, he broke in with Arkansas City, but when the Kansas State League exploded, he moved to Emporia of the Western League. He started with the Chicago Maroons in 1888, but was sold to Kansas City. Early in 1890, Long was bought by Boston for $6,700, to replace Joe Quinn, who had vaulted to the Brotherhood.

He was a peerless shortstop for the Beaneaters through 1902, but bad luck was his shadow. He hurt his arm. A restaurant he bought on Avery Street, Boston, failed. So did his health. On September 16, 1909, Long died of consumption in Denver—broke and friendless. His tragic finish inspired Harry C. Pulliam, National League

President, to propose a home for old professional players, but Pulliam himself died before the plan was realized. Both Herman Long and the home were soon forgotten. So was Pulliam.

4

The 1894 senior dinner at Brown University in Providence, Rhode Island, was held the night of June 15. At one o'clock in the morning, when few seniors were feeling much pain, Fred Tenney was called to the telephone.

"This is Frank Selee in Boston, Fred. Can you come up and catch for us tomorrow? All our catchers are hurt. We're in a bad way."

"Sure, sure," replied Tenney quickly. "I'll be there in time for the game."

It would never happen today. If a team were desperate for a replacement, it would pick one from the minor leagues, not from a near-by college. But Selee had seen Tenney play exhibition games against the Boston Nationals and had tabbed him as a prospect. Tenney leaped at the chance to turn professional. He had often wondered if he could play with and against such fellows as Hugh Duffy, Tommy McCarthy, Billy Nash, and Herman Long. Here was his chance to find out.

Tenney went to bed at four A.M. He arose early, looked for his absent roommate, until he found him sleeping under a tree on the campus, took a shower at the gym, had breakfast, and caught the train for Boston. He was put into the line-up by Selee, although a left-handed catcher, and did a creditable job, considering that he was playing with a broken little finger after the fifth inning.

He was pretty downhearted when he went home to Georgetown. He needed money to pay some college bills, but with a broken finger, how would he get it? He graduated from Brown, then returned to Boston to see the Nationals play a morning game, June 17.

"Mr. Billings wants to see you," Tenney was told at the gate.

After the game he saw Billings, who asked him if he wanted to sign with the Bostons. Tenney said, "With this finger, I can't play for a month."

"That's all right," said Billings, and offered Tenney $300 a month. Tenney's astonishment did not impede his acceptance. Then he screwed up his courage, and asked, "Could you advance me $150?"

"Certainly," replied Billings, "How do you want it?"

Tenney thought they were carrying a joke pretty far, but he took the money and departed. He rejoined the team in Philadelphia when his finger had mended. The Bostons stalled for rain, the umpire called the game, and the fans rioted. It took the Boston players two hours to reach their hotel, with the help of police. He had broken a finger in his first game; in his second game there was a riot. The Georgetown youth wondered what kind of a business he had got into.

Tenney caught twenty-four games in 1894 and hit .387, but Selee did not like his style as a catcher. His throwing was erratic. But as a first baseman Tenney was to prove himself one of several replacements the Boston champions of 1891-93 were to need before becoming the champions of 1897-98.

After training in Columbia, South Carolina, the Beaneaters anticipated a return to championship form in 1895. But instead of going up, they went down, into a fifth-place tie with Brooklyn. It was one of the Triumvir's most disappointing seasons. There were no pitchers behind Nichols, who won thirty-two and lost thirteen games. Even Stivetts lost as often as he won. Eight hurlers were tried, including Jim Sullivan of Charlestown, Cozy Dolan, and Frank Sexton, who had pitched to Tenney at Brown. He was wild as a pitcher with the Beaneaters, but when Sexton later became a doctor, he threw nothing but strikes.

To the Triumvirs, 1895 meant dissension and matrimony, which so often keep company. There was a tough catcher from New York named Jack Warner, who would just as soon fight as eat, and was frequently in trouble. Among the five Beaneaters married during the season were Duffy and Tenney.

Tommy McCarthy was injured and his place in the outfield taken by Tenney. At the end of the season, the Heavenly Twin was sold to Brooklyn. One season there, and he retired to enter business at 603 Washington Street, Boston, where a combination bowling alley and saloon bore the sign: "DUFFY AND MCCARTHY."

In 1895 the name of Jimmy Collins first appeared in the Boston line-up as an outfielder. This was another unhappy experiment. Collins had been bought from Buffalo after batting .332 in 1894. The twenty-one-year-old Collins replaced the popular Jimmy Bannon, a prime favorite with the fifty-cent bleacher fans at the South End Grounds, in right field, and was a bust. The fans jeered him: "Go hit a baskit, Collins," "When are yer going to git another hit?"

78

and "We want Bannon." The press became hostile. On May 17, when Collins's average had dropped to .205, Selee sent the youngster to Louisville, where by a stroke of luck he was given a chance to play third base when the regular incumbent, Walter Preston, went into a tailspin. Collins went on from there to become the best of all third basemen, although Selee tried him at shortstop early in 1896.

Years later, during a National League meeting in New York, Tenney walked into a room of old-timers such as John McGraw, Ned Hanlon, and Kid Gleason, and heard them talking about third basemen. They were comparing Bill Bradley with others.

Finally Tenney interrupted them impatiently. "What are you talking about Bradley for? What was the matter with Collins?"

"Oh, nothing at all, Fred," replied Hanlon. "We've already decided he was the best. We're just trying to pick the second-best."

Collins and Tenney did the Bostons no particular good in 1895, but they were to be invaluable to the champions of 1897 and 1898. So were a couple of other players acquired in 1895. In September, the Triumvirs gave Frank Connaughton and $1,000 to Kansas City for Catcher Martin Bergen. Bergen had been born at North Brookfield, Massachusetts, October 25, 1871, almost nine years after Connie Mack had been born in East Brookfield. He first played as a professional for Wilkesbarre, in 1893. Sold to Pittsburgh, he was later released to Lewiston, where he hit .376 in 1894. Washington offered him $225 a month, but he had already promised to play for Kansas City, which he did in 1895. Bergen was to become a wonderful catcher, but when twenty-seven years old and at the height of his career, in 1900, he was to kill his wife, two children, and himself.

After the 1895 season, the Triumvirs traded Billy Nash, their veteran third baseman and captain, to Philadelphia for Billy Hamilton. Nash had been with the Boston club since 1885, except when with the Brotherhood in 1890. He was thirty years old and still a good ballplayer, but Selee thought he had a promising third baseman in young Collins, who had done well at Louisville, and Selee wanted a center fielder like Hamilton to replace McCarthy.

Hamilton, who was born in Newark, New Jersey, but lived in Clinton, Massachusetts, was one of the fastest men and best base runners in the game's history. He was short and squat, standing five-six and weighing 165 pounds, but could run and slide like no one else, unless it was Harry Stovey or Ty Cobb. He set the National League stolen-base record at 115 while with Philadelphia in 1891, and set the scoring record at 196 runs while with the same team in 1894. In twelve seasons, six with Philadelphia and six with Boston, he was to bat .351, score 1,694 runs, and steal 797 bases. Selee used Hamilton as lead-off man in 1896, because of his speed and inclination to wait out pitchers for bases on balls.

The 1896 season was as disappointing as that of 1895. Although the Beaneaters climbed to fourth place, they finished seventeen games behind the pennant-winning Orioles. Duffy replaced Nash as captain of the team, getting "the limit for playing and a good round sum ($600) for handling the team." Duffy was a strict disciplinarian, and he and Selee had "a perfect understanding as to each other's duties." But the Beaneaters didn't win games. They made a good start, but slumped in May, and in July lost seventeen out of twenty-seven games.

Nichols won thirty games and lost only fifteen, and Stivetts had a 22–13 record, but behind them there was nothing until Fred Klobedanz, young left-hander, was bought from Fall River in the fall. Klobedanz had hurled a five-hit exhibition against the Bostons in the spring, and Selee offered to buy him on the spot, but Fall River made him wait. Ted Lewis, who was to be a valuable pitcher in subsequent seasons, was signed after graduating from Williams College. Lewis had been born in Machynlleth, Wales. Before he died, he was president of Massachusetts Agricultural College and the University of New Hampshire.

Billy Hamilton stole ninety-three bases his first season with the club, to set a Boston record that still stands, and he led the team by hitting .363. Tenney was sent to Springfield early in 1896, where in ten games he caught, played left field and first base, and made twenty-five hits. On Decoration Day, he played for Springfield at Providence in the morning, then rushed to Boston to play for the Beaneaters against Cleveland in the afternoon. Tenney not only could play two or three positions in one game, but he could play for two teams in two leagues in one day. Quite a fellow! He got into eighty-six games as a catcher and outfielder and led the team by hitting .342. The Beaneaters did not have much extra-base power in 1896, but in a game against Baltimore they made twenty-eight singles to tie a record. They didn't hit the ball very hard but they certainly tapped it artistically.

Boston Red Stockings, National Association champions. With four league championships in the five-sea-
son existence of the National Association, the Red Stockings were a dynasty. Slugging second baseman
Ross Barnes and pitcher A. G. Spalding led the team for more than five seasons. During that time,
Spalding won an astounding 205 games and pitched an average of 500 innings per season. Courtesy of
Richard A. Johnson

▲ Ivers Whitney Adams founded the Red Stockings on January 20, 1871, at a meeting at the Parker House in Boston. The fledgling team secured the services of several players who once played for the legendary one-season wonders, the 1869 Cincinnati Red Stockings. Courtesy of Richard A. Johnson

▲▶ George Wright, shown here in 1871, was the son of an English cricket star, and a great player in early professional baseball. He virtually invented the position of shortstop and led both the Cincinnati and Boston Red Stockings to unparalleled success before Boston's entry into the newly formed National League in 1876. Courtesy of Richard A. Johnson

▶ Harry Wright became the first manager of the Boston team after it joined the National League in 1876. Originally a cricket star like his father, Wright played center field for the Boston Red Stockings. In 1877 and 1878 he brought his team consecutive pennants. But in 1879 his younger brother and former teammate, George, and his team from Providence broke his streak. Courtesy of Richard A. Johnson

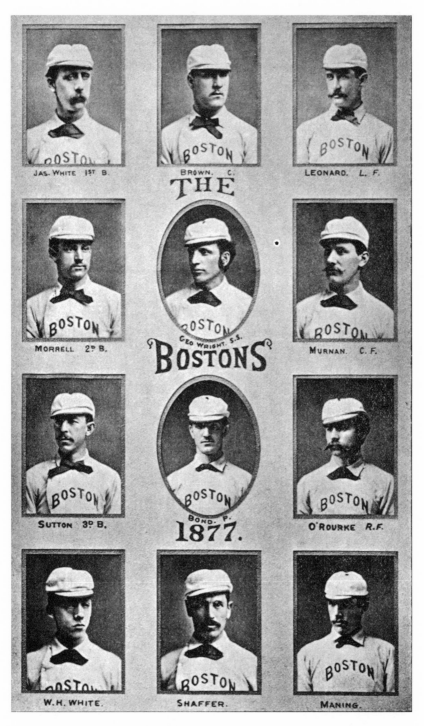

The 1877 Boston Nationals were the first of Boston's ten National League pennant winners. Pitcher Tommy Bond and first baseman Deacon White took the team to 40 victories in 58 games (of the 60-game season). White's .387 batting average and 49 RBI made him first in the league. Courtesy of Richard A. Johnson

Michael "King" Kelly, known simply as "King," was the first team-sport superstar in America. Like his boxing counterpart, John L. Sullivan, Kelly's talent matched his colorful character. His habits included more than his fair share of socializing. A multi-positional player, Kelly achieved a lifetime average of .307 and inspired a popular parlor song titled "Slide Kelly, Slide." On his deathbed, he reportedly told a teammate, "I'm sliding home." He died at the tender age of thirty-six, from the effects of his excessive, exuberant lifestyle. Courtesy of the National Baseball Hall of Fame

▲◀ John Clarkson, a native of Cambridge, Massachusetts, won 149 of 328 career victories with the Boston Nationals. In the 1889 season he topped the National League with 49 wins, 620 innings pitched, 73 games pitched, and 68 completed games. Clarkson was elected to the Hall of Fame in 1963. Courtesy of Richard A. Johnson

▲ In the span of six years, Frank Selee rose from player/manager of the Melrose, Massachusetts, town team to manager of the Boston Nationals. He led a series of pennant winners, starting in Haverhill, Massachusetts. He then journeyed west to Oshkosh, Wisconsin, and finally to Omaha, Nebraska. In his twelve seasons as Boston's manager, his team earned five pennants and dynasty status. An ambitious man of few words, his credo was "If I make things pleasant for the players, they reciprocate." Courtesy of Richard A. Johnson

◀ Star catcher Charles Bennett suffered a horrific, career-ending injury on January 10, 1894. He slipped under the wheels of a train while disembarking at a rest stop in Wellsville, Kansas. On August 27, 1894, the Red Stockings played a benefit game for their former star. The world heavyweight boxing champion, "Gentleman" Jim Corbett, played first base for the home team in the game against local collegians. They raised more than $6,000 for Bennett and his family. Courtesy of Richard A. Johnson

The South End Grounds, shown here in 1890, was the most elegant ballpark in the majors in the nineteenth century. It was Boston's first and only true double-decked, outdoor stadium. The park burned in the South End fire of 1894. It was rebuilt, but because of an insurance settlement that equaled only 60 percent of its value, the new park was a shadow of its former self. Home to eight National League champions, the park stood on what is now the Ruggles MBTA rail station, adjacent to Northeastern University. Courtesy of the Bostonian Society

Rhode Island native Hugh Duffy was one of the Beaneaters' "Heavenly Twins"; the other was fellow future Hall of Fame outfielder Tommy McCarthy. In 1894 Duffy won the National League Triple Crown with a record-setting .438 batting average, 18 home runs, and 145 RBI. Duffy served as both a hitting instructor and a roving goodwill ambassador for the Red Sox in his later years. Courtesy of the Boston Public Library

Standing five foot ten and weighing 150 pounds, Robert Lincoln "Bobby" Lowe was hardly the prototypical slugger. However, on May 30, 1894, the Boston Beaneater second baseman made baseball history. He socked four home runs in the second game of a doubleheader at the Congress Street Grounds on Boston's waterfront. Lowe was the first to achieve this feat, and his assault on the Cincinnati Reds came in consecutive at bats. Following his fourth homer, fans showered him with more than $100 in coins and bills. His fifth and final at bat produced a single. This photograph was taken several years later. Courtesy of Richard A. Johnson

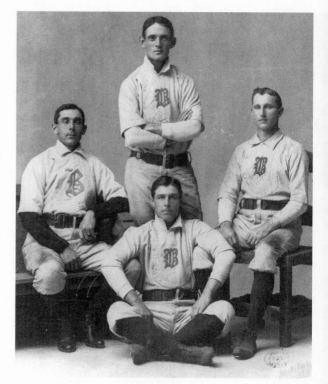

Second baseman Bobby Lowe, third baseman Jimmy Collins, first baseman Fred Tenney, and shortstop Herman Long led the infield for the Beaneaters, the National League champions in 1897. Though only Collins is enshrined in the Hall of Fame, Lowe was the first major leaguer to hit four home runs in a nine-inning game. Courtesy of Richard A. Johnson

Located near the Boston waterfront at A and Congress Streets (adjacent to the new convention center), the Congress Street Grounds was home to three major league teams. The Players League champion Boston Reds played their only season in the park in 1890. The American Association team of the same name played there in 1891. Following the fire that destroyed the South End Grounds, the Nationals played at the Congress Street Grounds from May 16 to June 20, 1894, about the time this picture was taken. The cozy bandbox featured a 250-foot left-field porch. Courtesy of Richard A. Johnson

Kansas City native, Charles "Kid" Nichols won 0 games or more for seven straight seasons, om 1891 to 1897. The crafty right-hander fin- hed his career with 362 victories and was elect- d to the Hall of Fame in 1949. Courtesy of the oston Public Library

In six seasons with the Boston Nationals, Jimmy Collins established himself as a great third base- man. He barehanded bunts and defensively recast the position. He also was an outstanding hitter, batting .309 for Boston and averaging nearly 90 RBI per season. He helped the Nationals win back-to-back pennants in 1897 and 1898. He anchored the best infield of the nine- teenth century, which included shortstop Herman Long, second baseman Bobby Lowe, and first baseman Fred Tenney. Collins moved to the Boston Americans in 1901. It was a major blow to both the team and the entire National League. Courtesy of G. Altison

▲ In an era when illiterate tradesmen were the primary players of professional baseball, Fred Tenney, a Brown University graduate, stood out as both a gentleman and a nimble first baseman. Tenney batted .294 over a seventeen-year career, while also inventing the 3-6-3 double play. Courtesy of the National Baseball Hall of Fame

▶ Walter "Rabbit" Maranville was a player beyond mere statistics. He came to Boston as a teenager in 1912 and soon became a fan favorite. In 1913, when Maranville was twenty, he was given a day in his honor at the South End Grounds. Friends and well-wishers from his hometown of Springfield, Massachusetts, made their way to Boston to celebrate the colorful antics of their hero. Among his tricks was a warm-up routine in which he sat on second base and threw perfect strikes to the catcher. He batted .308 in the 1914 World Series. Courtesy of the Sports Museum of New England

Braves manager George Stallings (center) with Bill James (left) and Dick Rudolph. Stallings, the son of a Confederate officer, was one of the most dynamic managers in baseball history. The former catcher was also a dropout from Johns Hopkins Medical School. He and Connie Mack were the only two managers to wear street clothes on the bench. Courtesy of the National Baseball Hall of Fame

Dick "Baldy" Rudolph won a league-leading 27 games as a member of the 1914 Braves "Big Three" pitching staff, which also included Bill James and Lefty Tyler. At twenty-seven, the right-hander enjoyed the greatest of his eleven years as a member of the Braves. He won two games in the 1914 World Series, with an earned run average of 0.50 in 18 innings. Courtesy of G. Altison

Big right-hander Bill James won 26 games and lost 7 (a .788 winning percentage) in the 1914 season. James won only 37 games in four major league seasons, excluding his two victories over the Athletics in the World Series. His World Series earned run average for 11 innings was a perfect 0.00. Courtesy of the National Baseball Hall of Fame

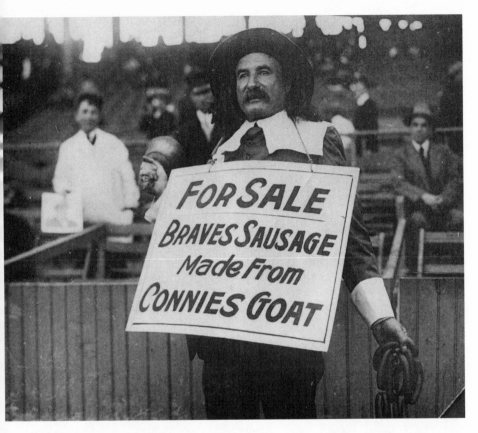

One intrepid Braves fan mocks Athletics manager Connie Mack prior to the fourth and final game of the 1914 World Series at Fenway Park. He, and members of the fabled Royal Rooters, gladly cheered for both the Red Sox and the Braves during the glory years of the teens. Courtesy of the Sports Museum of New England, Frank Bradley Donation

This issue of *Baseball Magazine* from February 1915 was devoted entirely to the unprecedented success of the newly crowned World Champion Boston Braves. Extensive articles about manager George Stallings, MVP Johnny Evers, and the saga of the 1914 World Series appeared within. Courtesy of Richard A. Johnson

The 1914 Miracle Braves who gathered at a reunion banquet in 1951 at the Somerset Hotel are (left to right): Fred Mitchell, Dick Crutcher, George "Lefty" Tyler, Hank Gowdy, Bill James, Paul Strand, and J. Carlisle "Red" Smith. Courtesy of George Sullivan

Hank Gowdy and Rabbit Maranville were the toast of Boston and all of baseball following the triumph of the Braves in the 1914 World Series. Gowdy batted .545, topping all hitters in the series. He socked the only home run to help win game three at Fenway Park. Maranville batted .308 and played his usual spectacular, flashy defense. Both were instrumental in opening Braves Field, then baseball's largest park, in 1915. Courtesy of G. Altison

Gene Mack illustrated Brooklyn pitcher Leon Cadore's reaction to the 26-inning marathon he and Braves pitcher Joe Oeschger hurled at Braves Field, May 1, 1920. The game started at 3 P.M. and was halted after four hours because of darkness. Courtesy of the Sports Museum of New England

CHAPTER VIII

THE GRAND CLIMAX

AFTER training at Savannah, Georgia, the Beaneaters began the 1897 season determined to end the three-year reign of Ned Hanlon's rowdy Baltimore Orioles, who were regarded as sure repeaters by the experts. The Beaneaters succeeded, but only after a bitter campaign that was decided on the last day of September.

"The Boston team of 1897 and 1898 was a great team because it had the best men in the league at every position." This is Fred Tenney's lavish testimony on the team that returned Boston to the top.

Bobby Lowe thought it the best of all teams because "it was a team of wonderful players. It had good hitters, fine fielders, and lots of speed. The boys had excellent habits, and every man was ready to sacrifice his own record for the good of the team."

The 1897-98 Beaneaters had no weaknesses that could be seen with the naked eye. They probably were the best of all Boston National League teams, the 1914 champions of George Stallings included. Baseball may have had another defensive infield as good as that of Tenney, Lowe, Long, and Collins, but surely it has never had a better one. The outfield of Duffy, Hamilton, and Charles Sylvester (Chick) Stahl, the latter having been bought from Buffalo after the 1895 season, contributed red-feather batting averages of .341, .344, and .359, respectively, in 1897. And those boys could catch 'em as well as hit 'em.

For example, there was Hugh Duffy's catch at the South End Grounds, August 6, which fans still boast of having seen. Joe Corbett, Baltimore pitcher, hit the ball to deep left, but Duffy pursued it, caught it with a desperate leap, and before touching the ground threw it home to get Joe Quinn as he was trying to score from third base. The story says the fans went mad from joy, but Duffy himself says it never happened like that. All he did was to make a leaping catch against the fence, a fairly common event in the undersized South End park.

The pitching staff was a model, with Nichols (31–12), Klobedanz (27–8), and Lewis (21–10) doing the bulk of the work, aided by Stivetts, Sullivan, and Charlie Hickman. There were four catchers: Bergen, Ganzel, Fred Lake, and George Yeager. Bob Allen, later a minor-league owner, was a clever and experienced reserve infielder.

This was a team of old-fashioned superstars, yet it barely defeated the Orioles. The Beaneaters had to come from behind to win. They took a critical series from the Orioles late in September and won by only two games. The Orioles, with McGraw, Jennings, Keeler, Robinson, Doyle, and Joe Kelley, were pretty good, too. They must have had the next-best men at every position.

Except for one important decision by Manager Frank Selee, the Beaneaters probably would not have beaten out the Orioles. Early in the season, Selee replaced Tommy Tucker, Holyoke first baseman who had been with the club since 1890, with Tenney. Selee made the move after Boston had lost three successive games to Baltimore, with Tucker at first base and Tenney in right field. Tucker left too many men on base and he played first base as if he were in a telephone booth. He was growing old.

Tenney had worked out at first base in practice, but few Boston players thought he would be given Tucker's job. When Selee moved him to the infield and put Stahl in right field, there was some resentment among the players. Tenney was not popular at first with the old pros. They called him "The Soiled Collegian." But Selee quickly eliminated the friction by selling Tucker to Washington, having seen that Tenney could take care of his new assignment.

The Soiled Collegian made the team and quickly became a sensation. Why, marveled experts, he was even better than Charlie Comiskey, the old Chicago wizard. A *Chicago News* reporter wrote: "Tenney's way is far different from that of other basemen. He reaches his hands far out for the ball, and stretches his legs, so that he is farther out from the bag on every throw than any other first baseman in the league." Tenney played wide and deep, as do modern first basemen, and he made plays that no first baseman before him had ever made. One of these was the "3–6–3" double play—first, to short, to first. He made it three times in one series, too.

82

"The play originated like this," explains Tenney. "One day a batter hit a slow, high bounder toward the second baseman, with a man on first base. Bobby Lowe grabbed the ball and barely got the hitter at first. I said to Lowe, 'If I had taken that ball, Bobby, I could have thrown to second and forced the runner.'

"'That's right,' agreed Lowe. 'The next time, you take it, and I'll try to get over to first for Long's throw.'

"It was not long before we made the first '3–6–3' double play. We were playing Cincinnati in Boston when the batter hit the ball over first. I grabbed it and threw to Long, then hurried to the bag and took Long's throw for a double play. It seemed that you could have heard a pin drop for ten seconds, and then the crowd just let out a roar. It had seen something new."

Tenney was exceptionally aggressive. With Cap Anson of Chicago trapped off third one day, he did not throw the ball, but simply ran across the infield with the ball and tagged the astonished Chicago manager. Such audacity from a collegian! Tenney wasn't a slugger but he excelled as a place hitter. In an exhibition game at Portsmouth, Ohio, Tenney once exhibited his skill at hitting them where they weren't. His first time up, the rival shortstop crowded second. Tenney said, "You're too far over. I'll hit the ball through the hole."

The shortstop laughed, so Tenney singled through the hole. His next time up, the shortstop played in the hole. Tenney said, "Now you're too far the other way. I'll hit the ball over second base." The shortstop's reply was the 1897 equivalent of "Nuts," so Tenney promptly singled over second.

The following day, the Portsmouth paper said: "We'd be willing to lose every day, if Tenney would only come back and hit some more balls through the infield."

Still active in the insurance business in Boston, Tenney is sometimes introduced by his friends: "Meet Mr. Tenney, the best first baseman who ever lived."

And then Tenney replies, with a smile: "Thank you, but you know as well as I do that there was only one first baseman—Hal Chase."

Less important than the shifting of Tenney to first base and the releasing of Tucker was the signing of two utility men during the season. One was Fred Lake, thirty-one-year-old catcher, who was bought from Kansas City, in June. This East Boston product later was to manage the Boston team in 1910. The other was Charles

T. Hickman, a graduate of the University of West Virginia, who was bought from New Castle of the Interstate League, in August. He had been a catcher in college. The Beaneaters bought him as a pitcher.

The Beaneaters got away to a slow start, losing their opening game at home to Philadelphia, April 19. But they were sixth May 15, third June 1, second June 7, and first June 21. Nothing helped catapult them to the top so much as a seventeen-game winning streak, which still stands as the club record. The Beaneaters won sixteen of the seventeen games at the South End Grounds. Through midsummer, the race was nip and tuck between the Beaneaters and Orioles. At the end of August, Baltimore had a microscopic lead. Tension mounted as the finish neared. Feeling ran high in September. So did attendances and gate receipts. The Triumvirs were glad their pass list totaled only two free customers apiece.

2

September was the month! It opened with Captain Duffy relieving Lewis with Nichols in the seventh inning, as Boston beat Chicago 7–4. "Duffy was hissed by a few people, but four fifths of the fans applauded the little captain." Allen, playing in place of the injured Long, hit a home run and knocked in five runs. But Baltimore also won.

The Boston team was idle the next day, so President Soden announced that henceforth Boston players would not egg on fans to rattle opposing pitchers. It seemed that Boston players, especially Herman Long, were inclined to conduct a raucous chorus of hooting, jeering, whistling fans when the rival team was in the field, the hymn of hate being dedicated particularly to the rival pitcher. For a few days thereafter, games were quieter at the South End Grounds. On this same day, Boston released Harry Staley, veteran hurler, to Toronto.

Boston defeated Chicago, 6–3 and 9–1, in a double-header September 3, and took the league lead. Darkhue White, the team's mascot, said, "Ah'll hoodoo dat man Anson." Kloby won the first game, Nichols the second. Jim Ryan, Chicago shortstop, said, "You might as well try to climb Butte Shasta on roller skates as beat this Nichols when he's out for the game." There were 9,000 fans in the park, and Tim Murnane wrote: "Think of 9,000 persons at a ball game on a Friday. Good clean sport, presented as the Boston club presents it, will draw anywhere. The game is the best game under the sun, and long may it prosper."

Trailing 2–6, Boston scored five runs in the sixth inning, to beat Cincinnati, 7–6, September 4. Allen, still playing shortstop in place of Long, who had an injured hand, speared Hoy's line drive to his right with his bare hand to save the day.

On Labor Day, September 6, Baltimore won two games from Pittsburgh and went ahead. Boston lost its morning game to Cincinnati, 5–3, but won the afternoon game, 10–2. The morning game drew 6,500 fans, the afternoon contest 12,000. When Lewis was beaten in the morning, Fred Lake, his catcher, "acted like a man who has to carry his own ashes out of the cellar." And, we are told "Ewing outgeneraled Selee matching batteries."

Both Boston and Baltimore matched victories for three days. On September 10, Boston beat St. Louis, 10–9, after trailing, 2–9. A three-run rally in the ninth won the game. Collins tripled off the right-field wall with two men on, then scored the winning run with a marvelous slide on Nichols's grounder to short. Boston took the lead again September 11, with an 11-to-0 victory over Philadelphia as the Orioles were tied, 3–3, by Chicago. Frank Selee missed this game to scout a player in near-by Everett, of all places and times!

Sunday, September 12, was an off day. Murnane wrote: "Outside of Duffy, Long, Tenney, and Bergen, the Boston players are a quiet lot. Two or three of them are likely to drop off into a trance if they are not jollied continually." On the same day, it was announced that Billy Rogers and George Appleton were arranging a trip to Baltimore for the big series, which would cost only $25 per person, if 100 fans would go. Those going were advised to take fish horns and police rattles, since "even 100 men can make a big noise if properly handled by a good leader."

By winning two games from Chicago while Boston was rained out, the Orioles regained the lead September 13. Three days later their margin was a full game, as New York beat Boston, 8–5, while the Orioles were tying Philadelphia, 4–4. The next day Boston beat New York, 17–0, a Boston record still, while Baltimore split a double-header and Baltimore's lead was narrowed to a half game. Both teams won September 18. Tenney worked hard this day, coaching at first base like a collegian. He had to, since both Selee and Bergen were unexplained absentees!

85

Baltimore's lead was again reduced to a gnat's eyelash when New York beat the Orioles, 10–9, and the Beaneaters were rained out September 19. But after a Sunday off, Baltimore again led by a full game September 21, for Boston only divided with Brooklyn, losing the morning game, 22–5.

"YELLOW BALL," shouted a headline. Brooklyn had scored twelve runs off Nichols in the first inning, after Catcher Charlie Ganzel had lost two foul flies. Nichols stuck it out until the fourth inning, when he was relieved by the rookie Charlie Hickman.

When Hickman marched out to the mound, Nichols soberly shook his hand, as if to say, "Charlie, I'm sure glad to see you. Good luck! I hope you don't get killed."

The next day the Beaneaters beat Brooklyn, 12–0, with Jack Stivetts and Jim Sullivan doing the pitching, while the Orioles lost to New York. This was the last home game of the season for the Beaneaters. They had won fifty-two out of sixty-five games at the South End Grounds. As they left for Baltimore and the pay-off series, the Beaneaters were only one percentage point (.706 to .707) behind their rivals.

With the team went some 125 Royal Rooters, bearing horns and rattles. A poet named Gill Burt was inspired to write a new verse for "Maryland":

> A hostile land is at thy door
>   Baltimore, my Baltimore.
> They's coming as they came before,
>   Baltimore, my Baltimore.
> If you don't take a sudden brace,
> I fear that you will lose the race,
> And drop down into second place,
>   Baltimore, my Baltimore.

The rooters left by train for Providence, where they took the boat to New York. They wore badges inscribed, "Boston Rooters," showing a bean pot producing lightning and a satan. In the group was Congressman John F. Fitzgerald, who was still waiting for "Sweet Adeline" to be written so he could sing it without any provocation the rest of his life. Nuf Ced McGreevey, whose saloon was popular with the players, went along. So did Fred Murphy, the young insurance man, who was later to become an executive in the club.

"BERGEN LOST IN THE SHUFFLE, BUT GAME WILL PROCEED," said a Boston headline. But the eccentric catcher showed up in time for the first game, the explanation being that he had forgotten that an exhibition scheduled for Orange, New Jersey, had been postponed, and he had gone there expecting to play. It is more likely that he spent the day at his North Brookfield home.

The first game was played September 24, and Boston won, 6–4. The 125 Boston rooters refused to be lost in the crowd of 13,000 spectators. They shouted, "Hit her up, hit her up, hit her up again for BOSTON!" and blew their fish horns.

When Hugh Duffy came to bat, a Baltimore fan yelled, "Go git yer shoofel, Doofey." And when Duffy promptly doubled, Boston fans shouted right back, "Doofey, it looks like yer got yer shoofel, all right." Baltimore fans didn't quite know what to make of these noisy people from the North. Didn't they know Baltimore was a five-to-two favorite to win two of the three games?

It was a tight game, with Baltimore scoring twice off Nichols in the first and ninth innings. Boston scored one run off Joe Corbett in the fourth, two runs in the fifth, two more in the seventh, and one in the eighth. Long, back in the line-up despite an injured hand, had a big day, making three hits. In the ninth, Doyle, Reltz, and Robinson singled to open the inning. Joe Quinn, the former Boston infielder, flied out as a pinch hitter, but McGraw singled. With bases full and one out, Keeler lined to Long for a game-ending double play. It wasn't as hard a chance as Long's leaping catch of Stenzel's liner with bases full in the eighth inning, or his earlier play on Robinson's grounder over second.

"Every time an old ball went out it was held by the crowd, until the home team had a beautiful bunch of white alleys to work on," complained Murnane. The next day he had more to worry about, for Baltimore won, 6–3, to regain first place.

Bill Hoffer, "the Wizard," outpitched Klobedanz, but the Boston hurler had some bad luck. Hamilton let two hits go through him, and Collins accidentally kicked a bunt by McGraw just before it rolled foul. Once Collins had told Jennings, "You bunt them, and I'll field them." Now the Orioles yelled, "We'll bunt them, and you'll kick 'em, Collins." Frank Selee did not feel much happier when he opened A. G. Spalding's telegram after the game, and read: "I congratulate you on yesterday's victory and more especially on

87

the absence of wrangling. Complete this entire series in a sportsmanlike way, and the game will be benefited."

The teams rested on Sunday and met in the deciding game on Monday, with Nichols again facing Corbett. Boston won, 19–10, a score that is partly explained by the crowd that overflowed the field until spectators were sitting on the ground within 20 feet of home plate, and partly by the pressure.

"Both teams blew up," explains Tenney, "but Baltimore blew higher than we did." He still has the last-out ball from that game, suitably inscribed.

The Orioles used four pitchers—Corbett, Nops, Hoffer, and Amole. At the end of the second inning, Baltimore led, 5–4, but Boston scored once in the third, three times in the fourth, and nine times in the seventh, before the Orioles scored again off Nichols. Tim Murnane wrote: "When Nichols is out for mischief he always wears one of those 'ain't-it-too-bad' sort of looks on his face." Duffy opened the seventh with a single, and ten more hits followed before the Beaneaters were retired. That day Collins made five hits, Long and Hamilton four each. So dense was the crowd in the outfield that the game produced fifteen two-baggers. The paid attendance was announced as 25,390, but another 1,500 got in by breaking down a fence. About 5,000 fans saw the game from adjacent housetops. Boston clinched the pennant by winning, 12–3, in Brooklyn three days later behind Klobedanz, while Washington was beating Baltimore, 9–3.

Captain Mike Griffin of Brooklyn said Boston's victory over Baltimore would tend to put foulmouthed players in the shade; and John M. Ward commented, "I think that Boston has played not only the best ball, but the cleanest ball as well." Herman Long led the cheering in the Boston dressing room after the game, while Frank Selee opened scores of complimentary telegrams.

3

The Temple Cup series between Boston and Baltimore opened Monday, October 4, in Boston. This was the fourth Temple Cup series, and the last. William C. Temple, Pittsburgh sportsman, had put up the cup in 1894 to be played for by the first and second teams of the National League. The competition was not a success, and it received its deathblow in 1897.

Baltimore lost the first game, then won the next four. It was the third time in four Temple Cup series that the second-place team had beaten the champions, one reason probably being that the series was an anticlimax for the pennant-winning team. "We didn't have any interest in the series in 1897, after winning the pennant, as we did, in the last week," says Tenney. "We had beaten Baltimore in the competition that counted, and this was just something extra."

On the morning of the first game, the *Globe* ran a reproduction of a McCutcheon cartoon in the *Chicago Record* that showed Boston's leading heroes to be Emerson, John L. Sullivan, and Klobedanz. Boston was proud of its Beaneaters, and 10,000 Bostonians turned out at the South End Grounds for the series opener.

There was no great tension among the fans or players. To them, this was an exhibition series. Kid Nichols gave way to Ted Lewis in the sixth inning, and said, "My arm grew lame in the second game in Baltimore last week, and I will now let some of the other boys finish the season, as I want to be right next season." Nichols remained with the team until the series ended, but he did not pitch again.

Leading 12–11, Baltimore wanted the game called because of darkness after the seventh inning, but Umpire Tim Hurst demanded that the game proceed. Boston scored the winning runs in the eighth on Stahl's double, Duffy's single, Long's double, and Bergen's grounder to Pitcher Jerry Nops, on which Duffy scored the winning run. The crowd swarmed onto the field, thinking the game was over because of darkness, but Hurst ordered the ninth inning played. Baltimore put two men on base, but Joe Kelley grounded to Long for the final out. Boston won, 13–12, but the headline said, "NO GREAT CREDIT TO YEAR'S CHAMPIONS! THEIR GAME HARDLY UP TO STANDARD."

Charlie Ganzel was not even in uniform for the first game, but instead served as an usher in the press box. Crowded conditions in the press coop, which was a rinky-dink affair just behind the plate, brought this blast:

The management in Boston is being severely criticized for the lack of courtesy and the grasping proclivities displayed at the Temple Game yesterday. The fact that every crank in the country was anxious to keep in touch with the game through the corps of newspaper correspondents sent to Boston was entirely disregarded. Instead of furnishing extra facilities to accommodate this rather important service even the ordinary and entirely inadequate equipment was rendered impossible. The wires and instruments lead to the front row of the grandstand, where a miserable unscreened press stand offers opportunities to practice dodging of foul tips and wild pitches. This space was sold yesterday, and correspondents, who also paid the price of admission, by the way, were driven to the slanting roof of the stand, accompanied by the telegraph operators, where they perched among the rafters and trusted a kindly Providence to keep the wires clear. As the wires were carried into the regions somewhere under the horde of spectators beneath and the switches and other paraphernalia of telegraphy were entirely out of reach in case of accident, the state of mind in which correspondents were kept was unenviable. Perhaps Mr. Selee doesn't care whether the public outside of Boston gets the news of the Temple Cup battles; but then the Temple Cup is a sort of national affair and baseball rooters are somewhat interested in it.

This was the game at which legend says one writer and his operator covered the game from the top of a telegraph pole. Baseball writers were nimble fellows in those days. Now they even demand elevators to carry them to luxurious press boxes perched like penthouses on grandstand roofs. The responsibility for the South End press box, of course, was not Selee's but the Triumvirs'!

Winning the first game had everyone in fine spirits that evening when the 1897 pennant was presented by former Mayor Curtis to Manager Selee, after the second act of Miss May Irwin's new comedy, *The Swell Miss Fitzwell*, at Tremont Theater. The Beaneaters were still celebrating their pennant victory while playing for the Temple Cup.

Joe Corbett, brother of Gentleman Jim, started the second game against Fred Klobedanz, who had to withdraw under fire in a six-run fifth inning. "Klobedanz threw commas, semicolons, Chinese laundry checks, North End streets, winding stairs, and his own name, but with no avail," wrote Murnane. Kloby quit after Reitz homered, and "Stivetts took his place and was nearly paralyzed by Clarke, who knocked his first pitch over the left-field fence for another homer." Boston kept fighting from behind, but never could quite catch up. After the second game, which they had lost, 13–11, the Beaneaters all attended a banquet at Faneuil Hall, where conviviality reigned.

The second game drew 6,000 fans, the third game about 4,000. Baltimore, with Bill Hoffer pitching, won, 8–3. Boston started Klobedanz again, but he was knocked out of the box in a four-run second inning. The Orioles got four more runs in the third inning off his successor, Ted Lewis, who was "still pitching with that tired

90

feeling." The game was called after seven innings because of darkness. Boston played "sleepy" ball.

Receipts for the first three games were divided as the series moved out of Boston. Net receipts were only $11,000, of which each club took half, a division that placed no premium on winning. The share of each Boston player for the three games amounted to only $310. World Series bat boys are better paid today.

On its way to Baltimore, this strangely casual rivalry stopped for an exhibition game in Springfield, where 3,000 fans saw Baltimore win, 8–6. For the third day in succession, Boston's starting pitcher was Klobedanz.

The next day the series resumed in Baltimore, the Orioles winning 12–11, as the Beaneaters played "saffron ball." Nops and Corbett hurled for the winners, while Selee varied the routine by starting Jack Stivetts, who had relieved the day before in Springfield. Lewis relieved Happy Jack in the third inning. The Orioles scored six runs in the first inning, after a pop fly fell among Long, Lowe, and Collins, only ten feet from second base. Anyone of the three could have caught the ball with "two fingers and a thumb," said Murnane. A "sunset muff" of Doyle's fly by Hamilton didn't help.

Needing to lose only one more game to end the series, the Beaneaters wasted no time. Marty Bergen, smartest of them all, had not even bothered to make the trip to Baltimore. Stivetts played the final game in center field in place of Hamilton. After singling in the sixth, Duffy left the game and caught a train for home. Charlie Hickman, starting pitcher, took Duffy's place in left field, and Jim Sullivan finished in the box. "Everyone took things good-naturedly," wrote Murnane, and added, "Boston was constantly doubled on the bases after making hits."

There were so few fans present that Boston players wanted to forfeit the final game and cup to the Orioles. The umpires, who were to get $100, objected. They settled for $50, and while Baltimore won, 9–3, with Hoffer allowing fifteen hits, the game was played in one hour and fourteen minutes. "As a burlesque, it was a great success."

In Pittsburgh the donor of the cup fumed on hearing reports that the games were fixed. He concluded, "The series has not been a good one by any means, and there has been general disappointment." He demanded an investigation. Instead, they gave his cup back to him. Unlike modern hockey fans, baseball fans could not stomach a postseason championship series between teams that had been playing each other for a championship all season.

4

Loss of the Temple Cup in 1897 had no ill effect on the Bean-eaters of 1898. They won one hundred and two games, but their percentage of .685 did not equal the all-time Boston record of .705 set the year before.

Because of the Spanish-American War, attendances sagged in all ball parks. Nick Young, president of the National League, said that seven of the twelve clubs in the league lost money, and he named Washington, St. Louis, Cleveland, Pittsburgh, New York, Brooklyn, and even Baltimore. The Triumvirs, who had enjoyed their best season financially in 1897, came out ahead, but not by much. Even in September, when the pennant race was hottest, the Beaneaters were playing to daily crowds of 1,200 and 1,400 at the South End Grounds. But there was no talk of stopping baseball because of the war. One day Bobby Lowe left a card game to buy an "extry" in New York, and read about Dewey's total victory at Manila.

If the Beaneaters of 1898 were stronger than the Beaneaters of 1897, it was because of a remarkable rookie pitcher, Victor Gazaway Willis, who won twenty-three and lost twelve games his first sea-son. The Delaware Peach, as he was called long before the days of the Georgia Peach, more than took up the slack of Kid Nichols's slump. The Kid for the first time in eight years failed to win thirty games. He won only twenty-nine and lost twelve games, for a .707 percentage.

Willis was born in Wilmington, Delaware, April 12, 1876. He broke in as a pro with Harrisburg of the Pennsylvania State League, in 1895, and pitched subsequently for Lynchburg and Syracuse. His 1897 record of twenty victories and seventeen defeats with Syracuse attracted big-league teams. Syracuse wanted $2,000 for him, but there were no takers. Faced with the prospect of losing Willis for $500 in the draft, Syracuse sold him to Boston for $1,000 and Catcher Fred Lake.

Tall, graceful, and right-handed, Willis had good control, a change of pace, and a sweeping curve. H. G. Merrill wrote in the *Wilkesbarre Record:* "While I am one of the few writers who give

92

the laugh to the chap who talks about strike-out records being a sure criterion of a pitcher's ability, in the case of Willis it is something worth considering, and is a criterion. With the Boston team behind him, Willis ought to be a terror."

Jack Ryan, former Boston catcher, who had handled Willis at Syracuse, said of the new pitcher, "Willis' drop is so wonderful that if anyone hits it, it is generally considered a fluke."

When Willis came through, the Triumvirs released the old favorite Jack Stivetts, whose size and swagger tickled Boston fans. That left Selee with a pitching staff composed of Nichols, Willis, the studious Ted Lewis, who led the league's hurlers, Hickman, and Mike Sullivan. Bergen and George Yeager were back as catchers, but when Yeager's hand was broken by a foul tip in September, William (Kitty) Bransfield was bought from Newport, Rhode Island. Late in the season, even Duffy caught a game at Baltimore. The infield was unchanged, but James Stafford, William Keister, and Jim Smith appeared as reserves. The outfield was the same, with Duffy in left, Hamilton in center, and Chick Stahl in right, but Dave Pickett served as a substitute.

Hamilton led the Beaneaters by hitting .367, and Collins led the league by hitting 15 home runs. Previous Boston players to lead the league in homers had been John Manning (6) in 1877, Charlie Jones (9) in 1879, Jones (9) again in 1882, Harry Stovey (16) in 1891, and Hugh Duffy (18) in 1894. Collins hit .337, Tenney .335, and Duffy only .319. It was not a good year for Captain Duffy. He was dropped to eighth place in the batting order, and did not get above .300 until three weeks before the season closed.

Most of the excitement occurred in September. Tenney injured a leg and was out for two weeks. Patsy Donovan, Pittsburgh manager, was quoted as saying: "Nobody is sorry for Tenney. I once saw him drop a throw, pick up the ball, and hit the other player in the back with the ball." When Tenney replied by saying: "Donovan is the meanest man I know," Donovan resorted to the line that was old even in 1898: "I was misquoted. I admire Tenney's winning qualities."

While Tenney was out, Boston lost nine of twelve games, yielding the league lead to Cincinnati the first day of September. A 6-to-6 tie with Cleveland in ten innings found two thirds of the crowd at South End cheering for Cleveland. Bergen had taken another unauthorized trip to his home in North Brookfield, a frequent failing

93

of his. President Soden was disgusted, and said, "The playing of the team the last two weeks is the worst it's been in years."

With Bergen absent without leave, Yeager, who had been substituting for Tenney at first base, had to catch. Who did Selee play at first base when the Beaneaters opened in New York, September 3? None other than Kid Nichols, the great pitcher. As the Beaneaters beat the Giants, 6–5, Nichols batted ninth behind Lewis, the pitcher. Selee was blasted by Murnane for "as poor a piece of judgment as ever befell the lot of a manager," and Nichols's own intelligence was openly questioned.

The next day, and until Tenney returned to the line-up, Charlie Hickman, a less valuable pitcher, covered first base. The slow return of Tenney and the loss of Yeager prompted Captain Duffy to growl about players getting soft. "There are too many doctors in the game now," the little leader of the nineties said contemptuously. He says the same today.

Boston was back on top September 5, as a result of two Labor Day victories over Washington. Willis won, 2–1, before 2,200 fans in the morning, Collins winning the game with a home run in the sixth inning. Nichols won, 6–2, before 4,000 fans in the afternoon. The year before, the Labor Day games at the South End Grounds had drawn 6,500 fans in the morning and 12,000 fans in the afternoon. Was it the war, or were Boston fans growing a little tired of the success of their Beaneaters? Certainly the rest of the league had tired of them. They were too cocky and too good.

Cincinnati, playing on the road, faded fast. The Beaneaters won nine games in a row and were sitting pretty until an old foe, the Baltimore Orioles, came along and won twelve games in succession. Tenney returned to the line-up, but then Billy Hamilton's trick knee popped out. Duffy moved to center, while Stafford went to left field. The Orioles cut the Boston lead to two and a half games on September 22, but that was the closest they could come. Chicago put an end to their winning streak, while Willis beat Pittsburgh, 2–1, with Duffy's double winning the game in the ninth. Murnane wrote, "When Mr. Willis is feeling well, all comers might as well draw four cards."

The Beaneaters just about clinched the pennant when they beat Brooklyn a double-header on September 26, while Washington was defeating Baltimore. But with a four-and-a-half-game lead, Selee again tortured the experts by starting Willis two games in succession. Willis beat Brooklyn, 3–1, September 27, but was frequently in trouble, although he finished the game. The next day, Selee again started Willis, and he lost after a four-run fourth inning. Duffy was chased out of the game by the umpire, and all Boston was in an ugly mood. The Triumvirs said things that could not be printed.

There was a notable improvement in dispositions the next day, when the Beaneaters beat Philadelphia by virtue of a six-run rally in the ninth inning. Collins tied the score with a home run with two teammates on base, and Stahl scored the winning run when Lewis's fly fell among three rival players in left field. The Beaneaters then wasted no time nailing the flag to the mast. They won nine of their last eleven games. There was no Temple Cup series awaiting them, and the Cincinnati Reds had rejected Selee's challenge to play a nine-game series for $2,500. Everyone agreed that the season, lasting until the middle of October, had been too long. By finishing first, the Boston players won a prize of $4,000.

But as good as they were—and the Beaneaters won sixty-one and lost only fifteen games at home—all was not beer and pretzels for the champions. Twice during the season they had been held hitless by rival pitchers. Jim Hughes set them down at Baltimore, April 22, beating Lewis, 8–0. Hughes walked three men, and there were three errors behind him. On a sweltering day in Philadelphia, July 8, Frank Donahue held the Bostons without a hit, beating Willis, 5–0. Donahue passed two men, and there were two errors behind him. The Beaneaters tied another record for futility when they left eighteen men on base against Baltimore.

Boston was mighty proud at the close of the 1898 season. What other city could boast of winning five pennants in eight years, and eight pennants since the National League was founded in 1876? Besides, new conquests were in sight. What if Duffy's average had slumped, and Bergen wasn't throwing to second base as well as he used to, and some of the snap had left Nichols's arm? The Beaneaters were still a young team, a nicely balanced and well-managed team. Surely no Boston fan in 1898 would have believed that his Beaneaters would not win another pennant for sixteen years.

CHAPTER IX

AN UNWELCOMED NEIGHBOR

SYNDICATE baseball brought an end to the reign of the Beaneaters in 1899—and perhaps carelessness had something to do with the slipping of the crown. Harry B. Von der Horst, owner of the Orioles, was so concerned about falling attendances in Baltimore that he bought control of the Brooklyn club after the 1898 season. He immediately tried to move his best Orioles to his new franchise. Ned Hanlon went as manager, Willie Keeler, Hugh Jennings, and Joe Kelley as players, but John McGraw and Wilbert Robinson chose to stay in Baltimore, much to Von der Horst's disgust.

But Brooklyn had all the help it needed to win the 1899 pennant. The Superbas had a lead of eight games over the Beaneaters at the close of the season. When the Giants protested the illegal use of Infielder George Wrigley by Brooklyn late in the season, the league's board of directors threw out eighteen games in which Wrigley had played. This did the Beaneaters no good whatsoever. They still finished second, four games behind the Superbas, even though they won ninety-five games to eighty-eight for the leaders.

Too many of Boston's regulars had off seasons. Perhaps they were due for slumps. Perhaps they took life too easy. They had been on top for a long time. Billy Hamilton dropped from .367 to .306. He was injured during most of the campaign and played in only eighty-one games. Hugh Duffy slumped from .319 to .279. Jimmy Collins, although still a youngster, had a bad season at the bat. He hit .337 and socked fifteen home runs in 1898, but in 1899 he hit .275 and socked only five home runs. Kid Nichols, now thirty years old, had his worst season, winning twenty-one and losing seventeen games.

But three Beaneaters had exceptional seasons, and they kept Boston in the pennant race. Fred Tenney led the team by hitting

.350, his highest average, and Chick Stahl batted .348. The sophomore right-hander, Vic Willis, enjoyed his finest season in the majors, winning twenty-seven and losing only ten games. Willis pitched a no-hit game against Washington at the South End Grounds, August 7, but he allowed a run, winning 7–1. Willis fanned five men, walked four, hit one, and three errors were made behind him.

Collins set a defensive record for third basemen by accepting 601 chances. Stahl became the second man in the history of the Boston club to make six hits in six times at bat, duplicating the feat of Sam Wise in 1887.

Yet it was a blue season in Boston. Attendances were not good. The Triumvirs were more unpopular than ever. There was dissension among the players. Marty Bergen, the eccentric catcher, kept everyone in a turmoil. When his son died during the summer, he was harder than ever to get along with. Bergen would catch a few games, then ask Manager Selee if he could return home for a few days. Selee would refuse permission, so Bergen would go home anyhow.

Bergen complained that the players kept reminding him of his son who had died. He resented a $300 fine Selee imposed when he took an unauthorized vacation. Black moods came on Bergen, who seemed to be happy only when on his farm in North Brookfield. Some players said they would not play for the Beaneaters in 1900 if Bergen was still with the club. That was all right with Bergen, who said he wanted to be traded.

In his letters to *Sporting Life,* Jake Morse explained that Bergen was a sick man who had undergone treatment at City Hospital. Once when the catcher did not accompany the team west, Soden had called him into his office and told him that he would have to "rise above his spells." Despite his mutations, the fans were sympathetic toward Bergen.

No word was heard of the catcher during the winter, until January 19, 1900, when his father returned from a few days' absence to find a terrible scene awaiting him at the farm. Using an ax and a razor, Bergen had killed his wife, his three-year-old son, his baby daughter, and himself. Some thirty-five years later, Connie Mack and George M. Cohan, who had close Brookfield ties, helped raise funds with which to erect a granite memorial to the gifted but ill-fated catcher. The inscription read: "In memory of Martin Bergen,

1871-1900. Member of the Boston National League Club. Erected in appreciation of his contribution to America's national game."

Poor Fred Klobedanz suffered a strange but less tragic fate, running afoul a labor union while working as a scene shifter, during the off season, at the Park Theater. He acquired a reputation as a strikebreaker and was literally hounded from the field. He drifted into the New England League, but bad luck pursued him. One day at Nashua, New Hampshire, he had a 4-to-1 lead in the ninth inning. With the bases full, the batter hit the ball back to Kloby. The pitcher threw home, but the ball got away from the catcher and went through a gap in the backstop. By the time the catcher had retrieved the ball, the three base runners had scored, and the batter was coming home from third. The catcher threw to Kloby at the plate, and the pitcher dropped the ball. The opposition had scored four runs and won the game on a simple bounder to the pitcher.

From a twelve-club league, the National League went to an eight-club circuit in 1900. Washington, Baltimore, and Louisville were eliminated, and Cleveland went to the Western League. From Washington the Beaneaters got John (Buck) Freeman, a little outfielder who had batted .319 and hit twenty-five home runs in 1899, and Big Bill Dineen, a right-handed pitcher. Dineen did his bit for the 1900 Bostons, winning twenty-one and losing fifteen games, but Freeman batted a mere .242 and hit only five home runs.

The great Beaneaters were no more. The tiny flaws of 1899 became major fissures in 1900. Duffy was able to play in only fifty games. Kid Nichols for the first time failed to win half his games, his record showing thirteen victories and fifteen defeats. Bergen was sadly missed. Bill Clarke, who took his place, led the league's catchers with twenty-seven errors. John Clements, the veteran left-handed catcher, was signed, but always had a sore toe or a lame arm, and caught few games. Tenney slumped from .350 to .284, and Willis was fearsomely wild throughout the season and could win only nine games while losing sixteen. The Bostons finished fourth, twenty games behind the flag-winning Brooklyn Superbas. For the first time in fourteen years, the Triumvirs had a team that could not win half its games.

The gloom was heavy at the South End Grounds as a new century was born. What if Buck Freeman did make two triples in one

98

inning? What if Herman Long led the league with twelve home runs? What if the Beaneaters scored thirteen runs in the first inning of a game against St. Louis? What if three Boston pinch hitters hit safely and scored runs in the ninth inning of a game against Philadelphia? What if John Barry did make two hits and score two runs in an inning? These were crumbs. The Beaneaters were moldering fast. Duff was through. Old Nick was through. Billy Hamilton was through. And even the Triumvirs were about through. Dark days lay ahead.

2

During the winter, a young bull came along to challenge the old bull. The old bull survived, but the young bull won the right to live beside the old bull. The young bull, of course, was the American League. The old bull was the National League. Part of the fight was fought in Boston.

Not wishing to battle the National League at first, Ban Johnson, president of the new league, originally did not intend to place a rival club in Boston. What prompted him to change his mind was the refusal of the National League to do business with him, and the threat of the National League to help reorganize the American Association as a rival of the new American League.

The Triumvirs, already having survived three wars, looked contemptuously on the new league. Only when Johnson, Connie Mack, and Charlie Somers went to work organizing a Boston club did Soden encourage Arthur Irwin, former National League player and manager, who had once won a game for Providence by hitting a home run through a hole in the fence at the South End Grounds, to put an American Association club at Charles River Park. But Soden was bluffing, and the American League went right ahead with its plans for a Boston team, while Irwin faded quickly into the background. Soden had no intention of fighting two clubs. One would be bad enough, although he confidently predicted: "Only one club will survive this battle in Boston, and that will be the same old National League club."

Soden fought the new intruders halfheartedly, like a weary Roman emperor facing a new horde of barbarians. There was little he could do. The issue would be resolved at the gate, by the public. In January, Connie Mack signed a lease for a large plot of land at the corner of Huntington Avenue and Rogers Avenue. A few days later, Hugh Duffy arrived in Chicago and announced that he would manage Milwaukee in the new league in 1901.

"Mr. Soden asserts that the Boston club has an option on my services, but I have just finished a two-year contract at Boston," he said. "The option is the usual National League reserve clause, and I received no bonus except for $600 for captaining the Boston team last season. I consulted my lawyer and was told to go ahead and better myself if possible. That, I think, I am doing."

Duffy told Boston friends that he was tired of playing at the South End and tired of being criticized for his handling of Boston pitchers in his capacity of captain. "I haven't had the full authority as captain, as anybody knows," he complained. The Triumvirs made no fight to hold Duffy. Conant said, "He's about through as a player. We'll let him go in peace."

But since Duffy's interest now was in the American League, he did his best to persuade his friends on the Beaneaters to make the same jump. The first and most important to take the leap was Jimmy Collins, best of all third basemen. This hurt the Triumvirs, for as late as Feburary 28, they had a telegram from Collins in Buffalo promising not to sign until he heard from the Boston Nationals. Soden was willing to let matters take their course, but Conant immediately dispatched Billings and Selee to Buffalo, telling them to go as high as $5,000 to keep Collins. That's what Conant told them out loud in the presence of newspapermen. What he whispered to them confidentially must have been something else, for Collins signed as player-manager of the Boston Americans at $4,000, which Somers assured him even if he were enjoined from playing with the new team.

From the Beaneaters, Collins won Chick Stahl, who was later to succeed him as manager of the Red Sox and to commit suicide before the 1907 season; Buck Freeman, the outfielder; and Ted Lewis, the scholarly hurler. Dineen and Willis almost took the plunge but decided to string along with the Beaneaters another season. Tenney, Long, Lowe, and Hamilton all refused to cross the railroad tracks to the Huntington Avenue Grounds.

But the Boston Nationals lost too many good men as it was. The Triumvirs let the enemy gain a foothold. They were too complacent, too confident. They underestimated the strength of Ban Johnson's new league. They were going to brush that fly off their noses when they got around to it, but they were too slow getting around to it. The fly turned out to be a hornet, and the Triumvirs got stung.

If they had been offered enough money, Collins, Lewis, Stahl, and Freeman would have remained with the Beaneaters. In Collins, the Triumvirs surrendered a valuable asset to the rival club, and the Triumvirs needed all the assets they had for this fight. Their one chance of winning was to make the newcomers look like minor leaguers by comparison. Instead, the newcomers made the Beaneaters look like minor leaguers, and the Boston sporting public enjoyed the spectacle.

The Triumvirs had become symbols of stinginess. In saloons and on street corners they were ridiculed by fans who took their cue from the newspaper writers. The South End ball park was an ugly little wart. Players were known to be dissatisfied with their small salaries. The smug attitude with which the Triumvirs regarded the new intruders cost them friends.

The Americans made a hit with a twenty-five-cent bleacher section. Kids like Gene Mack could cash in a couple of whisky bottles found in a dump, hook a ride on an open trolley, and see the Americans play for nothing. Their park was new, neat, and larger than the South End Grounds, of which the public had grown weary. And they presented some interesting new players in Ossie Schreckengost, Freddy Parent, Hobe Ferris, Lou Criger, George Cuppy, and Cy Young—especially the great Cy Young, who was lured from the St. Louis Cardinals.

Young pitched May 8, when the Americans opened their home season by beating Philadelphia, 4–2. "AMERICAN LEAGUE MEN GIVEN ROYAL WELCOME BY 11,500 ROOTERS," said a *Globe* streamer. General Arthur Dixwell, the old Beaneater rooter, threw out the first ball. Jimmy Collins got a bouquet, the new team got a great hand. The Nationals had already played several games at home, but they unhesitatingly played at the South End Grounds the same day the Americans made their debut a few blocks away. They beat Brooklyn, 7–6, in twelve innings. By letting Boston English and Boston Latin High School boys in free, they had a crowd of 5,500, about half what their new rivals drew. For years the Nationals would have to be satisfied with second place in Boston.

Jimmy Collins's team played fast, hustling baseball, stayed in the American League pennant race all the way, and finished second to Clark Griffith's pennant-winning Chicago White Sox. That was three places higher than the 1901 Selees finished in the National League steeplechase.

3

Although they had Tenney, Lowe, and Long in the infield, Billy Hamilton in the outfield, and Nichols, Willis, Dineen, and Pittenger on the mound, the 1901 Nationals were in no danger of being favorably compared with the great teams of the 1890's. Replacing Collins at third base was a newcomer, Eugene Napoleon DeMontreville, who appeared in the box scores as Demont. During the season, he was moved to second base, and the aging Lowe shifted to third.

Hamilton started in center field but was able to play only ninety-nine games. Fred Crolius was in right field, John C. Barry in left, and they had a lively competition misjudging fly balls, until Barry was sent to Philadelphia for Jim Slagle. Elmer Smith, Fred Murphy, John Gammons, and Fred Brown were other outfielders who made National League fans yearn for Hugh Duffy and Chick Stahl. The catcher was the good-natured veteran Malachai Jedidiah Kittridge, who was helped by Pat Moran.

The team had little batting punch. Tenney batted only .278. In May, a Cincinnati southpaw, Frank (Noodles) Hahn struck out sixteen Boston hitters. Captain Dutch Long whiffed three times. In September, a 1-to-0 game was lost to Chicago in seventeen innings, neither club producing an extra-base hit. That the Beaneaters were able to finish with a .500 record was due to their pitchers. Willis recovered to win eighteen, lose seventeen games. Dineen's record was a drab 14–19, but Nichols came back to win eighteen and lose fifteen games in his last season with Boston.

A promising young hurler was Charles (King) Pittenger, who had attracted Selee's attention by his extraordinary hurling for Brockton in the New England League several years earlier. The Pennsylvanian was to have a brief but brilliant big-league career, then was to die of diabetes when only thirty-seven years old.

This was the final season for four distinguished members of the club: Selee, Lowe, Hamilton, and Nichols. When the Beaneaters started to break up, they went to pieces in a hurry. Occasionally one of the pieces turns up unexpectedly today and is curiously regarded by modern connoisseurs of sports, like a strange object swept in by the tide. A newspaper clipping in 1946 turned up a relic from Boston's great era of National League champions.

The clipping:

Boston, Aug. 26 (AP)—Dave Ferriss, the Boston Red Sox pitching wizard, appears on the way to establishing a modern record for most games won by a pitcher in his first two seasons. Ferriss already has 44 victories, only three shy of the record of 47 set by Grover Cleveland Alexander.

The letter:

Kansas City, Aug. 29

Dear Sir—I was very surprised to read this article in our *Kansas City Star*. So I am writing to find out how come 47 wins for a pitcher's first two years is considered a record?

Either you have been misinformed, or you fail to recognize the existence of the National League as far back as 1890. All you need to do is look back to your newspapers of 1890 and 1891.

You will find that Charles "Kid" Nichols signed up with the Boston Nationals in 1890. During that year he won 27 games, and in 1891 he won 30 games for a total of 57. It seems to me the present day pitchers are a long way from reaching a record.

Were we to combine 1891-1892, we would have 30 and 35 wins for a total of 65 wins. In 1892 and 1893, he had 35 and 33 to total 68 wins. Notice, 35 wins in 1892, 33 wins in 1893, and 32 wins in 1894 for a total of 100 games won in three consecutive years.

However, I am told that Amos Rusie beat that by one game.

How do I know all of this? Well, you see, I am "Kid" Nichols' daughter. And in those first years of his professional career, he kept scrapbooks of the newspaper reports. . . .

Many of my Father's friends around here cannot understand just why you reporters in Boston have made no attempt to put him into the Hall of Fame.

It was in Boston he spent the best years of his life, and through his pitching ability was recognized in those days as the one who saved many a game for Boston. . . .

On Sept. 14th (1946) my father will celebrate his 77th birthday. He is enjoying good health. Able to work long hours at the Pla Mor bowling establishment, where he is employed. There he meets and discusses baseball with his old as well as new friends.

Sincerely,
Mrs. Harlan L. Everett, Sr.

P.S.—Notice number of innings pitched. Can Ferriss equal that?

The reply:

No, Ferriss cannot equal that, Mrs. Everett. . . . When your dad was in his prime, he averaged 400 innings and 30 victories per season over nine seasons. He and other great players like him set records so far beyond the reach of players today that we now ignore them and refer to modern records as those dating from 1900.

103

The game has changed so much, Mrs. Everett, that it is hard to compare the Dave Ferriss of today with the Kid Nichols of 50 years ago. Pitching staffs are twice as large now, the ball is livelier, the game is faster. Not better, maybe, but faster. There is more interest, more pressure now.

But even if the game changes, the ball gets livelier and the schedule grows longer, let us put the great players of every generation into the Hall of Fame. Your dad, Kid Nichols, belongs there right now.

In fourteen years as a big leaguer, Kid Nichols won 360 and lost 202 games for a .641 percentage. He completed 530 of 582 games he started. He completed the first fifty-six games he started for Boston, not being relieved until his second season with the club. He won thirty or more games in seven consecutive seasons, twenty or more games in ten consecutive seasons. Yet pitchers with less impressive records are in the Hall of Fame, while he, as of 1947, is not.

"I have yet to learn that Nichols has any wonderful, elusive curves and quick-breaking shoots," Pat Donovan of the Pirates once said, "but he has one thing that makes an effective pitcher, and that is command of the ball and speed to back it up."

Nichols was a model athlete. Malachai Kittridge described him as "the most perfect husband and father I have ever met." A half century has passed, but the Boston Nationals have yet to come up with a pitcher like old Nick, who, when out for mischief, always wore "one of those ain't-it-too-bad sort of looks on his face." Plenty of Braves pitchers have had his look. None has had his record.

CHAPTER X

THE TRIUMVIRS GO TOBOGGANING

⊜

HAVING lost the first round of their bout with the American League upstarts, the Triumvirs decided to give their ailing club a transfusion. First, however, they elected to cut off the patient's right arm. This they did by releasing Manager Frank Selee, after the 1901 season. Although Albert C. Buckenberger, who succeeded Selee, had enjoyed considerable success at Rochester, the replacing of a man who had won five pennants in twelve years was hardly a move designed to increase the popularity of the National League team in Boston.

It looked as though the Triumvirs were making Selee the goat for their mistakes. More than the fans, the ballplayers resented Selee's dismissal. Returning from Milwaukee, where he had managed the American League team, Hugh Duffy angrily said: "Selee should long ago have left this city and taken one of several good chances he had, instead of staying here at a very small salary."

Selee was not a high-priced man, making around $3,500 a season. He made a little money on the side when he and Sid Farrar, former Philadelphia first baseman and father of Geraldine Farrar, the opera singer, opened a haberdashery in Melrose. When Clark Griffith, manager of the American League White Sox in 1901, heard of Selee's release, he said: "That is a big mistake. Selee is one of the few great managers in the business."

Jim Hart, who had managed Boston in 1889 and had been succeeded by Selee, seemed to think so. Now president of the Chicago Nationals, Hart at once engaged Selee as Tommy Burns's successor. One of Selee's first moves was to get Bobby Lowe from Boston. Buckenberger was glad to be rid of Lowe, who was Selee's lieutenant. Selee managed Chicago three years, 1902-04, and in successive seasons finished fifth, third, and second, then was succeeded by Frank Chance, who won pennants in 1905, 1906, and 1907.

"Selee built the team that won three straight pennants for Chicago," says Tenney loyally, "and Chance got all the credit."

Selee had shifted Tenney from catching to first base, and he did the same for Chance at Chicago, although Jack Taylor, a pitcher who liked to work with Chance, objected to the change. The fellow who talked Chance into trying first base was Lowe, Chicago's captain in 1902.

"I see by the fielding averages that Chance is a good many points ahead of you," Billings said one day to Tenney. The Boston first baseman bristled, and replied, "Yes, but I'll tell you one thing: They'll trade you even." Billings complained no more.

Selee eventually resigned the Chicago job because of failing health. He later managed Pueblo, Colorado, but in 1909, only three months after Herman Long, he, too, died in Denver of consumption. He was then fifty years old. Alfred H. Spink wrote of Selee: "Few men in baseball were more popular. He was generous to a degree and extremely charitable. He had a host of friends."

Following the 1901 debacle, the Triumvirs disposed of other members of their 1897-98 champions besides Selee and Lowe. Buckenberger released Billy Hamilton when the outfielder would not go to spring training because of his son's illness. Bill Dineen was allowed to jump to the Red Sox. Kid Nichols drew his release, became a pitcher-manager of Kansas City for two years, then finished his career with St. Louis and Philadelphia in the National League.

About the only battle the Triumvirs won before the 1902 season opened was the one they fought for Herman Long, the veteran shortstop. Griffith came to Boston from Chicago and offered Long $4,000, or somewhat more than he had received in 1901. "I'm out for the money this time," announced Long, then went in to see Treasurer Billings. For once the Triumvirs opened their purse, and Long stayed.

In Buckenberger, the Triumvirs had an experienced manager who was only forty years old. Buck had been a minor-league second baseman for a few years, but when only twenty-three years old he was managing Terre Haute. He had also managed Toledo, Guelph, Ontario, Kalamazoo, Wheeling, Columbus, Syracuse, Pittsburgh, St. Louis, and Rochester before coming to Boston. In 1892 he succeeded Tom Burns as Pittsburgh manager. In 1893 he was president as well as manager of the club, and in 1894 he started the season as manager, but was replaced by Connie Mack. He began the 1895 season as manager of St. Louis, but was replaced by George Miller.

At Syracuse, Buckenberger had developed Vic Willis, the curveball artist who was now the best pitcher on the Boston team. When he came to Boston, Buckenberger boasted, "I can get players from Rochester who will replace all those fellows you've lost." He spoke as if Duffys, Collinses, Dineens, and Stahls grew on trees around Rochester. In his first season, Buckenberger opened with Fred Tenney at first base, DeMontreville at second, Long at shortstop, and Edward Greminger at third. His outfielders were Fred Murphy, Bill Lush, Pat Carney, Dick Cooley, and Dan McGann. Kittridge and Moran did the catching, as they had in 1901. Besides Willis and Pittenger, he had Sam Curran, Charlie Dresser, Malcom Eason, Roy Hale, Nelson Long, and John Malarkey for pitchers.

Buckenberger's first Boston team finished third, a lofty perch considering the personnel. Although Tenney batted .314, the Bostons had little punch, setting their all-time low with only thirteen home runs. Willis and Pittenger put the club in the first division. Pittenger won twenty-seven games, Willis won twenty-six. The only other Boston National pitcher of this century to win twenty-seven games in a season was Dick Rudolph, who equaled Pittenger's record in 1914. Pittenger's seven shutouts also set a modern Boston record, to be equaled three years later by Irvine Young. Willis finished forty-three of the forty-five games he started.

Despite their improvement, the 1902 Boston Nationals failed to win back the fans who had deserted them for the Boston Americans the year before. Jimmy Collins's team across the tracks had also finished third, but it was first in Boston popularity. The Triumvirs were still faced with the threat of players jumping to the other league, and after the season, Willis took the plunge. But he was too late. The leagues made their peace in January, 1903, and the peace commissioners returned Willis to the Boston Nationals.

The American League hotly pursued Tenney, but he remained loyal to Soden, for whom he had a great deal of affection. When Tenney was fined during the 1902 season for fighting with Fred Clarke of Pittsburgh, Buckenberger predicted, "Now he'll go to Detroit for sure."

But Tenney remained faithful, although Detroit had offered him

107

$5,000 for one season and $10,000 for two seasons—big money in those days. After the season, Soden gave Tenney his personal check for the amount of his fine, and also gave Tenney a three-year contract without the release clause. Tenney stuck, Willis was returned, but Herman Long was allowed to stay with the New York Highlanders. The Dutchman was near the end of the road. Tenney succeeded him as captain in 1903, another dismal season for the Triumvirs, especially since the rival Boston Americans won their first pennant and followed it up by winning the first World Series from Fred Clarke's Pittsburgh club. Buckenberger's second team finished sixth, winning only fifty-eight games. It was the worst record in seventeen seasons for the Boston Nationals.

Tenney had a good year, hitting .313, but Willis, understandingly disgruntled over his bad luck in having to stay with Boston, won only twelve out of thirty games. Boston led the league with 348 errors, but Pat Moran set a catching record with 214 assists. The most memorable day of the 1903 season was August 1, when Iron Man Joe McGinnity beat Boston, 4–1 and 5–2, in a double-header at New York, allowing only a total of eight hits. About the only satisfaction for Boston was provided by Pittenger, who pitched the first game. He hit four Giant batters with pitched balls, one more than McGinnity was able to hit.

This was the season when Boston began to play Sunday baseball in Chicago, Cincinnati, and St. Louis. It was also the first season for Edward J. Abbaticchio, the Italian football player from Latrobe, Pennsylvania. He played second base and shortstop for three years, quit to take care of his hotel in Latrobe, was traded to the Pirates, and then came back to Boston to finish his big-league career in 1910. Abbaticchio was a colorful player, especially when surrounded by such cup-of-coffee performers as Harry Aubrey, Frank Bonner, Thomas Leavenworth McGreery, Joe Stanley, Wiley Piatt, and Walter Williams.

2

Buckenberger rounded out his Boston stay by finishing seventh in 1904. It was the first time in twenty-nine years in the National League that the Boston team had finished so low. Unfortunately, the Boston Nationals liked life on a low level, and in following years it seemed that they might take up a permanent residence in seventh and eighth places.

108

While the Boston Americans were showing their fans three twenty-game winners in Cy Young, Bill Dineen, and Jesse Tannehill, the Boston Nationals were showing their followers three twenty-game losers in Willis (twenty-five), Pittenger (twenty-one), and Irvin K. Wilhelm (twenty).

When someone mentioned Tannehill on the bench, Willis said: "He's the fellow who dislocated his shoulder hitting fungo flies before a game we played in Pittsburgh a few years ago. They had to give him ether to put his arm back in place."

None of the Boston Nationals pitchers was in any danger of dislocating his arm in 1904, although Willis won eighteen games, a good record considering the club he was with. Willis also set a minor sort of record covering first base, for he made thirty-nine put-outs in forty-three games. It was a good thing he did, because nobody else was making them. It was every man for himself on the Boston Nationals.

This was the worst fielding Boston team of modern times, making a total of 353 errors for an average of .945. Phil Grier, who previously had had a trial with the Athletics and Milwaukee, set a record by making three errors in one inning at third base. Abbaticchio led the shortstops with 78 errors. As if this were not enough, Boston ended its season by making ten errors in a game against Chicago. Many new players were tried, best of whom were Tom Needham, an outfielder, and Jim Delahanty, second baseman. Delahanty was the fourth of the six Cleveland brothers, greatest of whom was Ed. Jim played with four clubs in the National League, three clubs in the American League. He played for Chicago and the Giants, was released to Little Rock, and then was taken up in 1904 by Boston, where he played two seasons before continuing his travels with a short visit to Cincinnati.

"It's strange that I should have played the outfield so much," said Delahanty one day in Boston. "I never liked it, and it wasn't until I got a chance here in Boston that I knew second base was my best position."

Delahanty was a fair ballplayer but not comparable to his brother Ed. He was often hurt, and while with Boston broke his ankle playing an exhibition game at Newark. A scrappy individual, later in his career he was to be a leader in the brief and unsuccessful revolt of the Detroit Tigers against Ban Johnson, president of the American League. At Boston, like all other National Leaguers, he was eclipsed by the darlings of the town, the Boston Americans.

Midway through the summer of 1904, the old Triumvirate lost J. B. Billings, who left Soden and Conant to function as a duet. The departure of Billings, a keen fan as well as treasurer of the club, shocked loyal followers of the Boston Nationals. It was sudden, unexpected, prophetic.

For nearly twenty-five years, Billings had signed the salary checks of Boston players, but on July 5, the players noted that Soden's signature had replaced Billings's. Where was Billings? He had not been at the game that day. What had happened?

"He's just on a little vacation," explained Conant. Billings had gone to his summer home at the Isles of Shoals.

Billings was not on a little vacation, but a permanent one, as far as the Boston team was concerned. Soden admitted that he had taken over Billings's duties as treasurer and that William Rodgers had been made assistant treasurer. Soden and Conant had bought Billings's stock, which amounted to only a few shares. For several seasons, Soden revealed, Billings had been drawing a salary as treasurer.

Billings had worked with and fought with Soden and Conant for many years. He was a nervous, sporty fellow with a consuming passion for figures, and he loved baseball. His most spectacular contribution was the purchase of King Kelly from Chicago for $10,000. Players liked him. While managing the Philadelphia Nationals in 1904, Hugh Duffy reflected on the years he had played in Boston, and said, "The man I miss most is Billings. He was a friend of the ballplayer."

Buckenberger was released at the end of the 1904 season, but Soden and Conant were slow to name their new manager. It was February, and spring training was near when Soden said to Tenney, "Clear some of those papers off the manager's desk, will you, Fred?"

That is how Tenney became manager of the Boston team. He worked steadily, signing players and arranging the exhibition schedule. One day Tenney asked, "How about signing me up for this year?"

"You've got your player's contract for $2,400," said Soden. "Sign that, and I'll see that you get what you deserve."

Tenney signed and said, "You're the only owner I'd ever do this for, Mr. Soden."

When Tenney talked about strengthening the team, Soden told

him, "We don't care where you finish, so long as you don't lose money with the team." Soden then offered Tenney a bonus if the club did not lose money. By working hard, Tenney collected this bonus the two seasons he served as manager for Soden and Conant. It was the only satisfaction he had. Tenney may not have been the best manager in the league but he soon became the thriftiest. Going into the stands with or without police protection to retrieve foul balls did not endear him to the public.

One day he accused an umpire, Bill Klem, of keeping balls that belonged to the club. When Klem denied the charge indignantly, Tenney attempted to search him. The result was a short but lively fight. But it was probably through his aggressive pursuit of baseballs that the club broke even, financially, and Tenney was able to collect his bonus.

If the Boston club did not make a practice of giving away autographed baseballs in 1905, it was more liberal with baseball games. Tenney's team finished seventh, losing 103 games, five more than Buckenberger's last team. The trading of Pittenger to Philadelphia for Harry Wolverton, third baseman, and Charlie Fraser, pitcher, did not help Boston. Fraser set a club record by giving 149 bases on balls.

The Boston Nationals had four 20-game losers in 1904—Willis (29), Fraser (22), Wilhelm (22), and Irving Melrose Young (21). The National League never had a more spectacular rookie than Young, the husky southpaw from Columbia Falls, Maine. He set rookie records that still stand, by pitching 378 innings, 41 complete games, and 7 shutouts. Although beaten 21 times, he achieved 20 victories, or two fifths of the games won by an inept ball club.

Since Cy Young was still pitching for the Boston Americans, they called this twenty-nine-year-old rookie Little Cy, or Young Cy. His parents had moved from Maine when he was seventeen years old so that Irving could become a fireman on the Boston and Maine Railroad, instead of a lumberjack in the Maine forest. For years he worked for sixty dollars a month as a fireman, pitching week ends for teams in Woodsville and Whitefield. Nathan Pulsifer, Bates graduate and Concord manager, gave him his chance in organized ball with the Concord New England League team, with which he won eighteen and lost fourteen games in 1904. Recommended by Scout Billy Hamilton, he was bought for $500 by the Boston Nationals.

111

In September, Barney Dreyfuss of the Pirates offered $7,500 for the sensational southpaw, but was refused. Little Cy was then being likened to Big Cy, a comparison that was somewhat premature. The star the baseball astronomers saw through their telescope was only a comet, after all, but a mighty bright comet at that.

Among the Boston rookies was Charles (Gabby) Street. Three years later he was to catch a ball thrown from the top of Washington Monument, but on June 5, 1905, he would have dropped a ball thrown from the porch roof, for on that day Gabby set a mark for other catchers to shoot at by making four errors. Street spent the next two seasons with San Francisco, about the farthest point on the American mainland to which Tenney could ship him. Later he was to be an outstanding catcher and manager, but not for Boston.

Most lucky of the luckless Bostons was Willis. He had lost twenty-nine games while winning only twelve, but this miserable record resulted in a trade that sent him to Pittsburgh in exchange for Dave Brain, third baseman, Del Howard, an infielder, and Vivian Alsace Lindaman, a pitcher. Willis promptly showed his gratitude for his release from boredom in Boston by winning over twenty games for the Pirates in each of the next four seasons. He helped pitch them to the 1909 pennant by winning twenty-two out of thirty-three games. He might have done as much for Boston if he had been given any help, but instead Willis left Boston with a modern National League record of twenty-nine defeats in one season. A fine memorial for the great curve-ball pitcher who died in August, 1947.

CHAPTER XI

DOVES WITHOUT WINGS

It was no secret that Soden and Conant wanted to sell their ball club. Soden, who had been president since 1877 and had borne the major responsibilities, was more eager to get out of baseball than Conant. Both had made fortunes in business, and the ball club had added to their incomes. The Beaneaters of 1897 were reputed to have made a profit of $120,000. When the 1898 team made a profit of only $90,000, J. B. Billings had moaned, "We lost thirty thousand dollars last year."

Fred Tenney hoped to head a syndicate that would buy the club. He approached friends in the Boston business world, but could not get the promise of $5,000, let alone $100,000. The Boston Nationals were not an attractive speculation, with the Boston Americans sweeping the town before them, the South End Grounds in a state of disrepair, and the team poor in talented players. So Soden and Conant still owned the club when the 1906 season opened.

Any inclination of theirs to hold onto the franchise was discouraged when the Boston Nationals for the first time in their history finished last in 1906. Tenney's team won only forty-nine games, and wound up sixty-six and one half games behind the Chicago pennant winners, a record for futility. One can only imagine the disgust of Soden and Conant as the 1906 Bostons fumbled and stumbled their way through a desultory campaign.

Boston was shut out no less than twenty-eight times, ten times by the Pittsburgh Pirates, and four times by Lefty Leifield of that team. Boston lost four consecutive shutouts in May, by scores of 0–5, 0–8, 0–1, and 0–5. On June 11, the team made eleven errors, and in the game Dave Brain, their new third baseman, made five errors to set the modern record.

Between May 17 and June 8, Boston lost nineteen games in succession, all of them on the road. This still stands as the club record. Curiously, Boston American League fans were still laughing at the Nationals when their own pets got mixed up in a twenty-game losing streak, dropping nineteen of the games at home. But when they ended the streak, there were nearly 5,000 fans present at the Huntington Avenue Grounds. The only solace for National Leaguers in Boston in 1906 was that their rivals across the tracks also finished last.

For the second year in a row, Tenney's team had four twenty-game losers—Gus Dorner (26), Young (25), Lindaman (23), and Frank (Jeff) Xavier Pfeffer (22). Dorner came from Cincinnati during the season, Pfeffer from Chicago. Although Irving (Little Cy) Young opened the season by pitching a shutout, he was not as effective as the year before. Nevertheless, John McGraw of the Giants offered $10,000 for him, only to be turned down. The powerful Young, who had shoulders like a wrestler, was popular with his teammates. When he married a Mattapan girl in September, they gave him a brass bedstead for a wedding present.

Among the characters tried in the 1906 line-up was Gene Good, a Boston musician and actor, a nifty little outfielder who was properly described as a light hitter. He weighed only 126 pounds. And there was Jack Cameron, a Bull Durham sign painter, who was picked off Boston Common, where he played in sand-lot games between the Shiney Dippers and Rusty Mugs.

Win Carlson, who now guards the press gates at Boston ball parks, remembers a line drive bouncing off Cameron's forehead back into the hands of his catcher, Jack O'Neill, who relayed the ball to first base for a double play. Thereafter, Cameron was tried in the outfield, where he was still in danger, but not quite so much.

O'Neill, the catcher, was a toughy. A foul ball broke his mask and cut his forehead one afternoon. With blood streaming down his face and over his uniform, he continued to catch.

"I wish you'd quit," begged the umpire.

"I wish you'd stick to your umpiring and let me catch," barked O'Neill.

It was Tenney who negotiated the sale of the club for Soden and Conant. He thought Barney Dreyfuss was buying the Boston team, because the Pittsburgh owner was present with George B. Dovey at the New York meeting October 3, when the club changed hands.

"I bought some stock myself, enough to be the second-largest stockholder," Tenney says, with a twinkle in his eye; "and I didn't even know who owned the club. I knew it wasn't Dovey, but I thought it was Dreyfuss. Actually, it was a Pittsburgh theatrical man named John Harris."

Harris remained in the background. The Dovey brothers, George B. and John S. C. (South Carolina), ran the team, for which they had put up $75,000 for the franchise, players, and grounds, the owners of the South End Grounds taking a back mortgage of $200,-000 at 3½ per cent. The Doveys were likable fellows, natives of Central City, Kentucky. In their youth, both had played for Dreyfuss's Paducah team, George at shortstop and John at second base. They operated their father's coal mine until it was flooded by a hidden river springing in Mammoth Cave, then spent several years railroading in the Middle West before fronting for Harris in Boston.

They opened a new office in the Paddock Building, and when J. B. Billings dropped in to give them some advice on signing players, he looked about the lavish quarters and said, "This reminds me of the office the Triumvirs used to have, it's so different." When Billings departed, he left a cabinet picture of himself to go with pictures of Soden and Conant. How often George Dovey must have looked at those pictures and envied the Triumvirs their success. The National League thought enough of Soden and Conant to make them honorary members of their organization, a well-deserved tribute to men who had helped save the league in its most troubled days.

When Tenney closed the sale of the club, he also carefully clinched his job as manager for 1907. Dovey's first team trained at French Lick Springs, Indiana. To show that National League fans in Boston could expect a new deal, Dovey negotiated for an electric scoreboard, and for new, cushioned seats in the right-field bleachers that would operate on the slot-machine principle. Dovey's Pittsburgh connections quickly became clear when he traded Abbaticchio to the Pirates for Clarence Beaumont, outfielder, and Claude Ritchey, second baseman. Beaumont had a good season in Boston, hitting .322 in 149 games.

Boston needed more than the Doveys, more than Beaumont's high average, more than Dave Brain's ten home runs that led the league, more than the league's best-fielding shortstop in Al Bridwell, and more than Pfeffer's no-hit, no-run game against Cincinnati, May 8,

115

for the Doves, as they were now being called, finished seventh in 1907.

They didn't know it at the time but they picked up a valuable player in midseason when they got William J. (Bill) Sweeney from Chicago, along with Newton Randall for Del Howard. Sweeney had attended St. Xavier College in Cincinnati for four years. During winter months, he helped his father make patent medicines, pink pills, and purple lozenges at their home in Newport, Kentucky. Sweeney was to make himself quite a ballplayer, although in 1907 he was only an infield sub who hit a mere .254.

In July, when Irving Young's record was 5–16, Dovey announced, "I'm ready to trade Young. He has been pitching his best, but a change would do him good. He would be more effective in another uniform." But no club came forth to claim Little Cy, who had opened the season by pitching a shutout, but finished with a 16-to-25 record.

The Doves had a bad streak in which they lost sixteen games in succession, five of the games being played at home. A St. Louis pitcher, Edward Karger, shut them out four times during the season. Only Brain and Beaumont hit well. Tenney slumped to .273.

Sorely disappointed, the Doveys resorted to an unusual dose of medicine: They fired the manager and also a stockholder. For a successor to Tenney they chose Joe Kelley of Cambridge. Kelley had played a few games for the Beaneaters in 1891, but he had played many more games against them as an outfielder–first baseman for the Baltimore Orioles, Brooklyn Superbas, and, more lately, the Cincinnati Reds. He had managed Cincinnati from 1903 through 1905, and in 1907 managed Toronto in the Eastern League.

Knowing that he was through with the Boston club, Tenney tried to sell his stock, asking $15,000, which would have given him a 25-per-cent profit. The club had lost money in 1907, partly because of bad weather on Saturdays and Mondays, the big days, and partly because of the losing streak in August.

"I'd sell my stock too, if I could get that kind of price," said George Dovey wryly. So Tenney held onto his stock even after he was traded to the New York Giants in December, along with Al Bridwell and Catcher Tom Needham, for five players: Frank Bowerman, catcher; Dan McGann, first base; Bill Dahlen, shortstop; George Browne, outfielder; and George Ferguson, pitcher. Harry Pulliam, president

116

of the league, did not like the idea of a Boston stockholder playing first base for New York and told Tenney to unload.

"Certainly I'll sell, but I won't give it away," said Tenney. When no buyer came along, he continued in his role of New York player and Boston stockholder.

When the three-for-five deal was made, Murnane wrote: "In Tenney, Needham, and Bridwell, Boston let go three men not especially favorites with the Boston public. Tenney played fine ball, but several of the players, it is said, would not return to Boston if they were forced to work under him."

It was one of baseball's biggest trades. Dovey wanted to send Tenney to Pittsburgh, but Kelley insisted on the New York proposition. The man he wanted in particular was Bowerman, the big receiver who had caught Christy Mathewson for eight seasons. If Kelley had only known that the gun was loaded! Bowerman took his job as manager.

For Bowerman and Tenney to be on opposite sides of the trade was a coincidence, for fourteen years earlier, in 1893, they were rival catchers in a thirteen-inning, 2-to-2 game played between Brown University and the University of Michigan, in Providence, Rhode Island. Bowerman picked Tenney off third base, and in the run down, Tenney crashed into him so hard that he dislocated Bowerman's knee, putting him out of action for the season.

The trade was well received in Boston. Paul Shannon wrote: "For the first time in five years, a real baseball team will perform for Boston at the South End Grounds." But McGraw had not made the mistake of giving away any priceless performers.

The Doves climbed only one notch to sixth place in 1908. They made the headlines all over the country by being victims of George (Nap) Rucker's no-hit, no-run game, September 5; by playing a seventeen-inning, one-to-one tie with Chicago, June 4; and by losing the last two games of the season to the Giants, thus necessitating a New York–Chicago play-off for the pennant, because of Fred Merkle's so-called boner earlier in the season.

Dave Brain was a stubborn holdout, so he was sent to Cincinnati, whence he was traded to the Giants. In June, Dovey at last traded Little Cy Young, sending him to Pittsburgh for two nondescript pitchers, Tom McCarthy and, of all people, Hiram E. Young, better known as Cy the Third. The original remained the best of the Cy

117

Youngs, for Little Cy was soon back in the minors, and Cy III lasted only one season with Boston.

Since both Boston clubs were finishing in the second division for the third straight year, this was considered a good year in which to recall ancient glories by playing an old-timers' game. The contest was held at the Huntington Avenue Grounds, September 24, with the Old Pros beating the Old Collegians, 7–5, in seven innings. Al Spalding returned to pitch a few innings. Behind him were George Wright, Jim O'Rourke, John Manning, Harry Schafer, Tom Bond, Frank Whitney, Mertie Hackett, and many others who had played on Boston's early pennant winners.

Captains of the college team were Walter I. Badger and Colonel Sam Winslow. Of Chubby Colonel Winslow it was written in the *Boston Evening Transcript:* "He had only one chance in right field, and that was to chase a rolling ball clear to the back fence. His throw in was a work of art."

Manager Joe Kelley umpired the game and that night made a speech at the Algonquin Club. He seemed disconsolate after mentally comparing the great old Boston players with the imposters he had at his disposal. The next season Joe Kelley was back managing in Toronto.

2

During the 1908 season, Bowerman had lost no opportunity to discredit Kelley's ability as a manager. There was also considerable friction between Kelley and George Dovey. In November, Dovey asked Kelley to resign. The president had been to Detroit to see Bowerman, and the husky catcher spoke of quitting baseball if he were not given the manager's job. Bowerman owned a big farm in Romeo, Michigan. His father was wealthy. He was independent, Bowerman said.

With Bowerman for his manager, Dovey could save Kelley's $5,000 salary, a needless burden. He had expected Kelley to play regularly, but the manager had done little more than pinch-hit. Kelley took his own time about doing it, but at last he resigned, and Bowerman was the new leader of the Doves.

And what a manager! By the middle of July he had quit. One report had him going through the motions, and dickering with McGraw to get back with the Giants. Another report said that he broke under the strain when his team went into a tail spin. Bowerman returned to his Romeo farm for a rest, the team being handled by Shortstop Bill Dahlen. Neither Bowerman nor the team was any better on his return, so he resigned.

The machinist replaced the farmer. Harry C. Smith, a veteran catcher who had been with Pittsburgh from 1902 to 1907, joining Boston in 1908, replaced Bowerman July 16, 1909. Smith was from Massilon, Ohio. He had been hurt at St. Louis a month before while making a wonderful barehanded catch just as he fell into the Boston dugout. He continued to catch, although his ankle and knee were injured, but when a rival base runner slid into him at the plate, he had to retire.

When Bowerman cracked up, Smith was on a scouting trip, so Dahlen handled the team. Smith returned to Boston to resume playing, only to find himself drafted as manager. Bowerman was given his unconditional release. Instead of signing with the Giants, he signed with Indianapolis. He was washed up as a big leaguer.

The biggest shock of the season was not Bowerman's failure to go through, but the sudden death of George Dovey. The president of the Boston club visited Owner Harris in Pittsburgh, scouted a couple of minor leaguers in Steubenville, Ohio, and left by train for Cincinnati. At Cedarville, Ohio, word was flashed that Dovey, only forty-eight years old and apparently in excellent health, had died June 19, of a hemorrhage of the lungs. His brother, John S. C., replaced him as head of the club, and the team went on losing games as usual.

The 1909 Doves won only forty-five and lost one hundred and eight games. It was the first of four consecutive seasons in which the team was to lose one hundred or more decisions. In their worst stretch, the Doves lost thirteen games in succession, all of them at the South End Grounds. Against Chicago, the Doves lost twenty-one of twenty-two games; against Pittsburgh, twenty of twenty-one games. The Doves did not once beat Chicago in Boston.

A good girls' softball team would have approximated the batting power of those 1909 Doves. Their .223 batting average was an all-time Boston low. Their slugging average (times at bat divided into total bases) of .274 was an all-time National League low. The Doves made only 182 extra base hits, of which 124 were doubles, 43 were triples, and 15 were home runs. Both Ruth and Lou Gehrig in a good year would hit for more extra bases than all of the 1909 Doves put together.

The Doves made more errors than any team in the league, a department of which they were to take charge the next four years. Already acquiring a reputation for getting involved in long, extra-inning games, the Doves played a seventeen-inning 3-to-3 tie with New York, in July, a more remarkable game because Jack Coffey, the Boston shortstop, did not have a single chance in the seventeen innings, which was hardly a point in his favor.

But the 1909 Doves excelled in one worth-while respect. They set a club record for themselves by stealing 190 bases. They couldn't hit, they couldn't field, they couldn't pitch, but, my, how those Doves could fly! The one fellow who liked to watch them play was their new trainer, Jimmy Neary, himself a former professional runner. Neary was to see fourteen managers come and go while he was trainer of the team for the next thirty-five years.

John S. C. Dovey was back as president of the Doves in 1910, but the club had its fifth manager in four seasons in Fred Lake, the catcher who while with the Beaneaters in 1897 had once "acted like a man who had to carry his own ashes out of the cellar."

It was a curious deal that brought Lake back to the Boston Nationals. The year before, he had managed the Boston Americans, called the Red Sox, to third place. It was the first time in four years that the Red Sox had finished in the first division, and Lake thought he deserved a salary raise. The case never reached a board of arbitration, however. John I. Taylor, Red Sox owner, simply hired Patsy Donovan, a scout who had been employed by Lake, to lead his team. Dovey then signed Lake to manage the Doves, and Harry Smith, gratefully we may assume, quietly returned to the ranks as a catcher.

Before the 1910 season began, Beals Becker, hard-hitting, fly-dropping outfielder, was traded to the Giants for Charles Lincoln (Buck) Herzog, second baseman, and Bill Collins, outfielder. This was only the first time McGraw traded Herzog. He was to trade him twice more before the player escaped the Giants for good, being by then reduced to a state of middle-aged decrepitude. (Lake found it necessary to suspend the moody Herzog during the season.) Becker did the Giants no great good in 1910, being used chiefly as a pinch hitter, but he hit a pinch home run against the Doves by way of saying, "Remember me?"

Alonzo Mattern, who had joined the team in 1908, set a Boston record by pitching in fifty-one games. Collins, who had played for Bloomington in 1909, tied a mark for first-year men by stealing

120

thirty-six bases. George Ferguson broke a lot of hearts, including his own, when he shut out the Cardinals for eight innings, fanned the side in the eighth inning, then walked the first four men in the ninth, and yielded three runs.

Clifton Curtis lost eighteen games in succession, a league record, while another Doves pitcher, Charles Brown, lost fourteen games in a row. But the Doves bought a twenty-year-old left-hander from Lowell, of the New England League, late in 1910, George A. Tyler, who gave promise as he allowed only three runs in the twelve innings he pitched. Tyler was to do the team considerable good in subsequent years. Remember the name.

George Paskert of Cincinnati embarrassed the Doves by stealing second, third, and home, successively, but this was nothing beside the embarrassment caused John McGraw by Fred (Liz) Beck, Boston outfielder. A time limit was set on a game played by the Doves and Giants at South End, because the Giants had to catch a train. In the first half of the final inning, the Giants scored eight runs and needed only to retire the Doves to win. The Giants failed in this seemingly simple task because Beck stood up at the plate and hit one foul after another, until the seconds ticked away, the game was called, the Giants lost a big inning and a sure victory, and McGraw narrowly escaped a stroke.

This wasn't Beck's only accomplishment, for the big, lazy left-handed hitter, who was such a soft touch for southpaw pitching, hit ten home runs to tie Frank Schulte of Chicago for league-slugging honors. Fifty home runs were hit out of the South End bandbox, one of them being Bill Sweeney's first big-league homer, to beat Chicago in the twelfth inning. But even though they saw more home runs than the fans of any other National League city, Boston rooters did no dancing in the streets. The Doves again trailed the field. In four seasons the Harris-Dovey combination had finished sixth once, seventh once, and eighth twice. Is it any wonder that they hung out a "For Sale" sign?

121

CHAPTER XII

A LITTLE HOME OWNERSHIP

THE small amount of stock still held by Fred Tenney was a factor in the sale of the Boston Nationals to a syndicate headed by William Hepburn Russell, a New York lawyer and city official, in December, 1910. Wanting the club, Hepburn represented Tenney's interest, from which vantage point he approached Harris and offered to buy the stock held by the Pittsburgh showman. Harris refused to sell but he offered $115 per share for the stock Russell represented. Russell refused the bid, not being sure that Tenney wanted to sell at that figure.

When Russell told Tenney he had turned down the Harris counter-offer, Tenney said: "What's the matter with you? You should have taken it. Call him back and tell him you'll take it."

Russell called Harris and said that he would accept the latter's offer, but then he found that the Pittsburgher had changed his mind and now wanted to sell his stock. The deal was arranged over the telephone, with a secretary recording the conversation at Russell's end of the wire. This was a wise precaution, for Harris later wanted to call off the deal, only to have Russell threaten court action.

Lined up with Russell were Louis C. Page and George A. Page, Boston publishers, and Frederic J. Murphy, Boston insurance man. The price paid for the club was $100,000. When Harris refused to turn over the club for $60,000 and absolute security for the remaining $40,000, Russell and Page raised the balance of the purchase price within forty-eight hours.

Peter Kelley, secretary of the club, read Harris's statement to the Boston press:

The National League men will be glad to know that Mr. Russell and Mr. Page have taken over the club, for they feel that it is much better to have local capital and ownership interested. I wish the new owners well, and I trust and hope they will flourish, and know they will.

They deserve well of the Boston public. While Mr. Russell, Mr. Page and their associates had forty or fifty days to complete the deal, yet they have paid over all the money involved and are now in absolute control.

Kelley also read a statement by Russell, the club's new president:

Mr. L. C. Page and myself have purchased and paid for a very large majority of the stock of the Boston National Club. I have been elected president and Mr. Page, vice-president. We have associated with us Mr. L. C. Page's brother, Mr. George A. Page, and Mr. Frederic J. Murphy.

Mr. Murphy becomes treasurer and Mr. George A. Page secretary of the club. Mr. Kelley remains with us in his present position as clerk, and will have daily charge of the offices of the club.

Both Mr. L. C. Page and myself expect to devote a great deal of time to the affairs of the club. We shall do this not only as a matter of necessity to the success of the club as a business enterprise, but also because both of us are ardent fans and we are extremely anxious to give Boston a National League club that will be recognized as a Boston institution, controlled by Boston men, and owned by Boston capital.

We shall do everything in our power to strengthen the club and advance it as rapidly as possible to a much better position in next year's standing. We shall not hesitate to pay good money for good players."

Mr. Page said: "I thoroughly concur in the statement by Mr. Russell."

John Dovey, now former president, left the club in the best of humor. He took all the baseball guides since 1893, which his brother had owned, and two famed baseball pictures he liked. The man who once said that next to a good game of baseball he most enjoyed a bout between two well-trained gamecocks "had a pleasant personality that endeared him to those who became acquainted with him during the Dovey regime in Boston."

Russell asked Tenney to manage the club, even though it meant buying off Fred Lake, the 1910 manager, whose contract had a year to run. Tenney, since figuring in the big 1908 deal with the Giants, had been released by McGraw before the 1910 season, and had been playing manager that year for Lowell in the New England League.

"I don't want to manage your team," Tenney told Russell. "You've got a rotten ball club."

"If you'll manage the team, Fred, I'll buy that stock you've been trying to get rid of."

123

"You will? Then you've got yourself a manager," agreed Tenney heartily.

The new manager told the owners that while they might not lose money with the ball club they had bought, if they wanted a winner they would have to tear the team to pieces. Tenney was told to go ahead and tear the team to pieces. The new owners were out to win back the Boston public. Fred Murphy, the treasurer of the club, who represented the $10,000 investment of James J. Phelan, Boston banker, and who now lives in Winthrop, recalls how liberal they were with passes as they tried to make friends.

It was Murphy's idea that the Boston Nationals sign Cy Young when he was released in August by Cleveland. Cy the First was then forty-four years old. For Cleveland he had pitched in only seven games, winning three and losing four. But Murphy argued, with other officers of the club opposing him, that signing Young would be a good publicity stunt. Young was the greatest pitcher in baseball history. He had been a prime Boston favorite while pitching eight seasons for the early Red Sox teams. In 1904 he had pitched a perfect, no-hit game against the Athletics in Boston.

Young agreed to pitch for the Boston Nationals when telegraphed by Murphy. He appeared in eleven games, winning four and losing five. In the first game he pitched at the South End Grounds he got a good going over in the early innings. Tenney relieved him, and the crowd booed the manager thunderously. The Rustlers, as they were being called after Russell, their president, came back to tie the score, only to lose in the tenth inning on a home run.

"I'm sorry, now, I took you out, Cy," admitted Tenney.

"That's all right, Fred," replied the pitcher. "There was nothing else for you to do."

Young pitched the last, the nine hundred and sixth, game of his big-league career with Boston, in Brooklyn, October 6, 1911. The man who had won five hundred and ten games in twenty-two seasons suffered his three hundred and thirteenth defeat. Brooklyn beat him, thirteen to three, making eleven hits off him in six and a third innings.

"The slaughter on Young in the seventh was brutal work. After Stark had popped to Sweeney, O. Miller tripled and Wheat singled. Northern, Daubert, and Daley singled, and Hummel hit for two bases and Tooley for one. He stole second. Coulson doubled," said a *Globe* dispatch.

124

"Then, with seven runs over the plate, Young passed the ball to Weaver and strolled to the clubhouse."

And that was the great Cy Young's exit. He never pitched another ball in the big leagues. For the Doves he had won four and lost five games. One of his defeats was by a 1-to-0 score against a promising young Philadelphia pitcher named Grover Cleveland Alexander.

2

A squirrel on a treadmill couldn't have produced more action with less progress than the Boston Nationals of 1911. After a long season of muscle stretching and brain busting, the Rustlers wound up in last place once more, and this time with only forty-four victories. Not until 1935, when the Braves were to win only thirty-eight games, were the Braves to achieve fewer victories.

Tenney shook up his team fiercely but he might as well have been sifting ashes. In January he traded Dave Shean, the Arlington infielder and former Fordham captain, who had hit only .239 in 1910, to the Giants for Arthur (Tilly) Shafer. The deal hinged not only on the return of Shafer from Japan, where he was coaching the University of Kioto, but on the approval of the Boston directors. Shafer got back from Japan, all right, but L. C. Page called off the trade after Russell had agreed to it.

A month later, Shean was traded to Chicago for Frank Pfeffer, who had pitched for Boston in 1906-08, and William Ingerton, a young third baseman. Shean, who is now a Boston marketman, was to play second base for Ed Barrow's 1918 world champion Red Sox.

Another deal sent Fred Beck, the home-run hitter, to Cincinnati for Harry Steinfeldt, third baseman. Beck got in bad by holding out. In midseason, Buck Herzog was sent to the Giants for Hank Gowdy, catcher, and Al Bridwell, the infielder who had figured in the Tenney-Bowerman trade in 1908. Other new players included: Jay Kirke, a powerful, left-handed-hitting outfielder; Mike Donlin, fly chaser from New York; and the veteran catcher from Chicago, Johnny Kling, who was acquired in midseason.

Kirke was a clumsy fielder who had been given a trial the year before by Detroit. It has never been decided whether Kirke or labor troubles drove the South End cigar factory out of Boston. The cigar factory was across the street from the right-field fence on Columbus Avenue. Every time anyone hit a long foul in that direction, there was a tinkle of glass, which caused the reporters to chorus in the press box, "There goes another window in the cigar factory." Eventually the factory moved to New Jersey, which was well beyond Kirke's range.

Kirke was weak against curves, a fact that led to a strange incident while he was playing at Louisville under Joe McCarthy. With men on first and third and Kirke batting, Louisville tried a double steal. The rival catcher threw to second, where the second baseman grabbed it and quickly returned it to the plate. The ball never reached the catcher, for Kirke stepped in and hit the ball over the fence.

"Now, what in the world made you do that, Jay?" asked McCarthy, when Kirke had been declared out for interference.

"Well, Joe," replied the hitter, "that's the first fast ball I've seen in three months, and I just couldn't resist the temptation to hit it."

He was slow of foot, but Kirke was a powerful thrower and a fabulous hitter. He used to hang his bats like hams in the cellar of his home, and could recite the feats he had accomplished with each of them.

One day after he had gone hitless, his wife was complaining around the house, when Kirke told her, "You take care of the housework, dear. Let me take care of the hitting."

Bill Sweeney came into his own in 1911, when moved from shortstop to second base. A side-arm thrower, it was said that "Sweeney when playing shortstop could make more fatal errors than any man living." Sam Carrick wrote in the *Boston Post* that fans were cool to Sweeney as a shortstop because "he could not make a graceful misplay," as could Jimmy Collins and Nap Lajoie.

The shorter throw from second helped Sweeney. He gained confidence and became a much improved hitter, finishing with an average of .314. Between May 24 and July 3, Sweeney hit in thirty-one consecutive games, belting the ball for .402 in the stretch, and bettering Hugh Duffy's mark of twenty-six made in 1894. He kept the streak going at the expense of some good pitchers, making two hits off Grover Cleveland Alexander in the twenty-sixth game, one hit off Christy Mathewson in the twenty-eighth game, and three hits off Rube Marquard in the thirty-first game. His record stood thirty-four years, until Tommy Holmes set a new club mark by hitting safely in thirty-seven consecutive games.

The Rustlers lost fourteen games in succession in May, all of them

126

at home, and later in the season lost sixteen games in a row. They made plenty of hits but suffered from poor pitching and fielding. Roy Miller, outfielder obtained the previous year from Chicago, led the league with one hundred and forty-six singles and hit .333, to trail Honus Wagner, league leader, by only one point.

A painful blow was struck by Fred Beck when he made his first appearance in a Cincinnati uniform in Boston. Old Liz hit a home run with bases full, to win the ball game, and seemed quite pleased at the discomfiture he caused his former teammates. Cincinnati also beat the Rustlers by a 26-to-3 score in June.

Clifton Curtis, Boston pitcher who had lost his last eighteen games in 1910, lost the first five games he pitched in 1911, giving him a record of twenty-three consecutive defeats. A mark of which the Rustlers could be prouder was made in the fourth inning of a game against Philadelphia, May 1. It took them eleven assists to retire three men.

The Rustlers were a scrappy ball club. Except for injuries, they probably would have finished higher. On their last western trip, they lost two of their best pitchers on successive days. Pat Flaherty, who had hurled for them in 1907 and 1908 and for Philadelphia in 1910, had his arm struck by a pitched ball. Although suffering great pain, he continued to pitch, finished his game, and scored a victory. X-ray pictures showed that his arm was broken. Flaherty was the southpaw who brought in the rule against quick pitches. The next day, Jeff Pfeffer hurt his arm while pitching and never again was effective. The Rustlers did not even have luck on their side.

CHAPTER XIII

TAMMANY AT THE HELM

⊗

DISSENSION, sickness, and finally death itself ended Russell's syndicate. He gave up an extensive legal practice in New York because of his health, then virtually committed suicide by buying the Doves.

He and the Page brothers could not agree. There was a furor when three players were traded for Kling, another when Herzog and Roy Miller were suspended for causing dissension, and still another when Herzog was traded to New York. Ed Hanlon, intending to move the club to Baltimore, tried to buy it for $169,000. Russell turned him down. A San Francisco sport, Jack Gleason, was ready to buy into the club in place of the Pages but failed to come through with the cash.

It was all too much for Russell. He died of heart trouble November 25, 1911, in New York.

John Montgomery Ward, New York lawyer, wanted the club. His angel, he thought, was James E. Gaffney, a New York political contractor with strong Tammany Hall connections. Ward paid $5,000 to William B. Winslow, representing the Russell interests, for an option on Russell's stock. Then he approached Gaffney, on the recommendation of a New York friend, John Carroll. These three, Ward, Gaffney, and Carroll, bought the club for $187,000, or $180 a share.

Ward was a baseball man, Gaffney was not. Ward had pitched for the pennant-winning Providence Grays in 1879. He had helped organize the Brotherhood and the Players' League in 1890. And he was then chairman of the National League playing rules committee. Gaffney was a fan, a close friend of Clark Griffith, and an avowed rival of Frank J. Farrell, owner of the New York Highlanders. One reason why Gaffney bought the Braves, it was said, was his desire to have a winning team before Farrell, in which he was successful, since Farrell never had a winner.

Ward was elected president, Gaffney treasurer of the new syndicate. But if Ward held the scepter, Gaffney wielded the power. He owned the club. Who was Gaffney? He was an East Side boy, reared in the gashouse district where kids grew up to be burglars, cops, or firemen. Gaffney became a cop for a little while, then turned to politics and was soon elected district captain. He served on the Board of Aldermen. He became a partner of Charles F. Murphy, a Tammany chieftain. The New York Construction Company, of which Gaffney was president, excavated for both Pennsylvania Station and Grand Central Terminal.

Who was Gaffney? He was the policeman who turned to politics who turned to contracting to become several times a millionaire. He was Tammany's Man of Mystery. He was a big, red-faced, healthy-looking specimen—modest, quiet, and retiring. Even while owner of the Braves, he was the subject of an inquiry into the awarding of contracts in New York.

Who was Gaffney? The *New York Herald* said: "Jim Gaffney is the most picturesque figure that the recent turbulent times have brought to the surface. As a power under cover, his position has been unprecedented."

Soon after they bought the club, Gaffney and Ward looked for a new site for their team. Failing to find one, they altered the old layout. The grandstand was enlarged, and the left-field bleacher was torn down. Right-handed hitters wept. Instead of being only 250 feet distant, the left-field fence was now 350 feet away.

Gaffney let Ward pick the manager but he selected the new nickname for his team. He called them the Braves—after Tammany. They kept their white uniforms and red stockings, but instead of the Old English "B" they bore on their bosoms, they now had the profile of a proud Indian. The new name caught on. It not only was original, it was aboriginal.

Although Fred Tenney had a year to go on his manager's contract, Ward dismissed him and announced that Johnny Kling, the ancient catcher who had finished out the 1911 season with the team, was the new manager.

"I don't want the public to think Tenney is being disciplined. I know he is a decent fellow," said Ward. "But after thinking it over, I thought I'd prefer a playing manager, and the best man to keep an

129

eye on players is the catcher. I talked with Kling at the National League meeting, and temperamentally he is the man I want. Tenney was up against it last season, but I found that the players I talked with wanted Kling."

Aware that the Boston Nationals had been in the control of out-siders since Soden and Conant sold to Harris in 1906, the New York proprietors made one concession to local pride. They hired as their secretary Herman Nickerson, former sports editor of the *Boston Journal* and a leading baseball writer of his time.

The Braves quickly showed that they could acquire new owners, new manager, and new nickname without changing their habits in the least. By the end of May they were in last place, and there they stayed. Cy Young the First reported for spring training, but after spending three weeks in camp, the veteran went to Kling and said, "There's no use fooling myself. My arm's gone." He was given his release.

A succession of misadventures befell the Braves before Ward resigned as president on July 31. On June 20, the Giants, who in one way or another did a lot of business at the expense of the Braves in this period, set a modern record by stealing eleven bases. In the ninth inning, Josh Devore stole four bases, second, third, and home, the first time he reached, and second base when he reached again later in the inning. The Braves scored ten runs in the ninth inning that day, so the Giants won only 23–12, instead of 23–2.

The next day, Rube Marquard of the Giants won his sixteenth successive game while beating the Braves. He was on his way to the modern record of nineteen consecutive victories, a streak in which he could show four wins over his Boston cousins.

A week later, with Brooklyn leading, 9–8, the Braves made four hits and drew a base on balls in the ninth inning, yet failed to score. After Ed McDonald was retired, Vin Campbell singled and was promptly picked off first base by Nap Rucker, Brooklyn pitcher. Bill Sweeney and Jay Kirke singled successively, and John Titus walked to fill the bases. Ben Houser then hit a ground ball that struck Titus, giving Houser a hit but retiring the side.

Early in July, the Braves lost a thirteen-inning game to Philadelphia, 13–11. Cliff Cravath, later to be the league's home-run champion, hit a home run with a man on in the seventh inning, then hit another home run with a man on in the thirteenth inning, to win the game for Philadelphia.

130

Such minor irritations as these increased the distemper already raging in the front office. Ward announced on July 31 that he had sold his stock to Gaffney and was resigning as president. Gaffney immediately elected himself president and soon let it be known that Johnny Kling would not manage the Braves in 1913.

The day Ward sold out, Pittsburgh beat the Braves, 7–6, in a nineteen-inning game. Otto Hess, a Swiss-born southpaw who had hurled a one-hitter against Chicago, in May, pitched the whole game against three Pittsburgh flingers. The score was tied, 2–2, at the end of the ninth. Each team scored twice in the eighteenth, but in the nineteenth Pittsburgh scored three runs, Boston only two. The day before, the Braves had beaten St. Louis in fourteen innings.

"I'm getting out just in time, by the looks of it," Ward told his friends. "This club is driving me bughouse."

Jay Kirke hit .320, but the fellow who really had a season was Bill Sweeney, captain of the Braves. This once weak hitter finished third among the league batsmen, with a .344 average. As late as August 7, Sweeney was making five hits in five times at bat against John Benton of Cincinnati, and taking the lead from Heinie Zimmerman of Chicago with an average of .374.

The 1912 Braves, despite Sweeney and Kirke, lacked pretty nearly everything that goes to make a good ball club. Best of the pitchers was Hub Perdue, who won thirteen and lost sixteen games.

This was a marvelous record beside that of Walter Dickson, who lost nineteen games while winning only three. Ed McDonald, third baseman, gave the Braves another distinction, striking out more than any other hitter in the league. It was a good thing Sweeney was around, for besides blistering the ball, he made 459 put-outs at second base, a record that was to stand twenty-one years.

A couple of baseball's most prized characters played their first big-league games with the Braves in 1912. One was Miguel Angel Gonzales, the Cuban catcher who was to win more attention for his catch-as-catch-can wrestling match with the English language than he ever would as a player or coach.

Gonzales, who had been brought up from the Havana Reds, caught just one game for the Braves, a seven-inning tie with the Giants, September 28. Mike went hitless in two times at bat. The Giants stole four bases on him, which he later shrugged off by saying, "She run. I throw. She safe."

But the Braves introduced a more colorful performer than Gon-

131

zales to big-league baseball late that season. He was one of the five shortstops they tried from April to September. The Braves bought him from New Bedford of the New England League. He weighed only 150 pounds at the time, but while one of the smallest of big leaguers, he had one of the biggest hearts and one of the longest names—Walter James Vincent Maranville.

2

They called him Rabbit Maranville because a little girl at New Bedford one day watched him bouncing around in a pepper game, giggled, and said, "You jump around just like a rabbit." Until then he had been known as Stumpy and Bunty.

Maranville was an imp. He was baseball's Peter Pan. His body aged, but his spirit remained young. He stood five-five and had the physique of a boy, but on the field he was a heavyweight, a giant. A mischievous sprite, he was a darling of fans, a worrier of managers, a tormentor of umpires.

He was just a rookie when he took a pair of glasses out of his back pocket, polished them carefully, and handed them to Umpire Bill Finneran in Brooklyn. A few weeks later in Philadelphia, he helped break up a fight between Art Fletcher, Phils shortstop, and Umpire Bob Hart.

"Gosh, Bob, you're hurt," said Maranville, viewing a tiny scratch under one of the umpire's eyes. "Here, let me put some iodine on it."

Hart meekly submitted to the Rabbit's gentle ministrations. Using a piece of cotton, Rabbit began applying iodine. As he went along, he discovered not one cut, but a succession of cuts. With repeated "Tsk-tsks," Maranville applied iodine until Hart's face was entirely painted.

"There, that'll do it," said the Rabbit with a relieved sigh.

"Thanks," said Hart gratefully, and went back to work. For a week the umpire looked like an Indian, a very angry Indian. The war whoop he emitted when he first looked at himself in a mirror would have done credit to an Apache.

Deciding to have a nice quiet card game in Philadelphia one afternoon, Maranville's teammates locked him in his room and retired to another room down the corridor. The game had been in progress only five minutes when one player, facing the window, looked up, whitened, and said, "Oh, my God!"

The other players turned about quickly, and there was Maranville, with his thin, pinched face and big ears, making faces at them through the window. He was kneeling on the narrow ledge that ran around the hotel at the twelfth floor.

Maranville is the character who waded in the pool of a St. Louis hotel late one night and caught a goldfish. The story goes that he promptly ate the goldfish, but this Maranville denies, saying, "I didn't eat him. I just bit him."

While playing for Pittsburgh in mid-career, he was arrested for reckless driving while on a trip to Boston with the Pirates. His wife emerged from a Pittsburgh theater late that afternoon to hear newsboys shouting, "Extry! Extry! Maranville in jail."

Maranville was fined $100 for driving under the influence when the case came up in court. His lawyer argued that Maranville could not have been intoxicated, because after being bailed out, he had played that afternoon against the Braves, had accepted nine chances flawlessly, and had knocked in the winning run in the ninth inning.

"How could anyone who was intoxicated give such a performance?" asked his lawyer.

"I don't know how," was the gist of the judge's reply, "but he did. One hundred dollars."

When the Pirates returned home, Mrs. Maranville took her husband to task for his unseemly conduct in Boston. After patiently listening to her pithy comments, the Rabbit at last dismissed the entire subject by saying: "Just think how lucky you are, my dear. Most wives don't know where their husbands are on road trips. But at least you knew that I was safe and sound in jail."

Although a brilliant fielder whether playing shortstop or second base, nothing Maranville ever did tickled fans quite so much as his vest-pocket catches. No matter how high the fly, the Rabbit would always catch it with his hands cupped under his belt buckle. The advantage of catching the ball in this unorthodox manner, he said, was that he could hold it against his stomach or chest if it hopped out of his small hands. The disadvantage, claimed other players, was the danger of catching the ball with the teeth instead of the hands.

Joe Cronin, for instance, could never make a true vest-pocket catch. The ball could not get past his chin. But the Rabbit never caught the ball with his teeth, and he rarely let a tall fly get away from him.

While on, a baseball trip to Japan in 1931, Maranville attempted

133

to teach the vest-pocket catch to native infielders, but he had little success. The Japs persisted in letting the ball hit them on the head, and after several of them had been knocked unconscious, the Rabbit quit in disgust.

Maranville went on the stage after one season, told a few jokes, sang a couple of songs, and closed his act by making a vest-pocket catch of a fly thrown up among the curtains by a stagehand. It was at the Old Howard in Boston's notorious Scollay Square that the stagehand decided to vary the routine. He threw a line drive that whizzed past Maranville's ear; then fled, with the frightened ballplayer chasing him. That ended Maranville's stage career. He was much funnier off the stage, anyhow.

During the trip to Japan, Maranville soaped Al Simmons's favorite bat before a game, with the result that Simmons set a new Japanese record for hitting foul balls. But the Japs liked Maranville, even if Simmons didn't. He was given his fortieth birthday party at the palatial home of Viscount Taketane Sohma.

Being small and having served in the United States Navy during the first World War, Maranville decided to sneak into a Japanese military review. He put on a Japanese Army uniform and promptly got himself arrested.

"I can march in English but I'm damned if I know how to march in Japanese," he said, after being rescued by his teammates.

One night on Broadway, the Rabbit thought he would stir up some excitement and asked Jack Scott, the big pitcher, to chase him, yelling, "Stop, thief." It was great fun for about three seconds, because after that Maranville was running for his life, like a little red fox being pursued by thousands of eager hounds. He escaped, from experience being familiar with Broadway's coverts and short cuts, but he never played the part of the fox again—at least, under those circumstances.

On and off the field, Maranville was always hogging the spotlight. When he went to bat he sometimes reached the plate by crawling between the umpire's legs, especially if it was a crabby umpire like Hank O'Day. Before a big crowd, he was a marvelous mimic and actor. If he made a good play, he swaggered and strutted like a bantam rooster, and got away with it because he was small and had class.

But he didn't need a big audience. Walking to the ball park in Rochester on a hot day, he turned to the two players with him and said, "Look, what are we walking up to the bridge for, when we could save ten blocks just by swimming across the river?"

"Swim? Are you nuts?" asked the players.

His sanity questioned, the Rabbit immediately dived into the river and swam to the other side. He waved to the dumfounded pair on the other bank, and walked briskly off to the ball park. The others used the bridge, despite the example set by the Rabbit.

Maranville was the third in a family of five children, born of an Irish mother and a French father in Springfield, Massachusetts. His father was a patrolman, on whose beat was a hotel that housed visiting New England League clubs. From what he learned about professional ballplayers, Papa Maranville was decidedly unhappy when his son Walter said he was going to play for Tommy Dowd at New Bedford, in 1911. Walter left without his father's blessing. His father wanted him to become a steam fitter.

Maranville learned quickly in the school of hard knocks and bad bounces at New Bedford. If he asked a teammate at the other end of the dinner table for a roll or baked potato, he always had his hands up to catch the requested ingredient before it hit him in the mouth. Dowd had no sooner signed him to play for $750 than he delivered Maranville to two relatives who sold him an insurance policy that cost $323.

It was a rough, tough league, but it turned out some great ballplayers, of which Maranville was one. When the Rabbit survived the games played between New Bedford and Fall River, he was ready to hunt lions with a switch. Confidence was one item that the Rabbit did not need when the Braves brought him up, late in the 1912 season.

CHAPTER XIV

THE MIRACLE MAN

NEAR the end of the 1912 season, Gaffney sat in the stands at the Polo Grounds and watched his pitiful Braves lose to the pennant-winning Giants. With him was a dark-complexioned man with a round face. This was the new manager of the Braves—George Tweedy Stallings.

Gaffney had seen Stallings do a fine job with the New York Highlanders of 1909 and 1910, only to lose his job to Hal Chase after leading his team to second place in the latter year. Nothing would please Gaffney more than to win a pennant with a manager who had been cast off by Frank Farrell.

"This club is a baseball horror," Stallings replied, when Gaffney asked him what he thought of the Braves.

"Well, you're the boss," answered the owner. "Make whatever changes you wish. We want a winner."

"I've been stuck with some terrible teams in my time," mused Stallings aloud, "but this one beats 'em all."

Two years from that day, Gaffney had his winner. The 1914 Braves were hailed as the bravest of all ball clubs. Stallings was known throughout the land as The Miracle Man.

He did it not with mirrors, but with psychology. Stallings was a brilliant strategist and tactician, but he excelled as a handler of men. His theme song was, "You can win, you must win, you will win." He was a salesman who peddled determination and self-confidence, and ballplayers liked to do business with him.

"There never was a ballplayer who did not want to get back to George Stallings," says Walter Hapgood, his associate for many years at Boston, Rochester, and Montreal. "He was rough and some-

136

times abusive, but players respected him because he was not mean and wanted only to win."

When he owned the Rochester club, one of his 1914 outfielders came into his office. It was six years since they had been together on the Braves.

"I'd like to play for you again," said Herb Moran. "Can you give me a job?"

"Why, Herb, we can't afford to pay you the money you'd want," said Stallings. "We're not a big-league club, you know."

"That's all right," replied the player. "Just give me a contract and I'll sign it. You fill in the figure with whatever you want to give me."

Off the field, Stallings was quiet and reserved. His players called him "George," "Chief," or "Big Daddy." But even when he was dining them at his plantation, The Meadows, in Haddock, Georgia, during spring training, his dignity survived.

On the field, Stallings was a firebrand—contemptuous, dynamic, blasphemous. He couldn't sit still on the bench, so intense was he during a game. He crossed and recrossed his legs, and always his upper foot bounced rhythmically, keeping time for his dancing nerves. He slid up and down the bench so much that he wore out the seats of four pairs of trousers in a normal season, and five pairs when he won the pennant in 1914. Superstitious, he couldn't bear to see paper on the field. One day Heinie Zimmerman tortured him by tearing a large piece of paper into small bits as he passed before the Boston dugout.

Stallings tongue-lashed his players for dumb plays. Years earlier when he had managed the Philadelphia Nationals, he had first called his players boneheads. When asked if he were not too rough on the players, he replied, "No. I go after players to find out if they're game. I've got no use for a player who isn't game. A game player fights back when bawled out, and that's what I like."

He admitted that sometimes in the heat of a game he went after players too fiercely. Once he asked a good pitcher to go to the bull pen at the start of a game. In the first inning, Boston's starting pitcher was hit hard. Stallings looked to the bull pen. There was no one there.

"Where in hell is So-and-so?" he asked.

"Here I am," replied So-and-so, from a comfortable corner on the bench.

Stallings flew into a rage, calling the pitcher every kind of bone-

137

head he could think of, which was a large number. The pitcher slunk to the bull pen, but it turned out that he was not needed. The starting pitcher settled down, and the Braves won.

Entering the clubhouse after the victory, Stallings saw So-and-so sitting with his head in his hands. He asked cheerfully, "What's the matter, old boy?"

"I was just wondering whether I should whip you right here in front of everybody or just quit the club," said the pitcher tersely.

Stallings immediately replied, "I apologize to you in front of the whole club. You know very well that I don't mean half the things I say during a ball game. Sometimes I go off half-cocked, but you never want to let that bother you."

On another occasion Stallings bawled out a pitcher on one of his minor-league teams, but with more costly results. The pitcher had given a succession of bases on balls, which were the bane of Stallings's existence, and had been taken out of the game.

"You base-on-balls bonehead!" roared Stallings. "Gwan to the clubhouse and burn up your uniform."

The pitcher trudged dejectedly to the clubhouse, which was in center field. A few minutes after he disappeared, smoke was seen rising from the chimney of the clubhouse. A player on the bench pointed it out to Stallings.

"What? Is he really burning up his uniform?" shouted Stallings. "My God, what a bonehead! Somebody go and stop him."

Stallings preferred working with mediocre players who hustled to star players who loafed. He used to say: "Give me a ball club of only mediocre ability, and if I can get the players in the right frame of mind, they'll beat the world champions. But they've got to believe they can do it."

Stallings built up his players. He made them think they were good. He put chips on their shoulders. He framed situations, such as letting Rabbit Maranville, still a green kid in the spring of 1913, win an argument from him. To break up a double steal by the enemy, Stallings claimed that Bill Sweeney, the second baseman, should take the catcher's throw, not the shortstop.

"I think it would be better if Maranville made the play," argued Coach Fred Mitchell, who had been rehearsed by Stallings. The two argued back and forth, with Maranville listening.

"Let me make the play. Sweeney has a sore arm. I'm quick enough to get over to second and either tag the runner coming down, or get

138

it back to the catcher in time to get the guy from third," boasted Maranville.

"The hell you are," argued Stallings. "It's the second baseman's play. It's right in front of him."

Maranville continued to protest, and at last Stallings said, "All right, have it your way. You take the throw. But you'd better be right."

In the next game the play came up twice, and each time Maranville took the catcher's throw and returned it to the plate in time to get the runner on third. That night Maranville boasted to Joe Connolly: "Well, I sure put one over on Stallings today. I argued him into letting me make the play my way, and damned if I didn't show him I was right."

Stallings was tickled when he learned that Maranville was getting chesty at his expense. He liked chesty ballplayers. Maranville and Johnny Evers were his favorites. The manager glowed when Evers, captain of the team, once told Grantland Rice: "Anybody that comes to this ball club will either hustle with the rest of us, or we'll drive him off the team."

When a Braves base runner was caught napping on the bases, being picked off, or failing to advance on a short passed ball, the Boston bench exploded like a string of Chinese firecrackers. While Stallings bellowed, "Bonehead," with embellishments, every other man on the team would be barking insults and invectives at their offending teammate. The Braves under Stallings were their own severest critics.

Wanting Hank Gowdy to pinch-hit one day, Stallings turned to the Boston bench, and said, "Now, you bonehead, get up there with a bat and see if you can hit the ball."

Not only Gowdy stepped toward the bat rack, but six other Boston players stepped with him. All were used to being addressed as boneheads.

Stallings was a baseball wizard. Asked what his system was, he always replied, "Play the percentages." To play the percentages, a manager has to know what the percentages are. Stallings knew them. No one ever knew them any better. He had a great baseball mind and when he discussed various plays at his daily morning meetings, even hardened veterans knew they were listening to a master.

"Stallings knew baseball as Einstein knows algebra," Tom Daly, late coach of the Boston Red Sox, once said. "It was a privilege just to sit and listen to him talk baseball."

Perhaps because inside baseball has been discounted by the lively ball, modern managers place less emphasis on skull sessions. But Stallings rarely let a day pass when he did not get his team together, usually at the hotel in the morning, and discuss tactics and strategy. Nothing was likely to be hit-or-miss on the ball club of a man who would use field glasses, as he did in Rochester, to steal the enemy's signals. He used to tell pitchers to concentrate on controlling a fast ball and a curve. "Then," he concluded, "and only then, should you try a pitch that's a little different. And when you have that, you've got a little extra 'baccy in your 'baccy pouch."

2

When Gaffney picked Stallings as his manager, he picked a man who had traveled far along baseball's highways and byways. Stallings had been born in Augusta, in 1869. By 1886 he had graduated from Virginia Military Institute and had gone to Baltimore to study medicine. He was thwarted in this desire by a fellow named Harry Wright, the same Harry Wright who had organized the Boston Red Stockings in 1871.

"You're too good a baseball player, young man, to be wasting your time in school," the Philadelphia manager told Stallings. The young man promptly traded his scalpel for a bat.

A catcher, Stallings was with Philadelphia only long enough to catch Gus Weyhing's no-hitter against Kansas City in 1887, and then he was released to Toronto. Stallings was a hustling player who never conceded defeat. Little more could be said for him. Certainly, big-league clubs did not fight for his services.

Stallings played baseball and saw the country. From Toronto he went to Galveston, from Galveston to Stockton . . . to Oakland . . . to Brooklyn, in 1890 . . . to San Jose . . . to Augusta, Nashville, and then Kansas City. He managed his first team in 1895, and led Nashville to a pennant. Then he successively managed Detroit, Philadelphia, Detroit, Buffalo, Newark, the New York Highlanders, and again Buffalo. Ill health kept him out of baseball in 1907.

One of Stallings's first moves as manager of the Braves was to bring in Fred Mitchell, who had played for him on the Highlanders in 1910 and had sided with him against Hal Chase. Mitchell, said to

140

be part Cherokee Indian, was the son of a Bolton, Massachusetts, apple farmer, who had broken in with the Boston Red Sox as a pitcher in 1901. While pitching for the Athletics three years later, he hurt his arm. He promptly became a big-league catcher.

"My Right Eye," was Stallings's nickname for Mitchell, who coached the pitchers and also directed foot traffic at third base. Stallings used to say of him: "Mitch is the greatest coach of pitchers I've ever seen." Stallings never underrated anyone on his side.

During his first season with the Braves, the crowd at the South End Grounds began to ride Stallings, for the Braves of 1913 were by no means the Braves of 1914. Returning from his third-base coaching box to the bench between innings, Mitchell made a little speech to the crowd:

"If you think you're so good, let's see you come out here and do any better. These guys may not be much good but they're doing the best they can, and if you don't like it, you can—"

The crowd drowned his last words with a loud, sarcastic cheer. But that's how Mitchell was—a straight puncher from the shoulder.

Even in 1913, Stallings did not like to lose. One day a kid in a Philadelphia uniform made him see red. The Braves had three men on base in the last of the ninth inning, with nobody out, and needed one run to tie. As Grover Cleveland Alexander walked in from the bull pen, Stallings got up to get a glass of water. But before he had returned to his seat, and even before he had taken his drink, Alexander had struck out three Boston hitters on nine pitched balls. Witnesses disagree, but Stallings either dropped the water pitcher or threw it.

The Braves showed a marked improvement under their new manager in 1913, finishing fifth, their highest level in eleven seasons. During the year, Stallings acquired most of the players who were to be regulars on the 1914 champions. Only Maranville, Gowdy, Tyler, and Hess of Johnny Kling's 1912 team survived to play on the 1914 Braves.

Joe Connolly, a Woonsocket boy and an outfielder, was bought on waivers from Washington. Leslie Mann of Springfield, another outfielder, came from Buffalo in a trade. Late in the season, Charles (Butch) Schmidt was bought from Rochester. At the season's close, the Braves drafted Dick Crutcher from St. Joseph, Larry Gilbert from Milwaukee, and Charlie Deal from Providence.

But the prize finds were the two right-handed pitchers, Bill James

141

and Dick Rudolph. Curveless Bill was a twenty-one-year-old Californian who had turned professional with Seattle in 1912. He was tall and rugged, and not only could he throw a ball hard, but he could throw it wet. He was a spitball pitcher, and while he lasted, a good one. The Braves got him from Seattle early in the 1913 season, but he was so wild that he won only six out of sixteen games.

Rudolph looked like Jeff in this Mutt-and-Jeff combination. He was a little fellow, but crafty. Bronx born, he had been an outstanding college pitcher for Fordham. In 1906 he pitched two shutouts over a Holy Cross team on which played Bill Carrigan, Jack Barry, and Jack Flynn. One shutout was a one-hitter.

Ed Barrow scouted Carrigan and Barry but discovered a Rudolph. He signed the little right-hander for his Toronto club in the fall, but not before Rudolph had pitched for Rutland in the Vermont League and New Haven in the Connecticut League.

The first hitter Rudolph faced for Rutland was a Plattsburgh lead-off man named Sullivan. Rudolph grooved the first pitch, and Sullivan hit it to right field for three bases. Rudolph recovered from the shock to retire the next three men and leave Sullivan on third base. He never forgot Sullivan. How could he, when Sullivan's real name was Edward Trowbridge Collins?

Rudolph pitched seven seasons for Toronto. His record was more impressive than his physique. In 1910 he pitched no-hit ball against Montreal for ten innings, but lost, 1–0, in the twelfth. He was given a tryout in the fall of 1910 by the Giants, but lost the only game he started to Philadelphia. He began the 1911 season with the Giants, but after a story appeared in a New York paper saying that he was "a groove-ball pitcher," McGraw sent him back to Toronto.

Rudolph had a 25-to-10 record with Toronto in 1912, yet his contract for 1913 was cut 25 per cent after the International League passed a rule limiting salaries. Rudolph signed his contract, but soon after the season opened he left the club, threatening to enter the law business of his brother. On May 4, Toronto solved the problem by selling him to the Braves for $4,000 and Pitcher Buster Brown.

Rudolph made a hit with Stallings in the first game he pitched for the Braves. He relieved with two men on, and promptly walked the hitter to fill the bases. With three balls on the next batter, and Stallings suffering audibly in the Boston dugout, Rudolph threw three curves over the plate in succession to end the inning.

"Well," said Stallings, who an instant before had been wondering

142

how far away he could send Rudolph and still keep him on the continent, "he's got some guts, at that, when he'll throw the curve in a pinch and get it over."

Before long, Stallings was calling Rudolph the smartest pitcher he had ever seen. Rudolph was smart enough to copy Christy Mathewson's curve and Bill James's spitball, which along with his own God-given control were to make him the most dependable pitcher on the 1914 Braves.

As if rehearsing for 1914, the Braves of 1913 began the season in last place and tried to see how high they could climb. By May 3 they were seventh, by May 10 they were sixth, and by August 23 they were fifth. They dropped back to sixth for a few days, but on September 6 returned to fifth place and stayed there.

Stallings kept drawing new cards as he tried to fill a winning hand. In all, the Braves used forty-six players during the season, and of them thirteen were pitchers, thirteen were infielders, and twelve were outfielders. One of the players who was with the 1913 Braves just long enough to get a plateful of Boston baked beans was Bill McKechnie, who was later to be their manager for eight seasons. Drafted from St. Paul, McKechnie played one game in the Braves outfield, going hitless in four trips, and then was sent on waivers to the New York Yankees.

"I'll eat all the hits he makes," said Stallings. He could have, too, for McKechnie batted only .134 for the Yankees.

Relations between the Braves and Red Sox reached a new high level in 1913, for the Braves were allowed to use the new Red Sox grounds, Fenway Park, for their Memorial Day double-header. The ancient South End Grounds were utterly inadequate by now, but Gaffney stalled off rebuilding the stands in the hope that he might locate a new site.

The Braves figured in a pair of one-hit games. George Suggs of Cincinnati held them to a solitary bingle in August, and two weeks later George Tyler, the Lowell lefty, allowed the Giants only one hit, a single by George McLean.

Maranville hit only .247, but he established himself as one of the best and most colorful shortstops in the league. He was a persistent little rascal, as he showed early in the season by being caught stealing three times in one game against the Chicago Cubs. A few days later he accepted eleven chances without an error against Cincinnati.

The Rabbit had to beat out Art Bues, Stallings's nephew, for his

143

job. In spring training he told Stallings: "What chance have I got if I have to fight your whole family? But I'll tell you one thing: If I ever get in there, you'll never get me out."

Stallings grinned, and answered, "That's the way to talk. But Bues has more experience than you, and I think we'll start with him."

Shortly before the season began, Bues got diphtheria, and Maranville had his chance. He was right. Stallings never did get him out of the line-up. As the Braves beat Christy Mathewson, 8–3, at the Polo Grounds in the opening game, the Rabbit made three hits in four times at bat. From then on he was a regular. His confidence grew and grew, until by the end of the season he was picking fights with none other than Joe Tinker, famous shortstop for the Cubs.

In midseason, and before he had been a big leaguer for even a whole season, Springfield fans gave Maranville a day at the South End Grounds. The Rabbit said he was embarrassed, but gave little evidence of it as he accepted the gifts showered on him. Nothing pleased him so much as the presence of his father in a box. At last he had been forgiven for leaving home to play professional baseball. He had his father's blessing.

With Hap Meyers, Maranville turned in a triple play. Meyers, the first baseman, was extremely fast. He stole 57 bases during the season, to set the modern Braves record.

Meyers was so fast that he almost ran into an unassisted triple play against St. Louis. With two men on base, Wilson Collins, Boston outfielder, lined to the St. Louis second baseman, George Whitted. Whitted stepped on second base for the second out, and needed only to run down the line a few steps to tag Meyers for the third out. But Whitted threw the ball to first base instead, thus ignoring his chance to make an unassisted triple play.

Arthur Devlin suffered a strange fate. On August 25, the Boston third baseman made a ninth-inning hit to beat Pittsburgh, and that night was released to Rochester for George Davis, a pitcher.

"I wonder where they would have sent me if I'd struck out instead of making a hit—Medicine Hat?" mused Devlin.

A postseason series had been arranged between the Red Sox and Braves, but this was canceled at the request of Gaffney. Maranville had been spiked, and Joe Connolly, a regular outfielder, had broken his leg. The season was over when the Braves clinched the pennant for the Giants by beating the Phils, September 27. It was the last favor the Braves were to do the Giants for a while.

144

CHAPTER XV

OVERTURE TO 1914

IF George Stallings was the Eisenhower of the 1914 Braves, his Patton was Johnny Evers.

Evers was 140 pounds of fighting fury, a skinny bag of bones with a big chin and a bigger heart. Apologists for Evers say that off the field he was quiet, reserved, and intensely serious. He had a deep, musical, and religious voice. He was kind to his friends, devoted to his family. In repose he was positively gentle.

But this was not the Evers that umpires, ballplayers, and fans feared, respected, and admired. The Evers they knew was a wildcat of a ballplayer, snarling at umpires and clawing at opponents. He was the Evers who wouldn't speak to his double-play partner, Joe Tinker, who would step all over an aggressive base runner sliding into a base, who would holler bloody murder if he thought an umpire missed one.

Evers was a famous player when the Braves got him from the Cubs in February, 1914, in exchange for Bill Sweeney and cash. He had played on the Chicago pennant winners of 1906, 1907, and 1908. He had made a bonehead out of Fred Merkle of the Giants, a good player who had neglected to run from first base to second on a hit that drove in the winning run. He had been immortalized in F.P.A.'s verse, which had for its punch line: "Tinker to Evers to Chance." He was the best second baseman in the National League.

Charles W. Murphy, owner of the Cubs, was the man who made possible the 1914 miracle of the Boston Braves. He had fired Peerless Frank Chance and made John Evers manager of the Cubs for 1913. The Cubs finished third, but what irked Murphy more was losing the city series to the White Sox.

"Evers is a great ballplayer, but too impulsive to be a manager

145

and a player at the same time," said Murphy. "We ought to have beaten the White Sox easily, and would have if the team had been properly handled. Evers's bad judgment cost us the series, and cost me about sixty thousand dollars."

So Murphy fired Evers, and then the National League fired Murphy.

The Federal League was being organized, and Evers used it as a threat to win a $25,000 cash bonus from the Braves. Stallings immediately made him captain of the team. No club in the league had better leadership than the 1914 Braves. Stallings and Evers were a hand-in-glove combination. A loafing player did not have a chance when caught between the crossfire of these two articulate leaders.

Evers was thirty-one years old. He had played twelve seasons for the Cubs, whom he had joined as a ninety-five-pound stripling late in the 1902 season. He was thrown into a deal by his home-town club of Troy, New York, for $250, because the captain of the Cubs had been injured. The captain was Bobby Lowe, the old Beaneater infielder.

When Evers joined the Cubs in Philadelphia, the manager took one look at him and laughed out loud. The manager was Frank Selee, leader of the great Boston teams of the 1890's.

"You'd better get a little rest before the game," Selee told the scrawny little kid. So Evers slept a couple of hours, then went out and played shortstop. He made two wild throws. In four games in Philadelphia he averaged nearly two errors a game. When the Cubs moved to Brooklyn, Selee shifted Evers to second base, where he played twenty-two games in succession without erring.

Evers is not listed with the very best second basemen, such as Eddie Collins, Larry Lajoie, Charlie Gehringer, and Rogers Hornsby, because he was a comparatively light hitter. But he compared with them as a fielder, and for alert, heads-up ball he was in a class with Collins. For sheer aggressiveness he was in a class by himself, and for this he was known as the Crab, just as he was also called the Trojan because his home town was Troy.

The double-play combination at Boston was Maranville to Evers to Schmidt. It was a good combination and the inspiration of considerable colorful phraseology by rival teams, if not of poetry by baseball writers.

Schmidt was a powerful man, an effective if not a graceful first baseman, but not a long-ball hitter. He hit only one home run in

146

1914, whereas Maranville, who was fifty pounds lighter, hit four. Schmidt had started out as a pitcher and had had a tryout with the New York Highlanders when Stallings was the manager. Control not being one of his specialties, he moved to first base, where Stallings had a good look at him in the International League. Stallings's confidence that Schmidt would be a suitable replacement for the fleet Hap Meyers was not shared by Boston experts when the season began.

The Braves opened the 1914 season with Charlie Deal at third base. In 1913, Deal had been given a trial by Detroit but was soon returned to Providence by Hughie Jennings, who thought him too inexperienced. A few weeks later, while Deal was hitting .312 for Providence, the Braves bought him. Deal was a good third baseman but a light hitter, causing Stallings to leap at the chance to buy J. Carlisle (Red) Smith from Brooklyn in midseason.

Smith was dissatisfied in Brooklyn and was known to be flirting with the Federal Leaguers. But he showed up in Boston and was offered a satisfactory contract by the Braves. As he was leaving the office after signing, he said, "I'll see you tomorrow afternoon."

"Tomorrow morning, you mean," said Gaffney.

"What do you mean? Does this club still have morning practice?"

"Yes, sir. Every day except Sunday," replied Gaffney.

Smith laughed and said, "Why, we quit having morning practice a month ago at Brooklyn." Smith reported in uniform bright and early the next morning.

Short and stocky, Smith was the best extra-base hitter in the Braves line-up, next to Joe Connolly. Smith was a native of Atlanta who had played for Auburn College before turning pro.

Stallings is supposed to have proved two theories with his 1914 Braves. One was that a small pitching staff could carry the whole load. The other was that everything else being even, it was profitable to use left-handed hitters against right-handed pitchers, and vice versa. Both propositions had been demonstrated long before Stallings appeared in Boston. Buck Ewing, while managing the Cincinnati Reds in 1895, used to bench Dummy Hoy against southpaw pitching.

But by employing two sets of outfielders in 1914, Stallings became known as a super-mastermind. The weakest part of the Boston team was its outfield. Stallings played eleven men there during the season, three at a time. The only outfielder who played regularly against both kinds of pitching was Connolly, a left-handed batsman. In center field, Stallings alternated George (Possum) Whitted, right-hander, and Larry Gilbert, left-hander. In right field he used Leslie Mann, right-hander, and Herb Moran and Josh Devore, left-handers. Ted Cather, a right-handed hitter, sometimes broke into these combinations, and Stallings also tried Wilson Collins, Tom Griffith, Jim Murray, and even Oscar Dugey, an infielder, in the Braves outfield, which was a sort of dump for fly chasers.

Devore, Whitted, Cather, and Moran were all acquired from other teams during the season. Whitted and Cather came from St. Louis, in July, for Hub Perdue, the veteran pitcher. Devore came from Philadelphia in exchange for John Martin, an infielder, in July. A month later the Braves bought Moran, a peppery little left-handed hitter from Cincinnati. Stallings was never satisfied with his outfield.

Devore was a small and speedy fellow who had once played for the Giants. He used to worry John McGraw, because while he was harmless and likable, he was also lazy and unpredictable. Once McGraw threatened to fine Devore and his roommate, Rube Marquard, $10 each for talking during a game about the lovely view from the hotel room they occupied.

Southpaw pitchers were Devore's hated enemies. Finally tiring of seeing Devore cringe as he batted against left-handers, McGraw one day ordered him to let Slim Sallee of St. Louis hit him.

"If you don't, it'll cost you ten dollars," said McGraw.

Devore gritted his teeth and turned his back into one of Sallee's curves. As he trotted to first he grinned broadly and shouted to McGraw, "Gee, Mac, it was easy."

Never again did Devore fear left-handed pitchers, but he still couldn't hit them. He struck out five times in succession in the 1911 World Series, four times in a row against the great Athletics southpaw Eddie Plank. Stallings used Devore only against right-handed throwers. Because he had played on Stallings's Newark winner in 1908, Devore was known as "Stallings's lucky player."

As a boy in Woonsocket, Joe Connolly had watched his older brother Willie play ball with Nap Lajoie. The day after games, he and his dog would look for balls lost in the woods where Lajoie hit plenty of them. Connolly had started out as a pitcher, but entered the majors as an outfielder. He was unique in that he hit Grover Cleveland Alexander and Walter Johnson better than he hit the speedy Pittsburgh right-hander Al Mamaux.

One day he walked up into the box as Alexander pitched to him.

148

Insulted, the pitcher told him, "Listen! If that ball isn't coming up there fast enough, just let me know." Connolly did not run up any more against Alex.

Connolly was the victim of a peculiar accident at Baker Field, Philadelphia, where the fences were so close that the outfielders played just behind the infield. Cactus Cravath smashed a low liner over Maranville's head, which Connolly charged. Just as he stooped for the ball it sailed and struck him flush on his big jaw. He woke up in the hotel, mere unconsciousness not warranting hospital treatment in those days.

Leslie Mann, then only twenty-three years old, was a Nebraskan who had been a star all-round athlete at Springfield College. In 1912 he beat the University of Vermont in a football game by returning a punt 75 yards for a touchdown, with only two minutes left to play. Emil Yde, Pittsburgh southpaw, once called Mann "the greatest hitter in the world against left-handed pitchers."

Yde complained, "If I knock him down with one pitch, Mann gets up and hits the next pitch against the fence."

But Mann did not like right-handers, least of all, their curves. The first time he batted against Christy Mathewson he singled on a fast ball. The second time he singled weakly on a curve. That was in April. Came October, and Mann had not made another hit off Matty.

Being an intellectual who was always asking questions and writing them down in a book for future reference, Mann asked Mathewson what had happened. Matty replied:

"When you hit the fast ball, I noticed that you liked to pull the ball. Then I threw a curve, and you fell away and were lucky to get a hit over second. After that, I threw you nothing but curves on the outside of the plate. You couldn't hit them with a paddle."

Commenting on the marvelous good luck enjoyed by the 1914 Braves, Connolly said, "We were so lucky that we even won games with Mann getting base hits off right-handed pitchers."

Mann was a good enough ballplayer but he was a better lecturer. When his active career was over, he promoted sand-lot baseball, and was once called by Judge Landis "the ambassador of American baseball." He made stirring talks to boys on the advantages of good clean living. One of his horrible examples was Rabbit Maranville, who somewhere along the line must have mended his ways, since he played in the big league until he was forty-three years old.

149

Unlike Connolly, who had turned from the mound to the outfield before turning pro, Ted Cather was a pitcher his first three years in organized ball. The Pennsylvanian broke in with Lancaster in 1910, winning twenty and losing nine games. Used in relief the next season by Toronto, he won three, lost four games, but with Scranton in 1912 he had a 13–10 record.

Brought up by the St. Louis Cardinals, Cather was shifted permanently to the outfield by Manager Miller Huggins, who rated him a better hitter than pitcher. He batted only .213 that year, but boosted his average to .284 in 1914, when he played for both the Cardinals and the Braves.

Larry Gilbert also began his pro career as a pitcher. He was a New Orleans boy who started out as assistant scoreboard keeper for the Pelicans, and became a southpaw hurler by throwing to hitters in practice. He broke in with an 18–7 record with Victoria, Texas, in 1910; then had a 17–5 record with Battle Creek, Michigan.

"I had to make good or walk from Battle Creek to New Orleans, quite a piece down the road," says Gilbert. He made good by shifting to the outfield. His bat was more potent than his arm. The Braves drafted him after he hit .283 for Milwaukee in 1913. He opened the 1914 season in center field for the Braves, when they played in Brooklyn. Twenty-six years later, his son Charlie opened the season in center field for Brooklyn against the Braves.

Gilbert was no great success as a big-league player, but there probably has never been a more successful minor-league manager.

The mildest character on the 1914 Braves undoubtedly was Hank Gowdy, a fair-haired skyscraper who was about as much like Johnny Evers as a violet is like a cactus. His fiercest invectives then, as now, consisted of "Criminy Sakes" and "Holy Cow!"

The Giants had taken him from Dallas, Texas, and given him a trial in 1911, but McGraw thought that the gawky rookie was lazy. He traded him along with Al Bridwell to Boston for Charlie Herzog. Gowdy spent 1912 with Boston as second-string catcher, but was with Buffalo most of 1913, hitting .313 before being recalled by Stallings.

Gowdy was a patient work horse for the 1914 Braves, catching 128 games, but he was a favorite target for Evers because of his good nature.

"Stallings is working me too much," Gowdy complained one day. "I'm stiff and sore all over."

150

"What?" yelped Evers. "You're playing too much? If I were you, Gowdy, I'd holler if he didn't play me. You ought to be thankful that you're in the game every day. What more can you ask?"

Gowdy, who was born in Columbus, Ohio, had been a peanut butcher as a boy, in the ball park there. The man who gave him his first chance to play professionally was Bob Quinn, a Columbus club official, later to be president of the Braves. Gowdy was a first baseman until he joined the Giants in 1911, when McGraw advised him to take up catching if he hoped to be a big leaguer.

Gowdy developed slowly and surely as a catcher. If he had any weakness in 1914, it was on high-foul flies hit directly over his head. It was to be much later that he was to have World Series trouble with a mask dropped under his big feet.

Behind Gowdy the Braves had young Bert Whaling, a native of Los Angeles who had been bought from Seattle in the fall of 1912, along with Bill James. The Braves paid $2,500 for Whaling, $5,000 for James. Whaling caught in about one third of the games, but batted only .209 in 1914.

When Evers was hurt and unable to play, either Oscar Dugey, an even-tempered Texan, or Whitted substituted for him at second base. Bill Martin, the team's other reserve infielder, was signed in midseason, but played little. Several big-league clubs were after him as he starred for Georgetown University in the spring, but their ardor cooled when he broke his leg.

The Braves of 1914 had other pitchers besides Rudolph, Tyler, and James, believe it or not, but none of them was very conspicuous. They included: the towering Texan, Eugene Cocreham; the southpaw from Syracuse University, Ensign Cottrell; the rookie Kentuckian, Richard Crutcher; the veteran southpaw who was born at Berne, Switzerland, Otto Hess; and big Paul Strand, a robust southpaw from the Northwest who was only twenty years old.

These pitchers, along with Perdue, who was traded to St. Louis during the summer, won twenty-five games among them. Rudolph, Tyler, and James won sixty-nine games, which explains why they are so well remembered while the others are forgotten.

CHAPTER XVI

THE TEAM OF DESTINY

THE years have grown into decades since the miracle of the 1914 Braves, and still baseball historians argue whether George Stallings's team was the weakest, the luckiest, or just the gamest club ever to win a pennant. In truth, the Braves of 1914 were all three—weak, lucky, and game.

Stallings did not expect to win the pennant when the Braves reported to their training camp at Macon, Georgia. He did expect to be in the race, and he did expect to finish in the first division. At one of his clubhouse meetings, he discussed the season's prospects with the players. He told them that the only team they need worry about was the New York Giants, winners of three successive pennants.

And that's how it turned out. The last of the seven teams the Braves caught and passed between July 19 and September 8 was the Giants.

The Braves made a dismal start. Lefty Tyler was beaten in the season's opener at Brooklyn, 8–2. The Braves lost their first three games before beating the Phils in Philadelphia. They won only four of their first twenty-two games. Their luck was atrocious. They lost game after game by one run. Evers was sick; Maranville had tonsillitis. Some of the pitchers were wild. The rest had sore arms.

Stallings moaned, "This bunch of mine is the worst-looking ball club I've ever seen. They can't do anything right. I've never seen such luck. But don't think we're a tail-end team. It'll take us a month to get back in shape, but then we're going to be hard to beat."

Stallings never gave up. He raved and raged like a maniac, sliding up and down the bench, bouncing his nervous foot furiously, and fining his players recklessly. There were no rules on the Braves except that players had to show up at the park every day in condition to play. They had only to keep within the law. No manager but Stallings could have handled such a wild crew.

"That'll cost you five hundred dollars," he'd rage at a player who had missed a hit-and-run signal.

"Make it a thousand dollars," the player would flare back at him.

"Now it's fifteen hundred dollars," Stallings would say.

Stallings never collected a fine. If he had collected all he imposed in 1914, players say he could have retired for life.

The Braves lost games but they never lost the spirit of winning. Stallings and Evers saw to that, one abusing them in the dugout and the other saucing them on the field. It was a hard team to play for, but if a man was game there was a fine frenzy in being one of these Boston Braves. The soul of the team was its will to win.

As Stallings had predicted, luck gradually changed for the Braves. Evers and Maranville became well. The pitching settled down once Stallings decided to use Rudolph, Tyler, and James as his three starters. Trading Perdue for Whitted and Cather added strength, and Herb Moran helped. Buying Red Smith from Brooklyn gave the team more punch at third base and put a power hitter behind Butch Schmidt in the line-up.

The Braves got a quick peek at daylight when they went into seventh place ahead of Brooklyn on June 25. But the next day they were back in the cellar, there to stay for three more weeks.

The Braves celebrated the Fourth of July by losing two games to Brooklyn. On the evening of the Fourth, a portentous day with baseball oracles, the Giants led the league with a 40–24 record. Fifteen games behind in last place were the Braves, with a 26–40 showing.

"We not only were in last place on the Fourth of July," Johnny Evers used to say, "but just after the holiday we lost an exhibition game to a soap-company team. That's how bad we were."

The Braves, who had won only twenty-six of their first sixty-six games, were to win fifty-two of their next sixty-six games. The Braves, who had scored only one shutout before the Fourth, were to score eighteen shutouts after the holiday, as Rudolph, James, and Tyler served a steady stream of goose eggs.

When the season was half over for the Braves, July 15, they were still eighth, eleven and a half games behind the Giants. Their record of 33–43 for the first half was unusually good for a last-place club.

153

In the second half of the season they were to win fifty-one games and lose only sixteen.

The Braves left last place behind them for good on July 19, when they won a double-header in Cincinnati. Trailing 0–2 entering the ninth inning of the second game, they scored three runs to win. As they left the field the players threw caps and bats into the air. They cheered like college boys. They almost smothered Stallings.

"Now we'll catch New York," the manager told his men. "We're playing thirty-per-cent better ball than any team in the league. They won't be able to stop us."

The Giants had been present to see the Braves leave last place. It was an off day for them in Cincinnati. When Dick Rudolph, their former teammate, visited them at the hotel that night, they laughed as he said, "We're going after you fellows now, and we're going to catch you."

"You're just wasting your time, Dick," the Giants said, but even then they were worried about this Boston team that had too much confidence for a club that was only in seventh place.

After a triumphant trip through the West, the Braves ran into a bad batting slump. It was then that their big three saved them. Rudolph, James, and Tyler allowed an average of about one run a game over a stretch of fifteen games. Leaving Cincinnati, the Braves went to Pittsburgh and scored four shutouts in five games. Tyler and James won the first, 1–0; Rudolph the second, 6–0; James the third, 1–0; and Tyler the fourth, 2–0.

They won one game when Maranville let a pitched ball hit him, with bases full. The score was 0–0, and Stallings had said to Maranville, "Get on somehow, even if you have to get hit."

The first two pitches by Babe Adams were strikes. The Rabbit was desperate. He leaned over the plate, hoping to be hit. He had his wish, for the ball struck him on the forehead. Adams was not the kind of pitcher anyone would choose to be beaned by. Maranville thought the Bunker Hill monument had fallen on him.

Umpire Charlie Moran regarded him suspiciously, and said, "If you can walk to first base, I'll let you get away with it." Maranville staggered to first, then had to be relieved. But the run he forced home won the game.

Three days after leaving the cellar, the Braves were fourth, so closely bunched were the clubs in the league standing. After being beaten in a one-hit game by Dan Griner of the Cardinals, the Braves

154

won nine games in succession. On August 10 they went into second place.

By this time the Giants were beginning to get the jitters, although their writers were saying: "The same thing happened in 1912. The Cubs and Pirates charged up, but the Giants went on to win by ten games."

But this was another year. The Braves went into the Polo Grounds in mid-August and won three straight games. Tyler beat Mathewson, 2–0, in ten innings, in the third game. The Giants filled the bases with none out in the last of the tenth and failed to score. A week later, August 23, the Braves tied the Giants for first place. It had taken these inspired madmen from Boston just five weeks to climb from the bottom to the top of the National League ladder.

The quick ascension left the boys a little dizzy. They spun into a slump that dropped them to second place, then to third. While they were spinning, Larry Cheney, of the Cubs, tossed a one-hitter at them.

It was in this series at Chicago that Evers and big Heinie Zimmerman started a memorable fight. Evers whacked Zimmerman with the ball on an attempted steal, and Heinie got up swinging. Seeing Evers in trouble, Maranville ran over and slugged Zimmerman, knocking him to the ground.

"I know who hit me. It was Moose Whaling," bellowed Zimmerman, while he was being held.

Maranville took Zimmerman by the arm, soothed him, and walked him off the field, saying, "Whaling didn't hit you. I did."

"The hell you did," protested Zimmerman. "No midget like you could give me a belt like that. It was Whaling or Butch Schmidt."

Zimmerman was so insistent that Maranville had not hit him that he challenged Schmidt. Then the big Boston first baseman lost his temper, and it took three teammates to restrain him. When Zimmerman later learned that he had walked off the field arm in arm with the fellow who had socked him, he lost his fond regard for Maranville.

This was a refreshing episode for the Braves. Their dizzy spell passed, and the Giants had time for only one deep gulp of relief before the tomahawk boys were chasing them again.

The Braves won a double-header from the Cardinals; then Tyler beat the Cards 2–0 as he pitched a no-hitter. On September 2, Rudolph and James won a double-header in Philadelphia as the

155

Giants lost to Brooklyn. The Braves had a one-game lead for first place. Whitted played second base when Captain Evers was indisposed with an upset stomach.

"Throw your straw hats away, boys. I'm buying you all some new lids when we get back to Boston," said Jim Gaffney, who had come over from New York for the series.

The Braves lost the lead the next day when Alexander outpitched Tyler, 7–4. Evers returned to the line-up—for about an inning. Umpire Bill Klem, not an upset stomach, eliminated him on this occasion.

A squeeze play by Gowdy with Smith on third base in the twelfth inning gave James a victory September 4, but the Giants beat Brooklyn to keep a half-game lead. Herby Moran was knocked cold as he tried to duck a bean ball thrown by Alexander, a relief pitcher. The ball glanced off the bat and hit him on the head.

"So you're the next hitter," Alexander said to Evers, who was swinging two bats. "I'll land one on the side of your head, too."

Evers went out to the mound with his two bats but hit him instead with his vocabulary. Either way, Alex figured to get hurt.

The Braves won the last game in Philadelphia, 7–1, with Cocreham pitching. The victory gave them a record of sixteen victories against six defeats on their long trip. It also put them in a tie for first place, with the Giants going into the crucial series with McGraw's team in Boston on Labor Day.

Joe Lannin, the new owner of the Red Sox, offered the Braves the use of Fenway Park for the remainder of their home games, and Gaffney gratefully accepted. It was at Fenway Park that the Braves set what probably is Boston's all-time one-day attendance record on September 7. The morning game drew 36,000 fans, the afternoon game 40,000. The paid attendance for the two games, Gaffney announced, was 74,163. Some 9,000 fans stood on the fringes of the outfield in the afternoon, most of them on Duffy's Cliff, which sloped up to the left-field fence.

The Braves won the morning game, 5–4, behind Rudolph by scoring two runs off Mathewson in the last of the ninth. After Gowdy was retired, Devore beat out a hit to Merkle. Moran doubled into the crowd in right field, and Evers drove in the tying and winning runs with a double to left, on which George Burns just failed to make a shoestring catch.

The crowd went nuts. Players had to fight their way off the field. George Stallings was engulfed in the dugout and could not escape to the dressing room for ten minutes, as fans crowded about and cheered him. The Braves were again alone in first place.

But not for long. The Giants caught them in the afternoon as Jeff Tesreau breezed to a 10-to-1 victory over Tyler. A four-run sixth inning finished the Boston southpaw, and it almost finished Fred Snodgrass, New York's center fielder. After almost being beaned by Tyler, Snodgrass reached first base by getting his sleeve in the way of the next pitch.

This was sufficiently annoying to the home folks, but Snodgrass did a dance on the way to first base, and from that sanctuary he brazenly thumbed his nose at Tyler. The park shook as Braves rooters shrieked in anger, but it took Tyler to stop Snodgrass. A bit of a comic himself, George pantomimed Snodgrass's muff of the fly that had lost the 1912 World Series to the Red Sox in this very same park. Snodgrass subsided.

When Snodgrass went out to center field after the Giants had scored four runs, the fans opened up a pop-bottle bombardment. As Snodgrass retreated hastily, the mayor of Boston, James M. Curley, jumped onto the field and tried to persuade a police lieutenant and Umpire Bob Emslie to put Snodgrass out of the game for inciting a riot.

"Mayor Curley became much more excited than Snodgrass or the crowd," wrote Bill MacBeth in the *New York Sun*. "Laying aside his official dignity, he precipitated himself upon the field and upon Umpire Emslie, demanding that Snodgrass be fired from the game."

Emslie resisted the mayor. So did the police lieutenant. But McGraw, probably feeling that Snodgrass was worth a good deal more to the Giants alive than dead, replaced the veteran with Bob Bescher.

The deciding game of the series was played the next day, before 17,000 fans, and James pitched a three-hitter to win, 8–3. The Braves again had sole possession of first place, and this time they had it to keep. McGraw started Rube Marquard, who went into the game with eight straight defeats behind him. The Braves quickly made it nine, finishing him off by scoring four runs in the fourth. Marquard was so wild that he forced two Boston runs over the plate.

In a game of sensational fielding, the best catch was made by Snodgrass, who went up the bank in left center to steal an extra-base hit from Gowdy. Although Mayor Curley had written to John K. Tener, president of the National League, demanding that Snodgrass be punished for thumbing his nose at Tyler, the Boston fans gave Snodgrass thunderous applause for his fine catch. Boston crowds have become famous for applauding good plays by visiting players, especially when the Braves or Red Sox are winning.

The Giants were bewildered and demoralized. McGraw had not even gone out on the coaching lines for the deciding game. The Giants were through, and the Braves rode high, wide, and handsome to the pennant, picking up speed as they went along.

They won a double-header from the Phils September 9, and in the second game, George Davis, the Williams College graduate, who was now attending Harvard Law School, pitched a no-hit game. Five Phils reached base on passes, two on errors by Red Smith at third base. Davis walked three men with none out in the fifth inning, but then fanned Ed Burns and got Cactus Cravath to ground into a double play.

The next day Evers was chased by Umpire Mal Eason and drew a three-day suspension. Evers complained, "I was swearing at the ball, not at Eason. He misunderstood me."

While Evers was out, Whitted played second base, and Moran patrolled center field. Evers returned to good standing just in time to be given a day by Boston fans. He said, "If anybody on this team cracks, it'll be me. This is the fourth time I've been through a tough fight like this, and I know what it's like. The others don't know and they don't care. You needn't worry about them."

Neither Evers nor his teammates cracked. They poured it on to the finish, clinching the pennant by beating the Cubs, September 29.

"Every man did his share," said Stallings. "It was team play that won. Stars couldn't have done it. There's no substitute in baseball for fighting spirit, and this team had it."

The Braves had it, all right, and the country loved them for it. American sports fans made the most of this chance to cheer for the underdog. The 1914 Braves were the all-time underdogs.

Stallings kept the Braves hustling after they had clinched the pennant. If he rested a regular, it was only for one game. He did not press for victories, but after a defeat he'd say before the next game, "I want this one." The Braves went on and won the pennant by ten and a half games from the Giants.

"We got discouraged," admitted Chief Meyers, Giants catcher, "because everybody in the country seemed to be pulling for the Braves and rooting against McGraw."

A coin was flipped in Philadelphia by August (Garry) Herrmann, chairman of the National Commission. Gaffney said, "Tails." It came down heads. Connie Mack smiled and said that the first two games of the World Series would be played at Philadelphia.

Evers was voted the most valuable player in the National League before the season ended and he won a Chalmers automobile. Evers got 50 points; Maranville was second with 44 points. Braves players generally felt that Maranville deserved the award more than Evers, but Maranville said, "I don't care, so long as one of our boys got it."

Playing at Brooklyn, Evers was spiked on the shin by Henry Myers. He stayed in and finished the game, but Gaffney worried. He called up Stallings and told him to be careful. There was only one more day to go, only two more games to play with Brooklyn.

In the ninth inning of the first game the following day in Brooklyn, Red Smith made a hesitant slide into second base and broke his leg. The Braves had lost their regular third baseman and one of their hardest hitters on the eve of the World Series.

The players were depressed, but Stallings immediately announced, "It's unfortunate, but we have another good third baseman. Charlie Deal will do the job perfectly. This is no one-man team. We'll go right on and fight it out."

Stallings benched his regulars for the second game of the doubleheader and sent out his "moss aggies" with instructions to show everybody what a scrub team could do if it wanted to. The moss aggies beat Brooklyn, 7-3. The season was over, and the Braves had ended it dramatically, with Smith breaking his leg, Evers being put out of the game by an umpire, and the scrubs beating the Robins.

Bill James led the league pitchers with twenty-six victories and seven defeats. He won nineteen of his last twenty games. His earned-run average was 1.90 per game. Rudolph, who had a twelve-game winning streak until beaten by the Cubs in August, finished with a 27-10 record. Bald Dick pitched six shutouts, all after the Fourth of July. The Braves had a team batting average of .251. Their only .300 hitter was Connolly, who battled Jake Daubert, of Brooklyn, for the batting crown, only to slump in the final weeks and finish at .306.

2

The Athletics, having won four American League pennants in five seasons, were two-to-one favorites to win the World Series. The

Braves had pulled off one miracle by winning the pennant. It was too much to expect them to pull off another by winning the World Series. The Braves, after all, were only a spirited team made up of a lot of ordinary ballplayers, while the Athletics, with their $100,000 infield and Chief Bender, Eddie Plank, and Joe Bush, came pretty close to being a team of all-stars.

The situation was ideal for a master psychologist like Stallings, and he made the most of it. He expressed nothing but contempt for the Athletics, nothing but admiration for his own team. He said he wouldn't scout the Athletics, although his assistants did secretly. He said he didn't care who they pitched. He said the Braves would win four games in a row, something that had never been done in a World Series. Stallings, it was clear, was whistling his way past the graveyard.

The Braves arrived in Philadelphia on October 7. The first game was to be played two days later. Stallings was talking with Walter Hapgood, of the *Boston Herald,* in his room when he suddenly asked, "How can we get their goats? We'll beat 'em, as it is, but we might as well make it easy."

"Don't ask me," replied Hapgood. "You've done all your own thinking until now, and have done pretty well."

An hour later Stallings called Hapgood and told him he wanted to see the baseball writers of both cities in his room. "And after we're together a while," said the manager, "I want you to ask me, 'When are you practicing tomorrow?'"

The writers convened in Stallings's room and chatted amiably until Hapgood popped the question: "When are you practicing tomorrow?"

"At two o'clock," replied Stallings.

Philadelphia writers looked up quickly. Jimmy Isaminger said, "But you can't. The Athletics are practicing at two o'clock."

"The hell you say," replied Stallings. He turned to Hapgood and said, "Get me Mack on the phone."

"Hello, Connie. I was wondering about practice tomorrow. I figure on taking my boys on the field about two o'clock," Stallings said, as the writers bent their ears. Then he listened to Mack, with growing impatience. Finally he roared, "But I don't want the field at noon or at four. I want it at two. If I'd made arrangements in Boston and you wanted to change, out of common decency to a visitor I'd have changed things to suit you. Well, you can have your

160

field at two, and at noon and at four, too. We'll still beat you four straight."

With that, Stallings hung up. Immediately the writers dashed for their typewriters. The next morning both Boston and Philadelphia papers carried front-page streamers: BRAVES FIND SHIBE PARK CLOSED TO THEM FOR PRACTICE. MACK TURNS DOWN BRAVES.

"Mack's courtesy is only a rumor," wrote a disillusioned Jim O'Leary.

Poor Connie was mystified by it all. He and Stallings had talked the day before about the Braves using Shibe Park, and the Boston manager had expressed no objection to the Athletics using the field between two and three.

"Why, that man called me unsportsmanlike and even threatened to punch me on the nose," admitted Mack in his bewilderment.

So instead of practicing at Shibe Park the day before the Series opened, the Braves practiced at Baker Field, the National League Park. Stallings explained that he wanted to practice at two o'clock so his players could get used to the shadows as they would be during the games.

If that ruse did not get the goats of the Athletics, Stallings employed another that did. In one of his skull sessions before the first game, Stallings told his players to ignore the Athletics throughout the Series, unless it was to insult them. Evers, Maranville, and other jockeys on the Braves investigated phobias and repressions of Philadelphia players.

As soon as the Braves walked onto the field, Eddie Murphy, Philadelphia outfielder, spied Maranville and shouted cheerily, "Hello, Rabbit." Since Maranville was one of his best friends, Murphy thought that this was the thing to do.

Maranville ignored him, so Murphy crossed the field and extended his hand. Maranville didn't see it, kept walking, and heard Murphy say bitterly, "What's the matter? You guys stuck up because you won a lucky pennant?"

The feud was on. When the announcer asked for Boston's starting line-up, Stallings chased him from the bench. The Braves unceasingly shouted insults across the field at the Athletics.

"It looks as though the boys are peeved," said Mack. "What have we done to get them so stirred up?"

During the games, the Braves gave their opponents the same acid treatment. They reminded the Athletics of debts they owed, troubles

161

in their families, and intimate personal shortcomings. Wallie Schang, young A's catcher, was ridiculed shamelessly, with the result that the Braves set a record by stealing nine bases in four games. On the bases, the Braves cavorted like dancers in a musical comedy chorus. The Braves acted like savages. They were uncouth and unmannerly. But they won the World Series in four straight games, and that is exactly what Stallings said they would do.

Connie Mack tried to be cozy before the first game, letting his prize southpaw, Eddie Plank, take hitting practice but starting Chief Bender, the crafty Chippewa, who had won seventeen games and lost only three during the season. He should have stuck with Plank, because the Braves hammered Bender for a 7-to-1 victory.

Dick Rudolph allowed only five hits and fanned eight. The Braves made eight hits off Bender, three off J. Weldon Wyckhoff, his successor. Bender was the first pitcher Mack had ever relieved in a World Series, although Coombs had to quit in 1911 because of an injury. Stallings used two left-handed hitters in the outfield, Connolly in left and Moran in right, but played a right-hander, Whitted, in center. Deal, the rangy third baseman who replaced the injured Smith, was dropped to eighth place in the batting order.

Gowdy led the Boston attack with a single, double, and triple. The Braves scored two runs in the second inning on Whitted's walk, Gowdy's run-scoring double, and Maranville's single. Gowdy's triple and Maranville's single gave them a run in the fifth. They added three runs and disposed of Bender in the sixth, on a single by Evers, a pass to Connolly, a triple by Whitted, and a single by Schmidt.

The Braves rubbed it in by working a slow-footed double steal in the eighth inning for their final run. With Schmidt on third, Gowdy on first, and Maranville hitting, Gowdy started for second, drawing the throw, and Schmidt slid home ahead of Collins's wild return throw. The riding the Athletics took then was ear-burning.

The Athletics scored their only run in the second inning, when Rudolph passed McInnis and Strunk's single rolled through Moran in right field. Asked if he were nervous, Rudolph said, "Yes. I was thinking about my daughter Marion, who was being born in New York."

In Dallas, Texas, a young newspaperman, Al Laney, now of the *New York Herald Tribune*, was losing his job because he was watching an electric scoreboard portray the game, while somewhat nearer at hand a train wreck required his undivided attention.

162

The Braves were more chesty than ever when they came out for the second game, but they had to fight for their lives to win it, 1–0. There were two vital plays. Both were made in the ninth inning and both favored the Braves. Plank and James had pitched shutout ball entering the ninth. The southpaw had allowed Boston six hits, while the Tribe's spitballer had given up only two hits, a single by Collins and a double by Schang.

With one out, Deal doubled over Strunk's head in right, the fielder misjudging the ball. James struck out, and Deal was trapped off second base. When Schang rifled the ball to Barry at second, Deal broke for third and slid in safely ahead of Barry's throw, although the Athletics protested Umpire Bill Byron's decision. Mann, who murdered left-handers, then lined the ball over Collins's head, and Deal scored the only run of the game.

In the last of the ninth, with one out, Barry was passed and took second on a wild pitch. Walsh walked, bringing up Murphy, who was so fast that he had not grounded into a double play all season.

"Get closer to the bag," Evers barked at Maranville, from behind his glove.

Maranville moved over and said, "I'm almost standing on it."

Evers growled, "Well, get right on it."

Maranville crowded the bag, and it was well that he did, because Murphy smashed the ball between James's feet, and it surely would have gone into center field except that Maranville was waiting for it, scooped it up, touched second, and threw to first for a double play that ended the game.

There was no holding the Braves as they returned to Boston. "Four straight, four straight," chanted the 300 Royal Rooters who had accompanied them to Philadelphia and paraded around the town in tribal regalia. Boston throbbed from excitement. The denouement to baseball's most wondrous fairy tale was at hand.

When the Braves left Philadelphia, Stallings ordered that all their traveling equipment, their road uniforms and trunks, be taken back to Boston. He proclaimed, "We won't be coming back. It'll be all over after the two games in Boston."

After observing a quiet Sunday in Boston, the teams went into the third game, before 35,520 fans at Fenway Park. Boston rooters were taking this Series more seriously than their cousins in Philadelphia. Both games in Shibe Park had drawn 20,562. At Boston 300 fans stood in line all night to get into Fenway Park.

163

Before the game, Evers drove around the field in his new Chalmers, but this was Gowdy's day to shine. He had contributed a single, double, and triple in the first game. In this one his offering consisted of two doubles and a home run. Hank remembers it as his biggest day in baseball. The Braves won 5–4 in twelve innings.

Stallings started Lefty Tyler, while Mack picked Joe Bush, speedy twenty-two-year-old right-hander, who had won sixteen games and lost twelve during the season. Bush went the distance, but Tyler was lifted for a pinch hitter in the tenth, and James finished.

This was the only game of the series in which the Athletics led the Braves. Three times they were in front. Three times the Miracle Men caught them. The Braves were lucky. They played a sloppy game but still they won.

The A's scored in the first inning on Murphy's double, Oldring's sacrifice, and Donnelly's muff of a fly by Collins. The Braves tied it up in the second, when Maranville walked with two out, stole second, and scored when Gowdy doubled in the temporary seats in left.

The Athletics took a 2-to-1 lead in the fourth. McInnis doubled into the left-field bleacher with two out, Connolly bravely diving into the crowd in an attempt to catch the ball. Walsh singled to score McInnis. The Braves bounced back immediately, Schmidt singling, taking second on an infield out, and scoring on Maranville's single. On his previous swing Maranville had blooped a fly down the right-field line, which fell among Collins, McInnis, and Murphy, and rolled to the fence. Maranville had circled the bases for a home run, but Umpire Hildebrand had ruled the ball foul.

Until the tenth inning, there was no more scoring. Then both teams got two runs. Schang singled, Bush fanned, and Murphy beat out a bunt. Both runners advanced as Evers threw out Oldring. Collins walked to fill the bases.

Evers then made what he always considered the dumbest play of his career. Baker hit a hard grounder at him, which he fumbled. Schang scored, but as Evers picked up the ball and cussed it, Murphy kept running and dashed over the plate as the Boston captain stood frozen in the field with the ball in his hand. The A's led, 4–2.

As the crowd edged tentatively toward the exits, Gowdy hit the ball into the center-field bleacher for a home run, leaving the

164

Braves only one run behind. The crowd returned to their seats. Devore batted for Tyler and fanned, but Bush passed Moran. Evers promptly advanced him to third with a single to right, and Moran scored the tying run on Connolly's fly.

James walked two A's in the twelfth inning, which some thought too dark to play, but was not scored on. Gowdy led off the Braves half by doubling into the handy left-field bleacher. Mann ran for Gowdy; Gilbert batted for James and was purposely passed. Moran bunted, and Bush, with an easy force play at third, threw the ball past Baker into the left field, to let Mann score the winning run.

"If we could win that game, we can't possibly lose tomorrow," said Stallings. He ordered Herman Nickerson, the road secretary, to cancel train reservations to Philadelphia for the following night. Nickerson thought that the Series might be affecting Stallings mentally, but he canceled the reservations as ordered, then prayed that the Tribe would win and end the Series.

They did, of course. How could they lose? It wasn't in the cards. From three days of rest, Rudolph went back to the mound and beat the Athletics, 3–1, before 34,365 fans. Instead of coming back with Bender or Plank, Mack started Bob Shawkey, a young right-hander who had won sixteen games and lost eleven during the season.

The Braves scored a run in the fourth inning, when Evers walked, reached third as Collins was abusing Connolly's grounder, and scored on Schmidt's soft hit over second base. The Athletics tied the score, 1–1, in the fifth, as Barry singled over third, reached second on Schang's grounder to Evers, and scored on Shawkey's single to center.

The Braves scored two runs in their half. With two out, Rudolph singled to center. Moran doubled to left, and with a 3-to-2 count, Evers singled to center, scoring both men. A young southpaw, Herb Pennock, pitched the last three innings for the Athletics and allowed two hits and no runs.

The Braves needed no more runs. Rudolph was the master. Boston fans squirmed uneasily only in the seventh, when Walsh walked and reached second base on a wild pitch with nobody out. But as Barry fanned, Gowdy pegged the ball to Evers at second, and Walsh was caught off the bag for a double play.

The fairy tale ended happily, as fairy tales must. The Braves were champions of the world. They were all heroes, but honored above

165

the rest was Hank Gowdy, the angular catcher who had batted .545, who had made six hits for fourteen bases, and who had handled Boston pitchers superbly.

Boston never knew a wilder baseball celebration than that which followed the fourth game. Thousands of fans swarmed around the Boston dugout, and Manager Stallings had to make a speech. Rabbit Maranville was dragged from the showers, and, half-dressed, he too spoke to the crowd from the roof of the dugout.

Then the crowd paraded with the band playing "Tessie" and "Along Came Ruth" around the park, through the Fens, down Huntington Avenue, and to Copley Square, where the beaten Athletics were serenaded in their hotel, the Copley Plaza. There were fully 5,000 fans in the human chain, and thrust to its head were all the Braves who came in sight, especially Maranville, who needed no thrusting.

Newspapers were filled with ghosted articles by Stallings, Evers, Gowdy, Maranville, and Rudolph. Inspired fans wrote poems that were printed. One was to Evers, with this opening stanza:

> Chubby Charlie from Chicago
> Must have made an awful squawk,
> When they named the Chalmers winner,
> Johnnie Evers, Troy, New York.

Another ode to Hank Gowdy concluded with this verse:

> When you're down on your luck and feeling fit
> For the hospital or the grave,
> Just think of a chap who wouldn't quit,
> Hank Gowdy, the Boston Brave.

Besides such lyrical tributes, the Braves drew down $2,812.28 apiece for their winning shares. They were toasted wherever the game of baseball was played. For them the winter was a long succession of banquets and parties. They were the rich little poor boys.

"A great team," said Connie Mack. "One of the greatest. It had wonderful spirit and just wouldn't be beaten."

Connie was so shaken by his experience that he immediately broke up his $100,000 infield and spent the next ten years in the second division.

166

During the winter, Rabbit Maranville met his old friend Eddie Murphy, the A's outfielder he had high-hatted in Philadelphia.

"Why, hello, Eddie," said Maranville largely, offering his hand. "Glad to see you again, old boy."

Murphy glared. He didn't see the hand. And he wasn't glad to see the Rabbit. Eventually he got over it.

CHAPTER XVII

A COUPLE OF NEAR MISSES

THE Braves began the defense of their championship in 1915 with a new slugging outfielder in Sherwood Magee, a new business manager in Walter Hapgood, and the same old fighting spirit. An extra incentive to repeat was in the title of "fluke champions," which had been bestowed on them by some depreciators during the winter.

"A fluke doesn't last from July through the middle of October against the best clubs in the game," argued Stallings. "We earned what we got by fighting for it and we had more ability than most people thought. Well, we've still got the ability and we've still got the fight. We're not going to wait until July this year."

During the off season, Stallings had been irked by Gaffney's trading of Possum Whitted and Oscar Dugey for Magee, the Philadelphia outfielder who had batted over .300 three years in a row. Stallings was glad enough to have another strong hitter but he hated to see Whitted go. He regarded Whitted as a key player on the 1914 Braves, because he could fill in acceptably for Evers at second base, aside from playing a good game in center field.

If anything, the Braves were less dignified than ever, even though they were champions. Spring training was a three-ring circus. Once a week Stallings would take the club from Macon to his 6,000 acre plantation, twenty miles away in Haddock. There they would have a frolic, with possum and coon hunts, honey-tree excursions, and fishing, topped off with a big dinner of roast turkey and country ham.

Big Daddy was a generous host. Players kidded him and played practical jokes on him, yet he always remained the boss. Maranville made the most mischief. He put on a bellhop's uniform one evening and delivered a fake telegram to Stallings as the manager was taking a bath.

"What are you waiting for?" asked Stallings irritably, with a quick look at the kid in the brass buttons.

"I'm waiting for my dime, you cheap skate," said the kid.

With an angry howl, Stallings leaped out of the bathtub and pursued Maranville into the corridor. And while he did not catch him, he made a good try to brain the fresh bellhop with a chair he threw down the stairs after him.

On a Saturday night in Macon, Maranville and Magee tried to break up a sidewalk meeting of Holy Rollers and succeeded to the point where the police were called. As Maranville and Magee fled before the angry crowd, they came upon a Salvation Army group marching down the street. Maranville grabbed a tambourine, and Magee took a drum, and between them they made that the most eventful Salvation Army meeting Macon had ever known. Just as Stallings and the police drove up, Maranville and Magee were starting the collection with five-dollar bills. So large were the receipts that the players escaped being jailed.

That was the spring when Stallings was always boasting of his prize imported Hereford bull. Stallings had 80,000 peach trees on his plantation but he was most proud of the bull. He intended having the beast insured for $25,000 but kept putting it off, until shortly after the season opened he learned that the bull had died.

The players were glad. They were starting to think that Stallings thought more of the bull than he did of them. During clubhouse meetings, he always talked of the bull, and the only way they could shut him up was to bellow in unison. This used to make him very angry. When the bull died, he was both angry and grief-stricken.

In Cincinnati, when the Reds were beating the Braves, Maranville made an untimely reference to the bull. After a Boston pitcher had given a succession of bases on balls and Stallings was frothing at the mouth, Maranville, at the other end of the bench groaned, "And—the—bull—died—"

Stallings couldn't believe his ears. He said nothing but sneaked a quick, wicked glance along the bench of solemn players. A few minutes later, a Boston hitter struck out on a ball that was over his head. "Go get some glasses. You're blind as a bat," Stallings raged at the player.

From the other end of the bench Maranville groaned, "And—the—bull—died—"

Shaking with rage, Stallings marched down the bench, asking,

169

"Who said that?" Nobody replied. Everybody was solemn as an owl. But just as he turned, the Boston hitter fouled out weakly, and Maranville shouted, "And—the—"

Stallings spun and caught him. He ran up to the Rabbit and nearly jabbed out an eye with his finger. "You—you little so-and-so!" he shouted. "I thought it was you. Out! Get out of that uniform. Back to the hotel. I'll get rid of you tonight. You're through."

But the Rabbit wasn't through. He lasted longer with the Braves than Stallings.

2

The Braves' pennant defense was unsuccessful. The Phils won their first, and to date their only, pennant under Pat Moran. While the Phils won only ninety games, the Braves finished seven games behind them in second place. The Phils built up their margin by winning fourteen and losing seven games against the Braves.

The collapse of Bill James, the injuries and sickness of Johnny Evers, Dick Rudolph's inability to equal his 1914 performance, and Sherwood Magee's disappointing hitting were hard blows. James became sick and spent most of the season at home. He is as good an example of a great one-year pitcher as the game has known.

Big Paul Strand, a promising young right-hander, also became sick and sat out the season. Ten years later he was to get another shot at the majors, this time as a slugging outfielder for whom Connie Mack paid Salt Lake City $50,000. He missed again.

Evers injured an ankle sliding into second base on April 18, as the Braves played Brooklyn, and had to be carried from the field. He did not play again until June 29, when he took part in the second game of a double-header against the Giants, hitting a home run, a double, and a single. Evers played only eighty-three games, batting .263.

Rudolph won twenty-two games, one of them with a home run with bases full, but was almost a .500 pitcher, for he suffered nineteen defeats. He probably would have done better if the team behind him had been as lucky as the team of 1914. Stallings longed for Whitted, who was helping the Phils win the pennant. Whitted could have substituted for Evers at second more acceptably than anyone the Braves had.

An injured shoulder bothered Magee, but probably not so much as the loss of Baker Bowl's handy fences. Magee had batted over .300 for the Phils three years in succession and in 1914 had hit fifteen

170

home runs. But for the Braves he batted .281 and hit only five homers.

When he reported at the park after a rough evening during spring training, Stallings told him, "You'd better take plenty of work in the outfield. Chase a lot of flies."

While shagging a short fly, Magee stepped in a hole, fell, and hurt his shoulder. He never was as good again.

Don Carlos Patrick Ragan, bought from Brooklyn in April, and Tom Hughes, a thirty-year-old veteran who had been bought for $3,500 from Rochester the previous September, ranked behind Rudolph on the Braves staff. Ragan's record was 17–12, Hughes's 16–14. George Tyler had an off season, winning ten and losing nine games. He pitched and lost a one-hit game to Brooklyn, 1–0, in September.

In midseason the Braves picked up two youngsters who were to become outstanding pitchers. Jesse Barnes, bought for $2,500 from Davenport, July 25, went on to win three games and lose none before the season closed. Ten days later a twenty-three-year-old southpaw, Artie Nehf, was bought from Terre Haute for $3,000. He won five, lost four games for the Braves. Four of his five victories were shutouts. One of his shutouts, against Brooklyn, was a one-hit game in which Brooklyn did not have a man left on base. Both Nehf and Barnes were to do their best pitching later for the Giants.

When Nehf was introduced to Johnny Evers by Stallings, the pitcher said, "This is the second time we've met, Mr. Evers."

"That so? When was the first time?" asked the Braves captain.

"When you managed Chicago. You watched me work out in the morning, then gave me the bounce in the afternoon."

"What, a good pitcher like you?" said the pained Mr. Evers. "Then that explains why they fired me in Chicago."

The Braves did not have a .300 hitter in 1915. As a team they batted .240, lowest in the league. Joe Connolly was top man at .298. In midseason the Braves picked up the veteran Fred Snodgrass, released by the Giants, but he batted only .215. His single kept the Braves from being victims of a no-hit game by Fred Toney of Cincinnati.

Jim Gaffney had a spat with his pal John McGraw early in the season, when he refused to let the Braves play the Giants if Benny Kauff, Federal Leaguer, played center field. After Umpire Ernie Quigley forfeited the game to the Giants, the game was played without Kauff in the New York line-up. The Braves won, 13–8, and their

171

victory was upheld while Quigley's forfeiture was overruled. Kauff returned to the Federal League for the rest of the season.

Stallings thought he had a lot of headaches but he found time to sympathize with John McGraw in a game played at Boston, in June. The Giants had men on first and third, with one out, when a long fly was hit to the Boston outfield. The runner on third would have beaten the throw home easily, but Larry Doyle, captain and second baseman of the Giants, was the runner on first. He reached up and caught the throw-in. The man on third was sent back to his base. He did not score. The game ended in a ten-inning tie.

One of the season's most remarkable games was played on the final day at Boston. The Giants won, 15–8, making twenty-four hits to seventeen for the Braves, yet the game required only one hour and two minutes to play. The boys were hitting the first good one that day.

There was a lot of talk of another miracle when July 15 found the Braves in last place. They climbed steadily until they were in second place on September 24. That was the closest they could come to the Phils, whose Grover Cleveland Alexander was winning thirty-one games and losing only ten. Alexander hurled his fourth one-hit game of the season against the Braves, September 29, to clinch the pennant.

The Braves felt that Umpire Bill Klem cost them the pennant in Philadelphia late in August. The Braves led in the first game of the double-header, when Alexander came to bat against Rudolph. Alex had been dusting off Boston batters all afternoon, and now Rudolph threatened to make him hit the dirt. The count went to three and two, and as Alex fell out of the box, Rudolph threw a curve that, the Braves said, bisected the plate. Klem called it a ball, Alexander got a walk, and the Phils won the game in that inning.

Losing the pennant was a bitter pill for the Braves, especially Evers and Stallings. Evers drew a five-day suspension for badgering umpires in the final month. Stallings slid up and down the bench, cursing base-on-ball pitchers. One day he tried two young college pitchers in relief. The first was wild, the second was wilder. While they were sitting on the bench feeling sorry for one another, Stallings rushed down to them, stuck his face close to theirs, and said, "Rah, rah, rah! Rah, rah, rah! Rah, rah, rah!"

Then he sat down, leaving the collegians to wonder if he was sane.

A major event in 1915 was the opening of Braves Field. Gaffney had been looking for a site for a new park ever since buying the Braves in 1912. He found what he wanted in the old Allston Golf Club on Commonwealth Avenue. It was a pretty location, with the Charles River meandering lazily in the background between grassy banks, and locomotives belching smoke and cinders in the Boston and Albany yards in the foreground.

The park was built with $600,000 raised by Arthur C. Wise, Boston broker, on a first mortgage. Wise had successfully undertaken the financing on Fenway Park when it was built three years earlier. The Allston lot measured 850 by 675 feet and contained 593,718 square feet of land. It was big enough so that Gaffney could build what he called "a perfect ball park." He wanted the playing field to be so large that it would be possible to hit a home run inside the field in any direction. The left-field foul line originally measured 402 feet, the right-field line 402 feet, and it was 550 feet to center field.

Instead of building the park on Commonwealth Avenue, the cagey Gaffney put it at the back of the lot, between Gaffney and Babcock Streets. By doing this he was able to sell the frontage at a handsome profit and also to do cleaners and launderers a good turn by putting his customers within easy range of smoke from the railroad yards when the wind was easterly.

Gaffney announced the purchase of the golf links December 1, 1914. Ground was broken March 20. The Braves continued to play at the South End Grounds, their home for forty-five years, until they began to move the infield sod to the new park. Then they played at Fenway Park, with the kind permission of the Red Sox.

Statisticians reported that 750 tons of steel and 8,200,000 pounds of cement were used in building a covered grandstand that would seat 18,000 fans, two uncovered pavilions that would seat 10,000 each, and a small bleacher in right field, the famous Jury Box, that would seat 2,000. A ten-foot cement wall surrounded the park.

Players who moved from the chummy South End Grounds to new Braves Field complained of loneliness. It was like moving from a modern three-room apartment into a nineteenth-century mansion. Ty Cobb, of the Tigers, stood at home plate one day, shaded his eyes with his hand like an Indian scout looking over the prairie, and said,

"One thing is sure. Nobody is ever going to hit a ball over those fences." He was right—for about five years.

The grand opening was held August 18, and B. M. (Business Manager) Hapgood had the time of his life inviting all the notables and dignitaries he knew, and some he didn't know. Among the 14,000 guests were 10,000 school children, who were packed into the left-field pavilion. The paid attendance was 32,000. The Braves claimed an attendance of 56,000, the largest ever to see a baseball game, although there were no more than 40,000 seats. At least 6,000 fans were turned away.

Clark Griffith, Gaffney's close friend, pitched the first ball, disdaining Rabbit Maranville's offer of shin guards. Miller Huggins, manager of the visiting St. Louis Cardinals, stood at the plate, and George Stallings was the catcher. Griffith pitched, Huggins swung and missed, and Stallings stuck the ball into his back pocket.

Present were thirteen mayors from near-by communities as well as Governor David I. Walsh. It took 400 elevated cars to handle the mob. Lost in the crush were the regular fans who had been so prominent in the South End Grounds. Hank Gowdy made the first put-out in Boston's wondrous new ball park, Maranville drove in the first run, Art Butler of St. Louis made the first hit, and Mel Webb challenged the first foul hit into the lofty press stand. With Rudolph pitching, the Braves made the occasion a complete success by beating the Cardinals, 3–1.

The Red Sox accepted an invitation to play the Boston games of the 1915 World Series at Braves Field and drew 42,300 fans for the game of October 11.

Until the ball was given the needle and fans became home-run conscious, Braves Field remained "the perfect park." Since then, successive owners have taken turns making alterations but they still haven't found a way to move 8,200,000 pounds of cement stands closer to the playing field.

4

Gaffney sold the Braves to a Boston syndicate of bankers on January 8, 1916. The reason given was that he and Harry Sinclair were going to buy the Giants, but the more likely reason, since that deal never came off, was that Gaffney had a chance to make a substantial profit. He was essentially a businessman, not a sportsman. He admitted selling the Braves for a lot more than the $187,000 he had paid for the team four years earlier.

The bankers who had financed the building of Braves Field, Millett, Roe, and Hagan, were part of the new syndicate. So were the politicians Louis A. Frothingham and David I. Walsh. Both Stallings and Hapgood owned some stock. The deal was closed January 14, when Gaffney and his partners, Robert H. Davis and Frederick R. Killeen, surrendered their stock, with John J. Toole, National League attorney, present to see that the stock actually changed hands. The National League would not countenance anything like syndicate baseball. Goodness, no!

Percy D. Haughton, famous Harvard football coach, was elected president, Arthur C. Wise, treasurer. Haughton was new to pro baseball, but in Boston it was taken for granted that anything he tackled was certain to be a success.

"Hope you will not be much disappointed in the transfer of club. Feel confident that with your co-operation we can make a success," Haughton wired Stallings. The Miracle Man stayed as manager and received a new, long-term contract.

In no time at all the new owners had a headache. Butch Schmidt, large and useful first baseman still in the prime of his career, announced that he was retiring from baseball to take care of his butchershop in Baltimore. It was known that the club had not satisfied Schmidt's salary demand in 1915, but he denied that he was quitting for any reason except that his business needed him. No amount of persuasion could induce him to change his mind. Schmidt stayed in Baltimore and worried about steaks and chops instead of worrying about base hits in Boston.

The Braves were lucky in replacing Schmidt. They bought Big Ed Konetchy, a Federal Leaguer in 1915, from the Pirates, along with Pitchers Elmer Knetzer and Frank Allen, for $18,000.

Spring training in 1916 was notable for two events. Percy Haughton lectured the players on the evils of profanity, a subject in which the former Harvard coach was well versed.

"Instead of swearing when something goes wrong," he told the gaping players, "say something else, like 'good' or 'nice'. It sounds a lot better and has the same result."

In an exhibition game that same afternoon, a ball took a bad bounce over Sherwood Magee's head at first base, giving the Giants a lucky run.

175

"Good!" shouted Magee. "Good, good, good!"

When he came into the bench still saying, "Good!" Stallings exploded, called Magee everything but good, and thus ended forever Haughton's ban on profanity.

B. M. Hapgood, as adventuresome a promoter as baseball knew until Larry MacPhail brightened the skies, arranged an exhibition itinerary that called for the Braves to sleep on a train something like twenty nights in succession after breaking camp. Most of the trains did not even have diners. The players endured it for a week, then rebelled.

Rabbit Maranville instigated a strike. The players continued to play, but they refused to shave and wore nothing but blue working shirts with loud neckties and fantastic caps. In three days they looked like a hobo convention. Confronted by Maranville, Konetchy, and Walter Tragesser, a small-town store owner in Georgia telephoned the sheriff and reported that some jail breakers were on the prowl. Crowds paid their respects in raspberries. Stallings and Hapgood threatened the players, then pleaded with them, but the players stuck to their beards and blue shirts. Hapgood's itinerary was modified.

The Braves made a better fight for the pennant in 1916 than they had the year before, for while they finished one place lower, trailing Brooklyn and Philadelphia, they were eliminated from the race only two days before the season ended. They trailed the pennant-winning Robins by a mere four games at the finish.

As late as September 4, the Braves were in first place, and they stayed so close in the sprint to the wire that World Series tickets had to be printed and orders taken, a costly and needless procedure. Alexander, who pitched sixteen shutouts in 1916, stopped the Braves on three hits on October 2, to put them out of the race. The Braves immediately returned the favor, eliminating the Phils by winning the second game of that double-header and winning two games the next day.

The Giants in 1916 won seventeen consecutive victories, all on the road, with Christy Mathewson beating Dick Rudolph, 3–0, for victory number seventeen. They then went into a devastating slump, and the next time he was in Boston, McGraw asked Stallings, "Do you think I ought to break up this rotten ball club of mine?"

"Why?" asked Stallings. "It's still a good club. Stick with it a while longer."

176

McGraw waited, and the Giants proceeded to set the all-time record with twenty-six consecutive victories. The last three triumphs were shutouts over the Braves in the Polo Grounds. Jeff Tesreau won, 2–0, over Rudolph in the first game, September 28. Ferdy Schupp beat Ragan, 6–0, in the second game, allowing only one hit, that by Konetchy. The next day Rube Benton won a 4-to-0 victory over Rudolph, Konetchy again making the only hit for the Braves.

The streak was ended in the second game by George Tyler, who beat Tesreau, 8–3, as Red Smith and Magee hit successive home runs. Despite their winning streaks of seventeen and twenty-six games, the Giants managed to finish only fourth, one of baseball's prize believe-it-or-nots.

The Braves had some good pitching from Rudolph (19–12), Tyler (17–10), and Hughes (16–2). Rudolph won ten games in succession. On September 12, he won the first game of a double-header, 1–0, then pitched the first nine innings of a thirteen-inning 3–3 tie in the second game.

Hughes, who had pitched a nine-inning no-hitter for the New York Highlanders in 1910, only to lose 5–0 to Cleveland in eleven innings, became the fifth Boston National hurler to pitch a no-hit game, when he shut out Pittsburgh, 2–0, June 16. Braves fielders had only three assists. Hughes clinched his no-hitter by striking out Honus Wagner for the second time. Slim Tom had the best won-lost record in the National League, but had the misfortune to break his hand late in the season.

Rudolph and Hughes shared the assignment for the Braves as they played a sixteen-inning scoreless tie with Cincinnati, June 3. Fred Toney and Pete Schneider did the pitching for the Reds. The Braves made only three hits in the sixteen innings.

The Braves had fine pitching, as indicated by twenty-one shutouts and nine one-to-nothing victories, but no hitting at all, to speak of. Their team average of .233 placed them last. Konetchy led the regulars with a modest .260 average. The Braves had little luck in either 1915 or 1916, but they couldn't complain after what they had in 1914. Not only was Hughes hurt, but Magee and Evers were seriously injured. Evers suffered through the season from neuritis in his throwing arm and played only seventy-one games.

Plagued by neuritis, a bad stomach, and an ornery disposition, Captain Evers was poorer company than ever. He rode the opposition, he rode the umpires, he rode his own teammates. Early in

177

August, Manager Stallings was suspended three days for telling Umpire Cy Rigler, "After your exhibition of umpiring this afternoon, you ought to be put in prison."

Thus, Stallings was not on the Boston bench for the double-header with Cincinnati, August 3. In the fourth inning of the second game, Umpire Byron allowed Bill Louden of the Reds to score because of interference at third base by Red Smith.

"What alibi are you going to give now for your dirty ball playing?" shouted Evers from the Boston bench. Teammates were not sure if Evers was joshing Smith, but Smith didn't think so, because he started swinging at Evers as soon as the inning was over.

When the belligerents were separated, Byron put Evers off the bench. Smith yelled after him, "If you're not yellow, you'll wait for me after the game."

Evers wasn't yellow and he waited. He waited in uniform until after the game, and then he and Smith had it out. As he left the clubhouse, Evers was crying from rage and predicting that he would retire from baseball. With two more years to go on a contract that paid him $10,000 a season plus bonuses, Evers didn't quit, of course. Neither did his neuritis.

CHAPTER XVIII

NEW OWNERS, NEW FAILURES

⊜

THE chief distinction of the Braves during the war years was provided by Hank Gowdy, who became the first big-league player to enlist, on June 2, 1917. He joined the Fourth Ohio Militia, which became the 166th Infantry of the 42nd, or Rainbow, Division. By October he was in France, a sergeant seeing service at Château Thierry, St. Mihiel, the Argonne, and the Lorraine.

That spring, when the Braves had returned from spring training, Gowdy, Evers, and Maranville all tried to enlist on Boston Common, but the Army wasn't quite ready for them. Gowdy was then getting a salary of $7,000, and Evers was calling him "the only catcher who could rival Johnny Kling." But baseball held no interest for Gowdy when duty called. His average had dwindled to a mere .214 when he left the Braves to put on a more distinguished uniform.

After their fine effort the year before, the Braves were expected to be pennant contenders in 1917, but they were never in the first division after May and finished sixth. Johnny Evers, always ailing, played only twenty-four games and was released to Philadelphia. Konetchy broke his leg. Hughes was unable to pitch until August because of an injured hand. Rudolph was a .500 pitcher, and Barnes lost twenty-one games, while winning thirteen.

Two great pitchers ended their big-league careers with the Braves in 1917. Ed Reulbach, who had pitched a one-hit game for the Cubs in the 1906 World Series, appeared in five games for the Tribe, winning none and losing one. The year before, he had come out of the Federal League to win seven and lose six games for the Braves.

Big Ed Walsh, one of the best of spitball pitchers, attempted a comeback with the Braves, after having pitched only fourteen games

179

in three seasons for the White Sox. He appeared in four games, and like Reulbach, he won none, lost one.

One Boston player who stood up was Art Nehf. The southpaw won seventeen and lost only eight games. Late in the season he pitched forty consecutive scoreless innings before Brooklyn put over a run against him.

The Braves of 1917 failed to hit much, but they were hit often. No fewer than forty-five Boston batters got in the way of pitched balls. Stallings said, "If you can't use your bats, use your heads." The Braves took him literally, and if they didn't bruise the ball, the ball certainly bruised them.

The first World War not only overshadowed baseball, but it caused the 1918 season to be terminated September 2. This was all right with the Braves, who finished seventh. In mid-June they were third, but even then were not playing .500 ball. The war season ended on a glorious theme, however. After losing their first fifteen games with the Giants, the Braves beat McGraw's team in the season's very last contest. Then they beat their chests, and said, "Wait'll next year."

Before the season opened, George Tyler had been traded to Chicago for Art Wilson, a catcher, Larry Doyle, a second baseman, and $15,000. Four days later the Braves traded Doyle and Jesse Barnes to the Giants for Buck Herzog. This was Herzog's second trip to Boston, he having played there in 1910 and 1911. The first one was enough, according to Herzog. He resented being traded from a pennant winner to a second-division club and was a holdout until the season began.

Another holdout was Rudolph, who did not join the club until May 27, and then proceeded to lose ten games while winning only nine. Rabbit Maranville enlisted in the Navy after playing only eleven games. Also lost to the armed forces during the season were Ray Powell, Walter Rehg, Ed Fitzpatrick, and Dana Fillingim, among others.

The Braves beat Brooklyn, 16–0, to set themselves a shutout record, but the season's most notable game for the Boston team, not excepting the solitary victory over the Giants, was the twenty-one inning contest played against Pittsburgh, August 1. Nehf went the whole way for the Braves, shutting out the Pirates through the first twenty innings. His opponents were Erskine Mayer, who retired in the sixteenth, and Wilbur Cooper.

In the twenty-first inning, Catcher Walter Schmidt singled off

180

Nehf. Cooper forced him, but the pitcher reached second as Whitey Ellam was being thrown out. Tom Leach then beat out a hit to deep short, putting Cooper on third. Max Carey singled to left, scoring Cooper, and Billy Southworth singled to center scoring Leach.

The Boston shortstop that day was James Lawrence Smith, who was later to set the pace for Joe Louis by walloping Billy Conn, his son-in-law, in a family quarrel. Since J. Carlisle Smith, who had once traded punches with Johnny Evers, was playing third, the Smiths were fairly well represented in the Braves line-up.

Three years of war-worried baseball were enough for Haughton's syndicate of Boston bankers. After rejecting a bid by Stallings and Hapgood because it was too small, they sold the Braves to a New York group headed by the somewhat mysterious friend of John McGraw, the derby-wearing, cane-carrying George Washington Grant. It was never proved, but it was generally believed, that with the advent of Grant the Braves fell under the control of the Giants. McGraw certainly had been put out when the Braves lined up against his proposal that managers as well as club presidents be permitted to attend National League meetings. It was McGraw who produced Grant, and for all Boston knew, he might have picked him out of a hat.

Investigation disclosed that the new owner had pioneered the moving-picture industry in England, having owned a string of cinemas for ten years before selling for a substantial profit in 1917. Grant had been a baseball fan since his youth in Cincinnati, where he had sold newspapers. While a young man, he had managed Kid McCoy when that busy fighter was bruising any chin that came within range.

Grant was a close friend of Charles Webb Murphy, who as owner of the Chicago Cubs had sold Johnny Evers to Boston, and of Charles A. Stoneham, owner of the Giants. He had offices in Wall Street with Stoneham and he had a box at the Polo Grounds beside Stoneham's. Both Grant and McGraw were interested in a Havana race track. Boston fans had reason to be suspicious of the deal that brought Grant to Boston. They wondered if the Braves were to be a farm team for the Giants.

The sale price was reported as $400,000. Grant owned the club, but Gaffney still owned the property. Grant said he had tried to buy the Braves from the Russell estate in 1911, but was beaten out by

181

Ward and Gaffney. Grant also said he would buy a home in Boston but he never did. He was just a New York commuter.

Grant, we are told by *Spalding's Guide*, "stuck to his post with grit and pluck" in 1919. It was a bad season at the gate, one reason being strikes in the Boston elevated system. Streetcar fares went up; ball-park attendances went down. The Braves made a poor start, suffered from injuries, ran into terrible weather, and were beset by a weak outfield. They finished sixth.

The Braves sold Konetchy to Brooklyn when they got a new first baseman in Walter Holke, a switch hitter. After playing three years for the Giants, Holke had been traded to Cincinnati along with Bill Rariden for Hal Chase. Then the Reds turned around and traded Holke to the Braves in exchange for Jimmy Smith and cash.

Jim Thorpe, a great athlete but ordinary ballplayer, was sent over from New York to finish his brief and unspectacular big-league career by waving weakly at curves. When Red Smith slumped at third, the Braves bought Norman (Tony) Boeckel from Pittsburgh on waivers. In August, Herzog was traded to Chicago for Charlie Pick and Les Mann, who had played in the 1914 outfield.

But the biggest deal of all, and one that strengthened suspicions of a strong Braves-Giants tie-up, was the trading of Arthur Neukom Nehf in mid-August for pitchers Cecil Causey, Joe Oeschger, and John Paul Jones, Catcher George (Mickey) O'Neil, and $40,000. Nehf was cheap at the price. As the Giants won four pennants from 1921 through 1924, Nehf turned in a total of sixty-six victories against thirty-seven defeats for them.

McGraw gave up on Oeschger, a pitcher he had acquired from the Phils, after seeing him pitch one inning against Brooklyn. The Robins made four whistling hits in succession off Oeschger, but did not score a run. One man was thrown out trying to reach third. Another was thrown out at the plate. And a third was thrown out stealing.

"There'll never be another miracle like that," said McGraw, and shipped Oeschger to the Braves.

Teammates had some trouble pronouncing Oeschger's name, but not nearly so much as they had spelling it. When he first pitched a spring-training game for the Phils in 1914, the umpire had carefully studied the name scrawled on his line-up, and then announced to the small crowd that Oyster was pitching for the Yannigans.

The 1919 season was spiced by some unusual events. Hank Gowdy

182

Day was observed May 23. The veteran catcher, playing his first game since his enlistment two years earlier, hit the first ball pitched to him for a single as thousands cheered.

Stallings nearly suffered a stroke July 11, when Cincinnati defeated the Braves, 4–2, in thirteen innings. Heinie Groh hit a homer to win the game, but Stallings suffered his crisis in the first inning when Bill Rariden, Cincinnati catcher, bounced a hit into the scoreboard for a home run. The boy in charge had neglected to close one of the inning spaces, and through this opening rolled Rariden's hit.

"My God!" shouted Stallings. "Even the ground help is against us."

But a month later luck and the ground help were on his side, for Ray Keating, Braves pitcher, got a home run when a ball he hit bounded through a hole in the fence.

A pathetic incident of 1919 was the attempted comeback of Curveless Bill James, the twenty-seven-game winner for the 1914 champions. James appeared in just one game, pitched five innings, and was through forever as a big leaguer.

Late in September, the Braves managed to be beaten, 3–0, by Chicago in a mere matter of fifty-eight minutes. They couldn't get the season over quickly enough.

2

May 1, 1920, was a cold, damp day. The clouds were low, the wind was east. Occasionally it sprinkled lightly. As Oeschger of the Braves and Leon Cadore of the Brooklyn Robins warmed up, they did not dream they were to pitch against each other for twenty-six innings and nearly four hours without a decision being reached.

They were both big men and strong. Cadore was a cunning right-hander, while the swarthy Spaniard, Oeschger, relied on a hopping fast ball. In the fourth inning, Brooklyn scored a run as Catcher Ernie Krueger walked, was advanced on Cadore's infield out, and scored on Ivy Olson's single. The Braves tied it up in their half of the fifth when Walton Cruise tripled and Boeckel singled.

There was no more scoring. Twenty-one more innings were played without either team getting another run. The game was called because of darkness, with the score 1–1. Oeschger set a record by pitching sixteen successive scoreless innings in a game. In sixteen innings, not consecutive, he retired the Robins one-two-three. The Robins made nine hits, drew four walks, and fanned seven times.

183

The Braves made fifteen hits, drew five walks, and fanned seven times. Brooklyn did not make an extra-base hit. Only three balls were used in the whole game.

It was the longest game ever played, exceeding by two innings the game of September 1, 1906, when Jack Coombs of the Athletics had beaten the Red Sox, 4–1, in Boston. Both pitchers complained that their arms were dead, but Cadore said, "The mental strain was worse. We kept thinking about that twenty-four-inning game. It was a relief when we got through the twenty-fifth inning."

The Braves had the good fortune to be unscheduled the next day, but the Robins went to Brooklyn, where the Phils beat them, 4–3, in thirteen innings. On May 3, the Robins went back to Boston, losing to the Braves, 2–1, in nineteen innings. When the Robins reached Boston, they discovered that Cadore was still in bed resting from his twenty-six-inning ordeal.

Aside from these marathon games, the Braves had little to offer their fans in 1920. They were third in mid-May, but steadily slipped down the standing until they came to a stop in seventh place, one position lower than they had finished the year before.

Oeschger, with a 15–13 record, was the only Braves hurler to win more games than he lost. Ray Powell, an outfielder who had been bought from Providence in 1917, led the team with six home runs. He batted a mere .225. Holke led the regulars with a .294 average.

George Stallings was pretty disgusted with it all. Since Gaffney had sold the Braves they had been steadily getting worse. They did not have the money with which to buy players they needed. Stallings shuddered at some of the baseball he watched, as on September 17, when St. Louis made twelve consecutive hits off Braves pitchers, ten in the fourth inning and two in the fifth.

With his contract about to run out, and Grant unwilling to renew it on the same generous terms, Stallings looked again to the minor leagues, whence he had come in 1913 to lead the Braves to their brief but magnificent moment of glory. The Miracle Man resigned as manager of the Braves on November 6, and with Hapgood he bought the Rochester franchise in the International League. Three weeks later, his former coach, Fred Mitchell, was signed by Grant to manage the Braves. Ed Riley, road secretary, succeeded Hapgood as business manager. Phil Troy succeeded Riley as road secretary.

My Right Eye had been released as coach of the Braves in 1916

184

so that he might coach Harvard College. Then he became a Braves scout. In 1917 he succeeded Joe Tinker as manager of the Chicago Cubs. After leading the Cubs to fifth place his first season, Mitchell won the pennant with them in 1918, but lost the World Series to the Boston Red Sox. He finished third in 1919, fifth in 1920, and then was succeeded by Johnny Evers.

Mitchell was president as well as manager of the Cubs for part of 1919. When William Wrigley bought the club, he gave Mitch a choice: "You can either be president of the Cubs or manager, but not both. What will it be?"

Mitch chose to be manager, and William L. Veeck, father of the present Cleveland Indians leader, became president. In his four years as manager of the Cubs, the stony-faced Mitchell had become a believer in strict discipline for ballplayers. If the Cubs had not converted him, the Braves most surely would have.

It was an unusual western trip during Mitchell's three-year reign with the Braves that the club did not collect $600 or so in fines from the players. The Braves were a lot of wild Indians in those days.

In a Pittsburgh café Ray Powell and Mickey O'Neil were hauled in for brawling after a game. It seems that some hill billies had started an argument with them, and the argument had led to a general demolition of furniture. For this escapade, Mitchell fined each of them $200. They were notified of the penalty in a billet-doux written by the road secretary, Phil Troy:

"You are hereby notified that you have been fined $200 by Manager Mitchell for being arrested for fighting and brawling in a Pittsburgh café. This amount will be deducted from your next pay check."

O'Neil studied the message carefully, then asked, "What do they mean by brawling? We only threw some chairs around."

The note fascinated the catcher. When the Braves reached Philadelphia, he got the key to the board announcing the hotel's daily events, and posted the letter there for everyone to see. O'Neil was not ashamed of his $200 fine. He was proud of it.

On another occasion, Mitchell overhead loud voices raised in an altercation outside a hotel entrance in Pittsburgh. A Southern drawl sounded familiar, so he investigated. He found four of his ballplayers, well lubricated, arguing about who was going to pay the sixty-five-cent taxi fare. All insisted on paying it, sure proof that they were not sober.

185

"Here, lemme pay it," demanded one loud voice. "I'll buy the whole damn automobile, if I want to."

Mitchell then made his dramatic entrance, saying, "Don't do that. Save some of your money, boys, so you'll be able to pay your fines."

The Braves finished fourth in 1921, their first season under Mitchell. It was the best Braves team in five years. Oeschger had his finest season, winning twenty and losing fourteen games. Dana Fillingim, who had been bought from Indianapolis in 1917, had his first winning record, 15–10. Jack Scott, who had been stumbling since the Braves paid $750 to Nashville for him in 1917, helped with a 15–13 record; and so did John Watson, a big Southerner who had been bought from New Haven the year before, by winning fourteen games while losing thirteen.

But what made the Braves of 1921 a first-division team was a midwinter trade that sent Walter Maranville to Pittsburgh for two outfielders, Billy Southworth and Fred Nicholson, Shortstop Walter Barbare, and $15,000. Southworth was an outstanding player, and if Barbare could not field like Maranville, his .302 batting average was considerably higher than the Rabbit's.

The Braves had Holke at first, Boeckel at third, Barbare at shortstop, and Horace Ford, a Tufts College graduate and a brilliant fielder, at second base. Southworth, Powell, Cruise, Nicholson, and Al Nixon patrolled the outfield. Gowdy, O'Neil, and Frank Gibson took care of the catching. Holke set a fielding record for first basemen, making only four errors for a percentage of .997. Powell set a Braves record by hitting eighteen triples.

From the middle of June until the end of August, the Braves held third place. Then they were passed by the Cardinals. September was a terrible month for the Braves. It started with the loss of a 1-to-0 game to Lee Meadows of Philadelphia. A week later Oeschger had a 6-to-0 lead and yielded eight runs to the Phils in the ninth. In the fourth inning he had fanned three Phils on nine pitches. Pittsburgh beat them a fifteen-inning game on a double by Maranville. The Cardinals scored six runs in the seventh inning to win, and then the Braves lost two twelve-inning games to Chicago in one afternoon.

This was the season the ball was hopped up for Babe Ruth. The Braves finished with a .290 batting average, as Cruise hit .346, Boeckel .313, and Southworth .308. Powell hit twelve homers to lead the team, but the most notable homer was the one Walton Cruise hit

186

into the jury box at Braves Field, August 16. It was only the second homer hit into that bleacher since the park was built in 1915. Cruise had also hit the first one while playing for the Cardinals two years earlier. No one had yet driven a ball over the left-field fence at Braves Field, but on August 25, Austin McHenry of the Cardinals became the first batter to hit the fence on the fly. The lively ball was making a bandbox of Gaffney's Acres.

The swarthy little Nixon had an unusual distinction one day while playing in Pittsburgh. He played all three outfield positions and had three put-outs at each position. He did not get into any record book, but Hod Ford did when he had twelve assists in a game to tie a thirty-nine-year-old record for second basemen. John Watson pitched and won a double-header from Philadelphia, 4–3 and 8–0, allowing only two hits in the second game.

With the Braves scoring more runs than they had since 1894, turning in triple plays, and walloping the ball in a manner remarkable for them, their attendances jumped appreciably. And with player fines helping to keep down road expenses, George Washington Grant enjoyed a profitable season in 1921.

He did not enjoy another. Luck changed so much for the worse in 1922 that Grant sold the club. The Braves, pepped up by their showing the previous season, were thinking of themselves as pennant contenders as the new season started. They finished in last place. At no time were the Braves higher than seventh.

Grant proved that he was a smart businessman by insuring his players against sickness and injury before the season began. Statisticians estimated that the Braves in 1922 lost 365 playing days because of injuries. Southworth was able to play only forty-three games, because of a dislocated knee. He coached a Boston fire department in his idle hours, and when the team won a championship, Southworth won a gold fireman's badge.

Before the season started, the Braves traded Scott to Cincinnati for Rube Marquard, veteran southpaw, and Bill Kopf, an infielder. Marquard had an 11–15 record in 1922. Scott complained of a sore arm at Cincinnati, was sent to New York, and there helped the Giants win the pennant. Joe Oeschger had a poor season, dropping thirteen games in succession in one stretch and winning only six and losing twenty-one games.

Fillingim complained of a sore arm and won only five games. The day before the season ended, he went to Grant, and said, "My arm feels much better now. I think I can work now whenever you need me."

"Well, we won't be needing you during the winter months, anyhow," said Grant dryly. "Unless it's to shovel snow."

In July the Braves replenished their treasury by selling Hugh McQuillan to the Giants for an estimated $100,000 and the veteran hurler Fred Toney. McQuillan was a promising young pitcher who had not had a winning season in three years with the Braves, but for the Giants he beat Carl Mays of the Yankees in a World Series game that fall.

"When McQuillan takes his cap off and runs his hand through his hair, he's all through," Jim O'Leary used to say in the press box.

McQuillan paid his former wife $500 a month alimony. Once he spent the $500 and was unable to accompany the Braves to New York, where his former wife lived, for a series with the Giants.

"There's the sheriff," a player would say, nudging McQuillan as they walked down the street in New York.

McQuillan would look hastily, shake his head with relief, and say, "Nope. He's not one. I know 'em all."

Gowdy was relieved when McQuillan was traded, because the pitcher was always tormenting him about his fear of germs. One day in Cincinnati, Gowdy entered the clubhouse, late as usual, and heard Gibson mutter, "I wouldn't let anybody do that to my mask."

Gowdy was all ears. He asked, "What's wrong? Who did what to whose mask?"

Gibson said nothing, but O'Neil explained, "Oh, that McQuillan. Spitting on your mask was a dirty trick."

"Spitting on my mask? On *my* mask?" shrieked Gowdy. Poor Hank was tempted to curse, but pluckily restrained himself. But the germs also had to be restrained, and this Gowdy accomplished by covering his entire mask with adhesive tape.

When Hank O'Day, the gruff old umpire, saw Gowdy walk to the plate wearing a white mask, he almost toppled and asked excitedly, "My God, man! What's that thing you're wearing? What is it? Tell me. What's going on here?"

The Braves set some inconsequential records in 1922. Ray Powell tied a mark for center fielders with ten put-outs and one assist. Boeckel went through nineteen innings of a double-header without having a single chance at third base. Bill Kopf, playing shortstop, started four double plays in a game. Fred Nicholson set a modern outfielding record with four errors in another game.

For some reason or other, Grant suddenly found himself very tired of the Braves.

CHAPTER XIX

THE JUDGE TAKES OVER

FOUR men were dining together at the Lambs' Club in New York. Two of them were easily recognizable, being famous in their fields. Everyone knew both John (Muggsy) McGraw, manager of the New York Giants, and George M. Cohan, actor, singer, composer, author. The other two men were Judge Emil E. Fuchs, then attorney for the Giants, and Harry M. Stevens, who with his brothers ran one of sport's most noted commissaries.

During the course of the evening McGraw looked across the dining room and commented: "Why, there's George Washington Grant. Did you know that you can buy his ball club for a half-million dollars?"

The other three men arched their eyebrows. They had not heard that the Boston Braves were for sale.

"Yes, the Braves can be bought," continued McGraw. He looked at Cohan, and added, "Now there's a club you should own, George. You like baseball and have always wanted a team. Here's your chance."

Cohan shook his head and said: "No, I guess not. I'm just a trouper, after all. I have no time for a baseball club. I'll stick to something I know."

McGraw turned to Fuchs, and asked, "Judge, why don't you buy it? You know the game and have the interest."

Fuchs surprised his listeners by replying quickly, "Sure, I'll buy it, but on one condition."

"What's that?" asked McGraw.

"That Christy Mathewson will help me run it."

Mathewson, the erstwhile superpitcher, was then living at Saranac Lake, New York, where he was undergoing medical treatment for a lung ailment. He had been gassed during the war. McGraw arranged

190

a meeting between Fuchs and Mathewson, and Matty welcomed the chance to head the Boston Braves. He assured Fuchs that his health was improved.

Fuchs gave Grant $50,000 for a thirty-day option on the Braves while he arranged for the purchase, which was announced February 11, 1923. The three new owners were Mathewson, Fuchs, and James MacDonough. Matty was elected president. Fuchs, who owned most of the stock, became vice-president. One of the men behind the scene was Charles A. Levine, the wealthy young adventurer who was to fly the Atlantic with Clarence Chamberlain a few years later.

The selling of the Braves from one New York party to another surprised Boston fans. No sum was mentioned, but Grant was believed to have made a nice profit on his four-year investment. Boston knew Matty well enough, of course, but knew only that Fuchs was a former judge and deputy attorney general of New York State, and that MacDonough was a New York banker with Boston connections.

"I never thought when I saw my first big-league game in Boston that I'd ever be president of the Boston team," Matty told his friends. He recalled that in 1899, while on his way to join Taunton in the old New England League, he had paid seventy-five cents to see Kid Nichols of the Beaneaters pitch against Cy Young of Cleveland at the Walpole Street Grounds.

But it wasn't Matty who was to make the biggest impression on Boston. It was Judge Fuchs. In the thirteen years he was to be connected with the club, the Braves were to experience a succession of weird adventures that would have left even Edgar Rice Burroughs cold and unbelieving. But Boston fans who went along on the wild ride were too dizzy at the finish to have any doubts about the reality of their experience.

Sunday baseball, lawsuits, dog racing, Babe Ruth, a president who made himself manager, Rogers Hornsby, notes and loans and stock snarls, Knot Hole gangs, radio broadcasting, press parties, and statements to the public—is it any wonder that the Braves binge of 1923-35 left Boston fans with the worst hangover they had ever known?

The chief actor in this strange, disconnected drama that was almost a farce but somehow proceeded inexorably to a tragic conclusion was Judge Fuchs. He was always on the stage—short, squat, dark, deliberate, polite, suave. There was an Oriental impassivity to his heavy features, a faint suggestion of menace in his careful cour-

191

tesy. The judge, everyone agreed who knew him, was a character.

He was nearly a millionaire when he bought the Braves, he says, and he wound up bankrupt. Fuchs was a fan who tried hard to be an owner, and Barney Dreyfuss once said that it couldn't be done. Fuchs also tried to be a manager, a financier, and a public-relations man. He was successful as a public-relations man.

Austen Lake of the *Boston American* knew and described him as well as anybody, once writing: "There was a day when Fuchs had it and spent it like a gamblin' man. He would pick up 200 casual guests, some of them pretty rowdy folks, and toss a dinner complete with prohibition wines, fruits-out-of-season, table gifts and variety leg shows.

"He was a sucker for a touch, a pushover for charities and a stooge for ambitious politicians."

Fuchs's best friends were among the press. He cultivated the baseball writers. He liked them; they liked him. He was agreeable, frank, and generous. During one spring training in St. Petersburg, Florida, he threw a gorgeous party for 300 guests. It was a swank party at a ritzy hotel. Judge Landis was there. So were government political figures. An operatic soprano attended. But the honored guest was not one of the big shots. It was Fuchs's close friend, the venerable and humble baseball writer Jim O'Leary.

His two favorite baseball people, says Fuchs, were Christy Mathewson and Ed Cunningham. Cunningham was sports editor of the *Boston Traveler* when Fuchs made him secretary of the Braves in 1926. Cunningham still attends the Judge closely, their friendship having survived all his many misfortunes.

"My board of directors," Fuchs used to call the baseball writers who covered the Braves: Burt Whitman of the *Herald;* John Drohan of the *Traveler;* Jim O'Leary and Mel Webb of the *Globe;* Ed Hurley of the *Record;* Joe Cashman and Nick Flatley of the *American;* and Paul Shannon of the *Post.* He frequently called in his board of directors for consultation. In his most affluent days, when he drew something like $5,000 a month as his salary and paid $1,500 a month for the clubrooms at the Copley-Plaza, they'd drop in of an evening, and he would order costly suppers and dinners, topped off, perhaps, with an act from the hotel floor show or from Keith's. For picking up checks, the Judge was in a class by himself.

Fuchs was born in New York City, April 18, 1878. He went through public school, then graduated from the New York Univer-

192

sity Law School. He served as a magistrate in New York City from 1915 to 1918. In 1922 he was attorney for Ralph A. Day, then federal prohibition director for New York.

He had played baseball only as a catcher on a settlement-house nine, but in spring training he liked to put on a uniform and play a gentle game of catch. It wasn't for this that he bought the Braves, but, as he once said, "I felt I'd be happier trying to make a living from baseball than any other business I know."

Fuchs is an elderly man now, but his mind is still sharp. He likes to go to the Boston ball parks and see the Red Sox and Braves play. He still remembers mistakes he made as a manager. He is not bitter toward baseball, but says, "It is now getting its just reward. It remained a good, clean, honest game while it struggled through adversity, and now is collecting a deserved dividend."

He brought no pennants to Boston, but the Judge feels that he made some worth-while contributions to the game in his adopted city. With a payroll of $80,000 under Grant, the Braves were the National League's Devil's Island. Fuchs boosted the club's payroll to $200,000 and eliminated the prejudice of players against performing for the Braves. He also, at considerable expense to himself, he claims, put over Sunday baseball in Boston. He promoted the game through a Knot Hole gang for boys and frequent Ladies' Days. He signed the first baseball broadcasting contracts for the Boston clubs. The Judge left something for them to remember besides his skill at picking up checks, his jokes, his legal tangles, and his statements.

The new owners kept Mitchell as their manager in 1923. They went along with the club they had inherited from Grant, except that in June they traded the battery of Watson and Gowdy to New York for the battery of Jesse Barnes and Earl (Oil) Smith. The deal was made while the clubs were in the West. Gowdy and Watson were given train tickets from St. Louis to Pittsburgh by Secretary Phil Troy.

Two days later, McGraw called Troy in Chicago and asked, "Where's Watson? He hasn't shown up yet."

Troy laughed and said, "I gave him his ticket. He probably cashed it in. Well, you wanted him."

"Is that so?" barked McGraw. "You haven't seen anything yet. Wait'll you have those guys I sent you for a while."

"Maybe so," said Troy. "But at least I know where they are. You can't even find Watson."

McGraw hung up. The next day Watson appeared. McGraw endured him a year, then said he was through with him. But Giants players pleaded with the manager that he let him pitch, because it might win the 1924 pennant for them. McGraw relented, and Watson helped win the flag.

Before selling the Braves, Grant had sold Holke to Philadelphia and bought John (Stuffy) McInnis from Cleveland on waivers to be the Braves first baseman. McInnis, who had starred for many years with the Athletics and Red Sox, enjoyed his first season in the National League, hitting .315, socking a home run with the bases full, and leading the circuit with thirty-seven sacrifice hits. The only thing he didn't enjoy was lining into a triple play against Pittsburgh.

At second base the Braves used Ford, at third base Boeckel, and at shortstop Bobby Smith, who had been drafted from New Orleans. Southworth, Felix, Powell, Nixon, and Bill Bagwell covered the outfield, while Smith, O'Neil, and Gibson did the catching. The Braves did not have one winning pitcher. Barnes had a 13–15 record, Joe Genewich a 13–14 record, but Tim McNamara won only three of sixteen games, and Joe Oeschger won only five of twenty games.

The Braves were third in mid-May, but they stepped on a banana peel and slid abruptly into the cellar. They had a bruising fight for seventh place all season with the Phils, and won it on the last day of the season by beating the Phils a double-header.

This was an eventful day because a young rookie up from Memphis, Ernie Padgett, made an unassisted triple play—in his second big-league game at shortstop. In the fourth inning, with Cotton Tierney on second base and Cliff Lee on first, and nobody out, Padgett caught Holke's liner, stepped on second, and tagged Lee. It was done so quickly and so simply that everyone wondered why it was the first unassisted triple play in the National League since Paul Hines, Providence outfielder, had made a somewhat dubious triple play against Boston in 1878. Padgett clearly did not know the answer, since he never made another play like it.

In May the Braves had beaten St. Louis, 7–6, in fourteen innings. They filled the bases with none out in the eleventh, but Boeckel lined to Howard Freigau, who started a commonplace triple play that required a couple of throws. Southworth won this game in the fourteenth inning when he hit one of the sixteen home runs that bounced off his bat that season.

Since 1921, Dick Rudolph had been a coach, but on May 17 he

194

decided that he was ready for a comeback. He outpitched Wilbur Cooper to win, 1–0, in ten innings. He allowed only eight hits, three of them to Maranville. He stopped Charlie Grimm, who had hit safely in twenty-five straight games. The Braves won the game in a manner painful to Boeckel. He singled, went to third on McInnis's single, and scored on Felix's grounder to Pie Traynor, because the third baseman's throw home hit him on the head.

"Rudolph Pushed the Headstone off His Tomb," said a morning headline, but he did not push it very far. His arm was as dead and lifeless as a liverwurst, after his one final spasm.

2

Like all owners, especially new and ambitious ones, Mathewson and Fuchs felt that they had to do something drastic before another season began. They thought of something very unusual. They fired the manager.

Fred Mitchell, a wise but deliberate baseball man, was gently removed from his job and made a scout. Replacing him was Dave Bancroft, one of the game's great shortstops. For nine years Banny had been performing miraculous deeds in and around the shortstop's station for the Phils, with whom he started in 1915, and the Giants, to whom he was traded in 1920. If Banny was quick afield, he was even quicker when it came to thinking.

When he joined the Giants in 1920, and was about to play his first game, Pancho Snyder, the catcher, said to him, "Now we'd better go over our signs, young fellow. They'll be new to you, and you've got to know them."

"Have you changed them any lately?" asked the young shortstop.

"No, they're the same, but—"

"Well, never mind," said Bancroft. "I know them already. I knew them when I was with the Phils."

Bancroft, who would be thirty-two years old before another season rolled around, was traded to the Braves along with two outfielders, Charles (Casey) Stengel and Bill Cunningham, November 12, 1923. Stengel was two years older than Bancroft, but a few weeks earlier he had hit two home runs off Yankee pitchers in the World Series, one of which he celebrated by thumbing his nose at the enemy even while circling the bases. "The paths of glory lead only to the Braves," said Stengel, when traded.

195

In return the Braves gave up Southworth, one of the best out-fielders in the league, and also one of the hardest men to sign to a contract, the veteran Oeschger, and an unrevealed amount of money. Bancroft was named manager to succeed Mitchell.

"The Giants without a doubt have given up the best shortstop in baseball," said McGraw, "but we want to help Matty over in Boston, we want to give Banny a chance to manage, and we want to help baseball in general."

The deal was of such magnitude that Fuchs was inspired to give out a statement, one of the first of a thousand or so official communiques he was to issue from his Braves office. The message to the Boston public concluded: "With the added strength just announced, the Braves of 1924 will be fighting it out with the best of them all for the highest honors of the game."

It was a typical Fuchs statement. The Braves finished eighth in 1924.

The worst blow suffered by the unlucky Braves was the death in a San Diego hospital of Tony Boeckel, for five years their third baseman, after an automobile accident. Boeckel and Bob Meusel, of the Yankees, were passengers. They were only shaken up when the car they were in collided with a truck, but a few seconds after the crash, while Boeckel was standing in the highway brushing himself off, he was struck by another car. He was only thirty years old, a happy-go-lucky fellow who was exceptionally popular with Boston fans.

The Braves, nevertheless, were up in the race until Bancroft was operated on for appendicitis July 1. Several days earlier in Philadelphia he had been hit in the stomach by a batted ball, and until he went under the knife was in constant pain. Another subject for an appendectomy was Rube Marquard, who was operated on May 12, and appeared in only six games.

Early in the season, the Braves sold their rowdy catcher, Earl Smith, to Pittsburgh. Smith and Jesse Barnes had each been fined $500 by Bancroft for throwing a chair out of a Philadelphia hotel window. Learning that Smith had thrown the chair, Bancroft returned the $500 to Barnes. Smith, as we shall see, was never to forgive Bancroft.

On July 17, Jesse Haines pitched a no-hit, no-run game against the Braves at St. Louis. Three Braves reached first on passes. On July 19, the Braves went into last place and stayed there for the rest of the season. That was the day that Herman Bell of the Cardinals pitched and won a double-header from the Braves, yielding them two hits in the first game and four hits in the second.

The Braves suffered still another indignity in a game against Chicago, when they had three men thrown out at the plate in one inning. Gabby Hartnett, Chicago catcher, made all three put-outs. Not a hitter in the league's first twenty-five, a pitcher in Jim Yeargin who won one and lost eleven, and not a pitcher who won as many games as he lost—this was how the Braves observed the tenth anniversary of the Miracle Men of 1914.

The most remarkable performance by a Braves player was either Jesse Barnes hurling 268 innings without a wild pitch or hit batsman, or Stuffy McInnis striking out only six times and drawing fifteen bases on balls in 146 games. Neither one, however, was given the key to the city.

So far as the Braves were concerned, the 1925 season began with a bang. In batting practice on April 10, a few days before the campaign opened, Bernie Neis drove a ball over the distant left-field fence. That had never been done even in practice since the park was opened August 18, 1915.

Players rubbed their eyes, and asked, "Was that a baseball or a golf ball you hit, Bernie?"

Neis, a rugged little 165-pounder who was a switch hitter, nonchalantly replied, "I must have muscles in my hair."

But Neis's wallop was no accident. The ball was full of bounce in 1925. The Braves turned in one of their highest batting averages, .292, yet were only fifth in batting. The Pirates led with an average of .307.

Frank (Pancho) Snyder, burly Giant catcher, drove the first official home run over the left-field fence. With the score tied 6–6, in the eighth inning on May 28, he teed off on Larry Benton's first pitch. The ball cleared the fence by about twenty feet, some fifteen feet from the left-field foul line.

But Snyder was not for long undisputed king of Braves Field sluggers. In the first game against St. Louis on July 7, with the score 1–1 in the fourth inning, Neis hammered a pitch by Art Reinhart, a southpaw, over the left-field wall and onto the Boston & Albany railroad tracks. This was a longer wallop than Snyder's, for it cleared the fence fifty feet from the foul line and cleared it by a greater margin.

For ten years nobody had homered over the left-field wall, which Ty Cobb once predicted would never be cleared, and then it was carried twice within six weeks.

Neis was one of several new players in Bancroft's line-up in 1925. He came from Brooklyn in exchange for Cotton Tierney. The veteran McInnis was given his unconditional release the day before the season opened, to make way for Maurice (Dick) Burrus, a methodical young man who had been drafted from Atlanta the previous fall. Burrus batted .340 to lead Boston hitters.

Second base was taken care of by Padgett and Walter (Doc) Gautreau. The latter was a lively, pocket-edition big leaguer from Cambridge who had starred for Holy Cross before signing with the Athletics. The Braves got him in July on waivers.

Bill Marriott played third base, until Andy High was acquired on waivers from Brooklyn in July. In the outfield the Braves had Jimmy Welsh, the choke-hitter for whom they had paid Seattle the equivalent of $50,000, Dave (Sheriff) Harris, Gus Felix, Les Mann, and Neis. Casey Stengel was released to manage the Braves farm team at Worcester. In May he was made president of the club, which resulted in one of baseball's strangest episodes.

With a chance to manage Toledo in 1926, Stengel wanted his release from the Boston club, to whom he still belonged. Fearing that Fuchs would not release him, Manager Stengel sat down and wrote a letter to President Stengel, asking for his immediate release. President Stengel at once granted the favor, no doubt having always held Manager Stengel in high esteem.

Judge Landis offered to declare the transaction null and void, but Fuchs said, "Never mind. If that's the way Stengel works, let him go. We'll be better off without him."

The Braves finished fifth in 1925. They were in last place until September, then uncorked a sprint. They might have reached the first division, if they had not lost sixteen of twenty-two games to the seventh-place Phils.

Larry Benton, a right-hander who had been bought from Memphis after the 1922 season, was the leading pitcher, with a 14–7 record. Genewich won twelve, lost ten games, and Johnny Cooney won fourteen and lost the same number. Gibson and O'Neil again handled the pitchers.

The National League's Golden Jubilee celebration was held at Braves Field, May 8. George Wright, who had participated in the

198

first game played by this Boston team fifty-five years earlier, and five years before the National League was formed, helped raise the flag. Also present were Honest John Morrill, Jack Manning, and Bill Conant, one of the Triumvirs. The Braves beat Chicago, 5–2, to make the old fellows feel at home.

3

The World Series of 1925, between the Pirates and Washington Senators, opened in Pittsburgh, October 7. The day before, the Braves had traded Barnes, Felix, and O'Neil to Brooklyn for Catcher Zach Taylor, and Outfielders Ed Brown and Jim Johnston. Judge Fuchs was quite amiable as he played bridge the next evening, even though the Pirates had lost the first game of the Series.

Bill McGeehan of the *Herald Tribune* entered the room, paused, and said, "Silence, gentlemen. I have some bad news for you. Christy Mathewson passed away today at Saranac."

Mathewson had been president of the Braves for three years. When he had taken the job, his doctor told him, "You'll last about two years if you go back to baseball."

So Matty went back to baseball. He spent no great amount of time in Boston, for he had to return frequently to Saranac Lake for medical treatment. Judge Fuchs ran the club. Once in a while Matty had his say, as when the ballplayers held out for more meal money. Phil Troy had limited them to four dollars a day, which in those days would have fed an average eater for a week.

"Four dollars isn't enough. We're starving," complained the players, who had been signing checks for all amounts, much to the joy of friends who dined with them. They went to Fuchs and protested.

"Let them sign their checks," Fuchs told Troy. "What difference does it make?"

But it made a difference when Mathewson saw the meal tabs. He called Troy, got the story, and then sailed into Fuchs. To Matty a ballplayer was only a ballplayer. They didn't like him, and he was not especially fond of them. The Braves meal limit went back to four dollars a day.

Shortly after Matty died, Fuchs was elected president of the Braves. Albert H. Powell, wealthy New Haven coal and real-estate man who had been buying stock in the club, became vice-president.

Several weeks after the 1926 season opened, on May 28, a tablet in Mathewson's memory was unveiled at Braves Field. It read:

In Memory of
Christopher Mathewson
Born—Factoryville, Pennsylvania
August 12, 1880
Died—Saranac Lake, New York
October 7, 1925
Gallant Sportsman
Courageous Soldier   Kindly Gentleman
"E'en as he trod this day to God, so walked he from his birth
In simpleness and gentleness and honour, and clean mirth."

It was during this season that a crisis developed in the ownership of the Braves. Powell came very close, a mere matter of twenty-five shares it is said, to getting control of the club. When he failed, he sold his stock to James V. Giblin for a reported $175,000. Giblin was a lawyer and public accountant from Fall River.

In midseason, irregularities in the Braves Field turnstiles, which may have cost the club as much as $50,000, were discovered. A shake-up in the front office personnel found Ed Cunningham, Boston sports editor, appointed the club's new home secretary.

The Braves slumped to seventh place in 1926. They had more trouble beating second-division teams than clubs in the upper flight. At home Banny's team won forty-four games. On the road it won only half as many. The Braves had most of their fun late in September when they harassed three pennant contenders, winning three out of four games from the Cardinals, three straight from Cincinnati, and two out of three from Pittsburgh.

One hilarious episode occurred in Brooklyn when, with bases filled and the score tied, 1-to-1, Babe Herman of the Dodgers doubled into a double play. As Vance rounded third, followed closely by Fewster and Herman, the Brooklyn third-base coach, Mickey O'Neil, shouted, "Hold up!" to Herman.

Vance thought the command was meant for him, and he slid back into third just as Herman slid in from the other side. Caught between them without any place to slide was poor Fewster. Herman was called out for passing Fewster, and Fewster was called out when Gautreau chased him into right field and tagged him.

"The trouble is," said Gautreau, "we don't play enough in Brooklyn."

200

Although Banny hit .311 and Henry Wertz, up from Worcester, was the only winning pitcher with an 11-to-9 record, the team's outstanding player was Ed Brown, the outfielder acquired from Brooklyn. He batted .328 and led the league by making 201 hits, few of them for extra bases.

Charles F. Adams and Bruce Wetmore, Boston businessmen, entered the Braves picture in 1927. Judge Fuchs was introduced to them by Edwin W. Preston, general manager of the *Boston Herald*, and they bought the stock originally owned by Powell and held by Giblin. Adams became vice-president. But for Adams, Fuchs might have had to sell his interest in the club.

The Braves again finished seventh, in their worst stretch losing fifteen consecutive games on the road. Lance Richbourg, an outfielder bought from Milwaukee; Eddie Farrell, an infielder who came from the Giants with Pitchers Hugh McQuillan and Kent Greenfield for Zack Taylor, Larry Benton, and Herb Thomas in a June trade; Jack Fournier, veteran first baseman signed after being released by Brooklyn; and J. Francis (Shanty) Hogan, a catcher now, but an outfielder when he got out of Somerville High School and played his first big-league game with the Braves the year before—these were new Braves regulars.

Brown set a National League record when he played in his five hundred and thirty-fourth consecutive game August 22, breaking the old record held by Fred Luderos. Johnny Cooney's arm went dead, and he did not pitch a game all season. He decided to start life anew as an outfielder.

Before Benton was traded to the Giants, he grooved a pitch for Big George Kelly, and Cincinnati's second baseman socked it over the left-field wall at Braves Field, thus joining Snyder and Neis as members of the lodge. Since Snyder had also hit his cross-country clout off Benton, teammates wondered how the pitcher would welcome the abbreviated Polo Grounds foul lines. He only became the league's leading pitcher with the Giants.

The Braves got tangled up, as usual, in extra-inning games. On May 14 they went eighteen innings against the Cubs, with the Cubs winning, 7–2. In their next game, May 17, they went twenty-two innings against the Cubs, with the visitors again winning, 4–3. Bobby Smith, the converted infielder, pitched the entire twenty-two innings against three Chicago pitchers. He yielded the winning run when Hack Wilson walked, Riggs Stephenson sacrificed, and Charlie

Grimm singled to center. This gave the Braves a record of forty innings played in two consecutive games—for two consecutive defeats.

It was a rough season for poor Banny, whose hair by now was fast turning silver. In Pittsburgh he ran afoul Earl Smith, who was still demanding the return of his $500 fine. Bancroft ignored the burly catcher, until just as he crossed the plate with a run, Smith swung, hit him on the jaw, and knocked him unconscious. Bancroft was woozy for two days, Smith was suspended for thirty days and fined $500. When Smith subsequently visited Boston, he had to climb over the back fence at Braves Field to escape being served a warrant by which Banny hoped to collect $15,000. He sprained an ankle in the process. *The Sporting News* headed its editorial on the episode, "Blackguards Always Are Cowards."

After the season, Dick Rudolph, who had been with the club for fifteen years, was released. Phil Troy, who had started out as the club's telephone operator in 1914 and been road secretary seven years, resigned. And Bancroft was told to make a deal for himself. He signed with Brooklyn. Of the $30,000 paid by the Dodgers, Bancroft got $20,000 as a bonus, and Fuchs took $10,000 for the minority stockholders.

Banny had proved to be an easy-going manager. Burt Whitman wrote in the *Herald:* "I feel that he cared immensely about playing shortstop and about going up there to bat in his turn, but never did enjoy himself thoroughly as a manager. He was the ball player first and last, not the manager."

New York Giants manager John McGraw meets with Christy Mathewson, his former star pitcher and the Braves president, and Braves owner Judge Emil Fuchs at spring training camp in St. Petersburg, Florida, March 1923. Within two years, Mathewson died of tuberculosis and the effects of trench gassing from his service in World War I. Courtesy of G. Altison

Veteran pitcher Richard "Rube" Marquard played the last four seasons of his Hall of Fame career with the Braves. In Boston he won 25 games and lost 39. The team finished near the bottom of the National League. In 1923 he was reunited with Christy Mathewson, a New York Giants teammate from 1908 to 1915, when Mathewson served as Braves president. Courtesy of G. Altison

New York Giants manager John McGraw was afraid Rogers Hornsby would undermine his authority, so he traded his superstar to the Boston Braves for a catching prospect, Shanty Hogan, and an outfielder, Jimmie Welsh. In 1928, his only season as a Brave, Hornsby won his seventh National League batting championship with an average of .387. He also led the league in walks (107) and slugging percentage (.632). Courtesy of the Sports Museum of New England

Braves owner Judge Emil Fuchs enjoyed donning a uniform and sharing the fun with friends. He is shown here with golfer Walter Hagan, business mogul Jack Taylor, and Braves pitcher and future Hall of Famer Rube Marquard during spring training in 1925. Courtesy of Robert Fuchs

"Sunday Baseball Cliffhanger" (July 13, 1930) by Gene Mack. When Sunday baseball was finally allowed in Boston, it came with the legal restriction that no inning start after 5:40 P.M. In the second game of a twin bill with the Cubs, the Braves won on a technicality. An eighth inning foul ball stint by Rabbit Maranville prevented the Cubs from finishing the game by the six o'clock curfew. They dropped both ends of the doubleheader. Courtesy of the Sports Museum of New England

Wally Berger, shown with Babe Ruth at spring training in 1935, stands as the greatest slugger in Boston Braves history. He clouted 199 home runs in eight seasons, most of them in the large expanse of Braves Field against a prevailing north wind. Though Ruth dominated headlines in 1935, it was Berger who carried the hapless Braves in their worst season with 34 homers and 130 RBI, tops in the National League. Courtesy of the National Baseball Hall of Fame

Fred Frankhouse by Gene Mack (1934). Right-hander Fred Frankhouse came to Boston via a trade with the St. Louis Cardinals for future Hall of Fame pitcher Burleigh Grimes. Frankhouse anchored the Braves pitching staff for five seasons. In 1934, his best year, he won 17 games and lost 9. Courtesy of Richard A. Johnson

On opening day in 1935, Babe Ruth thrilled a less-than-capacity crowd at Braves Field with a home run hit off fellow Hall of Famer Carl Hubbell. Courtesy of the Sports Museum of New England

Dizzy Dean and Babe Ruth at Braves Field. In his first at bats against fellow Hall of Famer Dizzy Dean on May 5, 1935, Babe Ruth struck out, walked, and grounded out. Before the game the two greeted fans and shared stories with a mob of reporters. Courtesy of the Sports Museum of New England

"The Braves Become the Bees" by Gene Mack (1936). The Braves changed their name to the Bees in 1936. Team president Bob Quinn pressed for the ballpark to be called the "Beehive" in print, but it retained the name Braves Field. The Bees fared no better than the Braves, and returned to their former appellation in 1941. Courtesy of Richard A. Johnson

Johnny Cooney spent 15 of 20 seasons with the Boston Braves. The son and brother of major league shortstops, he started as a pitcher and won 34 games before an operation shortened both his arm and his pitching career. Later, as an outfielder, Cooney batted .286 in 1,172 games. Cooney was well respected. Once, when the boat carrying the umpires failed to arrive in Boston, he umpired the game against the Giants. Both teams agreed he called a fair game in his unprecedented role. Courtesy of the Maxwell Collection

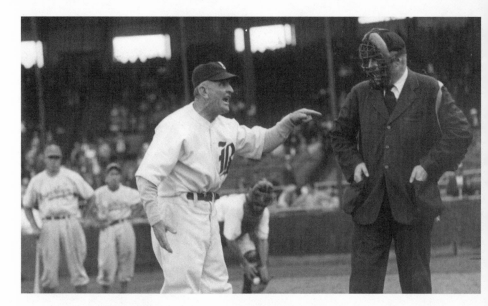

Casey Stengel makes his point, 1942. In 1938 Casey Stengel succeeded fellow Hall of Famer Bill McKechnie as manager of the Boston Bees. That year, the Bees reached fifth place. After that, the team lost an average of 90 games a season, perpetually mired in seventh place. Hall of Famer Warren Spahn, who pitched for Stengel with both the Braves and the Mets, remarked that he "played for Casey before and after he was a genius." Courtesy of the Maxwell Collection

"Casey Stengel Celebrates" by Gene Mack (1942). Manager Casey Stengel celebrates a rare Braves sweep in a doubleheader against the Phillies at Braves Field in 1942. The victories didn't save Stengel's job. Stengel departed Boston with a 59–89 win-loss record, good only for seventh place. Courtesy of Richard A. Johnson

Tommy Holmes signing autographs for fans outside Braves Field. After starring with the Newark Triple A farm team of the New York Yankees, Tommy Holmes got his chance at the majors with the Boston Braves. Holmes became the people's choice, the darling of the right-field jury box crowd. In 1945 Holmes led the league with 28 home runs, 224 hits, 47 doubles, and a .577 slugging percentage. With his 37-game hitting streak, he achieved a league record. He earned Player of the Year honors from the *Sporting News*. Courtesy of J. Brooks

The Braves were the first of the Boston teams to play under the lights when they faced the Giants on May 11, 1946, at Braves Field. Eventually, they played their night games in special satin uniforms, designed to enhance their appearance on another new addition on the baseball scene, the television. Courtesy of the Sports Museum of New England

The Boston Braves started the Jimmy Fund in 1947. Radio personality Ralph Edwards and several Braves players visited a boy known simply as "Jimmy" at Children's Hospital in Boston. The program inspired countless contributions, including this television to the Dana Farber Cancer Center. "Jimmy" was later revealed to be Einar Gustafson of New Sweden, Maine. Following the Brave's move to Milwaukee in 1953, the Red Sox adopted the Jimmy Fund. Courtesy of the Jimmy Fund

"The Spirit of '14 and '48" by Gene Mack. The Braves' pennant-winning season of 1948 invited comparisons with the Miracle Campaign of 1914. Courtesy of Richard A. Johnson

The 1948 National League Champions. Courtesy of Richard A. Johnson

"1948 Braves Highlights" by Gene Mack. Gene Mack sketched from the Braves Field press box and delivered a daily cartoon to the *Boston Globe* sports page. Mack, a relative of Connie Mack, was one of the great sports cartoonists during the golden age of the medium. Before ESPN and the daily "top ten," Mack captured the drama and style of the defining moments of each game he covered. Courtesy of Richard A. Johnson

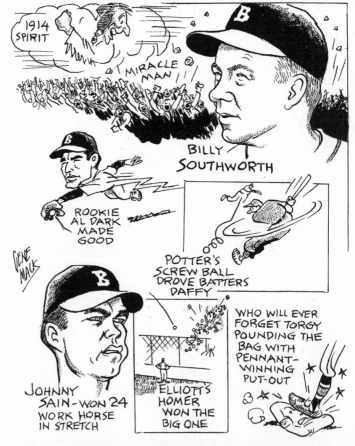

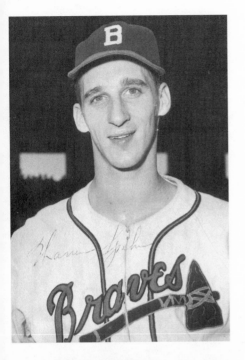

▲◄ Warren Spahn was the winningest left-handed pitcher of them all. He won 122 of his 363 victories in seven seasons with the Boston Braves. Casey Stengel sent Spahn back to the Hartford Chiefs as a rookie in 1942. His next uniform was that of an infantryman. Spahn served with distinction in combat and returned to Boston a decorated war hero. Courtesy of J. Brooks

▲ After his rejection by the Red Sox in April 1945, outfielder Sam Jethroe returned to Boston with a vengeance in 1950. Jethroe spent the better part of his career with the Cleveland Buckeyes of the Negro League, but he earned Rookie of the Year honors at age thirty-two. In his three seasons in Boston, Jethroe batted .261 with 49 home runs and 98 stolen bases. Courtesy of G. Altison

◄ Eddie Matthews, the only Brave to play in Boston, Milwaukee, and Atlanta, was the 1952 National League Rookie of the Year. His good looks and powerful swing made him a fan favorite during the team's glory days in Milwaukee in the late fifties. Courtesy of the Sports Museum of New England

When the National League pennant was unfurled in April 1949, it had been thirty-four years since a championship banner had flown over Braves Field. Fans didn't suspect that their team would play in Boston for only four more seasons, before heading to Milwaukee, the home of their Triple A affiliate. Courtesy of G. Altison

Braves Field was the largest ballpark in the country in 1915. It hosted two World Series for the Red Sox, one for the Braves, an all-star game, NFL football, Holy Cross and Boston College football and baseball, and countless schoolboy games. Its proximity to the rail yards symbolized the strong connection between the Braves and Boston's working and immigrant classes. Courtesy of Boston University Archives

CHAPTER XX

THE BOSTON PUNCHING BAG

☺

It was always a question of which talked louder and more often, Rogers Hornsby's bat or his tongue. He used both to express himself clearly, forcefully, and in a manner that left no doubt as to his intentions. The only difference was that his bat brought grief to the opposition, while his tongue brought trouble to himself and innocent bystanders.

One such innocent bystander was Jack Slattery, who was named manager of the Braves for 1928 after Dave Bancroft was released. A native of Jamaica Plain, a Boston suburb, and a graduate of Fordham University, Slattery had been a catcher of modest abilities with the Red Sox, Chicago White Sox, St. Louis Browns, and Washington. He had caught Nick Altrock and also Walter Johnson when he was young. Slattery had coached the Braves under Stallings in 1918 and 1919, replacing Fred Mitchell, who had become coach at Harvard. And Slattery had also coached Tufts College, Boston College, and Harvard.

"Slattery was sold to me by my board of directors," Fuchs has said, pinning the responsibility of Slattery's choice on Boston baseball writers. "He was a local man, and popular with writers and fans."

And whereas Bancroft had received a salary of nearly $20,000, Slattery would work for $10,000. Slattery did not get a fair shake. Circumstances lined up against him. When he was named manager November 2, 1927, Judge Fuchs issued a statement:

"We feel that we have in Mr. Slattery a well-grounded, matured judge of the game of baseball; a man of judgment, and while possessing the milk of human kindness, has the asset of firmness and the knowledge and demeanor which will instil confidence in the men under him."

203

On January 10, 1928, two days after they had signed him to a two-year contract, the Giants traded Rogers Hornsby to the Braves for Shanty Hogan and Jimmy Welsh. Since Hornsby had hit .361 the previous season and was recognized as one of baseball's greatest batsmen, there had to be a story behind the trade.

The story was variously reported as (1) Hornsby's desire to succeed McGraw as manager of the Giants, (2) Hornsby's throwing of Charles A. Stoneham, president of the Giants, out of the clubhouse after the loss of a game, and (3) Hornsby's altercations with Jim Tierney, secretary of the club and a pal of Stoneham's.

Hornsby has said that his trouble was with Tierney, not McGraw or Stoneham. Late in the 1927 season he became acting manager of the Giants when McGraw was ill. After a defeat in Chicago, according to Hornsby, Tierney began to blast Travis Jackson for making a costly error.

"You run your end, and I'll run mine," Hornsby told him. "Furthermore, see that our players are treated right at the hotels, and don't be grabbing off all the best accommodations for yourself."

Hornsby, according to the contract the Braves had assumed, was to get $40,000 a season. He was made captain and received $600 more. When the Braves reported to spring training, it was Hornsby, not Slattery, who got the play. Slattery was just the college coach trying to find his way around the majors. Hornsby was the star who had managed the St. Louis Cardinals to the world championship only two years earlier. Hornsby was getting four times as much money as Slattery.

"Where's Hornsby?" a visiting writer asked Slattery during a practice session.

"Look around until you see a guy swinging three bats," replied the manager. "That'll be Hornsby."

The writer looked around until he saw a player swinging three bats. It was Hornsby.

Rumors of trouble in the South filtered back to Boston. Hornsby was popping off about the way Slattery was running the club. There was no skull practice, no instruction, he complained. This might be all right for a college team, but it wasn't all right for a big-league club.

Early in April, Slattery was called back to Boston. It was somewhat unusual for a manager to leave his team just before the season was to open. It was expected that Slattery would be fired. There

204

were signs of rebellion in the press. Fuchs could read, and Slattery wasn't fired. He had just returned to Boston, he said, on a routine business trip. He said, "No one is closer to me than Captain Hornsby, who will be a wonderful help and inspiration. The spirit of the club is wonderful."

Six weeks later, when the Braves ended a dismal western trip, Slattery resigned as manager. Because of his growing reputation as an underminer of managers, Hornsby said that he would rather be traded than succeed Slattery, but he let Judge Fuchs change his mind. The Judge announced: "We shall continue in our efforts to build up a fighting and winning club for Boston."

The Braves finished seventh. They played .333 ball for Slattery, .325 ball for Hornsby. Altogether they won only fifty games. Still, it was a successful season for Hornsby, if not for the Braves. He batted .387 to lead the league in hitting and set a modern Braves hitting record. When players today complain that the east wind ruins hitters in Boston, managers always point to Hornsby, and say, "He played here a whole season and hit .387."

Hornsby seemed as much interested in his average as in the Braves. At that time, the sacrifice fly helped averages. On at least one occasion Hornsby bawled out a Boston runner on first base for not advancing to second when the great Rajah had hit a long fly to the outfield.

"Why didn't you go down?" growled Hornsby. "You cost me a time at bat."

Hornsby had the advantage, too, of a smaller playing field. The previous fall, Judge Fuchs had announced that stands would be built in left and center fields so that Shanty Hogan could hit more home runs. The trading of Hogan for Hornsby did not change the Judge's mind. The stands, which seated 6,500 persons, drastically changed the park, cutting the left-field line from 402 feet to 353 feet and center field from 550 feet to 387 feet. In left center the fence was only 330 feet away from the plate.

As so often happens when an easy target is set up, the wrong side hits the bull's-eye. By the middle of June, the opposition had hit thirty-two homers into the new stands to fifteen for the Braves. Judge Fuchs admitted that he had made a grave mistake, and had a thirty-foot canvas erected in front of the bleachers to stop cheap home runs. But before he did, Lester Bell, third baseman who had been acquired from St. Louis in a trade for Andy High, hit three homers in one game, and added a triple besides.

If Hornsby's luster as a manager gained no polish by the Braves' showing in 1928, neither did it tarnish much. He was tough enough, actually challenging the whole team when he found several of them smushed. There were no takers.

"I don't smoke, drink, or chew. I can hit to left, center, and right. They call me a great player. If you live like I do, you can be a great player, too," Hornsby told the Braves. They did everything but yawn in his face.

The Braves had for their road secretary in 1928 the manager of the Bruins, Boston's professional hockey team, Arthur H. Ross. He didn't get along with Hornsby either. When Ross left in the fall to start hockey practice, he said, "Well, I'm on my way to Montreal. See you later."

"So long," said Hornsby. Just like that!

On August 30 it was announced that Hornsby had been signed to a six-year contract, although it was obvious to everyone that if the Braves had to pay Hornsby $40,000 a year for six years, losing money at the rate they lost it in 1928, the club would wind up bankrupt. Come to think of it, the club became practically bankrupt without Hornsby—but it took longer.

A seventh-place team probably never had a more eventful season than the 1928 Braves. They scored only one shutout during the season, Ed Brandt, a rookie southpaw, pitching it in April against Brooklyn. Ed Brown stretched his playing string to 618 consecutive games until Hornsby benched him June 8 against Pittsburgh. At St. Louis, Lance Richbourg batted in six runs in the first three innings, with a homer in the first, a double with bases full in the second, and a triple with two on in the third.

George Sisler, whose eyes were supposed to be bothering him, was bought from Washington late in May and played first base the rest of the season. If he couldn't see, the thirty-five-year-old veteran felt his way to a .340 average.

Between September 4 and September 15, the Braves played nine consecutive double-headers. They lost five of these in a row, one to the Phils and four to the Giants. But the most important of the 103 games they lost was to the Cardinals the next to last day of the season, for that victory clinched the pennant for St. Louis.

Few Novembers have been as productive of important baseball events in Boston as that of 1928. The order of importance was as follows:

1. The sports referendum that would permit baseball to play on Sundays ended in a sweeping victory at the polls, after Judge Fuchs had backed a long campaign to have the measure passed.

2. Hornsby was traded to the Chicago Cubs in a $200,000 deal that brought the Braves a fine defensive second baseman in Freddy Maguire, three unproven pitchers in Percy Jones, Bruce Cunningham, and Harry Seibold, and a substitute catcher in Louis (Doc) Legett.

3. Judge Fuchs announced that, under the persuasion of Vice-President Adams, he would act as manager of the 1929 Braves, with the assistance of Johnny Evers.

In getting through the Sunday sports bill, Fuchs ran into all kinds of legal and political trouble. City councilors were alleged to have solicited bribes, there were hearings before the Financial Commission, and the attorney-general's office made an investigation. The councilors were cleared of having solicited bribes, but the Financial Commission blasted some of them and Mayor Malcolm Nichols for intimacy with the Braves.

Credit for putting the Sunday sports bill across went to the Outdoor Recreation League, headed by Claude B. Davidson, but Fuchs admits he spent close to $200,000 out of his own pocket. A million booklets and four million sample ballots were printed. Placards were placed in every streetcar. Fuchs pleaded *nolo contendere* to a charge of spending money to influence the vote on Sunday baseball and the Braves were fined $1,000 in Municipal Court.

About the same time they scored their victory over the Sunday blue law, the Braves traded Hornsby to Chicago. It was bruited about that the Giants had really paid Hornsby's $40,000 salary in 1928, and that they made this deal, but as Judge Fuchs tells the story, Hornsby was disposed of in this fashion:

Late in the season, when the Braves were in Chicago on their last western trip, Hornsby went to Fuchs and said, "Judge, what you need is a young club. Now, I have about one year left and could help Chicago. Why don't you let me make a deal for myself with Chicago? It would help everybody concerned."

207

Hornsby talked to Bill Veeck, Sr., in the latter's box at Wrigley Field, and apparently persuaded the president of the Cubs that he could do the Chicago team some good. Veeck called Fuchs, and asked, "What do you want for Hornsby?"

Fuchs couldn't tell him, he said, because he would have to talk to his board of directors. A meeting was arranged for Buffalo in November. Joe McCarthy was then managing the Cubs and lived in Buffalo. Besides, a grocery convention in Buffalo then made it possible for C. F. Adams to be present. This was important to the Braves, Fuchs said, "because Adams was a thousand times better businessman than I."

At the meeting in the Statler Hotel, Veeck immediately offered $50,000 and Maguire for Hornsby.

Adams protested, "But Hornsby has just won the batting championship. I'll tell you what we'll do. The Braves will give two hundred thousand dollars for any two Chicago players."

"Take it," said McCarthy to Veeck.

"You write out an agreement, and I'll write out a check," said Adams.

Veeck hedged. He asked, "Who will you take?"

"Cuyler and Hartnett," replied Adams.

Veeck shrugged. He said, "I'd lose my job. Wrigley would fire me. Now what do you want for Hornsby?"

Adams said, "One hundred thousand dollars and five players."

Veeck called up William Wrigley, Jr. on the long-distance telephone. He said, "They want one hundred thousand dollars and five players. That's one hundred thousand dollars and three players too much."

Wrigley's answer was short, for Veeck immediately hung up. He explained, "He said to give it to you."

The ballplayers the Braves received amounted to little, although Maguire was the Braves second baseman through 1931, and Socks Seibold was a starting but losing pitcher for four seasons. The cash came in handy, however, for with half of it the Braves a year later bought Wally Berger from the Chicago farm at Los Angeles.

If the prospect of Sunday baseball caused Boston fans to cheer and the Hornsby deal made them jeer, the revelation that Judge Fuchs himself would be the bench manager in 1929 made them leer. Fuchs insists that it was Adams's idea, and this is believable, since Adams was a businessman who would be likely to think of saving a

208

manager's salary by letting the club president take over his duties. But as he quickly learned, a manager is not so unimportant that anyone who can distinguish between a sacrifice bunt and a home run can be one successfully.

"If I don't make good," said Fuchs, "no one will realize it quicker than I, and it will be perfectly simple for me, as president, to remove myself as manager."

President John A. Heydler of the National League was cool to the idea, but Fuchs insisted: "The time has gone when a manager has to chew tobacco and talk from the side of his mouth. I don't think our club can do any worse with me as manager than it has done the last few years."

That's where the Judge was wrong. For the first time in six years, the Braves were to finish last.

Other owners had tried managing their teams, starting with Chris Von der Ahe of the St. Louis Browns in the 1880's. Charlie Ebbets had finished out a season as manager in Brooklyn, and Andrew Friedman had tried managing the Giants prior to McGraw. Friedman not only landed the Giants in the cellar, but he tried to convert Christy Mathewson from a pitcher to a first baseman. Fuchs didn't go that far.

Fuchs believed in playing unorthodox baseball. In his first spring-training game, he took out a left-handed hitter, Ernie Padgett, for a right-handed pinch hitter, Zach Taylor, with a right-hander, Jack Quinn, pitching.

"You can't do it!" shouted Evers, Fuchs's assistant. "It's crazy."

But Taylor batted and won the game with a single. The next day Evers apologized to the Judge before the players, saying, "I want to apologize for losing my temper, not because the play worked. The Judge is going to do some unorthodox things, but I'm willing to string along with him." The Judge seriously accepted the apology of one of the smartest baseball players who ever lived. Nobody was unkind enough to snicker.

Stories, no doubt exaggerated, are still told in Boston of Judge Fuchs, the Braves manager. One day, with bases full and nobody out in a close game, he reputedly turned to the bench and asked, "What shall we try now, boys?"

"What about a squeeze play?" someone replied.

"A squeeze? No," protested the Judge. "Let us score our runs in an honorable way."

209

The Braves had acquired Joe Dugan, a fine third baseman for the Yankees in his palmy days, on waivers. One day Fuchs told Dugan to play shortstop, and the veteran quipped, with a wink, "Where is shortstop on this field?"

"Show Mr. Dugan where the clubhouse is and how to take off his uniform," commanded the Judge coldly.

The Braves were losing to Jumbo Elliott, a capable Philadelphia southpaw, when Fuchs turned to Ed Brandt, a left-handed pitcher and hitter in the ninth, and said, "Ed, you go up now and hit."

Brandt looked horrified, and protested, "Me? Why, Judge, that fellow out there is left-handed."

Fuchs studied Elliott a moment, and admitted, "So he is."

The Judge has always enjoyed telling stories. The Braves had a 5-to-0 lead on one occasion when he gathered the players around to tell them his latest rib buster, the one starting, "Now there was one fellow named Pat and another named Mike. . . ."

Five minutes later Bob Smith shouted, "Hey, Judge. The score is tied, the bases are full, and there's no one out. Better get a pitcher ready."

"Oh, yes," said the Judge, irritated at being interrupted. "Art, run down to the bull pen and get warmed up. I'll tell you the rest of the story when you get back."

The Judge still doesn't think he was a failure as a manager. A reporter recently interviewing Fuchs asked, "Judge, tell me some of the funny things that happened while you were manager."

"Young man," said the Judge, rising hastily, but putting his arm about the reporter's shoulders affectionately, as he escorted him to the door, "the interview is ended."

The Braves made a fine start under Fuchs, winning seven of nine games in April. The Judge had surrounded himself with stars of the 1914 team, Maranville having been bought from the Cardinals and Hank Gowdy returning from Rochester as a player-coach. When the Braves showed signs of slipping, as they did in May, they lost Fuchs as manager. He had a big law case coming up in New York.

It was decided that Maranville should replace him as manager, but the Rabbit asked for a five-year contract, and Fuchs, in view of the Rabbit's unfortunate experience as manager of the Cubs in 1925, was willing to give him only a one-year contract until he had shown his ability to manage himself, as well as the team. Maranville refused, and the Braves stumbled along with Evers as acting manager.

210

Occasionally, Fuchs exercised his prerogative and sat on the bench.

The Braves were in last place from August 19 to the end of the season. They lost eleven games in a row in their worst stretch. Sisler batted .326 to lead the team's hitters. Harry Seibold won the most games, but had seventeen defeats against his twelve victories. The Braves had a remarkable collection of fading stars in Sisler, George Washington Harper, Dugan, Gowdy, Lester Bell, Maranville, and Maguire. Even Evers, forty-six years old, got into one game, the last game of his colorful big-league career. All he did was to make one error in the field.

With Bobby Smith pitching against Cincinnati on May 10, Earl Clark bounced off the fences to make twelve put-outs, a record that still stands. There were a few flies Clark couldn't reach. Cincinnati won the game, 5–3.

The Braves would have played the first Sunday game in Boston, but it rained April 21, and their contest with the Giants was postponed. Thus, the privilege went to the Red Sox, who could not play Sunday baseball at Fenway Park because of the proximity of a church. The Athletics beat the Sox, 7–3, April 28 at Braves Field. A week later, the Braves played their first Sunday game at home, losing to Pittsburgh, 7–2.

This game produced a weird triple play. With Heinie Mueller on third base, Rabbit Maranville on first, and nobody out, Al Spohrer bounced the ball back to Pitcher Burleigh Grimes. Mueller was caught in a run down, Spohrer was caught trying to reach second, and Maranville was caught trying to score.

One day Mueller, the player who is supposed to have built a hen coop in his cellar and then been unable to get it out the cellar door, tried to sacrifice a runner home. There was a run down, and the runner was tagged out despite Mueller's coaching. Then the ball was thrown to first for a double play. Mueller screamed that he hadn't run because his bunt was foul. Evers shooed him gently off the field.

On another occasion, with Harper on second and Dugan on first, Maranville singled to left, scoring Harper. When Lefty O'Doul threw the ball to third base, Maranville raced for second. As he slid in, he saw Dugan looked down on him, grinning, and asking, "What in hell are you doing here?"

Maranville scrambled to his feet and headed for first, saying, "Nothing. I'm on my way back."

All misplays of this nature in 1929 were attributed to Judge Fuchs, the president who aspired to be a manager. But to prove again his good nature, the Judge threw his customary party for "his boys" and friends at the close of the season.

3

The day before the 1929 World Series began, the Braves had a new manager in Bill McKechnie, the same McKechnie who had played one game for George Stallings on the 1913 Braves, and then had been waived to the New York Americans. Although he had batted only .134 for New York, Frank Chance used him in forty-four games at second base. Asked why, Chance replied, "Because McKechnie knew more baseball than the rest of my team put together."

McKechnie was another of those mediocre ballplayers who turn out to be excellent managers. Wilkinsburg Will managed the Pittsburgh Pirates from July, 1922, when he succeeded George Gibson, until 1926, when he was released because of dissension on the club brought about by the interference of Vice-President Fred Clarke. Under McKechnie, the Pirates finished third four times, and won the pennant once—in 1925—and took a seven-game World Series from Washington.

His next chance to manage a big-league team was with the St. Louis Cardinals in 1928. The Cardinals won the pennant, but were pulverized in the World Series by the mighty Yankees, losing four straight games, with Babe Ruth hitting three home runs in the final contest. Sam Breadon, president of the Cardinals, was so irked that he demoted McKechnie to Rochester, New York, in 1929, and promoted Billy Southworth from Rochester to manage the Cards. By July, Southworth had been replaced by McKechnie, under whom the Cardinals finished fourth.

"I made a mistake and I want to rectify it," Breadon told McKechnie, when he recalled him from Rochester.

Toward the end of the season, Breadon offered McKechnie a two-year contract, but added, "First, I want to give you a chance that has presented itself. Judge Fuchs of Boston has asked about you. I think you may be able to get a long-term contract, and as you know, we give no long-term contracts on the Cardinals."

McKechnie soon left the Cardinals, ostensibly on a scouting trip. He was scouting, all right, but it was a job with the Braves. He talked to Fuchs in New York, and they came to an agreement. Fuchs

212

then told him to speak to Adams, the power behind the throne. McKechnie saw Adams at Lexington, Kentucky, where the Boston sportsman was buying horses. Their discussion was brief. Adams said, "You'd better consider yourself the manager."

The Braves gave McKechnie a three-year contract. Later they gave him a four-year contract. He stayed with the Braves longer than Judge Fuchs.

McKechnie was quiet, shrewd, and sharp, and of course, dour, thrifty and canny, since both his parents had been born just outside Glasgow, Scotland. He was a strict disciplinarian, yet he got along with such rebellious characters as Alexander and Oil Smith. He played strict percentage baseball. He was conservative, a wonder when it came to handling pitchers, but no magician when it came to handling hitters.

His morals were of the best. He was a religious man. He was a family man. Guns and dogs were his hobbies. He became a thirty-third-degree Mason. He was kind, but did not throw his money around. Occasionally he'd treat a friend to a newspaper. McKechnie always had the respect of his players.

McKechnie's first Braves team finished sixth in 1930, not high, but higher than any Braves team had finished since 1925. The Braves were eighth in batting with a .280 average, but there was some improvement in their pitching. Seibold was practically a sensation with a 15–16 record, and Wee Willie Sherdel and Fred Frankhouse, who had been obtained from the Cardinals in a trade for Burleigh Grimes, were modest winners. The Braves had got Grimes, the stubble-bearded spitball pitcher, from Pittsburgh in April for cash and Percy Jones, a southpaw. Grimes did the Braves one favor before being traded. He beat Chicago to end a seven-game losing streak in May.

This was George Sisler's last season as a big leaguer. There was some fear at the start that he would not be able to carry on, and the Braves drafted Johnny Neun from Baltimore. But Sisler played 107 games at first base, and finished with an average of .309. Neun played 55 games at first base, and batted .325. The bald-headed catcher, Al Spohrer, hit .317, and Richbourg hit .304, to pace the veterans.

Old Tom Zachary, who had won twelve games and lost none for the Yankees in 1929, was waived to the Braves, for whom he won eleven games while losing only five. But while Zachary admitted

213

being thirty-three years old, Rabbit Maranville admitted to thirty-eight years. Playing his nineteenth season in the majors, Maranville got into 142 games, hit .281, and led the league's shortstops in fielding with an average of .965.

The Braves won only five of twenty-two games from the runner-up Cubs in 1930. Maranville played a characteristic role in one of the victories. The Braves won the first game of a Sunday double-header at Boston, July 13, behind Seibold, 2–1, and they had a 3-to-0 lead behind Smith entering the last of the eighth inning of the second game.

No inning could be started after 5:40 P.M. because of the Sunday baseball law, and the Braves made a valiant effort to keep the Cubs from getting to bat in the ninth. They failed by two minutes, but only after the imp Maranville had sprayed the stands with countless fouls as he tried desperately to delay the game. When Joe McCarthy was named manager of the Boston Red Sox seventeen years later, he was still talking about Maranville's exhibition of hitting fouls.

The Cubs managed to get Maranville out in time to enter the ninth inning, but they did not manage to win the game, even though they scored four runs. They had a 4-to-3 lead, but the Braves had the tying run on third base, the winning run on second, and only one out in the last of the ninth when the clock struck six. The law stepped in and stopped the game.

McCarthy protested the game, but the Braves were declared 3-to-0 winners. Since the Cubs lost the pennant by two games, and McCarthy lost his job to Hornsby, he had reason to remember that Sunday afternoon in Boston many years ago. It helped him land with the New York Yankees, with whom he had a certain amount of success.

CHAPTER XXI

A WARRIOR WITH A WAR CLUB

BRAVES fans did not get their biggest thrill of the 1930 season from their new manager, Sunday baseball, or Rabbit Maranville's stream of fouls. The frosting on their cake was a lanky, raw-boned blond from San Francisco, a free-swinging young giant named Wally Berger.

It was most unusual for the Braves to come up with the season's prize rookie. Not since Maranville, Gowdy, and Nehf joined them had the Braves landed a young star of Berger's magnitude. Berger was hooked from the Los Angeles farm of the Chicago Cubs as part of the deal whereby Rogers Hornsby regained title to Lester Bell, his favorite third baseman. The Braves also sent to Los Angeles Pitcher Art Delaney, George Harper, the veteran outfielder who made every catch look hard, and part of the cash they had received the year before for Hornsby.

Berger, born in Chicago but reared in Frisco, had played third base on the Mission High School team, for which Joe Cronin played second base. But while Cronin finished school, Berger quit in his junior year. He drove a laundry truck, worked on the docks, drove a team, and played semipro ball. Twice he was given trials and released by Nick Williams, San Francisco manager.

He signed with Butte in 1927, then moved to Pocatello, in the Utah-Idaho League. He hit .385 to tie Johnny Schinski, another Frisco boy, for the batting title. They flipped a coin for the championship and Berger won. Whenever they met, Schinski and Berger always flipped a coin to see who was champion. Berger always won. At the end of the season, Pocatello sold him to Los Angeles for $700. Two years later, after he had socked forty home runs and hit .335, Los Angeles realized a huge profit on their $700 investment.

Berger was a right-handed hitter who swung from his heels. He struck out often, but when he connected the ball traveled far and fast. On Memorial Day, against the Giants in Boston, Berger hit a ball over the outside fence in left-center field, a blow that might have carried 475 feet. It was the second ball he had hit over the outside fence and onto the Boston and Albany Railroad tracks in two days. During his first season with the Braves, Berger beat the Giants five games by one-run margins with his home runs. New York's Joe Genewich dusted him off one day, but Berger got up and blasted a game-winning homer. He had it, all right.

Recalling former Boston sluggers such as Babe Ruth and Buck Freeman who had moved on to other teams, Gene Mack wrote a poem that concluded with the verse:

> But now, my friends, the sad part ends,
> No more the days are flat;
> All Hubites roar as home runs soar
> From Wally Berger's bat.

Berger hit thirty-eight home runs in his first season, more than anyone in the history of the club. This was also a National League rookie record. Besides, Berger set league rookie records by batting in 119 runs and pounding the ball for 169 bases. He also hit twenty-seven doubles and fourteen triples.

Overshadowed by Berger in 1930, but a talented rookie nevertheless, was Randy Moore, a versatile twenty-four-year-old Texan. Having a broad chest, he could play third or first base, but preferred the outfield. The Braves bought Moore after he had hit .365 for Dallas in 1929.

The Braves had so much luck with Berger that they went back to Los Angeles in 1931 for another powerful right-hand-hitting outfielder, Wesley Schulmerich. They sent Bobby Smith, who had joined them as a shortstop in 1923 and been converted into a pitcher by Bancroft, to Chicago for Bill McAfee, an undistinguished pitcher, and sent Jimmy Welsh, who had been returned by the Giants for Eddie Farrell in 1929, to Los Angeles for Schulmerich.

Schulmerich had been an All-Western fullback for Oregon State in 1925 and 1926. He stood six feet and weighed 210 pounds. He had almost quit baseball for professional wrestling. He was rough and ready and he swung a forty-two-ounce bat. Asked if he had ever been East before, Big Wes replied, "Sure, when we played football in Nebraska, and another time in Milwaukee."

216

Schulmerich came with the recommendation of George Washington Grant, former Braves owner, who was then living in Los Angeles. He wasn't exactly a flop, for he hit .308 for the Braves in 1931, but neither was he another Berger. He hit only two home runs. He detested curves.

But the Boston Jury Box fans liked Schulmerich, the bowlegged Dutchman with the tremendous physique, the generous nose, and a willingness to pass the time of day with sociable customers. He was one of seventeen players of German extraction who reported to the Braves for spring training in 1931.

Another outfielder added by the Braves was Robert Lee (Red) Worthington, a Californian who had hit .375 for Rochester in 1930. He had been in the Cardinals chain system for four years, but was not fleet enough to qualify for the parent club.

McKechnie's second Braves team suffered a relapse in 1931, finishing seventh as it collapsed the last two months of the season. In August and September the Braves won only seventeen games while losing forty-three. They lost nine in a row, until Ben Cantwell beat the Giants, 5–0. In St. Louis, when the Cardinals had scored a run for nearly every fan in the stands, and were leading 12–0 behind Hallahan, Rabbit Maranville one hot afternoon gathered the Braves around him on the mound.

As everyone wondered what was going on, the Braves suddenly broke out of their huddle, lined up in a football formation, and with the Rabbit chirping signals, began to run football plays until the umpires intervened.

The 1931 Braves had one winning pitcher in Ed (Dutch) Brandt, a rugged southpaw who turned in a record of 18–11. Brandt won eight games and lost none through May. One of his defeats was a two-hitter lost to the Cardinals, 2–1. He allowed one hit in the first inning, the other hit in the ninth. Brandt, bought by the Braves from Seattle in 1927, had been a heavy loser in three previous seasons. Until 1931 he had more success as a pinch hitter than as a pitcher.

McKechnie had soft spots at both third base and first base. Buster Chatham was his regular third baseman in 1930, but he also tried Eugene Robertson, Billy Rhiel, Red Rollings, and Randy Moore. In 1931 he used Billy Urbanski, Charlie Wilson, Bill Dreesen, Bill Hunnefield, Moore, and a strong-armed young man promoted from

217

Williamsport, Bucky Walters. A few years after the Braves released Walters, he was one of the best pitchers in the game.

Urbanski was bought in midseason from Montreal for $30,000. He was a shortstop but had to wait until the next season for Maranville to move over. Everyone was eager to see the new Braves infielder in his first game, especially a young boy who had ghosted his way into the park.

"He looks pretty good, doesn't he?" said the boy to a companion. "He gets around all right."

He had no sooner spoken than Urbanski's hat flew off, revealing a knob almost as bald as Al Spohrer's.

"Why," exclaimed the disillusioned youngster, "Urbanski ain't even got any hair! And I thought he was just a kid."

Later the youngster grew up to be a big-league infielder himself. Eddie Pellagrini may have lacked some of Urbanski's talents, but at least he had more hair.

Sisler having been released to Rochester following the 1930 season, Earl Sheely, former White Sox star, was drafted from San Francisco to play first base. The veteran batted only .273 and was released to Los Angeles at the end of the season. His substitute, Flip Neun, was sent to Newark. Another veteran let go was Freddy Maguire, the stylish second baseman from Dorchester. Maguire had excelled in fielding and sacrifice bunting since coming from Chicago in the Hornsby deal, but more annoying than a hitter who can't bunt is a bunter who can't hit.

Through these various releases and acquisitions, Fuchs and McKechnie were gradually building a formidable team. They were encouraged when the Braves played .500 ball in 1932 and finished fifth, only one game behind Philadelphia. It was the first time since 1921 that the Braves had won half their games.

Maranville, now thirty-nine years old, was moved to second base, and Urbanski, the Perth Amboy barber, was installed at shortstop. As usual, the Braves pulled their first and third basemen out of a hat. Wilfred (Fritz) Knothe, up from Seattle, was the regular third baseman, but was helped by Moore, Walters, and Bill Akers. Starting the season, Arthur (The Great) Shires was the number-one first baseman, but he injured a knee and needed help from Berger, Moore, and Baxter Jordan, the latter being purchased from Baltimore.

Shires, who had previously tried to talk his way through the American League with the White Sox, was brought up from Mil-

218

waukee, where he had hit .385 in 1931. If the deal did not exactly fill the Tribe's needs at first base, it at least gave them a peerless loud-speaker, one who wore flashy suits, lived in elaborate hotel layouts, and displayed a bluster and swagger strange to the Braves, who modeled themselves after cigar-store Indians.

Boston fans knew Shires not only as the former eloquent first baseman for the White Sox, but as the articulate boxer who had scored a technical knockout over Spohrer in the Boston Garden ring January 10, 1930. Shires was then trying to promote a bout in Chicago between himself and Hack Wilson, strong boy of the Cubs. This trial by haymakers was spared the sports world through the timely intervention of Judge Landis.

The Shires-Spohrer fight drew 17,000 customers, who paid $32,700 to see Shires pitch and Spohrer catch. Spohrer was down for a count of nine in the second. At the end of the fourth he was wandering around the ring looking for the information window. His seconds graciously threw in the towel.

"Folks," said Shires from the ring, "I didn't want to hurt Al Spohrer. I want to hurt Hack Wilson."

Denied a chance to hurt Wilson, Shires returned to baseball and hurt his knee instead. Early in August, 1932, he applied for voluntary retirement, had an operation, and then tried to come back with the Braves. "They thought they had me down, but I was only reclining temporarily," he announced. But the Braves liked Jordan, and Shires went back to the minors. Once he complained, "All those hands that pat you on the back on the way up have got knives in them on the way down."

The 1932 Braves started fast, but lacked staying power. An extraordinary, and still unexplained, event transpired on Sunday, May 22, when a double-header with the Phils drew 47,123 paid customers. This still stands as the park's largest paid attendance.

On July fourth the Braves were second, but by the end of August they were sixth. Berger hit only seventeen homers. Schulmerich slumped to .260. But the Braves excelled in defense, fielding .976 for a new league record. They had some good pitching, too. Young Bobby Brown won fourteen, lost seven games. Huck Betts, slow-motioned veteran bought from St. Paul, and Cantwell won thirteen games each, and Zachary won a dozen.

One of their outfielders was Fred Leach, the station agent from the Ozarks. Fuchs had arranged his purchase from the Giants late in

219

the previous season, when McGraw was in Boston. "Would you take fifty thousand dollars for Leach?" Fuchs asked McGraw at breakfast. McGraw said he wouldn't.

That afternoon, with the score tied, Richbourg on third base, and one out, Leach made a spectacular catch of a ball against the left-field fence. What burned up McGraw was the fact that the drive was at least ten feet foul, and after Leach caught the ball, Richbourg scored the winning run.

"About that offer for Leach now," McGraw began, when he saw Fuchs that evening.

Fuchs laughed, and said, "What's the use of kidding? I'll give you ten thousand dollars for him."

McGraw began to sputter, then said, "I'll take it. I'll take it just to get rid of a man who doesn't know when he's ten feet in foul territory."

The tightest series of the season was played in Chicago, in August. The Cubs scored four runs in the ninth inning to win the first game, 4–3. The next day the Cubs won, 3–2, in nineteen innings, and then won the third game, 4–3, in fifteen innings. The Braves won the final game, 6–5, but by then the Cubs had gained the impetus that was to carry them to the pennant.

2

The flame of baseball interest in Boston burned brightly in 1933. Not only did the Braves finish in the first division for the first time in twelve years, but they were in strong contention for the pennant until the last month, when they lost a crucial series to the Giants in Boston.

The Braves set an attendance record for themselves by playing to 517,803 fans at home, even though the depression was still on. The big series with the Giants alone drew 150,000 fans to Braves Field.

McKechnie had solved his infield problem by using Jordan, a light but consistent hitter, at first base, and by getting Pinky Whitney from the Phils to play third. With Whitney came Hal Lee, an out-fielder, in exchange for Knothe and Schulmerich. Before the season began, the Braves bought back Shanty Hogan, beefy catcher who had spent five seasons with the Giants. The good-natured Hogan resumed his career with the Braves by getting so badly sunburned

220

in spring training at St. Petersburg that he could do nothing but eat for three days, which was no trouble at all for Hogan.

Worthington having broken his leg early in the season, McKechnie had Berger, Moore, Lee, and Joe Mowry, who had batted .342 for Minneapolis the previous season, for his outfield. The only difference between Berger and Mowry was that the former could hit anybody but Carl Hubbell, while the latter could hit nobody but Hubbell.

The Braves were six games behind the Giants as they began their six-game series with the leaders on August 31, at Braves Field. They had started the season in eighth place, worked their way up until they were fifth on July fourth, and taken second place on August 22. The Braves won nineteen games, lost only five at home, in August.

A 7-to-3 victory in the first game, with Ben Cantwell beating Roy Parmelee and Wally Berger hitting his twenty-fifth home run, had Boston fans tearing at the fences the next day, when the teams went into a double-header. Ten rows of fans stood against the outfield fences as 50,000 persons squeezed into the huge park. Another 15,000 fans had to be turned away, and many persons who had tickets could not get to the park because of the crush.

The Braves did not fare so well on this occasion. They had lost a regular when Randy Moore suffered a broken finger on his throwing hand while batting against Parmelee in the first game. The Braves called in Rupert Thompson from Albany to replace him. But the Giants had also lost a regular, for after hitting a homer in the first game, Johnny Vergez, their third baseman, was operated on for appendicitis.

The Giants won both games. The first went ten innings, and Hubbell not only outpitched Frankhouse, but he singled home the winning run. Mel Ott went to bat five times and drew five walks. The Giants won the second game, 5–3, and not only did Dolph Luque, a relief pitcher, get the decision over Brandt, but he broke a 3-to-3 tie by doubling into the crowd in the ninth. The Braves were shut out for seventeen innings before they scored three runs off Fred Fitzsimmons in the eighth.

Only 20,000 showed up for the fourth game, on Saturday, but the Giants didn't mind. They won 5–3, with Hal Schumacher beating Zachary. The Sunday double-header drew 42,000, even though the Braves were by now eight games behind. The Giants took the first game, 4–3, in fourteen innings, with Luque, the relief pitcher, again winning his game with a base hit. The second game ended in a 4-to-4 tie, and this was certainly a moral victory for the Braves, since Luque also appeared in this contest.

When the series ended, Judge Fuchs gave out a statement in which he praised the Braves for trying hard. The only person to resign was Weston W. Adams, who quit as traveling secretary to enter the investment business. But Bill McKechnie did not sleep well for a few nights. All he saw in his dreams were base hits flying off the bats of Giants pitchers.

After this catastrophe, the Braves had to take their tired bodies and bruised spirits on a long western trip. They won twelve out of twenty-three games, but lost ground to the Cardinals. Entering the last game of the season, the Braves were in fifth place, a half game behind St. Louis.

Berger had picked up the flu in Pittsburgh and had not played for three weeks. McKechnie advised him to return to his home in California, but the doctor wouldn't even let him return to his home in Boston. Berger stayed in Pittsburgh until he was well. The day he was to leave, the Phils were playing there. Berger strolled over to Forbes Field for a look at the pitchers. Hurling for the Phils was a newcomer, a Reginald Grabowski. Berger observed with interest that Grabowski liked to throw a dinky little curve.

"I hope that guy is still around pitching next season," said Berger to himself. But he was not very hopeful, he later admitted.

Berger had returned to Boston and rejoined the Braves. He was still feeling rocky and did not put on a uniform. He was not dressed, McKechnie noticed, when the Braves went out to play the last game of the season. The Braves started Ed Brandt, who usually could beat the Phils by throwing his glove onto the mound. The Phils started Reginald Grabowski.

Grabowski did all right with his dinky little curve. He had a 1-to-0 lead entering the seventh inning and had allowed only three hits. Berger, sitting on the bench, watched Grabowski for three innings, then went in and put on his uniform. Watching Grabowski's dinky little curve made him feel comparatively healthy.

Jordan opened the Boston seventh with a hit, and Moore singled him to second. Whitney tried to sacrifice but struck out instead. Lee grounded out, advancing the runners. The Phils elected to disregard Hogan and passed him intentionally. This brought up Maranville (.218) with two out and bases full.

222

McKechnie looked into the Boston dugout from the coaching box, and asked, "How do you feel, Wally?"

"I'm ready," replied Berger, grabbing his bat. "If he throws it near the plate, I'll put it out of the park."

On his first swing, Berger almost put his bat out of the park. The second pitch was a ball, the third a called strike. Grabowski became overconfident. He threw his dinky curve, and Berger straightened it out for him so forcefully that the ball went into the left-field bleachers on a line, a pinch home run with bases full.

Berger's wallop gave the Braves fourth-place money, for Bob Smith, who had relieved Brandt in the sixth, held the 4-to-1 lead to the end, and Chicago beat the Cardinals. It was a $7,100 homer, worth $242.82 to each player. Berger was mobbed by his teammates as he trotted home. Little Rabbit Maranville shinnied up and planted two $242 kisses on Berger's rosy cheeks. The crowd of 4,000 fans went wild, because Berger had knocked the Braves into the first division for the first time since 1921.

It was Berger's twenty-seventh homer of the season. He had hit .313, played in the first All-Star game at Chicago, and had been voted the best center fielder in the majors. He had some help, but not quite enough. The Braves set a fielding record of .978. Ben Cantwell, side-wheeling Southerner who had never quite arrived, turned in a 20-to-10 record, becoming the Braves first twenty-game winner since Joe Oeschger won that number in 1921.

Brandt won eighteen games, Frankhouse sixteen, and Betts eleven. If Bob Brown had repeated his 1932 performance, the Braves might have scrambled into the World Series. But Brown had hurt his arm playing badminton, a vicious pastime, and pitched only seven innings all season. In one of the seven innings, he committed two balks.

Although a stubborn holdout in the spring of 1934, Berger had to be satisfied with a $2,500 raise that gave him $11,500 for the season. He signed up in time to be present at Waterfront Park, St. Petersburg, the day Rabbit Maranville broke his leg sliding into the plate in an exhibition game with the Yankees.

Maranville, forty-two years old, but ready to start his twenty-fourth season as a big leaguer, had shown early in the game just how young he felt by hitting a home run off Russ Van Atta. The Yankees led, 3–2, when Maranville started the last of the eighth inning with a hit. He went to third on Hogan's single. There were

223

two out when the Rabbit and Urbanski, who was running for Hogan, started a double steal. Maranville had Frank Crosetti's return throw to the plate easily beaten, but he slid into Norman Kies, rookie catcher for the Yankees, and broke both bones in his lower left leg.

Strong men wept, then, on the field as they looked down on baseball's Peter Pan, who lay there drenched in agony's sweat. Somebody gave him a cigarette, which he puffed nervously as the break was set so that he could be moved. Umpire Bill Stewart gave Maranville the tying run and called off the game.

"I've got to stop sometime, so it might as well be this way as any," Maranville told those around him.

The baseball world grieved to learn that Maranville had reached the end of the trail in such an unhappy manner. Will Rogers wired the *Boston Globe:*

"When Rabbit Maranville breaks a leg right at the opening of the season that constitutes America's greatest crisis, and if anybody reading this had to ask who Rabbit is, then you should be made to show your citizenship papers."

Within a few days, Maranville was telling visitors how he could be back playing again for the Braves. "Sure," they agreed, and called themselves liars.

Maranville was laid up most of the summer. His leg failed to mend properly. He read box scores and answered fan mail. A woman had a daughter she wanted him to marry. The Rabbit answered on a post card so that his wife might see it: "I'm very much married right now."

But the Rabbit showed up in September, when Boston fans gave him a day. The weather was disagreeable, but 22,000 Maranville rooters turned out. So did John A. Heydler, retiring president of the National League.

Without the Rabbit, the Braves had infield trouble throughout the season. They opened with Hal Lee, the outfielder, at second base, but soon signed Marty McManus, the veteran who had managed the Boston Red Sox the year before. With McManus on third, Whitney moved to second, a position he didn't like. In August they brought up Les Mallon from Buffalo to play second base.

The Braves did well to finish fourth for the second successive season. Ben Cantwell, twenty-game winner in 1933, won only five games, but Fred Frankhouse, high-strung curve-ball hurler, and Huck (She-ain't-what-she-used-to-be) Betts each turned in seven-

224

teen victories; while Brandt won sixteen games. A midseason addition to the Boston staff was Flint Rhem, the man who once claimed he had been kidnaped on the eve of a World Series, and who on another occasion got a trowel from a groundkeeper and stopped the game to do some landscaping on the pitching mound. Rhem won a 1-to-0 one-hitter from Brooklyn a few weeks after he joined the Braves.

Berger slipped to .298, but he hit 34 homers and drove in 121 runs. Lee hit three homers in a game the Braves won, 16–13, in Philadelphia. Bill Urbanski went to the plate six times on June 13 without being charged with a time at bat, because he drew four walks and made two sacrifice bunts. Even Shanty Hogan had a record that had nothing to do with eating. He caught 121 consecutive errorless games from May 17, 1933, until August 4, 1934.

But about this time in their history, more attention was being paid to Braves owners than to Braves players. It wasn't so much a question where the Braves would finish, but if they would finish.

CHAPTER XXII

AND ALONG CAME RUTH

☻

COLONEL JACOB RUPPERT, owner of the New York Yankees, wanted somehow to dispose of Babe Ruth, baseball's most glamorous figure. When the 1934 season closed with the Yankees playing in Washington, everyone knew that Ruth was through as a regular player. At Fenway Park, 46,766 fans had crowded onto the field to see his farewell appearance with the Yankees. The pipestems that served as legs would no longer carry, with any alacrity, the barrel that served as a torso. Joe McCarthy, manager of the Yankees, knew Ruth was through. Ruppert knew it. And more than anybody else, Ruth knew it. He had already made it clear to Ruppert that he wanted to manage the Yankees.

Ruppert was in an embarrassing position. He was determined to keep McCarthy as his manager, and yet he felt that he had to treat Ruth discreetly. Ruppert did not want Ruth to play for another American League team and come back to Yankee Stadium, even as a pinch hitter, and break windows in the house he had built. And Ruppert was aware of the critical regard with which his treatment of Babe Ruth was being watched by the American public.

When Judge Fuchs of the Braves arrived upon the scene and offered to take Ruth, the husk of a mighty slugger, off his hands, Ruppert must have felt an urge to embrace this fine fellow from Boston. Here was his dilemma solved for him by a comparative stranger from the rival National League.

"Take him, and with my blessings," was the gist of Ruppert's reply. It took some restraint, we may be sure, for Ruppert not to appear too pleased. But like Fuchs, he, too, had an Oriental impassivity.

What did Judge Fuchs and the Braves want with the forty-year-old Babe Ruth?

226

Fuchs was a man sinking in stormy financial waters. He was in over his head and he was sinking even though a strong swimmer. He had been in the water too long. His resources were exhausted. In desperation he reached for a twig, a straw, a leaf. Ruth was a twig, and Fuchs reached for him.

Fuchs, through borrowing on Braves stock, had become indebted to Adams and Wetmore, among others. He tried repeatedly to free himself of the millstone around his neck. Jimmy Roosevelt was at one time interested in the club. On another occasion, a deal whereby Major Francis P. Murphy of New Hampshire and James M. Curley, Massachusetts political giant, were to come in as partners just missed fire.

The Braves made money in 1931, 1932, and 1933, but the Judge spent it as fast as it came in. He told newspapermen that the team's profit in 1933 was $150,000, but that the Braves had spent $159,000 for new players. The chief debt was a $200,000 note, which had several times been extended. A showdown was inevitable in 1935.

Adams said of Fuchs during the 1929 hearings on Sunday baseball, "To me Judge Fuchs has proven himself a gentleman, charitable to a fault, and so modest by nature that he has not fully replied to these charges.... From youth to manhood, it was the same story to Emil Fuchs, flawless, lovable, kind, and charitable—in magnificent tribute." But it was now six years later, and Adams and Fuchs were on opposite sides.

Before the National League meetings in December, 1934, Fuchs dropped an atom bomb into the laps of his horrified colleagues. He said that the Braves would conduct dog racing at Braves Field. The Braves, of course, would move in on the Red Sox and play their games at Fenway Park. "Over my dead body," was the equivalent of Tom Yawkey's quick reply.

A few days before the meeting, Fuchs formally applied to the Massachusetts Racing Commission for a license to conduct dog racing at Braves Field. Ford Frick, new National League president, called the action "absolutely preposterous." Bill Benswanger, president of the Pirates, said that he didn't think dog racing "a proper sport for a baseball field." Judge Landis was quoted as saying he would quit if Fuchs ran dog racing at Braves Field.

After the National League meeting, Fuchs announced that he would remain in baseball and not try to conduct dog racing. The league made no official announcement on the dog-racing issue.

227

Complaining that rumors of his loss of the club were embarrassing his home life with his family, the Judge gave out a statement December 17: "I am, and always have been, the majority stockholder of the Braves. . . . I was indebted to Mr. Adams to the extent of $289,000. I have paid him $210,000 of this amount, and the balance plus interest is not due until next Summer."

The next development in the dog-racing issue was the announced intention of the Gaffney estate trustees to oust the Braves and lease the park to the Boston Kennel Club. The Braves were now "homeless." A special meeting of the National League was held in New York, and there it became evident that the dog-racing issue was developed in order to win the league's backing on the solvency of the Braves.

The meeting lasted thirteen hours, and at the end, wrote Paul Shannon of the *Boston Post:* "Steve (Judge) McKeever of the Dodgers was asleep in his chair, and the others were in a coma." A couple of owners did not want to rescue the Braves, but it was decided that the National League would guarantee the rental on the park, which was cut from $40,000 to $25,000, and would loan the club $7,500 to meet spring training expenses. Fuchs was to remain as president.

Then the Judge thought of Ruth. In February, 1935, it was announced that the Yankees had turned over the Babe's contract to the Braves. They were doing this, of course, so that Ruth might have the chance he so long wanted to become an executive on a big-league club. Other American League teams gave waivers on Ruth, who had just returned from a trip to Japan.

Boston, to be sure, was all agog over the second coming of Ruth, who had started his big-league career as a pitcher for the Red Sox in 1914. Fuchs led the cheers; this was what he loved. The Red Sox had just paid $250,000 cold cash for a young manager named Joe Cronin. Well, the Braves had parried neatly with Ruth, and the Judge's broad smile clearly said, *"Touché."*

The occasion called for statements, correspondence, and a monster reception.

The Judge wrote to Mr. George H. Ruth on February 23, 1935, as follows:

My dear George:

In order that we may have a complete understanding I am putting in the form of a letter the situation affecting our long distance conversation of yesterday.

228

The Boston Braves offer you the following inducements, under the terms and conditions herein set forth, in order to have you sign a uniform contract plus an additional contract which will further protect you, both contracts to be filed.

1–The Boston club offers you a straight salary contract.

2–They offer you an official executive position as an officer of the corporation.

3–The Boston club offers you also the position, for 1935, of assistant manager.

4–They offer you a share of the profits during the term of this contract.

5–An option to purchase stock and become part owner.

6–The details of the amounts agreed upon will be the basis of a separate contract which shall be a personal one between you and the club, and as the case may be, with the individual officials and stockholders of the club.

In consideration of this offer, the Boston Club naturally will expect you to do everything in your power for the welfare and interest of the club and will expect that you will endeavor to play in the games whenever possible, as well as carry out the duties above specified.

You have been a great asset to baseball. . . . Your greatest value to a ball club would be your personal appearance on the field. . . . I have never seen you make a wrong play or throw a ball to the wrong base. . . . If it was determined, after your affiliation with the ball club in 1935, that it was for the mutual interest of the club for you to take up the active management on the field, there would be absolutely no handicap in having you so appointed. . . .

The Babe replied to the Judge's lengthy document with one so flowery as to make one wonder if the Judge wrote it for him:

So long as memory serves me I shall always remember with tender recollection and appreciation the farewell testimonial accorded me at Fenway Park. . . . I am mindful of the great battle and sacrifice you have made to give Boston a good ball club and a winner. . . . In the spirit of the memory of Christy Mathewson, which we both hold sacred, and who came to Boston with you almost fourteen years ago, and in the continuation of my long friendship with you, I pledge to the people of New England that we shall keep the faith.

How the Judge could put on a show!

Ruth arrived in Boston and signed a $25,000 contract on February 27 as player, assistant manager, and second vice-president. The Babe told an Associated Press reporter in New York: "I will take full charge of the Braves on the field next year. My main ambition still is to manage a big-league club, and I am going to Boston with the full understanding that it will be fulfilled."

229

One reporter cruelly closed his story of the ceremonious signing, with fans cheering in the streets, by writing: "The Braves owe $205,-000 on notes due April 5."

2

When Ruth reported to the Braves training camp at St. Petersburg, Rabbit Maranville greeted him with, "On this club, of course, you'll have to work your way up from the bottom." At which the Babe gave one of his deep belly laughs.

The Braves had no uniform big enough for Ruth except one that Shanty Hogan had outgrown, and this had to be cut down a little for the Babe. Ruth did not punish himself very much in training. His attitude was that of an exhibitor, not a competitor. He wasn't kidding himself about playing regularly with the Braves.

On the first day of practice Ruth spied two dozen new baseballs sitting on a table near his locker. He scowled at them and asked, "What in hell are those for?"

"They're baseballs," replied Hank Gowdy. "We use them in practice."

"Oh," grunted Ruth. "I thought I had to autograph the damn things."

McKechnie chuckled, and said, "You're lucky to get two dozen balls to practice with on this club, let alone autograph."

"Good," said the Babe, and he meant it.

Although he and Ruth had exchanged love notes when the deal was announced, it was obvious that McKechnie was none too happy about the situation. He said, "I've handled men like Alexander and Smith. I guess I can handle Ruth."

But Ruth was different. He was bigger than Alexander and Smith put together. Ruth was a reputation, a tradition, an intangible quality that could not be grappled with. Ruth was a law unto himself. How could McKechnie control his team with Ruth the untouchable always present? He couldn't, and the knowledge that he couldn't weighed McKechnie down and hurt the morale of manager as well as players long before the season started.

The Braves of 1935 were a disgrace to baseball. They lost 115 games and won only 38, the worst record for a National League team since Cleveland, in 1899, had lost 134 games and won only 20. The fault lay not so much with McKechnie, Ruth, or other players, as with the hopeless financial predicament into which the

230

Braves had at long last maneuvered themselves. The Braves' collapse was general.

Ruth played in twenty-eight games, the last of his career, and batted .181. He opened the season in left field against the Giants in Boston. It was a cold, raw day, and he had to face Carl Hubbell, but with 22,000 fans cheering him there was only one thing for the Babe to do, and he did it. He hit a home run and a double, and the Braves, with Brandt pitching, beat Hubbell, 4–2. In left field, the Babe made a wonderful running catch.

Four days later Ruth pulled up lame, but on Easter Sunday he hit another home run as Brooklyn beat the Braves, 8–1. He then caught cold and was out of the line-up a few days. He failed to hit when he returned. On May 5 he faced Dizzy Dean for the first time, struck out once, walked once, and grounded out once.

On May 21 in Chicago, where he had hit his historic called-shot homer off Charlie Root in the 1932 World Series, Ruth hit his third National League home run. Two days later he was hitless in four trips at Pittsburgh, and the next day he made only one hit in four tries. But the day after that, May 25, Ruth slugged three home runs against the Pirates. It was only the second time in his career that he had hit three homers in a game.

His first time at bat, with Urbanski on second base, Ruth homered into the lower tier in right off Red Lucas, who ten years earlier had been a Braves second baseman. In the third inning, with Guy Bush pitching and Urbanski again on second base, Ruth hit a three-two pitch into the upper tier. In the fifth inning he singled off Bush to score Mallon.

"If he'd ever lifted that one it would have been a home run, too," admitted Bush. "He really laid the wood on it."

Bush threw Ruth a slow curve in the seventh inning with nobody on base, and the Babe hit it fifty feet over the right-field stands, the first time a ball had ever been hit over in that particular spot. Ruth then withdrew from the game. He had made three home runs and a single, and had knocked in six runs. And still the Braves managed to lose. The Pirates beat them, 11–7.

As it turned out, Ruth should have quit, then and there. The next day at Cincinnati before 24,361 fans, he went hitless in four times at bat. Si Johnson fanned him three times. It was Ruth's only complete game in the National League. His last time at bat in the big leagues was in the Memorial Day opener in Philadelphia. A pitcher named Jim Bivin, who lost seven of nine games that season, retired him.

While the Braves were beating the Giants, 2–0, at Braves Field on June 2, Ruth called a meeting of Boston and New York writers and announced that he was going on the voluntary retired list. He was through with the Braves. Ruth was angry at Fuchs. He said, "I was being given the old run-around."

Ruth was mad because Fuchs didn't want him to attend a party on the *Normandie* in New York, as ambassador for baseball. He attended anyhow. He was mad because Fuchs wanted him to sell five hundred tickets for a retail clothier, autographing each ticket. He was mad because Fuchs wanted him to play an exhibition game in Haverhill when he had an injured knee.

Ruth had told Braves players that he was quitting before they went out to play the Giants. There was silence for a moment, and then the players rushed to him for autographs. Some of them had been panning him. The pitchers were especially critical of the Babe's fielding after he had let a drive bounce past him for a home run.

McKechnie put himself in the middle by admitting that he could get no discipline with Ruth on the premises. Judging from the record, he didn't get much more after Ruth had left. Fuchs said that if Ruth had not quit he would have been asked to resign for the best interests of the ball club. The club owed Ruth no money. That night Fuchs gave Ruth his unconditional release.

When Ruth left Boston for New York the next morning, McKechnie, a few fans, and several writers were at his hotel to see him off. "I'm sorry to see you go, Babe," said the manager. "It's too bad it worked out like this."

As the Babe left, he walked right smack into the middle of a wedding reception and was immediately showered with confetti that was intended for the bride and groom. The Babe left Boston with a laugh, after all.

The day Ruth retired, Judge Fuchs issued a statement in which he admitted that he did not have the capital to get new players, but said that he was ready to sacrifice his large equity in the club to anyone who would promise to retain the player assets of the team, and to protect the interests of the stockholders.

Fuchs was sinking fast. He had until August first to sell his equity in the club or surrender it to Adams and Wetmore. Bill Cunning-

232

ham, then of the *Boston Post*, asked Adams what he would do if Fuchs's efforts to sell the club failed.

"What do we do with a grocery store that doesn't pay expenses?" asked Adams.

"I don't know. What do you?" replied Cunningham.

"We close it up," said Adams. "And," wrote Cunningham, "his mouth shut like a steel trap."

Adams had been buying out minority stockholders who were hostile to Fuchs, and by this time owned 65 per cent of the stock, which had cost him $60 per share. He offered it, he said, to Fuchs for $35 a share, and to the National League for $30 a share. Adams was peeved at the National League for letting the Braves get themselves into such a mess. He told Frick, "If you find a real buyer I'll talk to him, but I'm too busy to bother with movie actors and others primarily interested in publicity. I've had enough of hot artists for a whole lifetime."

He tried hard to the end, but Fuchs was unable to meet the obligations due August 1. Nearly ten years after he had succeeded Christy Mathewson, the Judge stepped down as president of the Braves. They had been an eventful ten years in Boston baseball. Fourteen months later he filed a voluntary petition of bankruptcy. His chief sympathizers were sports writers he had wined and dined. While he had it, the Judge had run his show on an opulent scale. And who was going to give out the statements now?

3

The departure of Fuchs helped the 1935 Braves no more than did the departure of Ruth. The team had dropped into eighth place May 22, and it stayed there, finishing sixty-one and a half games behind the pennant-winning Cubs.

The Braves lost fifteen games in succession, all on the road, in July. The worst was still to come. From August 18 until September 14, The Braves won only two of the thirty games they played. Cantwell, two years earlier a twenty-game winner, lost twenty-five games and won only four. He dropped thirteen decisions in a row. Brandt lost nineteen games, won five. Frankhouse was a wizard, for he lost only fifteen games and won eleven.

Wally Berger bore up through it all. He hammered out thirty-four

233

home runs and set a Braves record by batting in one hundred and thirty runs. He hit three homers with bases filled.

Maranville came back at the age of forty-three and played twenty games at second base. This was his valedictory. When the season ended, the Braves wanted him to manage their farm at Allentown. He asked, "Allentown? Where in hell is Allentown?" The Rabbit was a little put out. He signed with Elmira, New York, instead. Elmira gave him $3,000, and the Braves kicked in an extra grand.

After Fuchs withdrew, McKechnie served as president pro tem. Ed Cunningham soon retired as secretary, Paul Curley as road secretary. Adams wanted an experienced man to head the club, if he had to hold onto it, since he was at this time investing heavily in Suffolk Downs, first horse track in Massachusetts. The man Adams wanted was Bob Quinn.

Quinn had been business manager of the Dodgers for two years, serving as peacemaker for warring Brooklyn directors. He was reluctant neither to leave Brooklyn nor to return to Boston. Quinn had been president of the Red Sox from 1923 through 1932. He had sold the club to Tom Yawkey and Eddie Collins and had worked for them in 1933 by heading their Reading farm.

He was one of the old school, kind and open, but aggressive and stubborn. He always seemed to have a well-paying job, but if being successful meant having winners, Quinn was not successful.

"Some men die in time to save their reputations," he once said. "I lived too long. I've had a great reputation for developing teams and players, but twenty-five years ago I went to Boston, and since then . . ."

In the big leagues he was nearly always connected with losers, with poor teams that lived from box office to pay roll. Quinn was a man on barrel staves trying to compete against well-equipped skiers in a cross-country race. As his destiny became clear, he grew bitter.

Probably the nearest Honest Bob Quinn ever came to doing a reprehensible deed in baseball was when he caught for a college team as a youth. He was exposed as a "ringer" because he could not give the school yell. But for an injured throwing arm, he would have had a trial with Frank Selee's Boston Nationals in the last century. When through as a player, he became an executive. For seventeen years he was with Columbus, Ohio, a club he helped organize. It won three American Association pennants for him, and finished in the second division only twice.

234

From 1917 through 1922, Quinn was business manager of the St. Louis Browns. Led by George Sisler, who hit .420 and stole fifty-one bases, they were barely edged out by the Yankees in 1922. Quinn was young and confident, then, as he headed a syndicate that bought the battered remains of the Red Sox from Harry Frazee in 1922, but he changed quickly. His Red Sox finished in last place eight times, in seventh place once, and in sixth place once before he sold the club to Yawkey and Collins.

"I'd rather lose ten thousand dollars finishing first than make one hundred thousand dollars finishing last," said Quinn, and nobody doubted his sincerity. He had become synonymous with losing baseball in Boston, so returning to that city to take over the Braves in 1936 was a challenge he welcomed. Alas, he could not meet the challenge as he and his friends hoped.

On the last day of 1935, the Boston National League Baseball Company bowed into retirement, 11,074 shares voting "Yes," and 1,404 shares voting "No" on the issue of financial reorganization. A few days later Boston National Sports, Incorporated, was organized. It owned just twenty-four players. Quinn was elected president; Leopold Goulston, a lawyer, vice-president; and Oscar L. Horton, a shoe man, treasurer. Because of Judge Landis's objections to his horse-racing connections, Adams was neither an officer nor a shareholder but he still controlled the club, because it owed him something like $325,000.

One of Quinn's first decisions was an unfortunate one. Wishing to remove the stigma of utter failure from his team, he abandoned the nickname of Braves, which the club had used for nearly a quarter century. Fans were invited to submit new names, and baseball writers asked to serve as judges. Thousands of nicknames, from Sacred Cods to Bankrupts, were submitted. The judges, solicitous of the headline writers, picked the short but singularly vapid title of Bees.

Braves or Bees, it was still the second division. As Shakespeare might have said: "What's in a name? That which we call a skunk cabbage by another name would smell as foul."

The reorganization of the club found John Quinn, son of the president, moving from the Red Sox as secretary, and George (Duffy) Lewis, who had been a coach, becoming traveling secretary. Even the playing field was reorganized, home plate being moved fifteen feet closer to the grandstand. And instead of being

235

called Braves Field, it was called National League Park, or, informally, the Beehive. There, on July 7, a disappointing crowd of 25,556 saw the National League win its first All-Star game, 4–3, in four tries.

The 1936 Bees were thirty-three victories and two places better than the 1935 Braves. They finished sixth. What helped more than a new nickname, an altered field, and new officers were some new ballplayers. The best trade brought Al Lopez, Castilian catcher, Tony Cuccinello, infielder, and pitchers Ray Benge and Bobby Reis from Brooklyn in exchange for Ed Brandt and Randy Moore. It was one of the best trades Quinn ever made. Benge was traded to the Phils for Fabian Kowalik, Whitney was traded to the same team for Mickey Haslin, and Rabbit Warstler was grabbed from the Athletics on waivers. Of the three, only Warstler helped.

Danny MacFayden, who had been a Somerville High teammate of Shanty Hogan's and had pitched for the Red Sox and Yankees in the American League, was the only Bees pitcher with a winning record. He had been picked up the previous season from Cincinnati on waivers, and done little. But with Lopez catching him in 1936, the Deacon turned in seventeen victories.

Lopez, seventh son of a seventh son, was crafty. Once, with a big run on third base, first base open, and three balls on the hitter, Lopez signaled MacFayden to knock the hitter down. Three times MacFayden shook him off. Knock a hitter down with three balls on him? Was Lopez daffy? But the fourth time Lopez gave the signal MacFayden conceded. He knocked the hitter down, and saw Lopez pick the overeager runner off third base.

Buck Jordan led the Bees by hitting .323. Hal Lee, who got into Quinn's hair by holding out in the spring, tore some of it out by the roots when he grounded into twenty-three double plays. The Bees took a 15-to-0 beating from the Giants in May, but they more than made up for it by beating the Cardinals, 20–3, in August. They scored eleven runs and made seven doubles in the first inning. Jordan, Cuccinello, and Gene Moore each made two doubles in this inning, to break a record that had stood since 1883.

Moore, freed from the Cardinals chain system, was the rookie find of the year, according to Bill Terry, Giants manager. The Bees got him from Brooklyn in a trade for Frankhouse. The first time Moore batted in Boston, in an exhibition game against the Red Sox, he homered over Fenway Park's left-field fence, although a left-

236

handed hitter. It took Ted Williams over five seasons to hit a ball over that barrier. Moore led National League outfielders in 1936 with thirty-one assists.

Before leaving the majors Moore became famous for his power to left field, his strong throwing arm, and his patience as a hotel lobby sitter. Certain chairs in hotel lobbies around the National League might well be inscribed: "Gene Moore sat here six hours without moving August —, 19—."

Moore explained his silence by saying: "I went to Waxahachie High School like Art Shires, and I just want to show we turn out all types there, quiet as well as noisy."

The Bees buzzed up another notch to fifth place in 1937. They did not have a .300 hitter, but they had two rookies in Jim Turner and Lou Fette who won twenty games each. Turner, who worked off seasons as a milkman, might have been returned to Indianapolis after spring training, except that a more highly touted rookie pitcher, Vic Frasier, had a tendency to homesickness.

Frasier was sent home to Dallas, and Turner remained to win twenty games, while losing eleven. He was the third rookie to lead a big league in earned-run average, for which he won the Nick Flatley Trophy as Boston's outstanding player.

Fette, who had won twenty-five games for St. Paul, and had cost about $30,000, was a fixture from the start. He won twenty games while losing ten. Neither Turner nor Fette was a strike-out pitcher. Both relied on good control. They kept the ball low, so that enemy batters hit the ball on the ground, which was kept damp and slow by the canny McKechnie.

Except for Cuccinello at second, the Bees presented a new infield. Elbie Fletcher of Milton, who as a high-school boy had gone to spring training in 1935, replaced Jordan at first. Jordan was a holdout, therefore an annoyance to Quinn.

"I can't even trade you," Quinn told Jordan. "Nobody wants you."

"You could," replied Jordan, "if you didn't want Dizzy Dean for me."

Rabbit Warstler, a little veteran who needed only one hot day to get himself in condition, played shortstop, while Gil English, Debs Garms, and Eddie Mayo took turns at third. Vince DiMaggio, Joe's older brother, was tried there, too, the Bees having bought him from San Diego for Thompson, Chaplin, and cash.

Soon returned to the outfield, Vince showed that he could run

237

like Joe, field like Joe, and throw like Joe. But if Joe was a picture hitter, Vince was a sketch. He batted .256 and led the league with 111 strike-outs, a mark he was soon to improve upon.

Boston fans were down on Berger, who in a series against the Cardinals had failed to hit in thirteen times at bat, and had struck out seven times. Never a Berger admirer, Quinn traded the blond slugger to the Giants for the talkative pitcher, Frank (Gabby) Gabler and $25,000. And don't think the $25,000 could talk louder than Gabler. It couldn't.

Despite all their fine pitching, the Bees never were above fifth place after the Fourth of July, but this was so good that Bill Mc-Kechnie was named the number-one big-league manager for 1937 by *The Sporting News*, "for his managerial skill and his ability in handling men, especially pitchers, enabling him to pilot a mediocre team to a fifth-place finish."

While the World Series was still being played, McKechnie signed a two-year contract at $25,000 a year, but it wasn't with the Boston Nationals. McKechnie had moved to Cincinnati, leaving the Bees poorer than they knew.

CHAPTER XXIII

A LITTLE COMIC RELIEF

NEVER a professed admirer of Bill McKechnie's conservative methods, although himself stubbornly old-fashioned, Quinn first tried to get Donie Bush, former big-league shortstop who had become a successful minor-league executive, to manage the 1938 Bees. Failing that, he turned to an old favorite who had worked for him at Brooklyn, Casey Stengel. A long-distance telephone call to the Texas oil fields on October 25 clinched the bargain.

Bargain? That became a hotly debated point in Boston. In six seasons under Stengel, the Bees were to finish fifth once, sixth once, and seventh four times. But whether the successive failures were Stengel's fault, or Quinn's fault, or the fault of an impoverished organization was and still is a matter of opinion.

"You judge a manager on where his team finishes," said Stengel once, in a philosophical moment. "If you're in the second division and fine players, you're too tough—a Hornsby. If you're in the second division and don't fine players, you're too easy. If you're first and easy on 'em, you're a great fellow—a Joe McCarthy. If you're first and tough on 'em, you're a driver—a Bill Terry."

As a losing manager, Stengel was unique in that he never lost his sense of humor, although he occasionally mislaid it. He was impatient and indecisive, yet he was baseball wise, a good teacher of young players, and an inexhaustible conversationalist. For writers following the Bees, it was more fun losing with Stengel than with a hundred other managers they could name. Unfortunately, Boston fans did not have the benefit of Stengel's company.

In the three years Stengel had managed in Brooklyn, the Dodgers finished sixth, fifth, and seventh. He had been replaced as Brooklyn manager after the 1936 season while he still had a year to go on his contract. Thus, he collected $15,000 in 1937 for not managing the Dodgers, while his successor, Burleigh Grimes, collected only $7,500 for managing them.

Boston eagerly awaited Stengel's appearance. He was remembered as the character who had finished his big-league career with the Braves in 1925. He was the character who had taken off his cap when announced as a hitter in Brooklyn, letting a sparrow fly out. He was the character who had upset his pitcher by disappearing down a manhole in center field during an exhibition game.

When playing right field for the Giants, Casey would pick up a stray paper and read to fans in the Boston bleachers, his comment running: "Ah, I see where this fellow Stengel had another good day yesterday. He booted one in the field, but it was a hard chance, and it says here he made three hits. Quite a hitter, this Stengel. Quite a hitter!"

As a boy in Kansas City, Casey, his brother Grant, and his father, Louis, had operated a sprinkling cart, but Stengel said, "I wasn't very good at sprinkling. The rest of the family had to carry me."

A rookie star who had batted .316 for Brooklyn in 1916, Stengel went to Coffeyville, Kansas, prepared to tattoo the pitching of Walter Johnson in an exhibition game. Johnson struck out twenty men. Stengel was four of them. The next day he burned up when a paper said: "Walter Johnson bested Earl Hamilton, 1–0, through the inability of Casey Stengel to hit in the pinches." The only pinches occurred when Stengel twice came up with Joe Kelly on first base!

As a raw recruit with the Kansas City club in 1910, Stengel let a ball carom off a post and bounce past him for three bases.

"Get those balls!" yelped his manager, Danny Shay. "Learn how to play those angles."

"Angles!" blurted Stengel, less than a year out of Central High School, and fresh as paint. "Why don't you go down to Kling's Pool Parlor and get yourself a billiard player?"

Released to Maysville, Stengel educated himself by taking practice slides into second base on his way to the outfield after each inning. There was an insane asylum behind the center-field fence, and Stengel's manager kept telling him that he would ultimately land there if he kept sliding like that.

He didn't. He landed with the Brooklyn Robins instead. The first game he played in the Polo Grounds, Stengel hit three line drives.

240

All were caught. On his way to the field after being robbed the third time, John McGraw, manager of the Giants, spoke to him.

"Young man, there's no doubt but what you're the best hitter on that team."

"Oh, thank you, Mr. McGraw," replied Stengel, grateful for being rated ahead of Zack Wheat by so eminent an authority.

"But," concluded McGraw, "look out for that wall in right field. We've just had it built, and I don't want you running into it and knocking it down with that hard head of yours."

It was while with the Giants that Stengel told Jack Scott, who had once pitched for the Braves, "I can't play center field when you're pitching."

"Why not?" asked Scott indignantly. "You play it for other pitchers."

"Yes, but your ears are too big," explained Casey. "When you're pitching, your ears get in the way, and I can't see the ball leave the bat."

Judge Fuchs, it will be remembered, had made Stengel president and manager of the Braves farm team in Worcester in 1925, and President Stengel had given Manager Stengel his release so that he could manage Toledo. He had such success there that he returned to the majors as coach of the Dodgers in 1932, under Max Carey. He succeeded Carey as manager in 1934, Quinn giving him a two-year contract at $10,000 a year. After his first season, Stengel was given a three-year contract at $15,000.

He lasted two more years. Under Casey the Dodgers became known as the Daffiness Boys. Johnny McCarthy joined the Dodgers as a first baseman in 1934. His first game was in Boston on a damp day. After a Boston hitter had singled, Catcher Ray Berres tossed the ball to McCarthy, saying, "Throw it out, John. It's wet."

The rookie tossed the ball into the dugout, and the Boston runner was allowed to dash from first to third. Berres apologized, "I forgot to ask for time out."

When McCarthy later explained the incident to Stengel, the manager shrugged it off, saying, "Well, don't let it worry you, kid. You'll get used to these guys after a while."

It was the morning after the Dodgers had lost a double-header in Cincinnati, in 1935, that Stengel entered the hotel barbershop and sat down heavily in a chair.

"Shave?" asked a barber, approaching.

"Yes," said Stengel, wearily. Then he added, "But don't cut my throat. I may want to do that myself."

Stengel had been a game ballplayer, and it wasn't courage he lacked as a manager. When he broke in with the Dodgers in 1912, Stengel was thrown out trying to steal second, Jimmy Archer to Johnny Evers. He made a hard slide.

"The next time you come down here, you busher, I'll shove the ball down your throat," yelled Evers shrilly.

"Yeah? Well, I'll be coming back—the same way," promised the rookie. "Look me over, Evers, because I'm going to be around for a long time. The name's Stengel."

He was around a long time. In Boston there are still two factions, one arguing that he was around too long, the other not long enough.

2

Stengel's first team trained in 1938 at Bradenton, Florida, instead of St. Petersburg. Quinn felt that the city fathers of St. Pete had given the Bees the run-around. They received no guarantee for training there, as did the Yankees. The clubhouse assigned the Bees at Waterfront Park was appropriately described by Quinn as a "kennel." The playing field was in poor condition. So were the stands. The Bees couldn't draw anybody. The hotels snubbed them. So Quinn indignantly moved his team out of one of Florida's most attractive cities, and the Cardinals gleefully moved right in.

Besides a new manager in Stengel, the Bees had two new coaches in the unrelated George (Long Pants) and Bernard (Mike) Kelly. By 1938 there were few holdovers from the Fuchs regime, only two players, MacFayden and Fletcher, and Trainer Jimmy Neary. The latter's successor, Ralph May, was already on the scene as an assistant.

Turner and Fette said that they were grateful to McKechnie for the chance he had given them, but they saw no reason why they should not pitch as well for Stengel. Some veterans said they were glad they no longer had to listen to McKechnie's usual first-day speech, the one beginning, "I want all of you to know that every job is open." And the writers were delighted by the stories and antics of Stengel, after years of having tried to worm story material from the cautious McKechnie.

One night Stengel heard the muffled voices of two newspapermen

242

through the wall of his room. He went to the door and asked Arthur Sampson of the *Boston Herald*, "Can I come in? I'll only stay a couple of minutes. I'm dead tired."

At five o'clock in the morning he was rolling around the floor of the room showing the astonished writers exactly how the flabby Wilbert Robinson, famed Brooklyn manager, used to get into and out of a rubber corset he always wore.

Stengel's first Boston team finished where McKechnie's last Boston team had finished—fifth. The Bees won two more games than they lost, yet neither Turner nor Fette was a winning pitcher. Between them they won twenty-five and lost thirty-one games. MacFayden, with fourteen victories against nine defeats, was the team's leading hurler, while Ira Hutchinson, Dick Errickson, Milt Shoffner, and John Lanning won more often than they lost, but not much more.

"They had courage," said Stengel, of the 1938 Bees. "All you had to do was tape 'em together."

The Bees picked up a new third baseman from the Cardinals in the veteran Joe Stripp; signed Johnny Cooney, now an outfielder, after he was released by the Cards; and brought up a slugging outfielder from the San Francisco Missions in Max West. West was a hard left-handed hitter, a clumsy fielder, and a game guy who was the apple of Stengel's eye, although sometimes a crab apple.

In his first season, West lost a game for Danny MacFayden by misjudging a fly, saved another game by holding the ball after a fine catch, even though knocking himself out against the left-field fence, overslid third base three times and underslid it once, sang "Yankee Doodle" to himself to improve his hitting, and hit a notable home run off Johnny Vander Meer.

Vander Meer had pitched the first of his two consecutive no-hit, no-run games against the Bees, in Cincinnati, June 11. Only three Bees had reached base on passes, and Vander Meer beat MacFayden, 3–0. Four days later the Cincinnati southpaw hurled another no-hit game against the Dodgers in Brooklyn.

On the next Bees visit to Cincinnati, Vander Meer had them beaten, 3–1, with two out and two men on base in the first of the ninth. Stengel wondered if he should remove West, a left-handed swinger, for a pinch hitter. He asked West, "How do you hit Vander Meer?"

"Good," was the quick and positive answer. On the strength of

243

that reply, Stengel let West bat, and with two strikes on him, West hit a home run to win the game, 4–3.

If this wasn't the most impressive hitting feat by the Bees during the season, then the three consecutive home runs by Cuccinello, West, and Fletcher on four pitches by Carl Hubbell certainly was. The most impressive hitting feat against the Bees was a home run with bases full by Gabby Hartnett off Lou Fette, on a drive that appeared yards foul to the Bees but was perfectly fair to Umpire Tiny Parker. It helped the Cubs win the pennant.

Exactly one week later, September 21, the blast the Bees had given Parker was a zephyr compared to the hurricane that hit Boston while the Bees were playing the Cardinals. As the wind increased, Beans Reardon, umpire behind the plate, said, "When the advertising signs go down, I'll call it."

But he called the game when Tony Cuccinello yelled for a pop fly behind second base, only to have Al Lopez wind up catching the windblown ball almost against the backstop. If he had waited, Reardon would have seen the advertising signs carried away by the wind, and he'd have gone with them.

Early in the season, Lopez had a thumb horribly smashed by a foul tip. Shoffner lost his appendix. MacFayden had his hand broken by a line drive. Ray Mueller broke a finger. Bobby Reis, infielder-outfielder-pitcher, had to catch. Gene Moore had an operation on an injured knee.

Moore's knee embarrassed Stengel before his father, in St. Louis. The Bees led, 5–3, in the last of the ninth, with two Cardinals on base and Pepper Martin batting. Martin hit a pop fly that Moore could not quite reach in right field. When he retrieved the ball, Moore threw to Fletcher, who relayed the ball home. Unhappily, the ball hit the corner of the plate and bounced into the grandstand, letting Martin jog in with the winning run.

"Say, Charlie, what happened in that last inning?" asked Stengel's father, after the game.

"What happened? You were there. You saw what happened," said Stengel irately.

"No, I didn't," insisted the old man. "I turned around to spit, and when I looked back, everybody was walking off the field."

The season concluded somewhat inauspiciously with Vince DiMaggio striking out four times against Harry Gumbert of the

Giants. This gave DiMaggio a new record of 134 strike-outs in a season.

"I give up," said Stengel. "All I can say is I helped Vince set a new strike-out record. Maybe somebody else can make him a hitter."

DiMaggio was one of five players given by the Bees to Kansas City for a talented shortstop who appeared at the Bradenton camp in 1939. The Giants had offered $40,000 for Eddie Miller, but the Bees got him for John Riddle, John Babich, Tom Reis, Gilbert English, DiMaggio, and cash. Miller brought the Bees two of the surest hands ever seen in baseball, a new version of the vest-pocket catch and an argumentative nature. He had already been owned by the Pirates, Reds, and Yankees. Stengel said, "I'm going to leave him alone. They say he's hard to handle."

The 1939 Bees also had a new first baseman in Buddy Hassett, who with Jimmy Outlaw came from Brooklyn for Gene Moore and Ira Hutchinson; a new outfielder in the thirty-five-year-old Al Simmons, who was bought from Washington; and a new pitcher in Sailor Bill Posedel, who came from Brooklyn in a trade for Catcher Al Todd. Posedel was the team's only winning pitcher. Fette won as many as he lost, but Turner won only four games. A line drive off Ival Goodman's bat flattened Turner's nose in June, and he was inactive for a month.

Hassett, one of Stengel's boys at Brooklyn, won the first-base job from Fletcher, who was traded to Pittsburgh for Bill Schuster. Buddy, who had a nice Irish tenor, sang even better than he hit, and he hit .309 to lead the Bees.

While batting against Red Ruffing of the Yankees in an exhibition game that spring, Hassett took two called strikes. Stengel called time, walked out toward Hassett, and said seriously, "This fellow's a pretty good pitcher, Buddy. You don't have to spot him anything."

Although Simmons contributed a lot conversationally and hit some mighty drives in batting practice, he was not an asset. The Braves sold him late in the season to Cincinnati, where Bill Mc-Kechnie was winning the first of two consecutive pennants. They should have sold him earlier, before he collided with Miller in short left field and broke the rookie shortstop's left leg in mid-July.

The 1939 Bees finished seventh, even though West hit a home run in every National League park, and Cooney hit the first home run of his big-league career, at the Polo Grounds. The loss of Cuccinello with a knee injury for six weeks early in the season was a serious handicap. Cuccinello returned to the line-up June 27, just in time to play in a 2-to-2 tie that went twenty-three innings and lasted five hours and fifteen minutes, against the Dodgers in Boston.

"Do you want to quit now?" Stengel asked Cooch, as early as the sixth.

"No, I can go nine," replied the infielder.

"What about now?" asked the manager in the tenth.

"No, it'll be over soon."

In the fifteenth inning, Stengel asked again, "Don't you want to quit now?"

"No," said Cuccinello firmly. "I'll finish if it takes all night."

The game went until dark. In the thirteenth inning, Otto Huber, a Boston pinch runner, fell while rounding third base with the winning run. He blamed his shoes. For the rest of the season, Stengel never put a pinch runner on base without first examining his shoes. To Casey, Huber was always, "the boy who put us in the Little Red Book."

A year later, the Bees and Dodgers played an even longer game in Boston, their twenty-inning contest lasting five hours and nineteen minutes before the visitors scored four runs in the final inning to win, 6–2. This game took an hour and a half longer to play than the twenty-six-inning tie between the same teams in 1920.

The Bees again finished seventh in 1940. Hard up for cash, they sold Lopez to Pittsburgh for Ray Berres and $40,000, Cuccinello to the Giants for Al Glossup, Manuel Salvo, and cash, and Fette to Brooklyn for $7,500. New players introduced included Carvel (Bama) Rowell, fleet second baseman from Citronella, Alabama; Chet Ross, a burly right-handed slugging outfielder; and Jim Tobin, an experienced pitcher acquired from Pittsburgh in a trade for John Lanning. Lost for half the season with an injured knee, Tobin won seven of ten games after returning to action.

Told that Ross had hit a 550-foot home run the year before at Evansville, Stengel exclaimed, "Why, that big park in Boston will seem like a bandbox to him, and he won't be able to breathe in the Polo Grounds."

Ross was a rookie find, hitting seventeen home runs and leading the Bees by driving in eighty-nine runs. He also led the league with 127 strike-outs, just short of DiMaggio's record. But it was the veteran Johnny Cooney who won the Walter Barnes Memorial

246

Trophy, given by the Boston baseball writers to the outstanding Boston player in 1940. Mike Kelly having gone to Pittsburgh to tell hitters to "get a good ball" for Frank Frisch, the thirty-nine-year-old Cooney began the season on Boston's board of strategy. But even though Gene Moore had been bought back from Brooklyn, the Bees found they needed Cooney in center field. In 108 games the veteran batted .318 to lead the team and finish third among the league's hitters.

Dispositions around the Beehive were not sweetened when Debs Garms, sold to Pittsburgh in March, led National League hitters with a .355 average, nor when Jim Turner, traded to Cincinnati, won two of every three games he pitched for McKechnie's champions. Garms had driven his family from Texas to Florida, arriving just in time to learn that he had been sold to the Pirates, who were training at San Bernadino, California. He got in condition driving back and forth across the continent before the season began!

Boston players were involved in two notable streaks. Hassett made ten consecutive hits from June 9 to June 14, to tie a league record. Miller played 42 games in succession and accepted 241 chances without making an error, from August 4 to September 11. His fielding average of .970 was a new record for shortstops in the National League. When the season ended, Miller was being compared with all the great shortstops, including Honus Wagner. As a fielder, that is!

3

Quinn, who during the winter had been honored by New York baseball writers for his outstanding contributions to baseball, moved his Bees to San Antonio, Texas, for spring training in 1941. The Bradenton ball park was a sand lot, and certainly a large city like San Antonio offered better prospects of drawing crowds to exhibition games.

Furthermore, Quinn and Stengel did not want any more rookies getting spiked by catfish, as George Metkovich had been one evening as he strolled over the Bradenton bridge to Palmetto. Hearing that the spine of a catfish had perforated Metkovich's foot, Stengel exclaimed, "Well, that's one time a fin got a Russian!"

San Antonio gave the Bees a new practice field, so new that it was worse than the old field they had left at Bradenton. Noting that the players seemed ill at ease in their spotless clubhouse, Stengel turned to Scout Rudy Hulswitt, and said, "Rudy, will you please go around and squirt tobacco juice over everything so the boys will feel more at home?" It was a simple assignment for Hulswitt.

The Bees looked to three former American Leaguers for help in Wes Ferrell, Earl Averill, and Babe Dahlgren. Ferrell and Averill were soon released, but Dahlgren remained until June, when he was sold to the Cubs. Dahlgren hit twenty-three home runs that season, more than any other right-handed hitter in the league, which hardly made the Bees look good.

Soon after the season opened, a new syndicate, headed by Quinn and composed mostly of Boston men, bought out Adams's 73-percent interest in the club. Francis Ouimet was elected vice-president, Joseph F. Conway, treasurer. Stockholders included Max Meyer, Dr. William Wrang, J. W. Powdrell, Richard Hevessy, Frank McCourt, Daniel Marr, Stengel, Guido Rugo, Joseph Maney, and Lou Perini. But what made Boston fans cheer more was the adoption of the old nickname—Braves.

But again more was needed than a new name, for even as Braves the club finished seventh in 1941. During the season, the Braves picked up such veteran castoffs as the Waner brothers, Lloyd and Paul, and Frank Demaree. Cooney, now forty years old, played 123 games and surpassed all the other aged stars by hitting .319, second in the league to Brooklyn's Pete Reiser. One of Cooney's hits was a ninth-inning single that spoiled a no-hitter for Bill Lohrman of the Giants.

In a spring-training game at San Antonio, a rookie shortstop for the Browns, Vern Stephens, had made an unbelievable play on a ground ball behind second. Ross made a sudden slide and sprained his ankle. A few days after he returned to the line-up in July, Ross slid and broke a fibula. After those accidents, the young slugger never fulfilled his promise.

Chased from a game the Braves were losing in Brooklyn, Stengel went into the clubhouse and found a phonograph blaring and several of his substitute players dancing around it. Instead of bawling them out, Stengel joined the dance and outdid all of them. Stengel was in a frenzy because he had just seen Garms sprain an ankle when tagged on the head by Phelps, the Brooklyn catcher.

A riot nearly developed at Brooklyn in August when Errickson, who according to Stengel threw as if his arm were in a splint, hit three Dodgers with pitched balls. A week later, in Boston, Whit

248

Wyatt of the Dodgers was only two outs from a no-hit game when Masi singled over second base. The Braves battled the Dodgers, but not very successfully, down to the very end, when Leo Durocher's team clinched the pennant in Boston—with the help of the umpires, the Braves said.

As the umpires came onto the field the next day, Stengel and some of his players got down on their knees before the Boston dugout and gravely salaamed to them. Umpire Larry Goetz said hotly, "You shouldn't do that."

"What are you sore about?" jeered Stengel. "Your favorite team won, didn't it?"

He then poured oil on the flames by adding, "MacPhail oughta be president of the league instead of the Dodgers, and Frick oughta be president of the Dodgers."

Stengel had reason to see red. Boston critics were roasting him. The breaks had gone steadily against him. And a few weeks earlier he had seen one of his players toss the ball to the opposing catcher so that a Boston runner could be tagged out while trying to score. Returning from first base, where he had been retired, a ball rolled to West's feet as he passed behind the plate. Thinking it a foul, West picked the ball up, tossed it to Mickey Livingston, Philadelphia catcher, and saw Frank Demaree tagged out as he raced homeward on the short passed ball.

While Stengel was still pondering how many dollars and how many days West should be fined and suspended for such an unprecedented offense, West bent over the water faucet in the dugout. Before the water touched his lips, a foul flew into the dugout from Paul Waner's bat, hit West on the mouth, broke his teeth, and sent him to a hospital.

Stengel shrugged his shoulders and asked the world, "What can a manager do? All Max worried about was that his wife was having corn on the cob for dinner that night and he wouldn't be able to eat it."

The Braves returned to Florida in 1942, picking Sanford for their headquarters. Hotel accommodations were not very good, and of food there was only an abundance of celery. When Stengel discovered after four weeks of rigorous training that his squad had risen from 6,949 pounds to 6,975 pounds, he said, "They didn't do that eating in this dining room, because I eat there myself."

Duffy Lewis complained of the treatment given the Braves during their stay at Sanford, but the hotel manager replied neatly, "Maybe our service and conditions weren't as good as you would have liked, but I guess they were as good as the ball team." What he meant was that the Braves had won four and lost thirteen games while at Sanford.

The Braves had several new players in 1942. One of them, Ernie Lombardi, had been bought from Cincinnati. The huge catcher batted .330 to lead National League hitters, becoming the first Braves leader since Rogers Hornsby had hit .387, in 1928. This was a feat, since rival infielders backed into the outfield when Big Lom batted. Another new regular, an outfielder bought from the Yankees, was Tommy Holmes, who batted .278.

West and Buddy Gremp played first base, Hassett having gone to the Yankees in the Holmes deal. Sisti, third baseman in 1941, moved to second base, and Froilan (Nanny) Fernandez, shortstop bought from San Francisco, played third, along with others. Holmes was the only Boston outfielder to play one hundred games. Lombardi, Phil Masi, and Clyde Kluttz, the latter developed in the Cardinals chain system, handled as ordinary a pitching staff as there was in the league. Al Javery and Jim Tobin won twelve games each but they lost more games than they won. The hardest throwing by a Boston pitcher was produced by Salvo the day he got into a "dusting party" with Whit Wyatt of Brooklyn. Each pitcher hit the other, but Salvo won the game, 2–0.

For the fourth year in succession, the Braves finished seventh. They won fifty-eight games, and had one given to them. As they trailed the Giants, 2–5, in the eighth inning the next to last day of the season in New York, 9,000 juvenile guests of the Polo Grounds management swarmed onto the field so that the game could not be finished. Umpire Ziggy Sears forfeited the game to the Braves, 9–0.

Eddie Miller, a holdout in the spring, was the leading Braves performer. He made only thirteen errors in 142 games, and set an all-time fielding record of .983 for big-league shortstops. But his $15,000 salary was a burden to the Braves, and his disposition was a burden to both Quinn and Stengel, so at the end of the season he was traded to Cincinnati.

There were two red-letter days in 1942 for Braves fans. On May 13, Tobin hit three home runs against the Cubs, in Boston, and he needed them all for he won only 6–5. It was a remarkable hitting

250

exhibition by a pitcher, but not a fluke for Tobin. The day before, he had hit a pinch homer, and during the season he hit six home runs to tie Hal Schumacher's record.

On June 19, against Truett Sewell of the Pirates, Paul Waner made his three thousandth big-league hit. Two days earlier he had beaten out a grounder to shortstop, a difficult chance that the fielder had momentarily fumbled. As the official scorer, Gerry Moore, pondered whether to rule it a hit or an error, Waner from his perch on first base vigorously shook his head and waved his hand. Moore ruled it an error.

"I don't want it to be a questionable hit," Waner explained later. "I want number three thousand to be a good clean hit that I can remember." And it was.

Waner was given a party in Boston. The National League gave him a plaque. He was only the seventh player in big-league history to make 3,000 hits. Shortly after his climactic blow, the thirty-nine-year-old batting marvel revealed that he could not see well enough to read the advertisements on the fences at Braves Field.

"You can't!" exclaimed Stengel. "Then how do you hit the ball?"

"Oh, that's different," said Waner. "The pitcher's so near that the ball looks as big as a grapefruit."

"But how do you see fly balls in the outfield?" persisted Stengel.

"I don't see them at first," said Waner blandly. "But I can tell by the sound as they hit the bat which way they're heading, and then I pick 'em up when they get out aways."

Stengel's good nature was sorely tried by the 1942 Braves, especially when they lost twelve games in succession. In midseason he suspended Tom Earley, an inoffensive fellow without great ability, for "indifferent pitching." In St. Louis he became so provoked that he played a catcher (Masi) and two infielders (Sisti and Fernandez) in his outfield against the Cardinals.

Fortunately, Lennie Merullo was playing shortstop for the Cubs the day he made four errors in one inning at Braves Field. Merullo had reason to be jittery, since his first son was born that day. The son is still called "Boots."

Baseball learned that it was not a phony war when players began to be drafted in droves and when Judge Landis ruled that no teams should train south of Mason and Dixon's Line in 1943. The Braves found a nice setup at The Choate School, in Wallingford, Connecticut. The food was excellent, living quarters comfortable, and practice conditions as good as could be had in a baseball cage. In the service when training began were such valuable players as West, Sisti, Gremp, Posedel, Rowell, Jim Wallace, Warren Spahn, and Johnny Sain, the latter three being the most promising young pitchers owned by the Braves.

Miller having been traded to Cincinnati for Eddie Joost, Nate Andrews, and cash, Bill (Whitey) Wietelmann, became the new Braves shortstop. Wietelmann was a keen, hustling player who had been developed on Braves farms, a light hitter, and one of the greatest letter writers baseball has ever known. He answered every fan letter he received.

Lombardi was a holdout all spring. A few days after he signed, the Braves traded their batting champion to the Giants for Connie Ryan, Hugh Poland, and more money than was at first admitted. Ryan moved in as the regular second baseman, and Joost went to third. The day after the Giants traded Ryan to the Braves he hit a home run with two men on base in the ninth inning at the Polo Grounds to beat the Giants, 3–2. McCarthy played first base until he broke his leg in July, when Kerby Farrell, a pitcher until then, took over.

Lefty Gomez tried to come back with the Braves, but the southpaw who had been a leading pitcher for the Yankees did not get into a single game. As he watched Tobin win games with the slowest knuckle ball in captivity, he said, "Here I am worrying about a sore arm, and the only thing that bothers Tobin is a hangnail."

Red Barrett, who came up from Syracuse with Andrews, talked the best game, but Al Javery, a rawboned right-hander who was called Little Abner, or Bear Tracks, produced the best pitching for the Braves. He won seventeen games, lost sixteen. A scratch hit in the first inning by Ray Hamrick of Philadelphia cost him a no-hit, no-run game in September.

The balata ball appeared in 1943, and the Braves pounded the rock for all of .233. It was pitching, not hitting, that put them in sixth place, although a crude young outfielder, Butch Nieman, won a half-dozen games for them, with home runs in the clutch. The Braves played their best ball in September. They even won a game from the pennant-winning Cardinals, after having dropped sixteen decisions in succession to Billy Southworth's team.

Although his team gained a notch, it was a miserable season for

252

Stengel. Two days before the opening game, he was hit by an auto-mobile in Kenmore Square and his leg badly broken. He was in St. Elizabeth's Hospital nearly two months, while his coaches, George Kelly and Bob Coleman, ran the team. For seven weeks he sweated it out while twenty-five pounds of metal, dangling from a spike driven through his heel, drew the bones into place.

Stengel couldn't stand listening to Braves games on the radio. As the team left on a long trip, he told Kelly, "When you get back, I'll either be out of the hospital, or out of my mind."

Tony Cuccinello visited him, and remarked, "You're looking better than the last time I saw you, Casey."

"Yeah?" said Stengel skeptically. "It must be because I've just shaved."

His wife, caring for an invalid mother in distant California, wanted to rush to him, but he told her, "Don't come unless you know how to set a broken leg."

"I'll sit up nights with you, dear," she argued.

"Oh, I have a nice night nurse now," he quipped. Edna stayed in California with her mother.

Frank Frisch visited Stengel at the hospital when the Pirates came to Boston. He asked if he could have the basket on which Stengel's leg rested. Casey asked suspiciously, "What for?"

"I want to grow petunias in it," admitted Frisch.

Stengel's broken leg brought him a lot of sympathy, more than he ever received when the Braves were breaking his heart. Some-body sent him a wooden leg. Frank Bruggey, old-time Philadelphia catcher, wrote: "It's too bad you weren't hit on the head instead of the leg. You'd be out there coaching now."

And Hollis Thurston, former big-league pitcher, wrote: "I always knew you couldn't take it. You took one look at your team and threw yourself in front of an auto."

But Casey Stengel was glad to walk out of the hospital on crutches, even if it meant that he had to watch the Braves. Nor did he have to watch them for so very long, at that.

CHAPTER XXIV

THE THREE LITTLE STEAM SHOVELS

THE window shades had been drawn too long. For nine years the Braves had lived in the darkened room of the second division, seeing no light, no sun, no hope. Old bones and old boards creaked loudly in the gloomy and empty mansion about them, and the ghosts of ancient conquests flitted uneasily in the murk. In the bare halls, Bob Quinn's declamations and the jests of Casey Stengel sounded now as hollow echoes. It was time that new tenants moved in, snapped up the window shades, and let in some light.

The new tenants, being contractors, did not merely move in. They stormed in on caterpillar treads, like steam shovels, clanking, banging, puffing, digging—always digging at the dusty cobwebs of lifeless traditions hanging in distant corners, always digging at the thick walls of bleak impoverishment that had encompassed the Braves and walled them into the second division.

The Three Little Steam Shovels bought the Braves in January, 1944. During the 1943 World Series, Lou Perini, Guido Rugo, and Joseph Maney made an offer to other members of the syndicate that had owned the club since 1941, saying in effect:

"We are tired of being assessed one thousand dollars here, and ten thousand dollars there, without ever getting any place. We are ready to sell our stock to you for what we paid for it, or we will buy your stock from you for what you paid for it. One or the other."

The other stockholders elected to sell, although it looked for a time as though Max Meyer, Brooklyn pearl merchant and a close friend of Stengel and Quinn, would buy. He thought better of it, and Perini, Rugo, and Maney, Boston contractors who had made fortunes building ammunition dumps, wharves, piers, roads, tunnels, and airports during the war, took over the Braves.

254

Quinn remained as president; Stengel was out as manager. The Shovels, and especially Perini, had wearied of Old Case. They thought his explanations of Braves failures evasive. Stengel had a trick of answering questions by way of Cape Horn. He might start talking about Fette's sore arm, but he would probably wind up telling how he had once bought some store teeth for Leo Durocher after punching him in the mouth, or how he had half taken off his Giants shirt and offered it to Umpire Bill Klem. And Casey had once, it was said, advised the Shovels to stick to their cement mixers and let him run the Braves.

The Steam Shovels had big ideas in mind, but there they stayed for a while. The war was still on, and promotional handsprings were out of order. For their manager in 1944 they chose Bob Coleman, who had been a coach under Stengel the year before. Coleman had caught for Pittsburgh and Cleveland, but had got flat feet chasing foul flies at Forbes Field. As a minor-league manager and developer of young players, he had won an enviable reputation, but he had never managed a big-league club.

Coleman, with Tom Sheehan and Benny Bengough for coaches, took over a bad ball club, and he took it over at a bad time. So many players had been inducted that those who remained, the aged, unfit, and exempt, did not have to toe the mark. There was nobody to take their places. In short order, some Braves veterans were taking advantage of the good-natured Coleman, and there was reason to believe that the Steam Shovels impeded his efforts to maintain discipline by interceding for favorite players.

The Steam Shovels were not baseball men. They were political contractors who had started from scratch and made good in a big way.

"Lack of baseball background is an advantage," Perini said. "We take a sound business approach to the game. As contractors we are planners, and we know that good organization will accomplish wonders. Baseball is a side line with us, but it is also a business challenge that we want to meet."

Perini, only forty years old then, was the youngest of the three new owners, but he and brothers Joe and Charlie owned 50 per cent of the stock. In 1936, he and Maney, senior member of the trio, had joined Major Murphy of New Hampshire in negotiating unsuccessfully for the Bees. All three Steam Shovels had been

Braves followers, and Maney, the only one who had been even a fair sand-lot player, had rooted hard for the 1914 champions.

When nine years old, Perini had organized the Ashland Dreadnaughts and promoted mail-order uniforms from Ashland merchants. The Dreadnaughts played their first game on a muddy field, and Perini recalls bawling out a teammate for sliding into a base.

"Don't slide and get your new uniform dirty," he yelled. "Let 'em tag you."

Perini, Maney, and Rugo were all sons of construction men. All had worked hard as youths. When the Boston subway was being built between Franklin and State Streets over forty years ago, Maney was a timekeeper for Coleman Brothers. Rugo, English High School quarterback before the first World War, had worked for the Bethlehem Shipbuilding Corporation. Now all were heads of their own companies, and they had been business associates on big construction jobs since 1935.

Spring training in 1944 was again held in the cage at The Choate School. It was enlivened at first by the meanderings of Nate Andrews, husky Braves pitcher from Rowland, North Carolina. A ballplayer getting off the train at Wallingford noted a citizen in some difficulty up the station platform. He quipped to a companion, "Probably a Braves player."

A few seconds later, when he could see the unfortunate citizen more closely, he exclaimed, "My gosh! It is a Braves player. It's Andrews."

Straightened out by Alcoholics Anonymous, Andrews went on to have a good season, winning sixteen games and losing fifteen. But the most discussed Braves pitcher of the season was Jim Tobin, the butterfly bowler who warmed up by having Doc May rub his knuckles vigorously for two minutes. Old Ironsides pitched two no-hit, no-run games, the first for nine innings and the second for five. Tobin was only the sixth pitcher in the club's history to pitch a no-hit game, the others being Jack Stivetts, Vic Willis, Frank Pfeffer, George Davis, and Tom Hughes.

Only two Dodgers reached base against Tobin at Braves Field on the dark and chilly afternoon of April 27, and both of them were Paul Waner. He walked to start the game, and he walked again with two outs in the ninth. No Dodger hit the ball safely. Three line drives to the outfield were easily caught. The nearest thing to a hit was a bunt that settled two inches foul. The inability of the Dodgers to hit Tobin's powder-puff delivery earned them a furious tongue-lashing from their manager, Leo Durocher.

Tobin, who during the previous season had been the first big-league hurler since 1886 to hit three homers in a game, became the first hurler to hit a home run as he pitched a no-hit game. He hit one over the fence in the eighth inning, to give himself a little more working margin. He won, 2–0.

Fritz Ostermueller, losing Brooklyn southpaw, commented, "The first time in my life that I see a no-hit game, it's pitched against me."

Tobin's five-inning no-hitter was against the Phils, in the second game of the June twenty-second double-header at Boston. The game was called because of darkness. Tobin, failing to hit a home run, was disappointed. Curiously, Old Tobe was the Braves pitcher in Cincinnati on May 15, when Clyde Shoun, Reds southpaw, hurled a no-hitter. Drawing a base on balls, Tobin was the only Boston player to reach base.

Besides Tobin's no-hitters, the 1944 season was eventful for its parade of players taking physical examinations for the service. The leading player surrendered by the Braves during the campaign was Connie Ryan, who was having his best season at second base. After starring in the National League's 7-to-1 victory in the All-Star game at Pittsburgh, Ryan was inducted into the Navy in July. Frank Drews was brought up from St. Paul to replace him. Personnel changed so often that the Braves tried ten different men at third base during the season.

Finishing sixth, the Braves did as well as they had in 1943, but they drew only 245,000 fans at home, the smallest attendance in either league. Joe Maney had decided to lure the fans with home runs, so while the team was on a western trip in May, he pulled in the right-field fence so that the second baseman could sit comfortably in the right fielder's lap. The right-field line was reduced from 340 feet to 320 feet, and the fence was only 10 feet high. Whereas fifty-nine home runs were hit at Braves Field in 1943, ninety-five were hit in 1944. And there were many more to come.

The Cardinals clinched the pennant by beating the Braves, 5–4, in Boston, September 21. The Braves gave four players and $50,000 for Milwaukee's second-base combination of Dick Culler and Tom Nelson. But the season's most unusual event was a hurricane that prevented the September fifteenth game with Brooklyn. The Dodgers left Brooklyn at 12:30 A.M. and needed seventeen hours for the five-hour trip to Boston, arriving there at 5:30 P.M.

The Braves had twenty-seven players wearing the uniform of their country before the 1945 season opened. They also had a new club president. On the occasion of his seventy-fifth birthday in mid-February, Bob Quinn announced that he was resigning as president of the Braves, and henceforth would direct the club's farm system. His son John, hitherto secretary, was named general manager.

"The world is changing upside down," said Quinn, "with men wearing white shoes, white pants, and silk shirts, and women wearing trousers. But the thing that surprised me most in my life was not the telephone, radio, or airplane. It was night baseball."

Night baseball had not yet come to Boston, but it was on the way. Let the war be won and over, and the Steam Shovels had some rabbits to pull out of their bonnets. When Perini succeeded Quinn as president, it was a signal that the Braves were ready to launch an attack for some of the patronage held by Tom Yawkey's fair-haired Red Sox across the railroad tracks.

But before they could fire their heavy artillery, the Three Little Steam Shovels had to stagger through one more war year. And although the Braves again finished sixth in 1945, and although their attendance advanced to 394,000, in many ways this was a most miserable and unhappy season.

The club trained at Georgetown University, in Washington, D.C., and enjoyed ideal weather. It was a good thing the weather was ideal, for nothing else was. Nelson, second baseman bought from Milwaukee, hurt his throwing arm and never lived up to advance notices. Andrews jumped the club in Chicago and flew home to Rowland, North Carolina. He rejoined the team, but later failed to show up at the park on a day he was to pitch. The Braves sold him to Cincinnati. Javery and Nelson were fined $300 each for missing a train from Philadelphia. Late in the season, Javery was suspended. Tobin was thought to be a troublemaker and was sold to Detroit, where he appeared briefly in the World Series.

Joost broke his toe in the second game of the season and was out for a month. Then he broke his wrist, played, hurt it again, and was operated on. He went home in disgust and was suspended.

258

While pitching batting practice just before the season opened, Wietelmann had the little finger of his left hand shattered by a drive off Ab Wright's bat. Two thirds of the finger had to be amputated. Culler hurt his arm, Carden Gillenwater was beaned, and Drews hurt his knee so badly in spring training that it had to be placed in a cast.

This wasn't all. Late in May the Steam Shovels closed their first major trade, getting Mort Cooper, Cardinals pitching ace, for Red Barrett and $50,000. Perini beat his chest then, but within a few weeks he was ready to beat his head against a wall. The Braves had been had. Cooper won only seven games for them, but Barrett won twenty-one games for the Cardinals. Barrett explained, "The difference between the Cardinals and Braves is that the Cards are fast enough to catch the line drives hit off me."

Learning that the Braves had given $50,000 besides himself for Cooper, Barrett had quipped, "The Cardinals should have thrown in Kurowski." Events proved him right. Cooper had his chipped elbow operated on in August.

The Braves lost a double-header in Brooklyn, July 29, giving them eight straight defeats and a good hold on seventh place. The next day Coleman resigned as Braves manager. Old Carpet Slippers, as the *Record's* Dave Egan had neatly christened him, had had enough of the big-league pressure cooker. He'd go back to the minors, where he felt at home.

Del Bissonette, his coach, succeeded him. The apple farmer from Winthrop, Maine, had been Brooklyn's first baseman for five years, and he had been successful managing the Braves farm at Hartford. He was determined and willing, but he sensed from the start that he was only the stopgap manager. Seventh when Bissonette moved in, the Braves finished sixth.

Despite the multitude of misfortunes that beset the team, one Braves player enjoyed 1945 very much. Tommy Holmes, shrill-voiced bag puncher from Brooklyn, knocked the cover off the ball. He batted .352, only to lose the league batting championship to Phil Cavaretta of the Cubs by three points. He hit .405 in home games. Holmes knocked in 117 runs, and he set modern Braves records by scoring 125 runs and by making 224 hits and 47 doubles. His 28 home runs was a Braves record for a left-handed hitter. He took advantage of the handy right-field fence, and so did a lot of other people, because 131 home runs were hit at Braves Field in

1945, which was one more than was hit in the malformed and notorious Polo Grounds. Chuck Workman hit 25 homers, 19 of them at Braves Field.

Admitting that something had been overdone when 131 home runs could be hit at Gaffney's "perfect park," and especially when a line-drive hitter like Holmes could whack 28 homers, the Steam Shovels after the season said they would move the right-field fence back about 20 feet.

Holmes's principal feat, however, was a consecutive hitting streak that extended through thirty-seven games. He made at least one safe hit in every game played from June 6 through July 8, batting .423 in the period. The All-Star game interrupted his string, and in the first game played after the glorified interleague exhibition contest, against the Cubs in Chicago on July 12, Holmes was stopped as Henry Wyse pitched a three-hitter against the Tribe.

Holmes started his streak in a notable series played at Philadelphia early in June. In this series, which consisted of a twilight game, a night game, and a double-header, the Braves won four games inside of twenty-four hours, and Holmes made ten hits.

His streak set a new modern National League record. Hornsby had hit safely in thirty-three successive games in 1922. The all-time league record was set at forty-four consecutive games by Willie Keeler of Baltimore in 1897, and this was the record Holmes wanted to break. Among the many curious reasons advanced for Holmes's clouting was a hard yellow bat that Johnny Frederick had used fifteen years earlier when with the Dodgers, and which had lain since then in Bissonette's attic.

For his mighty splurge, the darling of the jury-box fans was voted Boston's outstanding player for 1945 and given the Peter F. Kelley Memorial Plaque by the town's baseball writers. Better still, the Braves and their fans chipped in and gave him a new automobile. New automobiles being rather scarce in those troubled times, Holmes received his present several months after it was given to him.

2

Whereas Judge Fuchs derived considerable pleasure from giving out formal statements, the Three Little Steam Shovels enjoy giving a luncheon, a dinner, or a party and then making a dramatic announcement. The luncheons, dinners, and parties are always excellent, the announcements sometimes so. When the 1945 season had ended, the Shovels soon found plenty of chance to practice their specialty number.

Bill Sullivan, nationally known as a publicity man through his affiliations with Boston College, Notre Dame, and Annapolis, was introduced as the new tub thumper for the Braves. Bob Quinn, after a long and certainly an honorable career in organized ball, announced that he was severing connections with the Braves to take a job with a sporting-goods house. Ted McGrew became head of the farm system. But the most exciting revelation was the hiring of Billy Southworth as manager of the Braves.

"We decided we wanted the best manager in baseball for the Braves," said Perini. "Then we asked ourselves who the best manager was, and of course we had to answer, 'Southworth.' We determined to get him if it was at all possible."

During the 1945 World Series between the Tigers and Cubs, Perini approached Southworth and was told to see Breadon. Perini found the owner of the Cardinals reluctant to part with a manager who had won three pennants and one world championship for him in six years, and had never finished below third place. These Steam Shovels had pestered him until they got Cooper, much to his profit, and they had even offered him blank checks for players like Marion, Musial, and Kurowski. Now they were going to take his prize manager away from him. Breadon couldn't stop them. He couldn't keep Southworth from taking a job that would pay him $35,000 a season, with a bonus of $5,000 for finishing fourth, $10,000 for finishing third, $15,000 for finishing second, and $20,000 for winning the pennant.

"I can't stand in his way," admitted Breadon, "and I can't afford to give him that kind of a contract. He's yours if he wants to go."

If he wanted to go! Southworth never was a man to let sentiment interfere with business. The proposition was up his alley. All he asked was full authority over the club's playing personnel. He got it.

"We've got our manager," said Perini, at the luncheon at the Engineers' Club. "Now we'll try to give him players of similar ability."

The Braves were really on the warpath.

At Braves Field eight new light towers for night baseball sprouted and grew quickly, to stand against Boston's sky line as a symbol of Braves progressiveness. The Steam Shovels raided the Cardinals for Johnny Hopp, who cost them $35,000 and Eddie Joost, and then for

261

Ray Sanders, who cost them $25,000. They moved their training headquarters to Fort Lauderdale, bustling town north of Miami. Southworth introduced two new coaches in Johnny Cooney and Jake Flowers, a new trainer in Dr. Charles Lacks.

Southworth's leadership was quickly established. The man who twenty-five years earlier had captained the Braves ran his practices with startling efficiency. He was firm, decisive, almost grim. Asked what he thought the funniest incident of his baseball career, he replied, "There wasn't any. There's nothing funny about a play which may mean a ball game. Baseball has always been a serious business with me."

From the start, Southworth sought to build up Braves morale through discipline. He made rules, and players breaking them invited fines. He set a midnight curfew. He told players not to gossip about each other. He forbade second guessing after defeats. The worst of offenses was loafing, which was intolerable. Southworth reprimanded his players in private, and usually a day after the mistake was made. He said, "I try to treat players the way I liked to be treated—and never was—when I was a player."

Braves players responded to his methods. There was no idleness on the practice field. Everybody hustled and felt better for it. Even Perini and Rugo took off their coats one afternoon, and with shovels and rakes prettied up the pitching mound and batter's box. From Perini, the president, to Shorty Young, the clubhouse custodian, the new Braves organization was filled with a new determination.

During the 1946 season, the Braves made fourteen deals for players who cost them about $180,000. They went into the minors and bought for 1947 delivery the fabulous first baseman from Seattle, Earl Torgeson. He cost them $50,000, plus four players. They outbid the Detroit Tigers for a star college athlete, Alvin Dark, of Louisiana State University, by giving him a $40,000 bonus. They bought Danny Litwhiler from the Cardinals, Don Padgett from the Dodgers, Mike McCormick from the Reds. They signed Ernie White and Si Johnson as free agents.

Buying players wasn't enough, so they bought a team, paying $270,000 for the Milwaukee club of the American Association. This gave them a Double A farm in place of Indianapolis, their previous affiliate, which had hooked up with Pittsburgh.

The Steam Shovels promoted their team as aggressively as they rebuilt it. Not even Walter Hapgood, when he was business manager

262

during Stallings's regime, had shown a bolder imagination. Night baseball, with neon foul poles and shimmering sateen uniforms that made the players look like a men's chorus, was a spectacular contribution in Boston, a stronghold of daylight ball. The Braves played the first night game ever held in Boston on May 11, losing a 5-to-1 decision to the Giants, but winning a 35,945 decision at the gate. For the twenty-four night games played at Braves Field during the season, 568,083 fans turned out.

Another success for the Shovels was the signing of Boston College to play its home football games at Braves Field instead of at Fenway Park. The winning argument was a portable bleacher that seated 12,600 spectators. Built of tubular steel staging, it was the largest portable stand in the country. From the top row, spectators said they could see Nantasket Beach.

Bill Sullivan edited a *Braves Sketch Book,* selling 22,000 copies. Ticket schemes were initiated, and from near-by cities such as Lynn, Lawrence, and Worcester, fans were delivered by special buses at the gates. A moving picture, *Take Me Out to the Wigwam,* was made for off-season distribution. A suggestion contest drew 54,000 entries, and the winning suggestion was worth a new automobile. The Braves worked with an airplane company that flew fans from Cape Cod.

Then there were the Troubadors, or Three Little Earaches. At every home game, three musical tricksters gave a combination concert and vaudeville show, playing theme tunes for Boston hitters, such as "Has Anybody Here Seen Kelly?" for Tommy Holmes, and deriding shower-bound enemy pitchers with funeral marches.

The Braves treated their trio to a western trip. After a game in Pittsburgh, Hy Brenner, the trumpeter, got into a cab with a total stranger for a ride back to the hotel. Turning to the party beside him, Brenner complained, "This is one terrible town for cabs, mister."

"Yes, it sure is," agreed the stranger.

"The cab situation here is even worse than the Pirates," said Brenner, "and that's awful." The stranger laughed heartily. He kept on laughing. Brenner was puzzled by the prolonged hilarity, until he reached the hotel. There he learned that the stranger was Frank McKinney, new owner of the Pirates.

The 1946 Braves were unlucky, yet Southworth led them to fourth place, only one game behind the Cubs. The bad luck started the very first day of the season, when about 5,000 of the 18,261 fans who saw the home opener with the Dodgers left the park daubed with green

263

paint. Many of the newly painted grandstand seats had failed to dry. As irate customers paraded to the front office, the Steam Shovels forgot momentarily about removing soft spots from the outfield and worried only about removing green spots from silk stockings, worsted suits, and mink coats. The office supply of cleansing fluid was sadly inadequate.

The Braves ran an advertisement in the papers: "An Apology to Braves Fans: The management will reimburse any of its patrons for any expense to which they may be put for necessary cleansing of clothing as a result of paint damage."

Claims poured in, even from such unlikely places as California, Nebraska, and Florida—some 13,000 of them altogether. Two lawyers worked all summer on claims, over 5,000 of which were paid. The average claim was settled for $1.50, the highest for $50. The Braves had to open a "Paint Account" in a bank. Their wet-paint opener cost them nearly $6,000, but the Steam Shovels concluded that the free advertising and good will they got was worth it, although nothing to be desired on an annual basis.

Where Judge Fuchs's bowwows had failed, the wet paint succeeded in getting the Braves into Fenway Park. Tom Yawkey loaned his park to the Braves until their paint dried, and they played a Sunday double-header there against the Phils, winning two games before 20,735 fans.

Injuries tormented the Braves, the worst being the broken arm Sanders suffered at St. Louis when Erv Dusak ran into him at first base late in August. At the time, Sanders was hitting only .243, and had been a major disappointment. Hopp included a beaning by Monte Kennedy of the Giants among his various injuries; Rowell had a chronic backache; Johnny Barrett, obtained from Pittsburgh for Workman, and McCormick had knee operations.

A lively manipulator to start with, Southworth had, because of these ailments, the opportunity to devise countless new line-ups. Of the forty-nine players who wore the Braves uniform, twenty-one were pitchers. One of the latter was the infielder Whitey Wietelmann, who found that while he had a strong arm, it was not strong enough for a pitcher.

Johnny Sain, after spending three years in the Navy Air Corps, returned to win twenty games and lose fourteen. A simple pop fly that fell for a you-take-it hit in the first inning at Cincinnati, July 12, cost him a perfect no-hit, no-run game. Ed Wright, Si Johnson, and

264

Bill Lee, former Cubs ace, had winning records. So did Warren Spahn, cool young southpaw who rejoined the team after being released from the Army in June. And so did Mort Cooper, who won two more games than he lost. Cooper shut out the Dodgers in Brooklyn, 4–0, in the season's last game, forcing a pennant play-off between the Dodgers and Cardinals. Better still, he won himself $100 from Perini, who was then giving cash prizes for shutouts and new suits for home runs.

The Braves had only two .300 hitters, Hopp batting .333 and Holmes .310, but the Tribe's .264 was only one point lower than the average of the league-leading Cards. The Braves were the victims, April 23, of a no-hit game pitched by Ed Head of Brooklyn. With the fence moved back in all directions, although still only 390 feet to dead center, there was marked decrease in home runs at Braves Field in 1946.

Boston fans reacted so favorably to the Braves that the club set itself an all-time attendance record of 969,673, nearly doubling the old record of 517,803 set in 1933. It was an eminently successful season and it closed with the Braves trading Billy Herman, who had been acquired from the Dodgers in midseason, along with Wietelmann, Elmer Singleton, and Stan Wentzel to the Pirates for Bob Elliott and Hank Camelli.

With the Red Sox having won their first pennant in twenty-eight years, and about to enter the World Series against the Cardinals, Boston fans were not especially stirred by the deal for Elliott. But before another season was to end, Eddie Dyer, Cardinals manager, was to call it "the greatest trade ever made." The Pirates gained no player strength, and Herman failed as a manager, but Elliott played so well for the Braves in 1947 that he was voted the National League's most valuable player, Boston's first since Johnny Evers won the Chalmers Award in 1914.

When Herman learned that the Pirates had given Elliott for him, he said, "Why, they've gone and traded the whole team on me."

Elliott in 1947 led the league in no major hitting department, but he batted .317, hit 23 home runs, and drove home 112 tallies. He hit in the pinches and made vital plays afield. His improvement, he admitted, traced to peace of mind. Southworth put him at third base and left him there. At Pittsburgh, he had been shuttled between third base and the outfield by Frank Frisch.

Besides Elliott, the Braves had two invaluable assets in Sain and Spahn. Each won twenty-one games. Spahn, joining Jim Turner, became the second Braves pitcher to lead the league in earned-run average. The twenty-six-year-old southpaw hurled seven shutouts. He won his first eight games. Sain did not start so well. In his second game, Mize of the Giants hit three successive home runs off him at Braves Field, but Sain won, 14–5.

"If I could win that one," said the big right-hander, his chew bulging in his cheek, "I should win any of 'em."

A few weeks later, Sain suffered an attack of hives. When the doctor said it was probably some kind of food to which he was allergic, the pitcher's wife said, "I hope it's tobacco." But it wasn't, and John's cheek continued to bulge.

The Braves trained for a second spring at Fort Lauderdale. Jake Flowers having become president of the Milwaukee farm, Ernie White, sore-armed southpaw, became a coach. Ted McGrew had moved to the Pirates, so young Harry Jenkins was made head of the farm system. A veteran of sixty-five missions over Europe, he was given a private plane with which to fly himself around the fast-expanding Braves chain. Southworth held a clinic for farm managers so that players coming up to the Braves would play his style of baseball—running, heads-up, hustling baseball. The Braves had reached the point where they were thinking of everything.

They even thought of having clinics for Ladies' Day fans, but this was a mistake. At the first clinic, the Braves tried to show the fair fans the secrets of the hit-and-run play, but Hopp, on first, promptly missed Elliott's signal and failed to run. It made little difference. Few women knew what it was all about, anyhow, although that of course does not include Mrs. Lolly Hopkins of Providence, whose loyalty had won her season passes from both Boston teams, and who was so familiar with ball-park procedure that she used a megaphone to help disseminate her knowledge to players, umpires, fans, and official scorers.

Although Red Barrett had returned from the Cardinals, the player most closely scrutinized for signs of abnormality was the new first baseman, Earl Torgeson. Reports of his misadventures in the minor leagues, private life, and the Army had preceded the Torch.

When Ted McGrew scouted Seattle in 1946, he used to sit in the hotel lobby to see at what hour Torgeson retired. Learning that he was being watched, Torgeson would openly leave the hotel late at night, sneak in by a back entrance, and go to bed. While he slept, McGrew would still be sitting in the lobby waiting for him to come in. The scout never quite understood how Torgeson could be so fresh and wide-awake every morning, while he, McGrew, was so tired and dopy.

But Southworth was not one to encourage caprices by a promising young rookie, Torgeson himself was anxious to make good, and the most eccentric thing he did during spring training was to bring two right-footed shoes to Lakeland when the Braves played the Tigers. This, according to Red Barrett, was not goofy at all, since Torgeson played first base as though he always wore two right-footed shoes.

Torgeson hit savagely, early in the season, but after Frank McCormick was signed, Southworth took to benching the rookie against southpaws. Even so, Torgeson hit seventeen home runs and drove in seventy-eight runs while hitting .281. Late in the season, when McCormick had a chance to lead the league in hitting, if he could only play in 100 games, Torgeson offered to remain on the bench, but McCormick protested, saying, "I wouldn't want to lead the league like that. We'll keep going as we have." They did, and McCormick did not play in 100 games. Neither did he lead the league.

The Braves bought Johnny Beazley from the Cardinals, but despite some mysterious nose treatments, the sore-armed pitcher who once was a phenomenal rookie never regained his effectiveness. Always trying to improve on their two-man pitching staff of Sain and Spahn, the Braves traded the apathetic Cooper to New York for Bill Voiselle, who won eight out of fifteen games for them. Voiselle got some renewed confidence when Frank Gustine of the Pirates challenged him for throwing bean balls one evening. Voiselle was flattered to think that he actually had enough stuff to hurt somebody, and thereafter pitched much more successfully.

Red Barrett hurled a one-hit game against the Cubs in June, a rival pitcher, Hank Borowy, making a puny single with two out in the sixth inning. Later in the season, Barrett was otherwise distinguished when he served a pitch to Lucky Lohrke in New York, on which the Giants set a new all-time home-run record.

Every time you looked up, when at Braves Field in 1947, Elliott was making another winning hit against the Pirates, Southworth was changing his line-up, somebody was being given a new automobile, a Boston outfielder was making a poor throw, or Sain was making another base hit. The pitcher batted safely in fourteen consecutive games and finished with a .346 average.

Among the automobiles given away were a new Packard and Ford served up by the Steam Shovels on Appreciation Day, August 20, when the Braves celebrated their arrival at the million mark in home attendance. It was a dismal afternoon, yet 24,638 fans paid their way into the park and endured a long afternoon to participate in the lottery. Not even a 16-to-10 victory for the Pirates could chase them away.

It was an impressive sight to see the ushers carrying in ticket boxes, like grooms leading in greyhounds at a dog track, the stubs being dumped into a barrel, the barrel being spun, and Mrs. Hopkins, without her megaphone on this occasion, but wearing an orchid instead, dunking her hand in and pulling out a Packard—or the equivalent thereof.

Other feathers in the promotion department's bonnet were the appearance of Chief Wild Horse in full war regalia at the season's opening game, the delivery by helicopter before a night game of an issue of *The Saturday Evening Post,* which featured a story on "The Three Little Steamshovels," and the Blue Plate Special. This last creation was a combination ticket for dinner at the Hotel Somerset, a cab ride to the ball park, and a reserved seat. Speculation immediately began as to when the Braves would introduce combinations good for a shave and haircut, a boat trip around the Charles River Basin, three beers at Huddleston's café, a manicure, and a box seat.

It would have been a dull season without at least one engineering feat being performed by the Steam Shovels at Braves Field. With the team away two weeks in June, the surface of the infield was lowered eighteen inches, 1,500 tons of earth being trucked away in the process. But while the infield was dropping eighteen inches in Boston, the Braves were rising from fourth place to second in the West.

The season could not be allowed to end without at least one dinner party, so to make sure, the Braves figured in two of them. The first was a testimonial to Duffy Lewis, the club's esteemed road secretary. Among the 900 guests present were Lewis's mates in the famous Red Sox outfield, Tris Speaker and Harry Hooper.

The second dinner was held by the Braves in New York as the World Series ended. While the occasion seemed pretentious enough to demand the acquisition of a Ralph Kiner, or at least an Enos

Slaughter, those attending were nevertheless impressed by the new five-year contract for $250,000 given Southworth. The man who had got $5 in his first professional game in Portsmouth, Ohio, was to get $365 a game the next five seasons, from the Braves.

Thus, with the assurance of continued good leadership, a highly recommended shortstop in Al Dark, a new outfielder in Jim Russell, for whom Johnny Hopp was traded to Pittsburgh, a new muscle man in Jeff Heath, a full quota of fond hopes, World Series ticket plans to fit any contingency, and countless promotional tricks up their sleeves, the Braves spiritedly embarked in their mechanized canoes for the 1948 season.

CHAPTER XXV

LAST DAYS IN BOSTON

⊜

THE final five-year chapter of the Braves' history in Boston began with a skyrocket's blazing swoosh, faded quickly to a dim ember and ended abruptly in the total darkness of oblivion.

The 1948 season was the most exciting Boston had ever known. The old town almost monopolized the World Series, for the Braves won in the National League, and the Red Sox lost in the American League only by yielding a play-off game to Cleveland. Bitter feelings arose between Braves and Red Sox players in the final weeks, and a World Series between the two Boston clubs probably would have been sensational.

But Cleveland took care of the Red Sox, then took care of the Braves, and all Boston had to show for 1948 was a National League pennant, which was quite enough since it was Boston's first in thirty-four years.

The Braves were strengthened in every department. For the outfield they bought Jeff Heath from the St. Louis Browns, got Jim Russell from Pittsburgh, and drafted Clint Conatser from Buffalo.

One day Conatser looked around spacious Braves Field and said, "I like to hit in a big park like this."

"You do?" exclaimed Heath and added pityingly, "Then you belong to Ripley."

The infield had a new keystone combination consisting of Al Dark, rookie shortstop up from Milwaukee, and Eddie Stankey, veteran second baseman acquired from Brooklyn for Bama Rowell and $100,000. New pitchers included Vern Bickford, competitive right-hander from Milwaukee; Bobby Hogue, chubby relief artist from Dallas; and, in June, Nelson Potter, who threw what Umpire Red Jones used to call "fruit salad." To help Phil Masi with the catching,

Bill Salkeld had been obtained from Pittsburgh along with Russell for Johnny Hopp and Danny Murtaugh.

This gave Billy Southworth a team experienced almost to the point of decrepitude, but about which there were only two big questions: how many veterans could again have good seasons, and would the rookie Dark come through at shortstop? Experts apparently thought both deserved affirmative answers, for in preseason polls they gave the Braves a slight pennant edge over St. Louis.

They were right about Dark. While not the slickest fielding short-stop in Braves history, he was an outstanding competitor—the kind who would go from first to third on a bunt or catch a difficult pop fly with his bare hand. As a sophomore at Louisiana State in 1942 he had been the football team's best runner, passer and punter, which meant that he was good enough to make a blocking back out of Steve Van Buren. A Marine flier during the war, Dark had signed with the Braves for a $40,000 bonus while in Lou Perini's plane, which was flying Southworth to an exhibition game at Rome, New York, in July 1946. Dark stayed with the Braves the last three months of the 1946 season, but played in only fifteen games. In 1947 he helped Milwaukee win the American Association play-offs.

Dark was voted the National League's leading rookie in 1948, and, while described by one rival slugger as "the worst-looking .322 hitter I've ever seen," he was a smart, hustling youngster. One day when he took some extra hitting practice with the reserves, Bob Sturgeon said to him, "Son, ain't you been hitting pretty good?"

"Yes," snapped the rookie, "but is that any reason why I shouldn't hit better?"

Southworth did a superb job of amalgamating the Braves, most of whom were veteran players who had serious limitations in one respect or another. The brusque little manager manipulated his lineup so as to get the maximum results with the talents at his dis-posal and, when he won the pennant, some observers were willing to rate him with Steinmetz and Edison. Some of his lineup shifts obviously came out of a test tube.

Who won the pennant for the Braves? Southworth got most of the credit, but Rogers Hornsby said, "Bob Elliott made the Braves. He's the old-time type who hits and plays best in the clutch."

The league's most valuable player in 1947, Elliott dropped to .283 in 1948, but he knocked in a hundred runs and hit twenty-three

271

homers, enough to make his nickname, Mr. Team, a household word around Boston.

Until he broke his ankle in midseason, Stanky was a spark plug. And when he was hurt, Sibby Sisti stepped in at second base and played as he never had before and never has since. The Braves did as well with Sisti as they did with Stanky, and there were some sideline objections when Stanky was returned to the lineup for the World Series.

Tommy Holmes not only led the team in hitting with a .325 average, but actually saved the Braves four straight defeats in St. Louis when he threw out Musial at the plate from right field in the ninth inning one day. Torgeson and Masi both slumped to .253, but they played steadily on defense, and Torgy was safe the first fourteen times he tried to steal a base.

But the Braves really excelled in pitching. Warren Spahn was the southpaw ace, winning fifteen games, and Vern Bickford had an 11–5 record in his first season. Hogue, Potter and Shoun were outstanding in relief. The big wheel, however, was Johnny Sain, whose 24–15 record made him a twenty-game winner for the third successive season.

"Same old Braves," was the quip of the hour when the Braves lost six of their first seven games, but by May 13 they had worked their way up to .500, and on June 11 they went into first place. Although Stanky had broken his ankle July 8 in a collision at third base with Bruce Edwards in Brooklyn, the Braves at the All-Star Game intermission held a five-and-one-half game lead over Pittsburgh.

In June the Braves in fierce competition with other big-league teams had signed an eighteen-year-old left-handed pitcher just graduated from high school. The Braves gave Johnny Antonelli of Rochester a bonus of $52,000, but the turning point in negotiations came when Antonelli's father, a small contractor, boasted to Lou Perini, "I own two steam shovels. How many do you own?"

"I'm not sure," said Perini mildly. "About fifty-two, I think."

The big outlay of cash to an untried schoolboy irked veteran players. Mel Ott of the Giants said sourly, "John McGraw gave me $400 for signing, but of course a dollar went farther in those days."

None of the Braves was more annoyed than Sain, and to mollify him the Braves before the All-Star Game in St. Louis gave him a new and better contract covering the balance of the 1948 season and the 1949 season as well. Sain responded nobly.

272

By July 18 the Braves had an eight-game lead, but then their fortunes ebbed. Their lead was cut to two games by mid-August; Southworth had been booed after using Al Lyons, a pitcher, as a pinch hitter for Heath; and Jim Russell, who in one game had hit a home run and a double batting first left-handed and then right-handed, was in a hospital with a heart condition.

Late in August the Braves lost six out of seven games in Chicago and Pittsburgh, and on August 29 dropped off the top for the first time in ten weeks. Four days later, however, they were back up there to stay. Nothing did them more good than a double victory over Brooklyn at Boston September 6 which gave them a four-game lead over the Dodgers. Warren Spahn pitched perhaps the best game of the season, winning the opener 2–1 in fourteen innings, allowing only five hits and picking Jackie Robinson off base twice. Torgeson's double in the fourteenth was the winning hit. Sain then won the seven-inning nightcap 4–0 as 39,670 fans roared to see the Braves for the first time in many long years win the games they had to win.

After that it was a buggy ride. The pennant was clinched a week before the season ended by a 3–2 victory over the Giants in Boston as Elliott's home run with two on in the first inning gave the Braves all their runs. Bickford got credit for the victory, although Potter finished for him.

Great was the jubilation then. Players pounded each other on the back. Stanky and Southworth embraced. In the front office champagne flowed, and Perini, waving aloft Elliott's home-run ball, said, "I'm walking on air and tripping over clouds." Actually, he was walking on champagne bubbles and tripping over corks.

It would have been more fitting if the Braves had clinched the pennant the day before when Sain pitched on his thirty-first birthday, but the Giants beat him 3–2 as the Braves failed to score in the ninth after filling the bases with none out.

"If I'd won that one, it might have made me the most valuable player," admitted the man of few words. "I'd have liked that, but if I was voting, I'd vote for Musial."

When the official ballots were counted, it was Stan Musial, not Sain, who was voted the National League's most valuable player of 1948. But in a period of nineteen days, from September 3 to September 21, Sain had pitched and won six games for the Braves, allowing only ten runs. As a workout for the World Series, he pitched the day before the season ended, retired after five innings and got credit for a 2–1 victory over the Giants. Until then, Sain had won sixty-eight games for the Braves, and had finished every one of them.

The 1948 Braves probably had only one indispensable player. He was Johnny Sain.

2

The Braves went into the World Series against Cleveland with one of their heaviest hitters on crutches. Jeff Heath broke his ankle sliding home at Brooklyn four days before the season ended. The Torso had hit .310, walloped twenty homers, knocked in seventy-seven runs, and his performance against his former Cleveland teammates had been eagerly awaited.

Thirty-four years earlier, the Braves had suffered a similar blow before the 1914 World Series when Red Smith, their hard-hitting third baseman, broke his leg sliding in Brooklyn, also after the pennant had been clinched. The 1914 Braves got along well enough without Smith to beat the Athletics four consecutive games, but the 1948 Braves were far less successful without Heath.

Cleveland won a six-game series that was an anticlimax to the frantic American League pennant race. Not until the day after the season closed did the Braves know they were to play Cleveland. Most of them were at Fenway Park to see the Indians beat the Red Sox 8–3 in the play-off game which pleased them hugely.

Although tired and let down, Cleveland was favored 13–5 to win the Series, having a younger, better-balanced team than the Braves, who were generally regarded as the best of a rather poor lot of National League clubs. The favorites came through because while Braves pitching was good, Cleveland's was better; and while Cleveland's hitting was poor, Boston's was worse. But the Series was by no means a washout for excitement.

The first game, seen by 40,135 at Braves Field, will never be forgotten. Sain outpitched Bob Feller to win 1–0 with the winning run scoring in the eighth inning on Holmes's single after a hotly disputed pick-off play at second. Feller opened the eighth by walking Salkeld. Masi, running for Salkeld, was sacrificed to second by Mike McCormick. Sisti ran for Stanky, who drew an intentional base on balls.

With Sain batting, Feller suddenly whirled and threw to Boudreau, who had cut over from shortstop in a count play the Indians had exploited all season. Masi desperately dove head first into the base just as Boudreau touched him on the shoulder.

"Safe," said Bill Stewart, National League umpire at second base, turning his palms downward.

For a moment it looked as though Boudreau would have hysterics, but the argument was brief, and when play resumed, Sain lined out to Judnich in right. An instant later Stewart's decision became monumental, for Tommy Holmes sliced a single inside third base to score Masi easily from second base. It was the first 1–0 game in a World Series in twenty-five years, and long did arguments rage over Stewart's decision for action photographs indicated that Stewart might have been wrong. The umpire only said, "Masi's hand was on the base when Boudreau tagged him on the shoulder."

Sain was not unduly excited about his four-hit shutout. When a reporter asked, "Tough game, John?" he replied laconically, "Never had an easy one yet."

Bob Lemon defeated Spahn 4–1 in the second game at Braves Field as 39,633 fans watched. The Braves scored their run in the first inning, and might have got more except for a maneuver the Indians were making monotonous. A Lemon-Boudreau pick-off rubbed out Torgeson at second. Cleveland tied the score on Boudreau's double and Joe Gordon's single in the fourth, and Doby's single brought Gordon home with the winning run.

When the Series moved to Cleveland, it was evident why the Braves had preferred the Indians as World Series rivals. The three games in Cleveland's Municipal Stadium drew in turn 70,306, 81,897 and 86,288 fans. Cleveland was hungry for its first World Series since 1920.

Gene Bearden, angular rookie southpaw, a war hero and the money pitcher who had hurled the play-off victory against the Red Sox, shut out the Braves 2–0 in the third game. He doubled and scored the winning run in the third inning when Dark threw wildly to first base. The Indians made only five hits off Bickford, Bill Voiselle and Red Barrett.

Boudreau gambled on Steve Gromek, a knuckle-baller who had won only nine games during the season, to face Sain in the fourth game, and he won 2–1. The only run off Gromek was a homer by outfielder Marv Rickert, who had been recalled from Milwaukee when Heath was hurt. The Indians scored twice off Sain, on Mitchell's single and Boudreau's double in the first inning, and on

275

Doby's 410-foot home run to center in the third. Of the last seventeen men to face Sain, only one reached base. Ed Robinson got an infield single in the fifth when Sain failed to cover first base. Cleveland rooters gasped in the eighth inning when Hegan and Keltner had a disagreement under an infield fly as the tying run was crossing the plate for Boston, but the catcher held the ball.

With a 3–1 lead, the Indians went into the Sunday game saying, "Let's not go back to Boston. Let's finish it today." They had plenty of moral support, for the crowd of 86,288 was the largest ever to attend a World Series game, but what they needed was better pitching. Feller did not resemble the fellow who had lost 1–0 in the opener. Elliott hit a three-run homer off him in the first, and another homer in the third. Despite this, the Indians rallied for four runs off Potter in the fourth, giving Feller a 5–4 lead, but he just did not have it. Salkeld's homer tied the score in the sixth, and a six-run rally in the seventh disposed of Feller, Klieman and Christopher.

The 11–5 victory went to Spahn, who relieved Potter in the fourth and allowed only one man to reach base. He struck out five of the last six batters to face him. This loosely played game had a little of everything, including a balk by Satchel Paige, a squeeze bunt by Dark, and a single to right for Stanky when he threw his bat at the ball. The Braves had waited until the mattress was on fire before grabbing a fire extinguisher, but they were still alive and talking about miracles as the teams returned to Boston.

The sixth game, seen by 40,103 fans, was the most exciting of the series. Big Bill Voiselle, wearing No. 96 out of respect for his home town, started against Lemon. The Indians scored in the third when Mitchell doubled to left and Holmes could not hang on to Boudreau's bloop double to right. The Braves tied it 1–1 in the fourth on Elliott's single, Salkeld's walk, and Mike McCormick's single.

A home run by Gordon, followed by a walk to Tucker, Robinson's single, and a missed double play on Stanky's high throw, put the Indian's ahead 3–1 in the sixth. They made it 4–1 on successive singles off Spahn by Keltner, Tucker, and Robinson in the eighth, but the Braves came right back for two runs.

Holmes led off with a single, and after Dark had lined out, Torgeson moved Holmes to third with a double. Elliott walked to fill the bases, and Bearden replaced Lemon. Clint Conatser, hitting for Rickert, flied solidly to Tucker in center, scoring Holmes; and Masi, hitting for Salkeld, doubled high off the fence in left. Torgeson scored, but Elliott only got to third, and there the tying run died as Mike McCormick bounced sharply to Bearden.

The Braves had another chance in the ninth, after Spahn had fanned three Indians in a row. Bearden passed Stanky for a start, and Connie Ryan ran for the little veteran. With a sacrifice in order, Sisti was sent up to bat for Spahn, but after fouling off one bunt, he raised a puny little fly that Hegan grabbed four feet in front of the plate and turned into a double play on the anxious Ryan. When Holmes flied out, the Braves had lost their first World Series, and the popular hard-luck kid, Sisti, was the goat.

"So long, Skipper," said Sisti to Southworth, later that afternoon.

"So long, Sibby. You're still the best bunter in the league."

"Yeah, but I let you down today. I let you down."

Boston truly had a let-down feeling, first because of the Red Sox, then because of the Braves, whose hitters had looked as though they were trying to pick a lock with a shovel as they faced Cleveland pitchers. But for the Steam Shovels, 1948 had been a glorious success. The Series had set records with a total attendance of 358,362 and receipts of $1,633,685. Each Cleveland regular drew $6,772, each Boston loser collected $4,570. The Steam Shovels got $210,104 as their end.

The Braves had been in the limelight from opening day, when they gave the fans a $50,000 electrical scoreboard which was as large as a tennis court. They inaugurated Jimmy Fund Day, a charity for the Children's Hospital cancer research. On the night of June 15 their game against Chicago at Braves Field was the first to be telecast in Boston. They staged another Appreciation Day on August 8, giving away automobiles, television sets and World Series trips, and drew 41,527 bingo players for a single game with the last-place Cubs.

The Braves set their Boston attendance record at 1,455,438, despite miserable weather in the spring, and the faithful sun-tanners were so crowded in the jury box that one of them, Elmer Foote, complained, "We were better off when we were in the second division." By the end of 1948, it seemed that the Braves had established themselves as powerful competitors of the Red Sox for the favor of the Boston public.

3

It soon became clear that the Braves could stand everything but success. No sooner had a pennant been won than the club went to pieces, and as the seasons passed, the pieces kept getting smaller. The collapse of the Braves was sudden and complete. Nobody suspected it then, but the pennant conquest of 1948 was the last convulsive effort of a dying giant, the last flaming eruption of a volcano before it becomes a clinker.

The first intimation that all was not well came shortly after the season closed, when Coach Fred Fitzsimmons quit the Braves and signed with the Giants. Such a walkout was an abuse of baseball law, and Commissioner A. B. Chandler punished both Fitzsimmons and the Giants. More important, it indicated that Fitzsimmons was unhappy with the Braves, although he did not tell why.

Southworth, encouraged by his success, was more than ever a martinet as spring training began in 1949. His two-a-day sessions totaled six hours, he had time-table workouts, like an expediter he rushed all over the field with a clipboard in his hand, and he generally managed to antagonize a team that was in no mood to be driven.

While the manager's masterminding had annoyed the players in 1948, the pleasure of winning had made it tolerable, but then the team's front office while negotiating 1949 contracts told them, in effect, "Southworth won the pennant. You didn't. You should thank Lou Perini for bringing you here to play for such a great manager."

This was too much and, of course, placed Southworth in the most awkward situation possible with his players, some of whom gritted their teeth when they said, "Miracle manager my eye. He gets the credit we deserve."

Tension increased between manager and players at the Bradenton camp. Before one exhibition game, Southworth told his pitchers to run around the outfield. They did, then went into the clubhouse, showered, and dressed. The manager sent word from the bench that the players were to put on their uniforms and come out. They refused. After the game, Southworth blew up and said, "That's the last time anybody will ever put anything over on me."

The manager had the jitters. He began to stay up nights to check players into the hotel. Some needed checking, but many would be in their rooms asleep when Shorty Young, the manager's watchdog, would rap on the door at midnight, and ask, "Are you in?" He also broke rules he had set for them, and they knew it. Rumors circulated that Eddie Stanky might replace Southworth as manager, but that the Braves were on the verge of an open revolt, as written by Dave

Egan of the *Record-Advertiser,* was debatable. There was no doubt that dissension was racking the team.

When Egan's story was read to Southworth, he said, "I don't believe a word of it." Advised to ask the players for a vote of confidence, he refused, explaining, "It would be like an admission of guilt."

Red Barrett, a pitcher who was on Southworth's side, suggested such a vote, but was promptly rebuked. Stanky is supposed to have said, "If Southworth wants a vote of confidence, let him ask for it himself."

The Braves nevertheless got off to a good start, and were in first place as late as June 4. In view of their many misfortunes, they probably did well to finish fourth, twenty-two games behind the champion Dodgers. What hurt them most was the following:

Jeff Heath went on the disabled list early in May, because of a slow recovery of his broken ankle, and did not play until August.

Earl Torgeson suffered a shoulder separation May 14 as he slid into Jackie Robinson trying to break up a double play. The Braves bought Elbie Fletcher from Jersey City to play first base.

Phil Masi slumped badly and was sold to Pittsburgh.

Johnny Sain hurt his arm, and although he continued to pitch, he lost seventeen games while winning only ten.

Southworth did not defend Stanky when hit-and-run plays by the veteran with Spahn on first base on a hot day enabled Pittsburgh to rout the pitcher with a six-run ninth inning that won the game.

Lou Perini flew to Cincinnati July 26 "to see what is wrong with the Braves."

When Torgeson was almost ready to play again, in August, he suffered a broken thumb and Jim Russell got a handsome shiner in a fight that caused Southworth to fine each of them $250.

And on August 16 Southworth was given a leave of absence for the balance of the season because of ill health, and Johnny Cooney was appointed acting manager.

Southworth, who said he was being persecuted by the press, was on the verge of a breakdown, but the *Boston Globe* summarized:

The Braves were an old club, crabby, bitter, set in their ways. Players who could no longer deliver blamed their ineptness on Southworth. Victory, which sugar-coated the bitterness underneath last season, eluded the crippled Braves and left bare the acrid taste of defeat, futility and animosity.

Southworth, one of the great managers, could not cope with the situation. Perhaps he was too aloof, too domineering, too cocky, and while he did not need the friendship of his players, even he could not afford to lose their respect.

As with Mickey Cochrane, Joe McCarthy, Shono Collins, Bob Coleman and many others, the pressure of managing a difficult team became too great for Southworth. Polls of players after he had gone to his home in Sudbury, Ohio, indicated that a majority hoped he would not return. Late in the season, the bitterness of some players toward him was revealed when he was voted only a one-half share of the club's fourth-place World Series money, the vote being 11–8 on a show of hands.

The Steam Shovels had a problem: should they bring Southworth back in 1950, or should they trade the players who most strongly opposed him?

Since the manager had three years left on a contract that paid him $50,000 annually, they let their pocketbooks do their voting. Southworth came back. Stanky and Dark, the inseparables, were traded to the Giants for Buddy Kerr, shortstop; Willard Marshall, right fielder; Sid Gordon, third baseman and left fielder; and Sam Webb, pitcher.

In Boston, it was generally considered a good trade for the Braves, because Dark had slumped in his second season and Stanky seemed near the end of his playing career. The reasoning must have been erroneous. The Giants finished third with Dark and Stanky, one place ahead of the Braves, in 1950; and won the pennant with them in 1951.

A subdued Southworth returned in the spring of 1950. He relaxed his discipline, and said cheerfully, "We'll come back," but spring training consisted more of the players' passing judgment on the manager than vice versa.

The Braves had their first Negro player in Sam Jethroe, a center fielder who was the league's fastest runner, but not its surest catch of a fly ball. He stole three bases in a game, scored from second on an infield out, stole home, and struck out four times in a game.

The Braves had three excellent pitchers: Sain 20–13, Spahn 21–17, Bickford 19–14. Bickford pitched a no-hit, no-run game against Brooklyn under lights at Braves Field August 11. Tied for first as late as July 18, the Braves faded in mid-August and finished fourth, eight games behind the winning Phillies. Marshall failed to plug the hole in right, Stanky was missed at second, and the staff needed another starting pitcher.

The Braves wanted harmony in 1950, and they had harmony, but the bum couldn't hit, run, or throw.

Before the 1951 opener, the Three Little Steam Shovels had become two. Dapper Guido Rugo was out as vice-president. There were other changes. Tommy Holmes was made manager of the Hartford farm team. The Braves and Red Sox, broadcasting all home and away games, battled on the air waves. Braves Field looked neater with only one advertising sign on the outfield fence.

But there was nothing neater about the team, and with the club in fifth place on June 19, Southworth announced in Chicago that, for reasons of health, he was resigning as manager, with a year and a half to go on his contract. He had made a comeback of sorts after his 1949 breakdown, but had never fully regained his own confidence nor the respect of his players. His masterminding, so acceptable in 1948, had become irksome. He feuded with baseball writers. His responsibilities weighed heavily on him.

Tommy Holmes, who was promoted from Hartford to replace him, was an improvement socially. For ten years he had been a Braves outfielder, a consistent hitter, and a popular player, but not even his admirers could argue that he was temperamentally suited to be a leader of big-league ball players.

"I've got to be firm. Everything depends on it. It'll be a tough job," said Holmes. How right he was. Too many Braves veterans had played with him and knew him to be an agreeable fellow lacking experience and a manager's essential streak of meanness.

Braves executives must have known it, too, but with their club going nowhere, burdened by high salaries, and suffering from diminishing attendances, their first concern was to reduce costs. These factors also caused them to sell John Sain, thirty-three-year-old veteran with a 5–13 record, to the Yankees August 29—a deal which helped the Yankees win three more pennants, but which did not hurt the Braves, since it gave them $50,000 and Lew Burdette, a capable pitcher.

The Braves in 1951 had a 28–31 record under Southworth, a 48–47 record under Holmes, and while they finished fourth, twenty games behind the Giants, they had no idea of the fate awaiting them in 1952.

The Braves prettied up their park with some fancy fir trees around the outfield fence, which was lowered five feet in a bid for more home runs; and they wasted $50,000 before the season on a publicity stunt known as the "Rookie Rocket," which was a chartered plane flying Boston writers around the country to interview Braves prospects, most of whom were unknown then and are unknown now.

After a faltering start, a sadly disillusioned Holmes was replaced May 31 by Charley Grimm, popular and experienced manager of the Milwaukee farm club. Ridiculed by veteran players who probably were jealous of him, Holmes made two major mistakes: (1) he chose Jack Cusick as his shortstop, instead of Johnny Logan; (2) he coached at third base, a job for which he had neither the experience nor the judgment. "Maybe we were too hasty in giving Holmes the job," said Perini.

The Braves, who were 13–22 under Holmes, were 51–67 the rest of the season under Grimm. They never reached the .500 mark, never were in the first division. They finished seventh, and were eliminated as pennant contenders August 31. Sid Gordon won a bear with his bat, Torgeson fought Sal Yvars of the Giants, Spahn got a threatening fan letter from Chicago, but the Braves were a woeful team with only one real attraction—a powerful rookie third baseman, Eddie Mathews, who hit twenty-five home runs, three of them in one game at Brooklyn.

Nobody knew it then, but the Braves were playing their last game at Braves Field on Sunday, September 21, when the Dodgers defeated them, 8–2, before 8,822 fans. It was the largest crowd since July 5, when the Dodgers drew 13,405—and that was the largest crowd the Braves had at home any day during their eighty-first and last season in Boston.

4

When Lou Perini after the 1952 season promised Milwaukee fans that he would help them get a big-league team, nobody in Boston seriously thought that the team might be the Braves. The St. Louis Browns were the weak sisters who were always being associated with any franchise-shifting proposal. In any event, said cynics, sending the 1952 Braves there would not give Milwaukee a big-league team.

The serious drop in Braves home attendance in 1951 and 1952, however, worried many Boston observers, and one prophet had written in July, "One of these days the Braves may go on the road and never come back."

A strong hint that Perini had big thoughts stirring in the back of his busy little brain was the announcement November 13 that he and his brothers, Joseph and Charles, were ready to buy all the stock—about 45 per cent—held by eight minority stockholders. Terms were agreed upon in less than two weeks, and on November 26 it was revealed that B. Perini & Sons of Framingham, Massachusetts, had arranged to buy the stock held by C. Joseph Maney (20 per cent), Leon and Joseph Rugo, Frank McCourt, the Estate of Frank Allen, Joseph O'Connell, Daniel Marr, and Jay Cole.

Why did Perini want all the stock?

"Is it a preliminary towards moving the Braves to another city—Milwaukee, as alarmists will suggest?" wrote a Boston sports columnist. "Is it intended by Perini to let his friends get out from under?

"If this is only a friendly act, then Perini must foresee more hard times for the Braves. If it is only a business move, then he foresees a bright future."

Perini said he wanted the stock so he could be free to act quickly without worrying about friends. That Perini was getting ready to take a big plunge of some sort should have been pretty clear, but for some reason—maybe eighty-two years of association with the Braves—it wasn't.

Braves fortunes had sagged, then plummeted after the 1948 zenith had been reached, presumably because of these four major mistakes: (1) giving Southworth a five-year contract; (2) trading Dark and Stanky to the Giants; (3) playing too many night games; (4) making Holmes the manager before he was ready. The club's rise and fall is best shown by the following table of home attendances and estimated profits and losses:

Year	Position	Attendance	Profit (Loss)
1944	6	208,681	($133,022)
1945	6	374,178	(137,142)
1946	4	969,673	39,565
1947	3	1,277,361	229,153
1948	1	1,455,439	238,104
1949	4	1,081,795	147,934
1950	4	844,391	(316,510)
1951	4	487,475	(380,000)
1952	7	282,000	(580,000)

During the winter, there was no further intimation that the Braves might leave Boston before another season started. Baseball writers received the customary small but well-intentioned Christmas gift from the club. The Braves attended the annual Baseball Writers' Dinner in force, and Manager Grimm told how the Braves would improve in 1953 and other funny stories.

The purchase of Andy Pafko from the Dodgers was hailed as a great boost for Mathews, who would not have to face so much left-handed pitching; and in February there was a four-club trade the ramifications of which were a little difficult to follow without a bloodhound, but which experts applauded with choice adjectives when the Braves wound up with Joe Adcock and Jim Pendleton and without Earl Torgeson.

As the Tribe headed south for another training season at Bradenton, reports that Milwaukee was putting pressure on the Braves to surrender their rights there so that the Browns might move in were read with complacency in Boston. An eyebrow or two lifted, however, when Fred Saigh turned down an offer of four million from Milwaukee and sold the Cardinals to the Anheuser-Busch Company for $3,750,000.

There was a little uneasiness, but not much, in Boston when Joseph Cairnes, Braves executive vice-president, said that he had been offered $500,000 for the Milwaukee territory, with the idea that the Braves would move their farm team to Toledo.

"I wish they'd forget it until next Fall," said Cairnes, with real concern in his voice. A reporter concluded from this: "Who knows? By next October the Braves may want Milwaukee for themselves." He was getting warm.

The possibility that the Braves would immediately leave Boston seemed remote, because Perini was a Boston man who had called the Braves "a sacred trust," and who had once said, "As long as I own the Braves, they will belong to Boston." His most ominous warning had been sounded after the 1952 season: "We'll give the Boston fans two more years to support the Braves."

As the team's camp followers sunned themselves before the Hotel Dixie Grande, the morning of Friday, March 13, they had little more on their minds than Dixie Walker's prediction that Mathews would hit thirty-five home runs, and the speed Bill Bruton had shown to score from first base on a single two days earlier. At noon,

284

however, Sam Levy, baseball writer for the *Milwaukee Journal,* bustled into camp and asked John Quinn to call a press conference.

Levy said he had confronted Perini at his beach residence with a scoop by *The Sporting News* that the Braves would move to Milwaukee before the opening of the season, while the Browns would move to Baltimore. Levy had been asked to relay Perini's reply to the Boston press. It consisted of this:

"I can't say yes and I can't say no."

The implications of this evasion were so clear that within an hour the *Boston Globe* was on the streets with a front-page banner reading: BRAVES QUIT HUB.

Contacted by Boston writers that evening just before he flew to St. Petersburg to attend a dinner for August Busch, new Cardinals owner, Perini refused to elucidate, but said sadly, "You don't know all the letters, telegrams, and telephone calls I've been getting on this thing from the Midwest."

When the first excitement had worn off and cold logic had a chance to work, Boston writers concluded that this was probably a false alarm. Perini was stalling, waiting for the Browns to move to Baltimore before saying "No" to Milwaukee. How could he get a unanimous vote of approval from the National League for such a drastic experiment on such short notice? It was preposterous.

Thus, for those Bostonians who had talked themselves into a sense of security, it was a shock all over again when, at 12:05 P.M. on Saturday, Perini began his remarks to a remarkably well-attended press conference by saying:

"I have a difficult announcement to make. We are moving the Braves to Milwaukee. I shall make an application to the commissioner."

He was very apologetic. He was sorry for the loyal Braves fans of Boston, few as they were; sorry for the business Boston would lose; sorry for the baseball writers who would be shifted to other assignments. It was obvious, he said, that Boston could no longer support two teams, that it was a one-team town, and that the team it preferred undoubtedly was the Red Sox. A little shudder rippled through the assembly when he said, "Maybe some day I'll be back in Boston. Maybe some day Tom Yawkey will sell the Red Sox and I'll buy them."

Then it was only a matter of gears turning. Perini was a shrewd engineer. He made no mistakes. When the American League turned

285

down Bill Veeck's request to transfer the Browns to Baltimore, chances for the Braves to stay in Boston seemed a little brighter, but no National League owner would promise to veto the Braves move.

"We never took a nickle out of Boston," said Horace Stoneham, whose memory apparently did not carry back to the 112,000 fans the Giants drew in three days at Boston in 1933.

Gabe Paul of Cincinnati said, "How could I vote against the Braves? Lou is such a good fellow."

And that is how Perini and Milwaukee won. A Chamber of Commerce committee to save the Braves for Boston arrived late at St. Petersburg on the crucial day, March 18, and never did get into the National League meeting, which on an open ballot unanimously voted the Braves permission to move to Milwaukee. The American Association likewise agreed that the Milwaukee franchise be moved to Toledo, when paid $50,000 damages for its territorial loss.

Thus, at the Hotel Vinoy Park in St. Petersburg on March 18, 1953, ended the first chapter in the history of the Braves, which had begun at the Parker House in Boston, January 20, 1871. The club quickly trucked its equipment from Boston to Milwaukee. The 1953 tickets were burned, and Braves Field, which three years earlier had been bought from the Gaffney Estate, was locked up and allowed to go to seed, until sold in July to Boston University.

The name may be changed, the bronze plaques to the memories of Christy Mathewson and Tony Boeckel may be removed from the infield walls, and an atmosphere of collegiate athletics may henceforth prevail at the stockade beside the Charles, but it will be long before the spirits of Maranville and Evers, Berger, Waner, and many other great National League ball players stop cavorting at Braves Field in the memory of man.

STATISTICAL APPENDIX

TABLE 1

BRAVES WINNINGEST PITCHERS, YEAR-BY-YEAR

Year	Name	W-L	ERA
1876	Jack Manning	18–5	2.14
1877	Tommy Bond	40–17	2.11
1878	Tommy Bond	40–19	2.06
1879	Tommy Bond	43–19	1.96
1880	Tommy Bond	26–29	2.67
1881	Jim Whitney	31–33	2.48
1882	Jim Whitney	24–21	2.64
1883	Jim Whitney	37–21	2.24
1884	Charlie Buffinton	48–16	2.15
1885	Charlie Buffinton	22–27	2.88
1886	Old Hoss Radbourn	27–31	3.00
1887	Old Hoss Radbourn	24–23	4.55
1888	John Clarkson	33–20	2.76
1889	John Clarkson	49–19	2.73
1890	Kid Nichols	27–19	2.21
1891	John Clarkson	33–19	2.79
1892	Kid Nichols	35–16	2.83
	Jack Stivetts	35–16	3.03
1893	Kid Nichols	34–14	3.52
1894	Kid Nichols	32–13	4.75
1895	Kid Nichols	26–16	3.41
1896	Kid Nichols	30–14	2.83
1897	Kid Nichols	31–11	2.64
1898	Kid Nichols	32–12	2.13
1899	Vic Willis	27–8	2.50
1900	Bill Dinneen	20–14	3.12
1901	Vic Willis	20–17	2.36

Year	Name	W-L	ERA
1902	Togie Pittinger	27–16	2.52
	Vic Willis	27–20	2.20
1903	Togie Pittinger	19–23	3.48
1904	Vic Willis	18–25	2.85
1905	Irv Young	20–21	2.90
1906	Irv Young	16–25	2.94
1907	Patsy Flaherty	12–15	2.70
	Gus Dorner	12–16	3.12
1908	Vive Lindaman	12–15	2.36
1909	Al Mattern	16–20	2.85
1910	Al Mattem	15–19	2.98
1911	Buster Brown	7–18	4.29
1912	Hub Perdue	13–16	3.80
1913	Lefty Tyler	16–17	2.79
	Hub Perdue	16–13	3.26
1914	Dick Rudolph	26–10	2.35
	Bill James	26–7	1.90
1915	Dick Rudolph	22–19	2.37
1916	Dick Rudolph	19–12	2.16
1917	Art Nehf	16–8	2.16
1918	Art Nehf	15–15	2.69
1919	Dick Rudolph	13–18	2.17
1920	Joe Oeschger	15–13	3.46
1921	Joe Oeschger	20–14	3.52
1922	Frank Miller	11–13	3.51
1923	Rube Marquard	11–15	5.09
	Joe Genewich	13–14	3.72
1924	Jesse Barnes	15–20	3.23
1925	Larry Benton	14–7	3.09
	Johnny Cooney	14–14	3.48
1926	Larry Benton	14–14	3.85
1927	Joe Genewich	11–8	3.87
	Kent Greenfield	11–14	3.84
1928	Bob Smith	13–17	3.83
1929	Socks Siebold	12–17	4.73
1930	Socks Siebold	15–16	4.12
1931	Ed Brandt	18–11	2.92
1932	Ed Brandt	16–16	3.97
1933	Ben Cantwell	20–10	2.62

Year	Name	W-L	ERA
1934	Fred Frankhouse	17–9	3.20
	Huck Berts	17–10	4.06
1935	Fred Frankhouse	11–15	4.76
1936	Danny MacFayden	17–13	2.87
1937	Jim Turner	20–11	2.38
	Lou Fette	20–10	2.88
1938	Danny MacFayden	14–9	2.95
	Jim Turner	14–18	3.46
1939	Bill Posedel	15–13	3.92
1940	Dick Erickson	12–13	3.16
	Bill Posedel	12–17	4.13
1941	Jim Tobin	12–12	3.10
1942	Al Javery	12–16	3.03
	Jim Tobin	12–21	3.97
1943	Al Javery	17–16	3.21
1944	Jim Tobin	18–19	3.01
1945	Jim Tobin	9–14	3.84
1946	Johnny Sain	20–14	2.21
1947	Warren Spahn	21–10	2.33
	Johnny Sain	21–12	3.52
1948	Johnny Sain	24–15	2.60
1949	Warren Spahn	21–14	3.07
1950	Warren Spahn	21–17	3.16
1951	Warren Spahn	22–14	2.98
1952	Warren Spahn	14–19	2.98

TABLE 2
BRAVES WHO LED LEAGUE IN BATTING

Batting Average

1877	Deacon White	.387
1889	Dan Brouthers	.373
1894	Hugh Duffy	.440
1928	Rogers Hornsby	.387
1942	Ernie Lombardi	.330

Home Runs

1879	Charley Jones	9
1880	John O'Rourke	6
1894	Hugh Duffy	18
1897	Hugh Duffy	11
1898	Jim Collins	15
1900	Herman Long	12
1907	David Brain	10
1935	Wally Berger	34
1945	Tommy Holmes	28

Runs Batted In

1877	Deacon White	49
1879	John O'Rourke	62
1894	Hugh Duffy	145
1935	Wally Berger	130

Hits

1877	Deacon White	213
1894	Hugh Duffy	237
1911	Roy Miller	192
1926	Ed Brown	201
1945	Tommy Holmes	224
1947	Tommy Holmes	191

TABLE 3
BRAVES WHO LED LEAGUE IN PITCHING

Earned Run Average

1879	Tommy Bond	1.96
1899	John Clarkson	2.73
1937	Jim Turner	2.38
1947	Warren Spahn	2.33
1951	Chet Nichols	2.88

Strikeouts

1877	Tommy Bond	170
1878	Tommy Bond	182
1883	Jim Whitney	345
1889	John Clarkson	284
1902	Vic Willis	225
1949	Warren Spahn	151
1950	Warren Spahn	191
1951	Warren Spahn (Tie)	164
1952	Warren Spahn	183

Victories

1877	Tommy Bond	40
1878	Tommy Bond	40
1888	John Clarkson	33
1889	John Clarkson	49
1897	Kid Nichols	31
1898	Kid Nichols	32
1914	Dick Rudolph (Tie)	27
1948	Johnny Sain	24
1949	Warren Spahn	21
1950	Warren Spahn	20

TABLE 4
NO-HIT GAMES

1892	Jack Stivetts vs. Brooklyn, Aug. 6, 11–0
1899	Vic Willis vs. Washington, Aug. 7, 7–1
1907	Frank Pfeffer vs. Cincinnati, May 8, 6–0
1914	George Davis vs. Phila., Sept. 9, 7–0 (2nd Game)
1916	Tom Hughes vs. Pittsburgh, June 16, 2–0
1944	Jim Tobin vs. Brooklyn, Apr. 27, 2–0
1950	Vern Bickford vs. Brooklyn, Aug. 11,7–0 (Night)

TABLE 5
BRAVES AWARDS BRAVES ALL-STAR GAME SELECTIONS

Year	Name(s)
1933	Wally Berger, of
1934	Wally Berger, of; Fred Frankhouse, p
1935	Wally Berger, of
1936	Wally Berger, of
1937	Gene Moore, of
1938	Tony Cuccinello, 2b; Jim Turner, p
1939	Lou Fette, p
1940	Max West, of
1941	Eddie Miller, ss
1942	Ernie Lombardi, c; Eddie Miller, ss
1943	Al Javery, p
1944	Nate Andrews, p; Al Javery, p; Connie Ryan, 2b
1945	No game
1946	Mort Cooper, p; Johnny Hopp, of; Phil Masi, c
1947	Bob Elliott, 3b; Phil Masi, c; Johnny Sain, p; Warren Spahn, p
1948	Bob Elliott, 3b; Tommy Holmes, of; Phil Masi, c; Johnny Sain, p; Eddie Stanky, 2b
1949	Vern Bickford, p; Warren Spahn, p
1950	Walker Cooper, c; Warren Spahn, p
1951	Bob Elliott, 3b; Warren Spahn, p
1952	Warren Spahn, p

TABLE 6

THE SPORTING NEWS AWARDS

Year	Name

MAJOR LEAGUE ALL-STAR TEAM
(Team selected at end of season in a poll of players)

1928	Rogers Hornsby, 2b
1933	Wally Berger, of
1945	Tommy Holmes, of
1948	Bob Elliott, 3b
	Johnny Sain, p

MVP

1945	Thomas Holmes, of

PLAYER / PITCHER OF THE YEAR

1948	Johnny Sain, p

MANAGER OF THE YEAR

1937	Bill McKechnie (M.L.)

TABLE 7

BBWAA AWARDS NL

Year	Name

MVP

1914	John Evers, 2b
1947	Robert Elliott, 3b

ROOKIE OF THE YEAR

1948	Alvin Dark, ss
1950	Samuel Jethroe, of

There are 39 Boston Braves players and executives in baseball's Hall of Fame. The following list includes the years they were with the franchise.

Earl Averill	1941
Dave Bancroft	1924–27
Dennis "Dan" Brouthers	1889
John Clarkson	1888–92
James J. Collins	1895–1900
Hugh Duffy	1892–1900
Johnny Evers	1914–17; 1929
Burleigh Grimes	1930
William "Billy Hamilton"	1896–1901
Billy Herman	1946
Rogers Hornsby	1928
Joseph Kelley	1891, 1908
Mike "King" Kelly	1887-89; 1891–92
Ernie Lombardi	1942
Al Lopez	1936–40
Rabbit Maranville	1929–33, 1935
Richard Marquard	1922–25
Eddie Mathews	1952–66
Christy Mathewson, team president	1922–25
Thomas F. McCarthy	1885, 1892–95
Bill McKechnie	1913
Ducky Medwick	1945
Kid Nichols	1890-1901
Jim O'Rourke	1876–78, 80
Charles Radbourne	1886–89
Babe Ruth	1935
Frank Selee, team manager	1890–1901
Al Simmons	1939
George Sisler	1928–30
Warren Spahn	1942, 1946–64
Albert G. Spalding	1871–75
Casey Stengel	1924–25
Ed Walsh	1917
Lloyd Waner	1941
Paul Waner	1941–42
Vic Willis	1898–1905
George Wright	1876–78; 1880–81
Henry "Harry" Wright	1876–77
Denton "Cy" Young	1911

INDEX

References to modern-era baseball teams and their nineteenth-century predecessors are reflected in this index only if their team name is used (either by itself or combined with the name of the city, such as Giants or New York Giants). References to teams by their city and league (such as Boston National League Club, New York Americans, or St. Louis Unions) are listed in that manner. Defunct nineteenth-century clubs, however, have been listed in various instances without their team name (such as Indianapolis Baseball Club).

The entry "Seasons" includes each of the years covered by The Boston Braves. Those years in which the Braves or their nineteenth-century predecessors won the pennant are designated by an asterisk.

Cincinnati Reds, 27–28, 46, 49, 58, 73, 95, 116, 147, 169, 177–78, 182, 245, 257, 262
Clark, Earl, 211
Clarke, Fred, 107–8, 212
Clarke, William Jones (Boileryard), 90, 98
Clarkson, John, 49–54, 56–62
Clements, John, 98
Cleveland Baseball Club, 35, 38
Cleveland Indians, 185, 274–77
Cleveland Spiders, 52, 54, 60–62
Cline, Maggie, 45
Cobb, Ty, 41, 75, 80, 173, 198
Cobb, Mrs. Ty, 75
Cochrane, Mickey 280
Cocreham, Eugene, 151, 156
Coffey, Jack, 120
Cogan, Tom, 71–72
Cohan, George M., 97, 190
Cole, Jay, 283
Coleman, Bob, (Old Carpet Slippers) 253, 255, 259, 280
Collier's Saloon, New York City, 8
Collins, Bill, 120
Collins, Cyril Wilson, 144, 148
Collins, Eddie, 41, 142, 146, 162–65, 234–35
Collins, Jimmy, 55, 78–79, 81, 85, 87–88, 91, 93–97, 100–102, 107, 126
Collins, Shano, 280
Collins, Shono. See Collins, Shano
Columbus, Ohio, Buckeyes, 46
Comiskey, Charles, 82
Conant, William H., 22–24, 46–47, 50, 53–55, 57, 75, 100, 110–11, 113–15, 130, 199
Conatser, Clint, 270, 276
Cone, Fred, 7, 9–10
Congress Street Grounds, Boston (Brotherhood Grounds), 38, 56, 66, 68, 73
Conkey, John A., 5, 11
Conn, Billy, 181
Connaughton, Frank, 66, 79
Connecticut League, 142
Connolly, Joe, 139, 141, 144, 147–50, 159, 162, 164–65, 171
Connolly, Willie, 148
Conway, Joseph F., 248
Cooley, Dick, 107
Coombs, Jack, 162, 184
Cooney, Johnny, 198, 201, 243, 245–48, 262, 279

Coons, William, 18
Cooper, Mort, 259, 261, 265, 267
Cooper, Wilbur, 180–81, 195
Corbett, Jim (Gentleman Jim), 66, 90
Corbett, Joe, 81, 87–88, 90–91
Corcoran, Larry, 30, 36, 60
Cottrell, Ensign, 151
Coulson, Bob, 124
Crane, Sam, 21
Cravath, Cliff (Gavvy), 130, 149, 158
Criger, Lou, 101
Crolius, Fred, 102
Cronin, Joe, 133, 215, 228
Crosetti, Frank, 224
Cruise, Walton, 183, 186–87
Crutcher, Dick, 141, 151
Cuccinello, Tony, 236–37, 244–46, 253
Culler, Dick, 257, 259
Cummings, Arthur, 11, 26
Cunningham, Bill (player), 195
Cunningham, Bill (sportswriter), 232–33
Cunningham, Bruce, 207
Cunningham, Ed, 192, 200, 234
Cuppy, George (born Koppe, George Maceo), 62, 101
Curley, James Michael, 157, 227
Curley, Paul, 234
Curran, Sam, 107
Curtis, Clifton, 121, 127
Curtis, Edwin, 90
Cusick, Jack, 282
Cuyler, Kiki, 208

Daffiness Boys, 241
Dahlen, Bill, 116, 119
Dahlgren, Babe, 248
Daily, Hugh, 38
Daley, Bill, 56, 59
Daley, Jud, 124
Daly, Tom, 139
Dark, Al, 262, 269–71, 275–76, 280, 283
Daubert, Jake, 124, 159
Davidson, Claude B., 207
Davis, George, 144, 158, 256
Davis, Robert H., 175
Day, John B., 64
Day, Ralph A., 193
Deal, Charlie, 141, 147, 159, 162–63
Dealey, Pat, 40
Dean, Dizzy, 231, 237
Delahanty, Ed, 74, 109
Delahanty, Jim, 109
Delaney, Art, 215

298

Moore, Gene, 236–37, 244–45, 247
Moore, Gerry, 251
Moore, Randy, 216–18, 221–22, 236
Moran, Charlie, 154
Moran, Herb, 137, 148, 153, 156, 158, 162, 165
Moran, Pat, 102, 107–8, 170
Morrill, John (Honest John), 19, 21, 27–28, 31, 33–36, 39–40, 49–51, 56, 199
Morrisania Unions, Morrisania, N.Y., 6–7
Morse, Jacob C., 21, 97
Mowry, Joe, 221
Mueller, Heinie, 211
Mueller, Ray, 244
Mullane, Tony (Count), 68
Municipal Stadium, Cleveland, 275
Murnane, Tim, 18, 20–21, 28, 38, 50–51, 53–54, 67, 70, 72–73, 84–85, 87–88, 90–91, 94, 117
Murphy, Alphonse (Phonnie), 26
Murphy, Charles F., 129
Murphy, Charles Webb, 145–46, 181
Murphy, Eddie, 161, 163–64, 167
Murphy, Francis P. (Major), 227, 255
Murphy, Fred, 102, 107
Murphy, Frederick J., 86, 122–24
Murray, Jim, 148
Murtaugh, Danny, 271
Musial, Stan, 261, 272–73
Mutrie, James J., 52
Myers, Henry, 159

Nash, Billy, 51, 53, 56, 59–60, 77, 79–80
National Association of Professional Base Ball Players, 3, 8, 13–17, 31
National Brotherhood of Baseball Players. *See* the Brotherhood
National Commission, 159
National League, 15–18, 22–23, 25–26, 31, 33–34, 37–38, 46, 56, 58, 60–61, 63–64, 67, 88, 92, 95, 98–99, 102–3, 106, 108–9, 111–12, 115, 119, 121–22, 128, 130, 145–46, 155, 157, 159, 175, 177, 181, 193–94, 198–99, 209, 216, 224, 226–28, 230–31, 233, 236–37, 245, 247, 251, 257, 260, 265, 270–71, 273–75, 285–86
National League Park, Boston, 236. *See also* Beehive
Neary, Jimmy, 120, 242
Needham, Tom, 109, 116–17
Nehf, Artie, 171, 180–82, 215
Neis, Bernie, 197–98, 201
Nelson House, Poughkeepsie, N.Y., 47
Nelson, Tom, 257–58

Neshannocks Baseball Club, New Castle, Penn., 74
Neun, Johnny, 213, 218
New England League, 21, 55, 68, 70, 98, 102, 111, 121, 123, 132, 135, 191
New Hampshire, University of, 80
New Orleans Pelicans, 150
New York Americans, 212
New York Clipper, 9, 10, 11, 12, 39
New York Construction Company, 129
New York game, 4
New York Giants, 34–35, 52, 60, 63–65, 68, 94, 96, 108–9, 114, 116–21, 123, 125, 130–31, 136, 142–45, 148, 150–58, 170–72, 174–77, 180–82, 187–88, 190, 194–97, 201, 204, 206–7, 209, 211, 216–17, 219–22, 231–32, 236, 238, 240–41, 245–46, 248, 250, 252, 255, 263–64, 266–67, 272–74, 278, 280–83, 286
New York Graphic, 11
New York Herald, 129
New York Herald Tribune, 162, 199
New York Highlanders, 108, 128, 136, 140, 147, 177
New York (Brooklyn) Mutuals, 11, 14, 17, 28
New York Sun, 157
New York University, 193
New York Yankees, 143, 188, 195–96, 210, 212–14, 223, 226, 228, 235–36, 242, 245, 250, 252, 281
Nichols, Charles (Kid), 53, 55, 57–63, 65–67, 73–74, 78, 80, 82, 84–89, 92–96, 98–99, 102–4, 106, 191
Nichols, Malcolm, 207
Nicholson, Fred, 186, 189
Nick Flatley Trophy, 237
Nickerson, Herman, 130, 165
Nieman, Butch, 252
Nixon, Al, 186–87, 194
Nops, Jerry, 88–89, 91
Northen, Hub. *See* Northern, Hub
Northern, Hub, 124
Northwestern League, 55, 73

O'Connell, Joseph, 283
O'Day, Hank, 43, 134, 188
O'Doul, Lefty, 211
Oeschger, Joe, 182–84, 186–87, 194, 196, 223
Oldring, Rube, 164
O'Leary, Jim, 161, 188, 192
Olson, Ivy, 183

Olympic Baseball Club, 4
O'Neil, George (Mickey), 182, 185–86, 188, 194, 198–200
O'Neil, James F., 69
O'Neill, Jack, 114
Oregon State University, 216
O'Rourke, James (Orator Jim), 7, 11, 13, 18–19, 28–30, 118
O'Rourke, John, 29
Ostermueller, Fritz, 257
O'Tool, Bob, 21
Ott, Mel, 71, 221, 272
Ouimet, Francis, 248
Our Boys Baseball Club, 21
Outdoor Recreation League, 207
Outlaw, Jimmy, 245

Padgett, Don, 262
Padgett, Ernie, 194, 198, 209
Pafko, Andy, 284
Page, George A., 122–23, 128
Page, Louis C., 122–23, 125, 128
Paige, Satchel, 276
Parent, Freddy, 101
Parker House, Boston, 5, 286
Parker, Tiny, 244
Parks, William, 18, 20
Parmelee, Roy, 221
Paskert, George, 121
Paterson, N.J. Olympics, 46
Patton, George, 145
Paul, Gabe, 286
Pellagrini, Eddie, 218
Pendleton, Jim, 284
Pennock, Herb, 165
Pennsylvania State League, 68, 92
Perdue, Hub, 131, 148, 151, 153
Perini, Charles, 255, 283
Perini, Joseph, 255, 283
Perini, Louis, 248, 254–56, 258–59, 261–62, 265, 271–73, 278–79, 282–86
Peter F. Kelley Memorial Trophy, 260
Pfeffer, Frank Xavier (Jeff), 114–15, 125, 127, 256
Pfeffer, Fred, 46
Phelan, James J., 124
Phelps, Ernest (Babe), 248
Philadelphia Athletics (American League), 109, 124, 142, 148, 159–67, 184, 194, 198, 211, 236, 274
Philadelphia Athletics (National Association of Professional Base Ball Players), 9–12, 14–15, 20, 22
Philadelphia Athletics (National League),

17–18, 26, 28
Philadelphia Athletics (nineteenth–century American Association team), 37, 58
Philadelphia Athletics (pre–National Association of Professional Base Ball Players), 7
Philadelphia Nationals, 31, 55, 73, 110, 137. See also Philadelphia Phillies
Philadelphia Phillies, 79, 132, 144, 152, 158, 170, 172, 176, 182, 184, 186, 194–95, 198, 206, 219–20, 222, 236, 257, 264, 280. See also Philadelphia Nationals
Piatt, Wiley, 108
Pick, Charlie, 182
Picked Nine: 1871, 8; 1872, 10; 1873, 12; 1876, 21; 1889, 50
Pickett, Dave, 93
Pierce, Henry L., 5
Pittenger, Charles (Kid), 102, 107–9, 111
Pittsburgh Pirates, 58, 108, 112–13, 133, 155, 175, 180, 197, 199, 212, 227, 231, 245, 247, 251, 253, 263, 265–68
Plank, Eddie, 148, 160, 162–63, 165
Players' League, 56, 128. See also the Brotherhood
Playoffs, 1891 season, 61–62
Poland, Hugh, 252
Polo Grounds, New York City, 6, 58, 136, 144, 155, 177, 181, 201, 240, 245–46, 250, 252, 260
Porter, Charles H., 11, 13
Portland, Maine, Baseball Club, 4
Posedel, Bill (Sailor Bill), 245, 252
Potter, Nelson, 270, 272–73, 276
Powdrell, J. W., 248
Powell, Albert H., 199–201
Powell, Ray, 180, 184–86, 188, 194
Preston, Edwin, 201
Preston, Walter, 79
Prince, Charles Alfred, 59
Providence Grays, 28–29, 31–32, 36–40, 49, 128
Pulliam, Harry C., 76–77, 116
Pulsifer, Nathan, 111

Quigley, Ernie, 171–72
Quinn, Jack, 209
Quinn, Joe, 51, 56, 59–60, 63, 75–76, 81, 87
Quinn, John, 235, 258, 285
Quinn, Robert, 67, 151, 234–39, 241–42, 247–48, 250, 254–55, 258, 261

Radbourne, Charles (Hoss), 35–36, 38–40,

305

43, 56, 60
Radford, Paul Revere, 39
Ragan, Don Carlos Patrick, 171, 177
Randall, Newton, 116
Rariden, Bill, 182–83
Reardon, Abraham Lincoln (Beans), 244
Rehg, Walter, 180
Reinhart, Art, 197
Reis, Bobby, 236, 244
Reis, Tom, 245
Reiser, Pete, 248
Reitz, Heinie, 90. *See also* Reltz, Heinie
Reltz, Heinie, 87. *See also* Reitz, Heinie
Reulbach, Ed, 179–80
Rhem, Flint, 225
Rhiel, Billy, 217
Rice, Grantland, 139
Richardson, Hardie, 51–53, 56, 59
Richbourg, Lance, 201, 206, 213, 220
Rickert, Marv, 275–76
Riddle, John, 245
Rigler, Cy, 178
Riley, Ed, 184
Ritchey, Claude, 115
Robertson, Eugene, 217
Robinson, Eddie, 276
Robinson, Jackie, 273, 279
Robinson, Wilbert, 65, 67–68, 82, 87, 96, 243
Rodgers, William, 110
Roe, Mr., (banker), 175
Rogell, Bill, 69
Rogers, Billy, 85
Rogers, Fraley, 10–11
Rogers, Will, 224
Rollings, Red, 217
"Rookie Rocket," 282
Roosevelt, James (Jimmy), 227
Root, Charlie, 231
Ross, Arthur H., 206
Ross, Chet, 246, 248
Rowe, John Charles, 47, 52
Rowell, Carvel (Bama), 246, 252, 264, 270
Royal Rooters, 44, 86, 163
Rucker, George (Nap), 117, 130
Rudolph, Dick, 107, 142–43, 151, 153–56, 159, 162, 165–66, 170–72, 174, 176–77, 179–80, 194–95, 202
Rudolph, Marion, 162
Ruffing, Red, 245
Rugo, Guido, 248, 254, 256, 262, 281
Rugo, Joseph, 283
Rugo, Leon, 283

Ruppert, Jacob, 226
Rusie, Amos, 58, 103
Russell, Jim (nineteenth–century player), 21
Russell, Jim (twentieth–century player), 269–71, 273, 279
Russell, William Hepburn, 122–25, 128, 181
Ruth, George Herman (Babe), 41, 48, 74, 119, 186, 191, 212, 216, 226–33
Ryan, Connie, 252, 257, 277
Ryan, Jack (National Association of Professional Base Ball Players), 10–11
Ryan, Jack (National League), 66, 74, 93
Ryan, Jim, 84

Saigh, Fred, 284
Sain, Johnny, 252, 264, 266–67, 272–76, 279–81
St. Elizabeth's Hospital, Brighton, Mass., 253
St. George Cricket Club, 6
St. Louis Association, 60. *See also* St. Louis Browns, American Association
St. Louis Baseball Club (nineteenth–century National League team), 28
St. Louis Browns (American League), 203, 235, 248, 270, 282, 284–86
St. Louis Browns (nineteenth–century American Association team), 69, 73, 209. *See also* St. Louis Association
St. Louis Cardinals, 101, 121, 150, 154–55, 174, 186–87, 197, 200, 204, 206, 210, 212–13, 217, 222–23, 236, 238, 242–44, 250–52, 257, 259, 261–62, 265–67, 284–85
St. Louis Unions, 38
St. Xavier College, 116
Salkeld, Bill, 271, 274, 276
Sallee, Slim, 148
Salvo, Manny, 246, 250
Sampson, Arthur, 243
San Francisco Missions, 243
Sanders, Ray, 262, 264
Saturday Evening Post, 268
Satzman, E. G., 4
Schafer, Harry, 7, 13–14, 18, 26, 28, 118
Schang, Walter, 162–65
Schinski, Johnny, 215
Schmidt, Charles (Butch), 141, 146–47, 153, 155, 162, 164–65, 175
Schmidt, Walter, 180
Schneider, Pete, 177

67, 73, 82–83
Tufts College, 186, 203
Tuohey, George A., 44, 55, 65, 69
Turner, Jim, 237, 242–43, 245, 247, 266
Tyler, George A., 121, 141, 143, 151–58, 164–65, 171, 177, 180

Union Association, 21, 24, 38
Union Base Ball Grounds, Boston. *See* South End Base Ball Grounds
Urbanski, Billy, 217–18, 224–25, 231
Utah–Idaho League, 215

Van Atta, Russ, 223
Van Buren, Steve, 271
Vance, Dazzy, 200
Vander Meer, Johnny, 243
Veeck, William L., Sr., 185, 208
Veeck, William, Jr. (Bill), 286
Vergez, Johnny, 221
Vermont League, 142
Vickery, George, 70
Virtue, Jake, 61
Voiselle, Bill, 267, 275–76
Von der Ahe, Chris, 209
Von der Horst, Harry B., 96

Wagner, Honus, 41, 43, 127, 177, 247
Walker, Dixie, 284
Wallace, Jim, 252
Walpole Street Grounds, Boston. *See* South End Base Ball Grounds
Walsh, David I., 174–75
Walsh, Ed, 179
Walsh, Jimmy, 163–65
Walter Barnes Memorial Trophy, 246–47
Walters, Bucky, 218
Waner, Lloyd (Little Poison), 248
Waner, Paul (Big Poison), 248–49, 251, 256, 286
Ward, John Montgomery, 29, 56, 63, 68, 88, 128–31, 182
Warner, Jack, 78
Warstler, Harold (Rabbit), 236–37
Washington, D.C., Baseball Club, 49–51
Washington, D.C., Nationals, 6
Washington, D.C., Olympics, 9, 13
Washington Monument, 112
Washington Senators, 59, 199
Waterfront Park, St. Petersburg, Fla. 223, 242
Watson, John, 186–87, 193–94
Weaver, Orlie, 125
Webb, Melville (Mel), 45, 174, 192

Webb, Sam, 280
Welsh, F. G., 5
Welsh, Jimmy, 198, 204, 216
Wentzel, Stan, 265
Wertz, Henry, 201
West, Max, 243–45, 249–50, 252
Western Association, 57
Western League, 76, 98
Wetmore, Bruce, 201, 227, 232
Weyhing, Gus, 140
Whaling, Bert, 151, 155
Wheat, Zack, 124, 241
White, Darkhue, 84
White, Edward H., 5
White, Ernie, 262, 266
White, Jim (Deacon Jim), 11, 13, 15–17, 19–21, 27, 36, 52
White, William, 26
Whitman, Burt, 192, 202
Whitney, Frank, 19, 118
Whitney, Jim (Grasshopper Jim), 30–31, 33–36, 38–39
Whitney, Pinky, 220, 222, 224, 236
Whitted, George (Possum), 144, 148, 151, 153, 156, 158, 162, 168, 170
Wietelmann, Bill (Whitey), 252, 259, 264–65
Wilhelm, Irvin K., 109, 111
Wilkesbarre Record, 92
Williams College, 4, 80, 158
Williams, Nick, 215
Williams, Ted, 237
Williams, Walter, 108
Willis, Victor Gazaway (Vic, Delaware Peach), 92–95, 97–98, 100, 102, 107–9, 111–12, 256
Wilson, Art, 180
Wilson, Charlie, 217
Wilson, Hack, 201, 219
Winslow, Frank, 38
Winslow, Sam (Colonel Sam), 118
Winslow, William B., 128
Wise, Arthur, 173, 175
Wise, Sam, 33, 36, 50, 97
Wolverton, Harry, 111
Workman, Chuck, 260, 264
World Series, 1914: Game One, 162; Game Two, 163; Game Three, 164–65; Game Four, 165
World Series, 1948: Game One, 274–75; Game Two, 275; Game Three, 275; Game Four, 275–76; Game Five, 276; Game Six, 276–77
Worthington, Robert L. (Red), 217, 221